*France Overseas: Studies in
Empire and Decolonization*

SERIES EDITORS:

A. J. B. Johnston, James D. Le Sueur, and Tyler Stovall

FRENCH ST. LOUIS

FRENCH ST. LOUIS

Landscape, Contexts, and Legacy

EDITED BY
Jay Gitlin, Robert Michael Morrissey,
and Peter J. Kastor

UNIVERSITY OF NEBRASKA PRESS
Lincoln

Publication of this volume was assisted by Les Amis.

Library of Congress Cataloging-in-Publication Data
Names: Gitlin, Jay, editor. | Morrissey, Robert Michael,
editor. | Kastor, Peter J., editor. | A Great City From
the Start: the Founding and Lasting Significance of
St. Louis (Symposium) (2014: Saint Louis, Mo.)
Title: French St. Louis: landscape, contexts,
and legacy / edited by Jay Gitlin, Robert
Michael Morrissey, and Peter J. Kastor.
Description: Lincoln: University of Nebraska
Press, 2021. | Series: France overseas: studies
in empire and decolonization | Includes
bibliographical references and index.
Identifiers: LCCN 2020051245
ISBN 9781496206848 (hardback)
ISBN 9781496227379 (epub)
ISBN 9781496227386 (mobi)
ISBN 9781496227393 (pdf)
Subjects: LCSH: Saint Louis (Mo.)—History. |
French Americans—Missouri—Saint Louis—
History. | Saint Louis (Mo.)—Ethnic relations.
Classification: LCC F474.S257 F74
2021 | DDC 977.8/66—dc23
LC record available at
https://lccn.loc.gov/2020051245

Set in Adobe Jensen by Mikala R. Kolander.
Designed by N. Putens.

This book is dedicated to the late Elizabeth Gentry Sayad. The book and the original conference were her ideas. Elizabeth cared deeply about culture and history and wanted her city to have the best of both. She will be missed.

This book is also dedicated to the people of St. Louis who care about their past as much or more than the citizens of any city. We hope they will always keep their *esprit français*. We also hope that all St. Louisans will find something of interest in this book that will sustain their sense of pride in their city and themselves.

CONTENTS

ILLUSTRATIONS

FIGURES

GENEALOGIES

GRAPHS

ACKNOWLEDGMENTS

This book began as a gathering of scholars, a symposium held at the Missouri History Museum in Forest Park in St. Louis on Friday, February 14, 2014, to celebrate the 250th anniversary of the founding of the city. As we said in the dedication, the idea of symposium and a new scholarly book came from Elizabeth Gentry Sayad. Mrs. Sayad was the founder, in 1994, and chairman emeritus of Les Amis, a group whose mission was and continues to be to promote education, preservation, and awareness of French Creole heritage and culture in the mid-Mississippi Valley. We also wish to thank Mimi Stiritz, past president of Les Amis, and current president Kina Shapleigh for the group's critical support and sponsorship of this book. Anne Juneau Craver, lawyer, translator, and scholar, not only wrote one of the book's finest and most groundbreaking essays but also has been an indispensable help in all aspects of the project behind the scenes.

Another major co-sponsor of this project from its inception was Yale University, through the Redpath Seminar program of the Yale Alumni Association. Two YAA directors, Eleanor (Nory) Babbitt and Diane Morrissey, provided critical leadership and organization of the original symposium. They worked in conjunction with Yale Club of St. Louis and John McClelland, president of the club at that time, to help organize the scholarly gathering. Other co-sponsors of the event that became this book are the Missouri History Museum, Washington University, and the Mercantile Library of St. Louis. We would like to thank Frances Levine, president and CEO of the Missouri History Museum, and Managing Director of Administration and Operations Karen M. Goering, who supported this project from the beginning. We hope the folks at MoHist will sell this book proudly in the museum bookstore, the Louisiana Purchase—obviously the best name of any such shop in the country.

Washington University was a crucial sponsor of this project. We are grateful to former chancellor Mark Wrighton and Assistant Vice Chancellor for Alumni Relations Susan Lipsitz Cohen for their gracious welcome and co-sponsorship. Our good friend Iver Bernstein, professor of history, African and African American Studies, and American Culture Studies at Washington University, was essential in helping to connect the various participants. We also must thank honored guests Principal Chief Scott BigHorse of the Osage Nation; Délégué du Québec au Midwest, Eric Marquis; French Consul General in Chicago, Graham Paul; and, of course, the Mayor of St. Louis at that time, Francis G. Slay. Coordinating it all and doing a magnificent job was the Executive Director of STL250, Erin Budde.

Historians William Foley and Claiborne Skinner, both of whom have written excellent and important books on the French colonial period in the Midwest, were valuable collaborators in the project. Katherine Mooney (Florida State), Karen Marrero (Wayne State), and Alexandre Dubé (Washington University) each gave wonderful talks at the symposium. Finally, John Neal Hoover, the executive director of the St. Louis Mercantile Library Association, participated in and supported this endeavor from start to finish. His assistance and wise counsel have been invaluable throughout.

Former editor in chief at the University of Nebraska Press, Alisa Plant, was essential in welcoming this project to their outstanding list. We are honored to be included in their important series France Overseas: Studies in Empire and Decolonization. Senior Editor and Interim Editor in Chief Bridget Barry has guided us with a sure hand and answered every question promptly and kindly. Above all, we thank the contributors for their hard work and their patience. Frozen custard at Ted Drewes this summer, on us.

FRENCH ST. LOUIS

INTRODUCTION

A French City in North America

JAY GITLIN, ROBERT MICHAEL MORRISSEY,
AND PETER J. KASTOR

This book has its origins in a symposium at the Missouri History Museum to celebrate the 250th anniversary of the founding of the city in 1764. The symposium, entitled "A Great City From the Start: The Founding and Lasting Significance of St. Louis," was sponsored by the Redpath Seminar Fund of the Association of Yale Alumni, Washington University, the Missouri History Museum, and an active group of local history boosters, Les Amis. Les Amis was organized in 1994 as a permanent support group for French heritage programs of the Missouri Department of Natural Resources. Its origins are rooted in the French Heritage Relief Committee formed during the flood of 1993 for the preservation and support of the endangered historic resources of Ste. Genevieve and the surrounding historic French colonial corridor. We thank Mimi Stiritz, the past president of the group, for her support. We also dedicate this volume to Elizabeth Gentry Sayad, former president of the group, who passed in 2017. Elizabeth was a patron of history and the arts and a historian herself. Her vision and enthusiasm sustained this project and encouraged all of us to keep the history of St. Louis and the regional French and Creole Corridor alive.

A bit to the surprise of the editors, who were involved with the planning of this symposium from the beginning, the public interest in this event was incredible. The museum's largest hall was filled to capacity and a crowd gathered in another room to watch on closed-circuit television. The editors were interviewed on a local NPR show. Jay did several television spots upon his arrival in the city. Taxi drivers knew about the event and asked questions about the city's early history. We should not have been surprised. St. Louis cares as deeply about its history as any city in America.

That said, it is our hope that this volume will provide what we think the history of the city has lacked: an outside perspective, meaningful context, and comparative connections. The history of St. Louis, like that of so many other cities, has always been mixed with a strong dose of mythology. It has perhaps had more than its share of boosterism, focused on dramatic moments like the 1904 World's Fair, and feel-good local institutions like Ted Drewes Frozen Custard, established in 1929. The founding moments in particular have often been treated in a very celebratory mode by a certain heritage community in the city. And while those stories have their place, in 2019 some of these celebratory and uncritical ways of seeing the city as a study in heroic entrepreneurialism and frontier community building might seem particularly tone-deaf and off point. After all, to many St. Louisans and outsiders alike, the image of St. Louis has in recent years been characterized in large part by narratives of urban strife and injustice, racial inequality, and, especially, the crisis of Ferguson. It goes without saying that many Whiggish accounts of early St. Louis do little to help us understand some of the difficult issues in the life of the city, or its present-day identity. By contrast, a more expansive and more inclusive approach can inform us on important parts of St. Louis's early history—diversity, ethnic relations, slavery, power, and resistance—that not only contribute to a more complex story, but also may help put the challenges and the successes of the present in the context of the city's longer trajectories. In their most useful moments, the historians in this book bring new perspectives and frameworks, as well as a certain healthy detachment, to a reconsideration of what the early history of St. Louis was all about.[1] We think this history is both relevant and important to include as part of local, regional, national, and even transnational stories.

St. Louis's Early History

Although these essays are diverse in focus, they join—and are representative of—recent efforts among historians to move the history of St. Louis beyond some rather tired narrative frameworks, parochialisms, and origin myths. It bears mentioning at the outset that early St. Louis historiography has long been characterized by a kind of "founders-obsession."[2] Specifically, many accounts of the history of early St. Louis begin with and centrally focus on the relatively narrow stories of key individuals, most importantly Pierre Laclède and Auguste Chouteau. While these characters were undoubtedly important and interesting, and while Chouteau's *Journal* understandably shaped many early historical accounts, the focus on them has often limited the ways historians have conceived of the early history of the city, keeping their vision local (and even narrowly based on families) at the expense of making connections to larger trajectories and historical contexts.[3] Happily, recent historical work has begun to transcend these old limitations, and this book aims to continue the trend.[4]

Not counting several mug books from the nineteenth century, the more modern and professional history of St. Louis began to be written in the 1940s with the work of Charles Peterson and John Francis McDermott. Peterson, an architect and employee of the National Park Service, was a pioneering advocate of historic preservation. His book, *Colonial St. Louis: Building a Creole Capital*, appeared in 1949 and provided a detailed look at construction practices and the built environment.[5] McDermott, a descendant of the city's French founding family, wrote many articles and edited several important volumes. He placed an emphasis on the Chouteau fur-trading family and—although an excellent historian—began the proprietary aspect of St. Louis historiography.[6] The somewhat private link between collections and scholarship continued with a beautifully illustrated book by a former director of the Missouri Historical Society, Charles van Ravenswaay. *Saint Louis: An Informal History of the City and Its People, 1764–1865*, which was published posthumously in 1991 and contains chapters such as "The Royal Family of the Wilderness" that could be seen as filiopietistic.

William E. Foley and C. David Rice, *The First Chouteaus: River Barons of Early St. Louis* continued the emphasis on the Chouteaus, but transcended some of the parochial aspects of earlier work, connecting the world of the Chouteaus to changing regimes and international diplomacy, Indian policy, and the business of the fur trade.[7] Foley and Rice provided a point of departure for Jay Gitlin's *The Bourgeois Frontier: French Towns,*

French Traders, and Western Expansion.[8] That book revisits the trope of St. Louis as a gateway to the West, looking at French Creole merchants and fur traders as "occupying a cultural and social space of accommodation while pursuing an economic agenda of development and change."[9] Thus francophone businessmen (and women) played a pivotal role in westering and the transition from Indian country to settlement frontier. Although intended to be western history, Gitlin's book also situated St. Louis and other francophone places such as New Orleans, Detroit, and St. Paul within the regional history of the Midwest, constituting the pioneer urban landscape of Mid-America. Meanwhile Peter Kastor's first book, *The Nation's Crucible: The Louisiana Purchase and the Creation of America*, provided another critical frame through which to view French Louisiana, examining not only the ways in which Louisiana adjusted to the nation, but also the ways that Louisiana "helped Americanize the United States."[10] Both books opened a door to new perspectives on this region—what Jay has dubbed the "Creole Corridor." The trend has been clear: new work on colonial St. Louis has increasingly placed the city in the context of broader historical trajectories while avoiding the pitfalls of exceptionalism and a kind of parochialism that at times resembles family squabbles.

More recently, four histories of early St. Louis have appeared. J. Frederick Fausz, *Founding St. Louis: First City of the New West*, has done two things far better than any previous historian of the city. Above all, he brings a deep understanding of the local Native communities, especially the Osages, and a persuasive conviction that they were partners in this city-building enterprise. As he observes in one chapter heading, St. Louis was a colonial but also an "Indian Capital."[11] Fausz also explored—following in the footsteps of McDermott—the roots of St. Louis founder, Pierre Laclède, in the French province of Béarn, connecting the first family narrative to a broader context in the Atlantic World. On the other hand, Patricia Cleary's book, *The World, the Flesh, and the Devil: A History of Colonial St. Louis* consciously attempted to transcend the focus on founders by focusing instead on St. Louis as an imperial outpost and "cosmopolitan" borderland. Like Shannon Lee Dawdy's important study, *Building the Devil's Empire: French Colonial New Orleans*, Cleary's account of colonial St. Louis provides examples of "rogue colonialism" where imperial plans met frontier realities. Cleary provides a clear exposition of Spanish rule in colonial St. Louis and her special focus on women and gender provides a fascinating look at the "intimate frontiers" of a critical contact zone. Cleary's book also has an iconoclastic approach, unafraid to upset some of the local elites in a city that considers its history a family affair.

Like Fausz, Jacob Lee centers Indigenous history and the deep context of Indigenous placemaking in which St. Louis took its place in the eighteenth century. His book *Masters of the Middle Waters: Indian Nations and Colonial Ambitions along the Mississippi* is not primarily a history of St. Louis, but it artfully uncovers the long trajectory of Indigenous and imperial contestation in which the city developed.[12] The most recent entry in the evolving historiography of early St. Louis, *St. Louis Rising: The French Regime of Louis St. Ange de Bellerive*, by Carl J. Ekberg and Sharon K. Person, revisits the story of founders. But Ekberg and Person break new ground by elevating a *different* founder—Louis St. Ange de Bellerive—as even more central to the founding of early St. Louis than the vaunted Chouteau clan. Critiquing and largely dismissing the much-studied *Journal* of Auguste Chouteau, Ekberg and Person should not be thought of as having replaced one kind of "founders-obsession" with another, for in their case there is a larger point: to place St. Louis in the context of a long trajectory of *imperial* development, and in particular in the context of imperial institutions. By emphasizing the role of the early settlement's military and legal institutions as well as their leaders (St. Ange de Bellerive and the notary Joseph Labuxière), the authors reconnect St. Louis to the deeper history of the Illinois Country and New France and deemphasize that "Royal Family of the Wilderness."[13]

What all of this recent work does so well is to consider the larger frameworks in which colonial St. Louis developed. St. Louis was never just a local place, and its inhabitants—Indigenous, enslaved, European, Creole—lived in complex networks that stretched well beyond the city's limits. Understanding this is an exercise in reframing. As much of early American history scholarship of the past generation has recentered early American places as part of larger geographical units—the Atlantic World, "continental history," and the like—we have gained a wholly new way of understanding their relevance not so much to a national story of the eventual United States, but to larger processes and patterns of history: "borderlands," "encounters," "conquests."[14] If the French past of St. Louis has always been relatively difficult to fit into the nation-state teleologies that have dominated the telling of North American history, the move away from nationalist narratives and toward these other frameworks in history scholarship has been salutary for thinking about the meanings of St. Louis's past.[15]

This recentered significance is the ground that these essays collectively claim for early St. Louis history. Reframed in the terms described above, St. Louis has an importance that not only transcends celebration by a small heritage community, but clearly merits the attention of a regional and national audience of both "civilians" and academic specialists. It is no accident that the history of French North America has increasingly taken space in such journals as the *Western History Quarterly* and the *William and Mary Quarterly*. In part this is because French areas like St. Louis disrupt tired narratives of colonial and western history, and make us reconsider the basic trajectories of the past. For instance, Andrew Wegmann's essay in this volume shows us a regional north-south frontier, a Creole "community that maintained a culture and identity in both St. Louis and Louisiana that defied expected practice in the antebellum decades." Viewed from St. Louis, Native and non-Native relations look different, not only as a history of domination and resistance, but also as a more complex history of collaboration and accommodation. Gender looks different too: women had economic agency rarely found in Anglo settlements, as Patricia Cleary reveals in a study of clothing, and as Robert Englebert illuminates in his study of intercolonial networks of women in French North America. In short, while St. Louis was not exceptional and shared features with other places in colonial America, Canada, and Overseas France, it was distinctive and provides a necessary comparative perspective within our national narrative. And as the essay by Craver points out, the French community and with it the French language, the market for French consumer goods and services, and a French print culture endured for a *long time*. Most observers of the history of the city and region continue to assume that French culture in Creole St. Louis had been "obliterated by 1821": the claim of historian Marshall Smelser in 1938. Remarkable new sources explored in this book document that the city continued to have a visible and audible French presence as late as the 1850s.

The Structure of the Book
Part 1. Fashioning a Colonial Place: St. Louis between Empire and Frontier

The book begins by exploring the larger imperial and colonial context in which the city was born. Despite how Laclède supposedly predicted that his new city would one day be one of the "finest in America," St. Louis was not founded with a knowledge of future industrial greatness. It was, however, founded on the edge of a colonial empire, at the crossroads of Indigenous communities, and in a well-developed, century-old colonial world: the Illinois Country. Far from predicting a future industrial power-house, Laclède and his generation had goals more specific to the eighteenth century, and hoped to connect the interior of the continent to networks of culture and trade in an Atlantic World economy. Recent work on New France, Louisiana, and the Illinois Country region makes it possible to see the significance and importance of early St. Louis, not just by looking forward to what was to come, but also by looking backward to see the complex contingencies and processes that brought it about. This section of the book sheds light on these colonial contexts that helped to shape the place that the French named St. Louis.

Bob Morrissey's essay puts the founding of St. Louis in the context of French colonial history in the mid-Mississippi Valley region. Morrissey shows how the French settlements in the Illinois Country were created by a distinct collaboration between imperial priorities and local practice. Founded in the late seventeenth century, the French settlements of the Illinois Country were some of the most remote European settlements in all of colonial America, in terms of their distance from colonial and administrative centers in Louisiana and New France. Their colonial inhabitants were also vastly outnumbered by Indigenous peoples, a fact that rendered claims to imperial control on the part of the French administrators in this place in some ways laughable. And yet the French settlements of Kaskaskia, Fort de Chartres, and neighboring villages were not lawless, anarchic, or isolated from forces and structures in the Atlantic World. Indeed, inhabitants in these settlements pursued an often-purposeful partnership with colonial officials and policies. For their part, colonial officials did not attempt a hardheaded and inflexible policy of absolutism in these marginal frontier colonies. Rather, in economic, social, and political matters, colonial officials and colonists, together with Indigenous neighbors, developed an "empire by collaboration": a distinctive political culture that colored much about life here. When St. Louis was founded, nearly 1500 people lived in the region in settlements that had been around for almost one hundred years. Their political culture strongly colored the early town of St. Louis, as it continued to operate at the edge of empire, albeit now Spanish.

Robert Englebert's essay also places early St. Louis in a larger colonial, imperial, and social context, locating early St. Louis within a river world defined by trading and legal networks extending to Louisiana and to Montreal and Quebec. In particular Englebert brings attention to the often-overlooked role of women in these networks and these processes of connection. By focusing on the well-documented family of Marie-Catherine Giard and her daughters, Englebert challenges the outdated notion that the fur trade and colonial economy were exclusively male domains. Indeed, Englebert "places women at the center" of the French Creole networks responsible for St. Louis's early growth and development. In this way Englebert not only challenges the myth of St. Louis as an isolated frontier outpost in the wilderness, but he restores gender balance to our understanding of who actually powered the growth of the early city.

If the colonial and imperial context help to give the early history of St. Louis meaning, so too does its position within Indian country. The essay by J. Frederick Fausz explores the significance of that context, arguing that the Osage were as much the founders of the city as French merchants. Fausz tells us that in early St. Louis, the fur trade provided the basis for increasing wealth, "affluent consumerism," and "multicultural goodwill." The regional economy also contributed maize, wheat, tobacco, lead, and other items of trade and sustenance. The model of alliance and trade exemplified by St. Louis and this "Sutler Trading Empire" stood in contrast to the

Anglo-American model of a "Settler Farming Empire" that emphasized conquest and coercion over commerce. Without ever romanticizing the participants or the events of the past, Fausz presents a nuanced yet bold and powerful portrait of a town created by multiple founding cultures, thus restoring the agency of Native and French people and their place in our histories.

If early St. Louis grew in the context of diverse people building, resisting, and collaborating with empire in the remote Mississippi Valley frontier, Patricia Cleary's chapter raises questions about cultural identity in the village's early years. Focusing on clothing and the ways in which people self-fashioned through dress and personal adornment, Cleary marshals fascinating evidence to show how people made choices and constructed identity in this dynamic zone of racial, imperial, and gender difference. Among her conclusions is the important point that clothing choices transcended simple categories of French, Spanish, Indian, or African; many early St. Louisans displayed hybrid and shifting identities in their choice of self-presentation. Additionally, Cleary amplifies the main themes of this section when she demonstrates how the consumption of clothing and fashionable wares "tied the people of this region to vast webs of commerce that spanned Asia, Africa, Europe, and North America." St. Louis's early history cannot be understood in the parochial and teleological ways it has been told, as a mere prelude to a nineteenth-century industrial rise. Rather, these chapters emphasize how it was part of a distinctive and well-established colonial world defined by global processes that shaped the eighteenth century.

Part 2. St. Louis and New Orleans: A Regional Perspective

If colonial context has been important to the reframing of early St. Louis, so too has the context of regionalism. In 1903 two great cities struggled to commemorate the centennial of the Louisiana Purchase, and both of them failed. New Orleans could only mount a low-key affair that was brief and drew little attention. Civic leaders in St. Louis had the more ambitious plans, but they did not come together until the following year. Despite the delay, the Louisiana Purchase Exposition (now colloquially known as the 1904 World's Fair) outshone the commemoration that had occurred in New Orleans the year before, much to the chagrin of civic leaders in New Orleans. A century later, it was New Orleans that laid claim to the bicentennial of the Louisiana Purchase, hosting a year of commemorative events. St. Louis devoted more energy to celebrating the centennial of the 1904 World's Fair than the bicentennial of the event that the World's Fair sought to commemorate.

Those two moments—in 1903–4 and in 2003—revealed the complex relationship between the Crescent City at the mouth of the Mississippi and the Gateway City in the mid-Mississippi Valley. Both were products of French imperial ambitions in the eighteenth century. Both became the subjects of U.S. territorial expansion at the turn of the nineteenth century. Both would emerge as contenders for the title of the great western city in the expanding United States. Both were fueled by the slave economy and both were remade by emancipation. And in the end, both St. Louis and New Orleans were overshadowed by regional competitors.

The history of St. Louis and its surrounding region only makes sense in relation to the history of New Orleans. Together, they tell the story of francophone urban culture in North America. Considered within their multiracial and multiethnic contexts, they come together to form a revealing story of migration, intercultural contact, and periodic conflict.

As Lawrence N. Powell shows, St. Louis and New Orleans grew together after 1763, but always in competition. While St. Louis and New Orleans both became economic engines in nineteenth-century America, they proceeded on profoundly different trajectories. Access to resources, environmental differences, and specific choices by settlers and regional elites alike produced two very different economies. White residents of New Orleans eagerly sought to develop their status as a hub for plantation agriculture, whether that meant extending enslavement, supporting nearby plantations of extraordinary size, or shipping the products of the plantation system. In sharp contrast, St. Louis's role in regional trade focused on the produce of small freeholds rather than large plantations. The city itself became the site of early industrial development long before New Orleans. New Orleans functioned as the only urban center in a region dominated by rural plantation life, while the plantations that surrounded St. Louis were fewer in number and smaller in size, even as the number of towns in Missouri and Illinois quickly outnumbered town development in Louisiana and Mississippi.

Despite these regional differences, social connections and cultural practices continued to link the two cities. Andrew Wegmann reconstructs these elusive sinews to reveal the ways that free people of color in New Orleans and St. Louis sought to realize their own visions of security and prosperity. Like Powell, Wegmann describes important differences. New Orleans was at the center of a horrific slave system, but was also home to a community of free people of color whose social and economic status were unique in the slave South. St. Louis never became a plantation society in a manner similar to its southern neighbors, but free people of color faced greater restrictions and fewer opportunities than their counterparts in New Orleans. Despite these differences, Wegmann shows the important connections that linked free people of color in both cities. As Wegmann argues, the "cultural histories and practices [in New Orleans and St. Louis] mirrored each other far more than most scholars have been willing to admit, and they exchanged far more than just products and profits within a system of riverine trade."

Part 3. Visualizing Place: New Sources and Resources for Telling the Story of St. Louis

In addition to important reframing and new contexts, many recent advances in the history of early St. Louis have happened as a result of new historical methods and the discovery of new sources. John Lawrence analyzes an extraordinary firsthand account that attempted to make sense of the similarities and differences between the lower- and mid-Mississippi Valley. In 1803 Pierre-Clément de Laussat, the newly arrived French colonial prefect in New Orleans, sought to make sense of the vast French domain he was supposed to govern. So he struggled to gather information on the towns and settlements clustered around New Orleans. His correspondence provides not only a glimpse at early nineteenth-century life, but also a vision of how imperial officials understood the complex multiracial population of North America. Lawrence's essay provides the first analysis of Laussat's correspondence, and as a result is as much a project in documentary editing as it is one of historical analysis. Lawrence's essay demonstrates just how little European officials actually knew about the mid-Mississippi Valley, a place where much of geographic and commercial knowledge belonged to the Native peoples who wielded governing authority in the region. By walking us through the process of interpreting Laussat's account, Lawrence provides a master class in documentary analysis.

Another exciting new development in understanding the early city has come from digital technology. A team led by Bob Moore at the National Park Service (Gateway Arch) has created a remarkable visualization of the urban plan of early St. Louis based on original records and utilizing a 3-D modeling program that allows us to imagine the texture, the shape, and the scale of life in the early frontier city in the late eighteenth century. Explaining this project, Moore first narrates a bit of architectural history of the city, especially the loss of historic buildings through the nineteenth and twentieth centuries. Unfortunately, much has been destroyed, and so it is impossible for us today to walk the streets of early St. Louis and gain a sense of that long-ago world, as we can in certain historic landscapes of North America. Moore then explains one solution to this problem: a new method of computer rendering that allows a highly detailed and accurate visualization based on maps, plans, and other sources. Samples of the resulting visualizations accompany the article and illustrate how we can now "see" the colonial world of St. Louis as never before.

Part 4. Maintaining the French Connection of St. Louis

The final section looks at the Frenchness of St. Louis in the nineteenth century and the present. The essay by Craver will astonish many readers, who will discover that the French community of St. Louis remained vibrant as late as the 1850s. Craver has prepared a wonderful map of the city's various French institutions and retail shops in the nineteenth century, revealing the very important French imprint on the city's culture at that time. Lionel Cuillé, head of the city's Centre Francophone, details the contemporary French community in the city, exploring cultural institutions with a long history in St. Louis, as well as ways in which francophone immigrant populations—including from former locations of French empire outside of North America—have made their mark on the "Frenchness" of today's city. In one section of the essay, "Francophone 2.0," Cuillé describes a vibrant French-speaking community to be found in traditional groups and gathering places, but also connecting through social networks online.

Jay Gitlin's conclusion is the final essay in this volume, and it brings the main theme of this book—the importance of seeing early St. Louis in larger perspective—to a crescendo. Gitlin emphasizes that our St. Louis, the one in Missouri, was only one of several, including one laid out in Minorca only two years earlier (1762), and that St. Louis did not become a great city, but remained a suburb of the capital city, Port Mahon, the home of a unique sauce known as "mahonesa"—our mayonnaise. The French also founded a settlement named St. Louis (São Luís) in Maranhão, Brazil, in 1612. Today that St. Louis is a city with a million inhabitants. Places named St. Louis can be found all over "France Overseas," including Quebec, Martinique, Guadeloupe, and Guiana. The point is that St. Louis, Missouri, although distinctive, can and also should be understood in a variety of broader contexts that shed additional light on its history and make its story relevant to a wider range of historians and fields. St. Louis was cut from an imperial mold and resembled other such colonial places. As a colonial and imperial city, it was connected to the emerging world economy. It was, therefore, modern, fashionable, and cosmopolitan from the start.

For related reasons, it is also relevant to us now, and not just as heritage for a certain segment of St. Louis society. Reframed in broader contexts, the French past speaks to present-day concerns and to a diverse audience, and in ways that were not obvious before. To take one example, back in 2009, Jay Gitlin gave a talk in St. Louis at a symposium sponsored by Les Amis. At the reception, he had a wonderful conversation with a young woman of color who taught French in one of the area's schools. She related the problems of teaching this perceived "European" language to mostly Black students who could not necessarily see why they should care, notwithstanding the French background of the city. One way forward, he explained, was to complicate our understanding of the experience of those French people, so often caricatured as Old World and stuffy and quintessentially "white," who in reality had a complex experience with exclusion and identity. After all, St. Louis fits squarely in the broader history of French North America, including Louisiana and Quebec. During the Quiet Revolution in that Canadian province, a young woman named Michèle Lalonde wrote a powerful poem, "Speak White" (1968). Lalonde did not invent the phrase. It was a common expression used by Anglo-Canadians to insult French Canadians when they used their own language. In short, instead of asking them politely to use English, Anglos commanded that the Quebecois "speak white," instead of French. Lalonde, in her poem, connects the various forms of disrespect and oppression, hegemony and resistance. She concludes by saying, "We are not alone. Nous savons que nous ne sommes pas seuls."

So when we see that language can become color, we can see the ultimate meaning of difference in North America, and how the past can speak to present-day struggles for inclusion and equality. I will recognize you as a person, but only if you look, act, and speak like me. This is but one example among many that pushes us to revisit the early history, the French history, of St. Louis, where French people were by turns the excluded as well as those drawing the lines of social difference. The work of the historians in this book allows us to reimagine the rich broth of St. Louis's past. As Lionel Cuillé points out in his essay, today's St. Louis Francophones are as likely to be from Burkina Faso or Senegal as France. In the early twentieth century, there were jazz musicians in New Orleans who grew up hearing parents speak French and Senegalese. That young teacher was very pleased to know about Michèle Lalonde. These essays, we hope, will push us to tell new stories about a complex city that has defied simple categories throughout its history.

Our volume shows how innovative and interesting the new work on St. Louis has been. Far from local and parochial, historians have placed the early city in broadest frameworks, using cutting-edge methods and sources to recast its relevance. Gateway to the West, outpost for eastern capital and culture, St. Louis straddled various geographical and political divides. St. Louis encompassed cultural, racial, and sectional communities and, at the same time, connected a vast region as a gathering place of peoples, cultures, and goods. As the nineteenth century went on, St. Louis prospered. St.

Louis ranked first in steamboat ownership in 1860, and steamboats defined St. Louis's hinterland. Floating extensions of heterogeneous and democratic urban space, steamboats magnified the city's ambitions and influence.

One visitor compared St. Louis in 1859 to Marseilles with its cacophonous waterfront. By the twentieth century, St. Louis had become the home of ragtime and blues. The last American city to be founded under the French regime, St Louis retained what author Charles Dickens referred to as a "French shrug" as late as 1842.[16] One could find traveling Indian delegations in the streets and buffalo tongues in the shops, French confections at M. Massot's store, and the latest Paris fashions on Fourth Street. French and American, eastern and western, southern and northern, multiracial, multicultural, and multilingual, St. Louis may not be the geographic center of the nation, but its history—and its future—may hold the key to understanding our sense of self and our sense of purpose.

NOTES

1. Arenson, "Double Life of St. Louis."
2. See, for instance, Ekberg and Person, *St. Louis Rising*, xi–xii.
3. For the *Journal*, see Hoover and Ames, *Auguste Chouteau's Journal*. For a critical analysis of the way the Chouteaus have dominated the memory and history of early St. Louis, see Gitlin, "From Private Stories to Public Memory," 3–16.
4. For a summary of the ways historians have reframed early American Midwestern history, including the geographical space in which St. Louis took its place in the eighteenth century, see Morrissey, "Le Pays Des Illinois."
5. Peterson, *Colonial St. Louis*.
6. For some of McDermott's key works, see McDermott, *Frenchmen and French Ways; French in the Mississippi Valley*. Jay Gitlin has examined McDermott's work in an essay, "Recovering the Chouteaus."
7. Foley, *First Chouteaus*.
8. Gitlin, *Bourgeois Frontier*.
9. Gitlin, *Bourgeois Frontier*, 120.
10. Kastor, *Nation's Crucible*.
11. Fausz, *Founding St. Louis*.
12. Lee, *Masters of the Middle Waters*.
13. For the authors' self-described "astringent critique of much of what has been written about St. Louis's early years," see Ekberg and Person, *St. Louis Rising*, chap. 1.

14. Aron, *American Confluence*. For these larger geographical frameworks, see Greer, "National, Transnational, and Hypernational Historiographies"; Usner, "Rescuing Early America"; Hinderaker and Horn, "Territorial Crossings."
15. Gitlin, *Bourgeois Frontier*, 2–3; Cleary, *The World, the Flesh*, 5.
16. Dickens, *Works of Charles Dickens*, 17:145.

BIBLIOGRAPHY

Arenson, Adam. "The Double Life of St. Louis Narratives of Origins and Maturity in Wade's Urban Frontier." *Indiana Magazine of History*, September 1, 2009.

Aron, Stephen. *American Confluence: The Missouri Frontier from Borderland to Border State*. Bloomington: Indiana University Press, 2006.

Cleary, Patricia. *The World, the Flesh, and the Devil: A History of Colonial St. Louis*. Columbia: University of Missouri, 2011.

Dickens, Charles. *The Works of Charles Dickens: American Notes and Pictures from Italy*. Vol. 17. London: Chapman and Hall, 1905.

Ekberg, Carl J., and Sharon Person. *St. Louis Rising: The French Regime of Louis St. Ange de Bellerive*. Urbana: University of Illinois Press, 2015.

Fausz, J. Frederick. *Founding St. Louis: First City of the New West*. Charleston SC: History Press, 2011.

Foley, William E. *The First Chouteaus: River Barons of Early St. Louis*. Urbana: University of Illinois Press, 1983.

Gitlin, Jay. *The Bourgeois Frontier: French Towns, French Traders, and American Expansion*. New Haven: Yale University Press, 2011.

———. "From Private Stories to Public Memory: The Chouteau Descendants of St. Louis and the Production of History." In *Auguste Chouteau's Journal: Memory, Mythmaking & History in the Heritage of New France: Essays Accompanying a New, Annotated Translation of the Narrative of the Settlement of St. Louis Together with a Reprint of John Francis McDermott's Glossary of Mississippi Valley French*, edited by John Neal Hoover and Gregory Ames, 3–16. St. Louis Mercantile Library, University of Missouri–St. Louis, 2010.

———. "Recovering the Chouteaus: John Francis McDermott and the Emergence of Franco-American Scholarship." Unpublished essay, 2010.

Greer, Allan. "National, Transnational, and Hypernational Historiographies: New France Meets Early American History." *Canadian Historical Review* 91, no. 4 (December 2010): 695–724.

Hinderaker, Eric, and Rebecca Horn. "Territorial Crossings: Histories and Historiographies of the Early Americas." *The William and Mary Quarterly* 67, no. 3 (July 1, 2010): 395–432.

Hoover, John Neal, and Gregory Ames, eds. *Auguste Chouteau's Journal: Memory, Mythmaking & History in the Heritage of New France: Essays Accompanying a New, Annotated Translation of the Narrative of the Settlement of St. Louis Together with a Reprint of John Francis McDermott's Glossary of Mississippi Valley French*. St. Louis Mercantile Library, University of Missouri-St. Louis, 2010.

Kastor, Peter J. *The Nation's Crucible: The Louisiana Purchase and the Creation of America*. New Haven CT: Yale University Press, 2004.

Lee, Jacob F. *Masters of the Middle Waters: Indian Nations and Colonial Ambitions along the Mississippi*. Cambridge MA: Belknap Press of Harvard University Press, 2019.

McDermott, John Francis. *The French in the Mississippi Valley*. Urbana: University of Illinois Press, 1965.

———. *Frenchmen and French Ways in the Mississippi Valley*. Urbana: University of Illinois Press, 1969.

Morrissey, Robert Michael. "*Le pays des Illinois* Finds Its Context: The Early History of Illinois in a Continental Perspective." *Journal of the Illinois State Historical Society*, III, nos. 1–2 (2018): 9–30.

Peterson, Charles E. *Colonial St. Louis: Building a Creole Capital*. Saint Louis: Missouri Historical Society, 1949.

Usner, Daniel H. "Rescuing Early America from Nationalist Narratives: An Intra-Imperial Approach to Colonial Canada and Louisiana." *Historical Reflections/Reflexions Historiques* 40, no. 3 (January 1, 2014): 1–19.

PART I

Fashioning a Colonial Place

St. Louis between Empire and Frontier

I

EMPIRE BY COLLABORATION

St. Louis, the Illinois Country, and the French Colonial Empire

ROBERT MICHAEL MORRISSEY

In 1772 a pamphlet was published in Philadelphia. Signed by "un habitant de Kaskaskia," it was entitled "Invitation Sérieuse aux Habitants des Illinois" (an Earnest Invitation to the Inhabitants of Illinois). Like so many other pamphlets published in Philadelphia in this period, it was a call to action, a manifesto. Its themes were self-reliance and economic enterprise. Addressing himself to his fellow colonists in the now four-generations-old settlements on the Mississippi River, the author predicted that the middle Mississippi region was going to be the wealthiest on the planet. He listed all the many things that the colonists could produce if they worked hard and stood on their own feet. They could make silk, raise animals, and produce wine and numerous other commodities for export. Of course this was typical booster stuff in some ways, and yet it is still remarkable because of the author's incredible optimism. The author urged his fellow colonists to expect "the perfection of their settlements." The middle of the Mississippi Valley clearly was not unaffected by the enlightenment optimism of this revolutionary age.[1]

And yet while many pamphlets of this era feature similar themes, there is something fascinating and different about this one. For even as this author invoked values of self-reliance, and predicted the bright future of his colony, an important purpose of this pamphlet was to urge the British empire, which had taken control of the east side of the Mississippi River in the wake of the Seven Years' War, to establish a civil government in Kaskaskia and give the colony a more robust imperial apparatus. As the author put it, "We are true and zealous subjects of his Britannic majesty and we doubt not at all that in a short time . . . the administration of civil government will be established among us. We are able at present only to desire these happy results."[2]

Think about this for a second. This is 1772. In Massachusetts they are about to throw tea in the Boston Harbor. Many other inhabitants of American colonies, including many other pamphleteers in Philadelphia, are expressing these same values of self-sufficiency and economic optimism.[3] But most of these other authors are invoking these values in order to argue for colonial independence. The colonists in the Illinois were doing the opposite, calling not for less, but for more, imperial government. To make this even more surprising, remember that these people were French, calling for the *British* government to rule them.[4] Indeed, in 1768, their counterparts in New Orleans, facing the same situation of a new imperial administration in their colony, had revolted against the Spanish.[5] Expressing the opposite sentiment, these Frenchmen in the middle of the Mississippi Valley called not for independence, but for government, for empire. Why?

The answer to this question lies in the distinctive political culture that defined the Mississippi Valley settlements of the Illinois Country from their creation. When the anonymous "habitant of Kaskaskia" called for a mixture of self-reliance and imperial support, he was summarizing the political tradition that had defined colonial life there since 1673. Here on the remote edges of empire, governments could not achieve top-down control, much less absolutism. But nor could the people who settled here go it alone. Instead, people and governments created a mutual order that was idiosyncratic and distinctive, an order which I call empire by collaboration.[6] It was this political tradition, its pragmatism and flexibility, that shaped the way francophones adapted to change in the early generations of St. Louis.

Most of the chapters in this book concern the early years of St. Louis. By contrast, I want to look back to the colonial history that provided the context for the development of the frontier city. I want to focus in on the very beginnings of colonial settlement in the mid-Mississippi Valley, and I want to argue that a distinctive political culture developed there out of a unique collaboration between imperial visions and local practice. This matters, I suggest, because it defined a pragmatic, flexible kind of politics that continued in the early American West, especially in the "bourgeois frontier" so nicely described by Jay Gitlin in his important book of that title.[7] It also provides needed corrective to a French colonial history still often dominated by the exaggerated themes of absolutism and dysfunction.[8]

When St. Louis started in 1764, there were already roughly 1500 French Creole colonists and slaves living in what was considered the Illinois Country, the network of villages along the Mississippi River at the junction of the Missouri, Illinois, Ohio, and Mississippi. These were substantial colonies that provided grain and livestock for New Orleans, in most years shipping many boatloads—small *pirogues* as well as larger *bateaux*—of flour in an annual convoy.[9] Many people here were wealthy and cosmopolitan, as exemplified by their consumption of fancy cloth, china, metal goods, and other objects from the Atlantic economy.[10] Their consumption and exploitation of human bodies from the Atlantic and Indian slave trades also testifies to the power of the colonies.[11] The economic largesse and refinement of the Illinois Country were undeniable, even a generation before an Illinois Country silversmith, Louis Robitaille, made an extraordinary sugar bowl that today survives in the collections of the Yale Art Gallery.[12] Meanwhile, their alliance with the Illinois Indians was especially strong. And their stone fort, Fort de Chartres was, in the words of one British writer, the "finest stone fort in North America."[13] These were impressive colonies.

And yet, when they were founded, these colonies were not part of the French government's plan for its North American empire. To the contrary, they were almost accidental, and certainly did not reflect the well-ordered operation of an absolutist state. In the 1660s, taking over New France as a royal colony, French ministers looked to limit settlement in the West. Losing money and facing danger during the notorious Beaver Wars, the French wanted to systematize fur trade with Algonquian allies in the Great Lakes, which they hoped to manage rigidly at several key spots, most importantly Michilimackinac. Ministers like Louis Colbert even hoped to limit Jesuit missionaries, arguing that they should try to settle Indians nearby Quebec, where they would teach Indians to speak French and Latin, teach them to dress as Frenchmen, to farm in the French style. They would, as the French

FIG. I. This sugar bowl was made in the very early nineteenth century in Saint Genevieve, Missouri, by the Canada-born silversmith Louis Robitaille (b. 1768). It is an extraordinary object that reflects the refinement of what was already by the late colonial period quite a cosmopolitan place, no rustic backwater. The sugar bowl is in the collections of the Yale University Art Gallery. Reproduction permission and photo credit: Yale University Art Gallery.

minister said, "Frenchify them."[14] The vision for the French Empire was for compact, intensive settlement, not extensive.

But if the government wanted tight settlement in the St. Lawrence valley, others disagreed. Indeed, it was the Jesuits who were the first to defy all of these plans. In the 1660s, rather than establishing reductions nearby Quebec, they began to establish new missions further and further to the West. In 1673 Jacques Marquette entered the Mississippi Valley for the first time, and established the mission of the Immaculate Conception on the Illinois River. This was not just another distant mission, it was the *most distant* mission that the Jesuits had ever established. Flying in the face of the government's call for Frenchification, the Jesuits here translated prayers into the Illinois language and made an idiosyncratic version of Christianity that was purposefully defiant of French imperial visions. After only a few years, the Jesuits celebrated this as one of the best missions in their system. In some ways, it was a finger in the eye of the colonial administration.[15]

After the Jesuits came Robert La Salle. If the French minister wanted to establish control over the West at places like Michilimackinac, La Salle had a totally different plan. Going straight to the King to propose a new program of exploration and settlement, La Salle envisioned a whole new empire in the Mississippi Valley, oriented to the south. As everybody knew, La Salle's ambition was to capture the fur trade of the West away from the Montreal traders, which is why the Quebec governor La Barre protested energetically against what he called La Salle's "imaginary kingdom."[16] To be sure, La Salle never achieved his would-be empire—he died before the Louisiana colony could take shape. But the first part of La Salle's new empire did become a reality at Fort St. Louis, in Illinois. It was a defiant imperial outpost, totally against Quebec's priorities.

Thus these earliest settlements in the middle of the country went contrary to the plans of the imperial administration in Quebec. Meanwhile, the young men that the priests and La Salle brought with them to the Illinois were only more defiant. Guides and *engagés*, or hired workers, included men like Michel Accault, who one priest chastised as "a base fellow," "disloyal," and "famous for his debaucheries."[17] These men deserted, married Indian women *a la façon du pays* (or, outside of the church), and sought their own self-interest. For instance, hired to help Father Louis Hennepin on a mission expedition, Accault abandoned the priest, stealing Hennepin's boat to go on a fur trading expedition to the Sioux in the north. As he told Hennepin, "everybody ought to be free."[18] And though he was deemed a scoundrel, he succeeded. After La Salle died, Accault the libertine had grown so wealthy that he purchased one half of the concession of the Illinois Country, transforming himself from what Hennepin viewed as a wayward *coureur de bois* into an official landlord.

Given how they conflicted with official plans, one might imagine that the French governors would try to shut down the settlement and mission in Illinois soon after they were established. But this was not an option. As it happened, the Illinois Indians were among the most powerful Native

FIG. 2. This map, entitled *L'Amerique septentrionale ou la partie septentrionale des Indes Occidentales* was published in Paris in 1689 by Jean Baptiste Nolin. It was the work of acclaimed cartographer Vincenzo Coronelli, and it showed the newly claimed Mississippi Valley region of North America where fledgling French colonial outposts grew up over the next several generations. Despite the bold and confident claims of maps like these, the reality on the ground was more complex; European colonists were extremely thin in this extensive empire, and European power was quite attenuated. Image courtesy Rare Book and Manuscript Library, University Library, University of Illinois, Urbana-Champaign.

groups in the Great Lakes. The French needed to keep these Indians as allies, and especially in the 1680s and 90s as the wars against the Iroquois threatened French interests. While other Great Lakes Indians declined in strength in this period, the Illinois expanded their influence and became "the Iroquois of the West," as one French observer wrote. Critically, they did this by expanding power to the southwest, building alliances with the Osages, Missouria, and other Siouan speakers in the plains. Quebec needed the Illinois, and so they needed to support the wayward settlements in the Illinois River Valley. This is why French officials made these unplanned settlements part of the empire, and tolerated Accault—an illegal fur trader—as an official landlord. French officials could not dominate; they had to collaborate.

Meanwhile, the same was true of the people on the ground—the Jesuits, fur traders, Indians, and La Salle's men. Normally hostile to one another, these people collaborated too. Most dramatically, the Jesuit priest Jacques Gravier began to perform Catholic marriages between the illegal fur traders like Accault and Illinois Indian women, a practice the Jesuits had explicitly criticized previously. Merging diverse agendas, together with imperial support, these colonists, proprietors, fur traders, and Indians created a community that reflected nobody's original idea of what empire should look like, but which represented a pragmatic collaboration.

In 1698 La Salle's Louisiana finally got off the ground as a fledgling colony. Accault, the Jesuits, and the Illinois Indians soon moved their settlement to the south, where opportunities for trade were better. From a growing settlement at Kaskaskia, they traded bison skins at a new tannery on the Ohio River, established under the jurisdiction of Louisiana. They traded beaver at Mobile. But the French also joined the Illinois Indians in their most important economic activity in this period—captive or slave trading. Carrying Pawnee, Osage, and Comanche captives from the West, they brought them east to Algonquian Indians, and to Carolina.[19]

All of this was so lucrative that many Frenchmen settled down and began to farm in permanent villages. Jesuits continued marrying illegal traders to Indian women, who joined their French husbands on French-style farming operations. Ironically, many of these women did indeed "Frenchify," in many ways assimilating to a French agrarian village life, just as Colbert had hoped for back in the 1670s.[20] And yet, when imperial officials began to learn about this unplanned colony, they were not thrilled. They issued arrest warrants for men like Michel Bizaillon, who had finished a contract with the Jesuits only to become an illegal slave trader. They issued two arrest warrants for a man named Jacques Bourdon, a notorious slave trader who officials complained was "guilty of treason."[21]

By 1715 Canadian officials sent an expedition to Illinois to investigate rumors of disorder there. What the expedition discovered was extraordinary. Far from just a little fledgling settlement, there were 150 Frenchmen living in the settlement of Tamaroa, which had just merged with the larger village of Kaskaskia. They were trading slaves and using them to cultivate their fields. As one member of the expedition reported: "[The illegal settlers] are living there at their ease; as grain thrives in that region they have built a mill, and have a great many cattle. They get as many savage slaves as they wish, on the river of the Missouris, whom they use to cultivate their lands."[22] Totally unplanned, this was a disturbing development. As one Canadian official put it: "This settlement is a dangerous one, serving as a retreat for the lawless men both of this Colony [i.e., Canada] and of Louisiana."

And yet, the imperial officials did not issue more arrest warrants. They did not try to shut the colony down. They did not stamp their feet and complain about "rogue colonialism" or disorder. Instead they took a completely different tack. Here's what the intendant of Canada wrote to the minister in France: "But as we see no possibility of preventing [the settlement], we believe, Sir, that we might render it useful for the service of the King and of the Colony by sending there a dozen Soldiers, Commanded by an officer, who could build a fort there, and gradually establish order among those Frenchmen."[23]

As this document makes clear, this was empire by the principle of "if you cannot beat them, join them." Hardly a rigid top-down system, this was the essence of what I call "empire by collaboration." At the margins, French imperialism was in fact directed not by planners in Versailles, but by an uneasy alliance of empires, colonists, and Indians.

In 1718 the French government did finally move the Illinois settlements into the official jurisdiction of Louisiana. A year later they sent the first commandant to the region. When he arrived, this commandant, Pierre Dugué de Boisbriant, made no arrests. He did not shut down the colony. Far from prohibiting the slave trade, as officials in Louisiana had urged, he expanded it, sponsoring an official policy whereby the colonists would purchase slaves from Missourias, Osages, and Illinois Indians to solidify alliances. He did not prevent intermarriages between Frenchmen and Indian women, even though the officials back in Lower Louisiana banned the practice in the 1710s. Perhaps most significantly, when Boisbriant appointed his local administration, he selected from among the "most worthy" colonists to populate the new government. Who did he pick as militia captain? None other than Jacques Bourdon, the illegal slave trader with two warrants outstanding when Boisbriant showed up in the colony. This was collaboration—letting the autonomous colonists determine the nature of the colony on their own.

And the founding of the colony was just the beginning. For the rest of the eighteenth century, the colonists and Indians continued to force the French government to collaborate. In the 1730s, the French fought an initially unwanted war against the Fox Indians, largely because the Illinois Indians insisted on it.[24] The provincial government in Illinois looked the other way when French colonists violated the strict requirements of the Coutume de Paris on matters of land tenure and inheritance. The Louisiana government allowed the colonists in Illinois to conduct slavery along idiosyncratic lines, sometimes in violation of the Code Noir.

And yet the colonists and Indians were not independent. Indeed, the colonists and Indians welcomed empire. The Illinois Indians, benefiting from alliance, were some of the most reliable Indian allies for the French government through the 1740s. For their part, the inhabitants of Illinois gladly utilized the government and even gained a reputation for being overly litigious. In the 1740s, inhabitants volunteered to build military installations, and they always labored to produce huge grain surpluses to supply New Orleans.

In short, contrary to myths often associated with the French empire in North America, the colonists were neither submissive nor anarchic. The government was not absolutist. Instead, the relationship between people and the government was collaborative, opportunistic, and often quite functional. The frontier conditions of the colony meant that everybody—colonists, officials, Indians, even slaves—had power, and nobody could dominate. And in this context, people got along not always through clashes and not merely by what one scholar calls "creative misunderstandings," but by pragmatic collaboration.[25]

All of this helps us understand the *Invitation Sérieuse*, the ambitious manifesto by the habitant of Kaskaskia in 1772. Envisioning a peculiar mix of self-reliance and imperial support, the *Invitation* expressed a longstanding political tradition in this region. To be sure, the *Invitation Sérieuse* never produced tangible results for the inhabitants of Kaskaskia. Although the British government promised to send a provincial government to Kaskaskia in 1774 under the terms of the Quebec Act, the American Revolution changed the priorities of the British Empire. By the late 1770s almost all of the francophone colonists of the Illinois Country moved, most of them to the west side of the river, to colonies like St. Louis and Ste. Genevieve, now under the control of the Spanish government.

But it is important to remember the attitudes they brought with them when they arrived. Anglo settlers who arrived in this region in the 1780s and 90s stereotyped the French Creoles as submissive peasants, dependent on authority, incapable of the competition, initiative, and self-reliance necessary for participation in a democratic and capitalistic future. The opposite was nearer to the truth. French *habitants* who stayed in Upper Louisiana and congregated in St. Louis in the 1760s and 70s knew how to facilitate their own interests as well as those of empire. Many of them swore loyalty to the Spanish government and assimilated by, for instance, Hispanicizing their names. Outward declarations and performances of a new imperial identity signaled an opportunistic desire to work with the new administration. And yet, there were limits as colonists continued to pursue their own agendas. If the Spanish Antonio de Ulloa intended that the now Spanish village of St. Louis would adopt Spanish customs, or feature submissive Creole subjects ready to take orders in a top-down manner, he was soon disillusioned.[26] Although Creoles accommodated the new government, as when Creole trader Charles Gratiot held his nose and "be[came] a Spaniard," in reality he was likely simply acting pragmatically.[27] By the time the American Regime began in St. Louis, Creole inhabitants of the region were so skilled in currying favor with imperial governments while at the same time pursuing their interest that they even likely invented a new tradition: political lobbying.[28]

And these practices were a direct outgrowth of their history within an empire by collaboration. Far from stuck in their ways, the inhabitants of Illinois had always been flexible and pragmatic, and their defining characteristic was self-interested enterprise, not submission or anarchy. In their dealings with government, they had been opportunistic and practical. Looking forward to the history of St. Louis, they would continue to make a multicultural order by pragmatically partnering with the powerful forces that aimed to control the early West.

NOTES

1. Brauer, "Earnest Invitation," 261–68.
2. Brauer, "Earnest Invitation," 267.
3. Bailyn, *Pamphlets of the American Revolution*.
4. To be sure, it is worth noting that the authors of the "Invitation" likely had a fairly liberal version of colonial government in mind, as they revealed when they suggested Connecticut—the most liberal of all the thirteen British colonies—as the model for their new provincial government. See Carter, *Great Britain and the Illinois Country*, chapters 6–7.
5. Meneray, *Rebellion of 1768*; Dawdy, *Building the Devil's Empire*, chap. 6.
6. Morrissey, *Empire by Collaboration*, 7–10.
7. Gitlin, *Bourgeois Frontier*.
8. For a great discussion of this theme, see Greer, "Comparisons: New France," 470.
9. Ekberg, *French Roots in the Illinois Country*, chap. 6.
10. White, *Wild Frenchmen and Frenchified Indians*.
11. Rushforth, *Bonds of Alliance*; Ekberg, *Stealing Indian Women*; Vidal, "Africains et Europeens au pays des Illinois."
12. Barquist, "Refinement in the Illinois Country."
13. Pittman, *European Settlements*, 46.
14. Belmessous, "Assimilation and Racialism," 323.
15. Morrissey, "Terms of Encounter," 44.
16. De La Barre to King, Nov. 4, 1683, C11a, 5:137v, ANOM.
17. Hennepin, *New Discovery*, 1:182, 289.
18. Hennepin, *New Discovery*, 1:204.
19. Rushforth, *Bonds of Alliance*; Gallay, *Indian Slave Trade*.
20. White, *Wild Frenchmen and Frenchified Indians*, 8; Morrissey, "Kaskaskia Social Network."
21. Vaudreuil and Begón to Ministre, Nov. 15, 1713, C13a, 34:4, ANOM.
22. Ramezay and Bégon to French Minister, November 7, 1715, CSHSW, 16:332.
23. Ramezay and Bégon to French Minister, November 7, 1715, CSHSW, 16:332.
24. Brett Rushforth, "Limits of Alliance."

25. Richard White, *Middle Ground*, x.
26. See "Ulloa Sends and Expedition," in Louis Houck, *Spanish Regime in Missouri*, 1:9.
27. Gitlin, *Bourgeois Frontier*, 39.
28. See Gitlin, "Old Wine in New Bottles."

BIBLIOGRAPHY
Primary Sources

ANOM. Correspondance à l'arrivée. Sous-série C11a, Canada et colonies d'Amérique du Nord; Sous-série C13a, Louisiane. Archives Nationales d'Outre Mer, Aix-en-Provence, France.

ANF. Archives de la Marine, Sous-série B1, Archives Nationales de France. Paris, France.

Bailyn, Bernard. *Pamphlets of the American Revolution, 1750–1776.* John Harvard Library. Cambridge MA: Belknap Press of Harvard University Press, 1965.

Brauer, Lydia Marie, trans. "Earnest Invitation to the Inhabitants of Illinois by an Inhabitant of Kaskaskia." In *Transactions of the Illinois State Historical Society for the Year 1909*, 261–68. Illinois State Historical Library, 1909.

CSHSW. *Collections of the State Historical Society of Wisconsin.* 20 vols. Madison: Madison State Printer, 1888–1931.

Hennepin, Louis. *A New Discovery of a Vast Country in America, by Father Louis Hennepin. Reprinted from the Second London Issue of 1698.* Edited by Reuben Gold Thwaites. 2 vols. Chicago: A. C. McClurg, 1903.

Houck, Louis, ed. *The Spanish Regime in Missouri: A Collection of Papers and Documents Relating to Upper Louisiana Principally within the Present Limits of Missouri during the Dominion of Spain, from the Archives of the Indies at Seville.* 2 vols. Chicago: R. R. Donnelley & Sons Company, 1909.

Meneray, Wilbur E. *The Rebellion of 1768: Documents from the Favrot Family Papers and the Rosamonde E. and Emile Kuntz Collection.* New Orleans: Howard-Tilton Memorial Library, 1995.

Secondary Sources

Barquist, David L. "Refinement in the Illinois Country: Louis Robitaille's Sugar Dish." *Yale University Gallery Bulletin* (2004): 58–67.

Belmessous, Saliha. "Assimilation and Racialism in Seventeenth and Eighteenth-Century French Colonial Policy." *American Historical Review* 110, no. 2 (2005): 322–49.

Carter, Clarence Edwin. *Great Britain and the Illinois Country, 1763–1774*. The American Historical Association, 1910.

Dawdy, Shannon. *Building the Devil's Empire: French Colonial New Orleans*. Chicago: University of Chicago Press, 2008.

Ekberg, Carl J. *French Roots in the Illinois Country: The Mississippi Frontier in Colonial Times*. Urbana: University of Illinois Press, 1998.

——. *Stealing Indian Women: Native Slavery in the Illinois Country*. Urbana: University of Illinois Press, 2007.

Gallay, Alan. *The Indian Slave Trade: The Rise of the English Empire in the American South, 1670–1717*. New Haven CT: Yale University Press, 2002.

Gitlin, Jay. *The Bourgeois Frontier: French Towns, French Traders, and American Expansion*. New Haven CT: Yale University Press, 2011.

——. "Old Wine in New Bottles: French Merchants and the Emergence of the American Midwest, 1795–1835." In *Proceedings of the Thirteenth and Fourteenth Meetings of the French Colonial Historical Society*, edited by Philip P. Boucher, 35–57. Lanham MD: University Press of America, 1990.

Greer, Allan. "Comparisons: New France." In *A Companion to Colonial America*, edited by Daniel Vickers, 465–88. Malden MA: Blackwell, 2005.

Morrissey, Robert Michael. *Empire by Collaboration: Indians, Colonists, and Governments in Colonial Illinois Country*. Philadelphia: University of Pennsylvania Press, 2015.

——. "Kaskaskia Social Network: Kinship and Assimilation in the French-Illinois Borderlands, 1695–1735." *William and Mary Quarterly* 70, no. 1 (January 1, 2013): 103–46. https://doi.org/10.5309/willmaryquar.70.1.0103.

——. "The Terms of Encounter: Language and Contested Visions of French Colonization in the Illinois Country, 1673–1702." In *French and Indians in the Heart of North America, 1630–1815*, edited by Robert Englebert and Guillaume Teasdale, 43–75. East Lansing: Michigan State University Press, 2013.

Pittman, Philip. *The Present State of the European Settlements on the Mississippi, with a Geographical Description of That River, Illustrated by Plans and Draughts*. London: Printed for J. Nourse, 1770.

Rushforth, Brett. *Bonds of Alliance: Indigenous and Atlantic Slaveries in New France*. Chapel Hill: University of North Carolina Press, 2012.

——. "Slavery, the Fox Wars, and the Limits of Alliance." *William and Mary Quarterly*, 63, no. 1 (January 1, 2006): 53–80. https://doi.org/10.2307/3491725.

Vidal, Cecile. "Africains et Europeens Au Pays Des Illinois Durant La Periode Francaise (1699–1765)." *French Colonial History* 3, no. 1 (2003): 51–68. https://doi.org/10.1353/fch.2003.0012.

White, Richard. *The Middle Ground: Indians, Empires, and Republics in the Great Lakes Region, 1650–1815.* New York: Cambridge University Press, 1991.

White, Sophie. *Wild Frenchmen and Frenchified Indians: Material Culture and Race in Colonial Louisiana.* Philadelphia: University of Pennsylvania Press, 2012.

2

BETWEEN OBLIGATION AND OPPORTUNITY

St. Louis, Women, and Transcolonial
Networks, 1764–1800

ROBERT ENGLEBERT

In November of 1778, St. Louis resident Marie-Marguerite Dupuis sued fur-trade merchant Pierre Durand for misconduct and breach of contract. Marguerite had procured passage with Durand and his *engagés* from St. Louis to Montreal in order to join her husband, Jean-Baptiste Louis Bardet dit Lapierre, who was away settling family business in Canada. Durand was to personally escort Marguerite and provide food and shelter throughout the voyage; in turn, he was to be paid a sum of four hundred *livres* upon safe delivery of his passenger.[1]

Marguerite explained that things started off reasonably well, but that part way through the journey, somewhere between Petit Rocher and Chicago, Durand began withholding food and became increasingly temperamental. She charged that Durand eventually became abusive, hurling obscenities and slipping away to eat the best food in private. Marguerite contended that she was forced to eat and live with the *engagés* against all sense of propriety.

When it became clear that Durand would not continue on to Montreal, citing low waters and insufficient provisions, Marguerite confronted the merchant, asking for ninety-three *livres* in furs to cover expenses her husband had already paid. The sum consisted of forty-eight *livres* as an advance; twenty *livres* for four jars of *tafia* (rum), fifteen *livres* for a ham, and ten *livres* for fifty pounds of flour. Durand refused, arguing that he did not have a receipt for any such transaction. The situation worsened, as Marguerite recounted how Durand gulped down the four jars of *tafia* all by himself and became increasingly belligerent. Left with few options, she secured passage back to St. Louis by way of two merchants, Leduc and Ducharme, each of whom transported her on separate legs of the voyage home.[2]

Marguerite's case was heard at St. Louis before Lieutenant Governor Fernando de Leyba, the highest colonial authority in Spanish Upper Louisiana. Durand denied any culpability whatsoever, and de Leyba called on three of the merchant's *engagés*—Augustin Monpetit, Joseph Poitevin, and Étienne Cardinal—to testify to the veracity of the allegations.[3] The employees in question had won a suit against Durand for unpaid wages earlier that month, which the merchant still had not paid. Their testimonies, however, were surprisingly muted, confirming most of Marguerite's story, but falling well short of outright condemnation. Perhaps the *engagés* held out hope that their former patron would finally make good on wages owed. Unfortunately, like so many colonial legal proceedings, the surviving records leave us without sense of closure. Durand emerges as an unscrupulous character and Marguerite likely won her case, but there is little in the archives to detail verdict or final resolution.[4]

The case of Marguerite Dupuis v. Pierre Durand is noteworthy for a few reasons. First, the sworn statements of Durand's former employees give voice to laborers who were mostly illiterate and left few records;[5] indeed, all of the *engagés* marked an X beside their names after having heard written record of their testimonies read aloud. The case also offers insight into the frequency of travel on the river highways of the continent. During the latter half of the eighteenth century, hundreds of merchants, voyageurs, and travelers set out annually on the waterways of North America.[6] Notwithstanding tropes of isolation and wilderness that abound in fur-trade literature, the apparent ease with which Marguerite hitched a ride home demonstrates that this particular route between St. Louis and Montreal was relatively well-trodden.

Finally, there is Marguerite Dupuis's account of her voyage, which presents an exceedingly rare and salient glimpse into women's travel experiences. Through this, a number of things immediately become evident: that women were able to procure passage out of St. Louis with fur trading outfits; that one could pay for a level of comfort and good treatment, but was ultimately subject to the rigors and perils of travel, not to mention the character and good will of their escort; and finally, that women had legal recourse in St. Louis when the terms of travel were breached.

For decades now, scholars have challenged traditional gendered notions of the fur trade as an exclusively masculine homosocial space, pointing to the centrality of intermarriage between French men and Indigenous women, the salient role of kinship, and the work of female merchants.[7] Beyond participation in the trade itself, we also know that women traveled the river highways of the continent as part of several waves of French migration from the St. Lawrence Valley to the *pays d'en haut* and *pays des Illinois* during the eighteenth century. For example, Marguerite Dupuis, Marie-Charlotte Levasseur, Marie-Anne and Marie-Josephe Robidoux, and Marie-Louise Gibeau, to name only a few, comprised a group of *Canadiennes* who relocated to the middle Mississippi Valley in the years following the end Seven Years' War in 1763.[8] For the most part, however, these women show up in one locale and then pop up again in another, leaving only ephemeral impressions gleaned from disparate sources. Therefore, while women's participation in the fur trade has been clearly established, their involvement with other facets of these continental river networks is still largely underdeveloped. This chapter seeks to remedy this imbalance, at least in part, through an examination of the role of St. Louisan matriarch Marie-Catherine Giard and her daughters in the creation, maintenance, and expansion of transcolonial French-creole networks of communication and exchange in the latter half of the eighteenth century.[9]

This study builds on a small but growing body of literature that deals with the ways in which women exercised power and authority in French colonial society in North America.[10] Whether it was the power of widows to run farms and businesses; the role of wives in managing family wealth; women's use of French colonial law; or nuns and lay women's work in education and healthcare; women were instrumental in shaping colonial society. As Jan Noel has recently noted, daily practice frequently subverted societal gendered hierarchy and divisions of labor in New France, thereby dispelling notions of rigid and unchanging patriarchy.[11]

The situation was similarly fluid in the small cluster of French-creole villages at the edge of empire along the middle Mississippi River. Some scholars have shown that French-creole women had remarkable personal and economic freedom, while others have argued that some women's actions tested the limits of permissibility and threatened to radically disrupt the social fabric.[12] In line with the more general shift, which gives closer consideration of class and race in the study of women's history in early America, French-creole relationships with both free and enslaved Black and Indigenous peoples, complicate our historical understanding of gendered societal norms.[13]

This chapter deals primarily with white French-creole women and more specifically with wives of merchant elites at St. Louis in the latter half of the eighteenth century. It does so because of the abundant source material for this particular family, a cache of dozens of letters, which provide rare insight into these women's lives. As Robyn Burnett and Ken Luebbering have noted, the relative paucity of sources creates challenges for telling women's stories during the colonial period.[14] Though certainly not representative of all of colonial society, Marie-Catherine Giard and her daughters reframe our gendered understanding of colonial St. Louis as a nexus for transcolonial French socioeconomic exchange. It places women at the center of French-creole networks and demonstrates that they were critical to the construction, maintenance, and operation of this transcolonial world. While scholars like Jan Noel, Leslie Choquette, Kathryn Young, Catherine Ferland and Fernand Grenier, Emily Clark, and Jennifer Spear, have linked women in New France and Louisiana to the French Atlantic World, this study extends those networks into the interior of the continent.[15] Looking out from St. Louis allows us to question how French-creole women helped to shaped the periphery of empire.

As the Seven Years' War drew to a close France carved up and divided its mainland colonies between Spain and Britain. The Treaties of Fontainebleau (1762) and Paris (1763) effectively put an end to its empire in North America. French creoles initially continued much as they had before.[16] News of imperial regime change was slow to reach Louisiana, and when St. Louis was established in 1764, it was founded as a French town named for his Most Christian Majesty. Under Spanish rule, St. Louis was bolstered by migrations from Canada, Lower Louisiana, and from communities across the Mississippi River in British Illinois Country.

Recent scholarship has characterized the early development of St. Louis in a number of divergent ways: a center of harmonious French Indigenous relations; a bastion of old French political and legal customs; and a place where social disruption and political instability threatened to tear the town asunder.[17] All of these histories reveal different facets of St. Louisan society from its founding until the end of the eighteenth century. And yet they all speak to the ways in which St. Louis was connected to the world around it. Jay Gitlin notes that St. Louis quickly emerged as a crucial trading town at the fulcrum of an extensive French-creole corridor, which ran from Detroit to New Orleans.[18] People and consumer goods flowed along the waterways of the interior of North America to form intricate networks of a socially integrated French river world.[19] This chapter pushes us to rethink the nature of early St. Louisan society, how it was connected to the world around it, and who made that possible. It demonstrates, moreover, that women like Catherine Giard and her daughters, who have typically been invisible in the archives and rendered inconspicuous in historical narratives, were instrumental in the development of St. Louis, its ties to this broader transcolonial French river world, and by extension to the Atlantic world that lay beyond.

Marriage Alliances

Marie-Catherine Giard was born in Kaskaskia sometime in the 1730s to parents who had emigrated from Canada.[20] In 1764 she married Jean-Gabriel Cerré, a *canadien* merchant from Montreal, who had established himself as a successful fur trader throughout the 1750s.[21] Like many young men from Canada, Cerré followed a well-established matrilocal marriage pattern and put down roots in Illinois Country.[22] Catherine's father, Antoine Giard, had been a successful farmer and churchwarden, who leased land and periodically rented out a couple of Black slaves as labor.[23] By the early 1750s, Catherine's father had passed away and her mother had remarried.[24] New France's civil code—*la coutume de Paris*—protected the inherited wealth of widows and daughters, as well as the property they brought into marriage. After the fall of New France, new imperial regimes introduced their own legal codes, which played out unevenly, often resulting in pronounced legal pluralism.[25] This was certainly the case for Illinois Country and Upper Louisiana, where French colonial civil law was regularly employed throughout the remainder of the eighteenth century within the framework of English, Spanish, and American legal regimes. In accordance with *la coutume* Madame Lafontaine retained a portion of her late husband's estate, while her daughter Catherine Giard's inherited wealth was held in trust until her marriage.

French colonial legal provisions may have given the appearance of separate gendered financial spheres, but business was still very much a family affair and couples worked to build collective wealth in the form of a community of goods. As Jan Noel has appropriately noted, "historians of pre-industrial societies have long recognized that family farms and artisanal shops depended on the work of both sexes."[26] In this particular instance, it was Catherine's wealth that afforded her *canadien* husband a position of landed financial security in Illinois Country from which to grow a trans-colonial commercial empire. By 1769 Gabriel Cerré had relinquished his hereditary rights to family property back in Canada and was leasing out some of his wife's inherited land at Fort de Chartres.[27] It might be going a bit too far to say that Catherine worked as an equal partner alongside her husband. After all, like most women, she was captive to the patriarchal structures—legal, social, and religious—of the day.[28] Still, Cerré family wealth increasingly came to depend on Catherine Giard, and, eventually, her daughters.

Shortly after American occupation of Illinois Country in 1778, George Rogers Clark pressured Gabriel Cerré to supply the Virginian army, going so far as to post soldiers outside the family home. Other merchants, like Charles Gratiot at Cahokia, saw doing business with Clark as a potential financial windfall and volunteered to supply the Americans. Unfortunately, devalued American currency and worthless promissory notes dashed any hope of full repayment. In 1781 Cerré and Gratiot both migrated across the Mississippi to St. Louis in Spanish Upper Louisiana.

The Giard-Cerré family's relocation to St. Louis happened to be good timing. The young town at the confluence of the Mississippi and Missouri Rivers had just repelled an attack by British and Indigenous forces in 1780, which ushered in a period of relative peace and tranquility. In addition, St. Louis had displaced Kaskaskia as the premier fur trade center of the region. Gabriel Cerré's ties to Montreal positioned the family to take advantage of old French-creole trade networks that cut across new colonial borders and spanned British, American, and Spanish territories. Catherine Giard and her daughters (the Giard-Cerré women) proved instrumental in developing and maintaining these French-creole transcolonial networks, while simultaneously securing family wealth and social standing at St. Louis.

Back in 1772, at the tender age of six years old, Catherine and Gabriel's eldest child, Marie-Anne (Manon), accompanied her parents on a voyage to Montreal. When they returned to Illinois Country the following year, Manon remained behind under the watchful eye of Cerré's relatives where she attended a school for girls founded in the seventeenth century by the sisters of the Congrégation de Notre-Dame.[29] The same year that the family relocated across the Mississippi River to St. Louis, Manon married Pierre-Louis Panet, a Montreal lawyer from a politically and financially well-connected *canadien* family.[30] The marriage bound the Cerré and Panet families together over vast distances and solidified French-creole networks of kin and commerce.

Gabriel Cerré wrote to Manon in 1782 to convey his and his wife's blessing of the union, and implied that his eldest child had selected her husband, stating "... nothing made me happier than learning this news and the choice you have made."[31] Yet Manon was only sixteen years old, young enough that her paternal uncle, Toussaint, was made legal guardian only days before the wedding for the expressed purpose of authorizing the union.[32] It could hardly have been a coincidence, moreover, that Panet's father had spent close to twenty years working as a notary for Cerré's former business partner and friend Jean Orillat.[33] Discussing her own nuptials years later, Manon's youngest sister, Julie, detailed how their parents had consented to let her marry a recent French arrival to St. Louis, but only after carefully vetting the suitor.[34] And so, while it is certainly possible that Manon and Julie chose their respective matches, it is also quite clear that parents played an important role in setting up marriages, and that short of controlling the process outright, exerted enormous influence over such decisions.[35]

Despite Cerré's effusive remarks of mutual joyous parental consent, Catherine Giard's account of the Cerré-Panet union nearly a decade later was far more somber in tone. Writing about the hardship of separation between mother and daughter, she reminded Manon of her duty to her husband, while at the same time lamenting, "Had it been in my power you would not have left your paternal home, but it was a great sacrifice that I made."[36] Notwithstanding both parents' penchant for rhetoric, Catherine's mournful explication elucidated a nuanced gendered reality. Both obligation and sacrifice constrained the actions of this St. Louis matriarch, while at the same time positioning her at the center of budding family commercial networks.

In 1786 one of Catherine's middle children, Marie-Thérèse (Thérèse), married Auguste Chouteau, a Louisiana creole who had helped establish St. Louis with his step-father, Pierre Laclède Liguest.[37] Nearly a decade later, Catherine's youngest daughter, Julie Cerré, married Antoine-Pierre Soulard, a French officer, who like many other French *émigrés* had taken refuge in America in the wake of the French Revolution.[38] Soulard established himself in St. Louis, working as both first surveyor general of Spanish Upper Louisiana and *adjutant pro tem* to the lieutenant governor.[39]

Each of the Giard-Cerré unions was a quintessential elite French-creole marriage alliance, "designed to increase family fortunes economically, socially, and politically."[40] The Cerré-Panet nuptials solidified Cerré's longstanding commercial ties to his *canadien* homeland, while the Cerré-Chouteau union bound together two of the wealthiest families of Upper Louisiana. But this was more than just renewing old commercial ties and merging family wealth. Manon and Thérèse's marriage alliances linked the immensely profitable Osage fur trade out of St. Louis, over which the Laclède-Chouteau clan held exclusive license, to British capital, goods, and markets at Montreal. In doing so they sustained and stimulated the flow of Atlantic goods into the interior of North America.[41] Later, the Cerré-Soulard marriage gave the family an inside track regarding politics, land acquisitions, and titles. In 1797 Catherine and Gabriel's only son, Pascal Léon, followed a similar pattern to that of two of his sisters and created ties with an established St. Louisan family through his marriage to Thérèse Louise Lamy.[42] Taken altogether, these strategic marriage alliances set a foundation of family legitimacy, commercial wealth, and access to the highest levers of power. And yet, it was the unions of the Giard-Cerré women that ultimately proved to be the pillars upon which family prosperity rested.

Women and the Transcolonial Economy

In 1796 French *émigré* Victor Collot cataloged large quantities of Atlantic goods being shipped down the Ohio River to French-creole communities in Illinois Country and Upper Louisiana. Among other things, the Frenchman's list included French, Portuguese, and Spanish wine; French and Spanish brandy; gin from Holland; textiles of all sorts, such as coarse blankets, woolen and cotton goods, and a variety of silks; dresses; shoes; hats; cutlery; clocks; silver and gold watches; silver teaspoons; tea sets and English china; looking glasses and window glass; jewelry; ladies' parasols; and a few small coaches. Goods for the fur trade were listed separately, reinforcing notions of a vibrant consumer culture in the middle Mississippi valley.[43]

The veritable embarrassment of riches was hardly a new phenomenon, and historian Natalia Belting argued that French creoles had long enjoyed considerable material wealth, going as far as to write: "It may be an exaggeration to say with the early historians of Illinois that Kaskaskia was the 'Versailles of the West'; but it is also an exaggeration to paint the settlement as a rough frontier village. No community could be that if its women wore satin and taffeta gowns and embroidered slippers with silver buckles, its men red silk breeches, fine linen shirts and silk stockings, or if its children were laced in corsets."[44] Taking advantage of his wife's ties to Canada, Auguste Chouteau exploited a number of crucial Cerré commercial contacts for the importation of British goods to St. Louis. By 1798 the fur baron was using over twelve different suppliers in Montreal. In 1800 alone, he ordered Indian textiles, Irish and Russian fabrics, over 143 rods of Scottish fabric, over fifteen dozen black silk handkerchiefs, several dozen leather shoes, including a dozen fine leather shoes, an additional two dozen boys and children's shoes, six pairs of women's shoes, ninety-nine Indian cotton shirts, large numbers of bracelets, ribbons, silks and satins, red and blue cloth, six dozen ivory combs, and several large barrels of wine.[45] The goods were procured in Montreal and shipped to St. Louis via Michilimackinac along the canoe routes of the fur trade. It was Chouteau's attempt to recreate what he understood to be "good society."[46]

From expansive libraries to the finery of household adornments, a world of Atlantic goods was meant to engender a particular culture of respectability, etiquette, and education. This was a far cry from Nicolas de Finiel's 1803 depiction of St. Louis as a wretched place that became a muddy bog when it rained and whose local inhabitants went hungry when provisions from private gardens and local Indigenous peoples grew scarce.[47] The town had seemingly outgrown its early nickname, *Pain Court*, or at the very least not all suffered deprivation equally.[48] Wealthy families dined using only the finest tablecloths, napkins, and silverware, and drank a variety of imported wines and coffee.[49] By the turn of the nineteenth century, it appeared as if you could get almost anything you wanted in St. Louis if you were part of the merchant elite. The town had an increasingly diverse population that was connected to commercial *entrepôts* and transatlantic markets. St. Louis was, in a word, cosmopolitan.[50] This is not all that surprising, however, considering the confluence of continental rivers and the long history of cosmopolitanism in the region dating back to the Mississippian era and the later migrations of Indigenous peoples.[51]

The Giard-Cerré women actively took part in the transcolonial market economy. For example, in June 1793, Catherine Giard sent her daughter Manon a package with tissue and cloth (Polish and Indian), a number of handkerchiefs (one of which was embroidered), an embroidered vest for Manon's husband, a parasol for Amélie (Manon's daughter), three types of grains, and a sack of pecans for the grandkids.[52] That same month, Julie Cerré wrote to sister Manon, complaining that she wanted to send a few small gifts, but that Mr. Quesnel was leaving with her father's canoes and that she could not get things together in time.[53] Two weeks later, she sent another note to her sister and enclosed a ring with the letter.[54] In 1804 Thérèse received a portrait of her sister and nephew from Montreal, and wrote back that she hoped to return the kindness in due course. Goods flowed back and forth between mother and daughter, sisters, friends, and associates, in what amounted to the material cultural expression of a French river world.

When Catherine Giard died in 1800, she was matriarch to one of the wealthiest families of St. Louis with an estate valued at 25,940 *piastres*. This included multiple properties, coaches and carriages, livestock, wardrobes, and all sorts of goods, from imported liquor, silverware, and glass, to exotic fabrics. Like many of the elite families of St. Louis, Catherine and her husband were literate and had built an extensive library ranging from religious texts and world history to the *Voyages of Cook*.[55] Of course not all of this came from Canada. After all, St. Louis lay at the intersection of transcontinental waterways that tied it to imperial commercial *entrepôts*, from Montreal, Detroit, Michilimackinac, and Pittsburgh in the north, to New Orleans and the islands of the Caribbean in the south.

Among the items indexed for Giard's estate were twenty-one enslaved individuals categorized as black or mulatto, a reminder of the terrible human cost of French colonial wealth.[56] Most slaveholders in Illinois Country counted a handful of enslaved individuals each, which were deployed primarily as domestics, farmhands, and boatmen.[57] The Giard-Cerré family were somewhat exceptional, however, in that they became one of the largest slaveholders in Upper Louisiana, with as many as forty-three enslaved black/mulatto individuals according to the census of 1791.[58] Some enslaved peoples traveled the river highways of the continent. For example, Gabriel Cerré allegedly took a couple of enslaved Black individuals to work as boatmen on his voyages, and his daughter Manon brought a Black female slave with her on a trip from St. Louis to Montreal in 1791.[59]

The old French *Code Noir* and newer Spanish colonial edicts provided provisions for the treatment of enslaved peoples and the conduct of slaveholders, though there was variability in how closely the rules were followed, in particular when it came to intimate relationships.[60] And yet, as Jennifer Palmer has so recently demonstrated, for the French Atlantic, "intimate bonds" were not strictly physical intimacy, but included an array of close quotidian interactions that domestic relations fostered.[61] There is little to indicate that Cerré's family back in Canada had much familiarity with the transatlantic African slave trade.[62] Catherine Giard's family on the other hand had held peoples of African descent in slavery and her father had rented them out as labor on several occasions. Catherine, moreover, had served as godparent for the baptism of a number of these enslaved individuals.[63]

Catholic baptism drew free and enslaved people into complex webs of fictive kinship, which reinforced racialized colonial power relations and provided networks of resistance.[64] Aside from Catherine's granddaughter's insinuation that the St. Louisan matriarch had a respectful or close relationship with those she held in slavery, noting that "she almost always spoke to her slaves in Negro French," there are few details regarding Madame Giard's interactions with her slaves.[65] We do know, however, that Catherine's husband was away on business almost every year; indeed, she frequently complained about it.[66] Cerré's long voyages meant that Catherine was left in charge of managing local affairs and agricultural production on the family's diverse land holdings. This included overseeing both household and farm slave labor.[67]

Women in the Illinois Country and Upper Louisiana were regularly left to manage family business when their husbands were absent.[68] Men could divest their patriarchal authority to their wives through a power of attorney (la procuration générale), and women could likewise grant that same third-party authority to friends, family, or associates to dispense with specific tasks (la procuration particulière).[69] Women could therefore exercise a great deal of authority within the gendered confines of frontier colonial society.

St. Louis was initially established as a center for the exchange of peltries and the conduct of Euro-Indigenous diplomacy, and the fur trade remained a vibrant industry into the 1830s. As the eighteenth century wore on, however, farming slowly began to assert itself in Upper Louisiana.[70] The Giard-Cerré family became one of the largest grain producers of St. Louis in the late 1780s.[71] In 1791 alone, the family produced three hundred bushels of wheat and five hundred bushels of corn, which put them among the top three or four agricultural producers in town.[72] During the French regime the Illinois Country had gained a reputation as Louisiana's bread basket and Catherine's work helped maintain old trade networks with New Orleans.[73] When she died, all but three of those held in slavery were willed to her children and their spouses in St. Louis, leaving just enough labor to help Cerré—by then an aging widower—maintain the household. The divestment of slaves was testament to the salient role that Catherine had played in managing and growing the agribusiness portion of family wealth out of St. Louis.

Women's Voyages

The fact that women's engagement in the transcolonial economy could largely be done from the comfort of their homes, either through the consumption and exchange of goods, or the domestic management of slave labor, makes it easy to lose sight of the fact that women also traveled the rivers of the continent. Sedentary domesticity was interrupted by moments of transcolonial mobility, often characterized by at least a single long migratory voyage. For instance, Auguste Chouteau's mother, Marie-Thérèse Bourgeois, traveled up the Mississippi with her four children to St. Louis shortly after its founding.[74] Other women, however, made more than one long river voyage during the course of their lives.

We saw in the opening story that Marguerite Dupuis traveled from St. Louis to Montreal to meet up with her husband. But this was not her first voyage. Born in Canada in the parish of La Prairie in 1744, Marguerite married Joachim Demolier at Montreal in 1765 and migrated with her husband and brother to Illinois Country sometime over the next seven years. Widowed in 1772, Marguerite remarried that same year to another transplanted *Canadien*, Jean-Baptiste dit Lapierre, a master blacksmith. At some point over the next six years, Marguerite and Jean-Baptiste moved to St. Louis, while her brother married into the Crely family and remained at Kasksakia.[75] And yet this is where Marguerite's story ends. Like so many women, we are left with only glimpses of their travels.

Take for instance the case of the Robidoux family. Marie-Anne Robidoux and daughter Marie-Josephe emigrated to St. Louis from Montreal sometime in the early 1770s. It is not entirely clear if Joseph-Marie returned to fetch his mother and sister after his father passed away in 1771, or if the two ladies procured passage to St. Louis with a fur trading outfit. What we do know is that Marie-Anne decided to stay in St. Louis with her son, while Marie-Josephe returned to Montreal in the early 1780s, where she married and lived out the rest of her days.[76]

Catherine Giard and her daughters did not travel all that frequently, but there is some evidence that long river voyages were not entirely uncommon either. Catherine voyaged from Kaskaskia to Montreal with her husband in 1772 and gave birth to their son, Pascal Léon, the following year in Canada. The trip had, in actual fact, been to bring Catherine's daughter Manon to Montreal for schooling.[77] Katharine Corbett contends that "a few fur merchants sent their sons to school in Canada and Europe, but not their daughters."[78] Indeed, Manon's brother was also sent away for schooling in Montreal for a brief time, while her sisters were kept in St. Louis. Perhaps the decision to educate Manon in Montreal had to with her being the eldest child of a merchant, who up to that point only had daughters. Or perhaps it was part of a long-term strategy for maintaining long-distance family-commercial ties. Still, Manon's experience is a reminder that women also took part in these voyages, were occasionally sent away for school, and became key members of these transcolonial networks.

A formal education continued to be hard to come by in St. Louis until the 1830s.[79] In 1794–95, Marie-Josephe Rigauche opened a school at the request of the Spanish governor, and Angélique La Grange Pescay also opened a school for girls, but both had limited success. Jean-Baptiste Truteau likewise worked as a teacher after returning from an expedition up the Missouri River in 1794. Most local education, however, appears to have been predominantly obtained by private tutor. Both of Manon's younger sisters managed to acquire a basic education in St. Louis, though Thérèse Cerré sheepishly admitted in a letter to her Montreal aunt-in-law in 1796 that she had meant to write sooner, but for her poor writing and fear of being judged.[80]

Family-commercial networks often played a role in sending children away for schooling. For example, Thérèse Cerré and Auguste Chouteau sent their son Aristide to be educated in Montreal in 1800. John Lyle, an important Cerré family business associate, was charged with safely transporting Aristide, and *oncle* Panet was expected to tend to the young man's education. Chouteau was quick to point out, however, that *tante* Manon would ease their minds and sooth their hearts by acting as a second mother to their son.[81] Constrained as she was within the gendered stratum of responsibility for the well-being of her nephew, Manon's role as surrogate parent provided a bridge between the parents in St. Louis and the child in Montreal by watching over and safeguarding the emotional well-being of both during their separation.

Women and children traveled the river highways regularly enough that it aroused neither shock nor suspicion. At times, plans to travel fell through, such as in 1799, when Julie Cerré's trip to Montreal was canceled because the canoes left too late in the season.[82] In 1790 Manon took advantage of her father's frequent travels to hitch a ride back and visit family in St. Louis. It had been nearly twenty years since she had left the shores of the Mississippi and she set off from Montreal with her eldest child, Léon, in tow. Manon's daughter, Amélie, stayed behind in Canada, and traveled with her father to visit his parents in Quebec City.[83] Manon and her husband swapped letters that year to keep each other updated on their children's development.[84] Though women's travel was somewhat infrequent, even for those from elite merchant families, the few trips that the Giard-Cerré women did make were instrumental in renewing family bonds and strengthening transcolonial ties.

Correspondence and Women's Networks

When women were not traveling the rivers of the continent, they remained interconnected through regular correspondence. If the canoe brigades of the fur trade and the movement of goods, furs, and people were the physical manifestation of a French river world, then information through correspondence, whether by letter or word of mouth, was the intellectual and social underpinning of such French-creole networks. The Giard-Cerré letters, therefore, serve as a reminder of how transcolonial networks functioned. The Giard-Cerré women were careful to indicate who carried their letters and who told them about family, friends, and associates abroad.

Catherine Giard was particularly sensitive about the reliability and security of letters as the lifeblood to long-distance family networks. In 1795 she scolded Manon and complained about the infrequency with which she received her letters. Frustrated over lengthy delays and sporadic news that came only "indirectly" from third parties, she posited, "I have reason to think that you trust your letters to [unfaithful] persons, or to those who at the very least are careless, since it has been years without hearing of your state of well-being."[85] The St. Louis matriarch pointed out that Andrew Todd, a close Cerré business associate, carried her letter and brought news whenever he came to visit, and pleaded for Manon to take advantage of his services in the future.

Mr. Todd delivered Giard-Cerré family correspondence for at least several years and Catherine wrote again to Manon the following autumn to explain that he was staying with the family for few days, preparing for his voyage, and had agreed once again to carry their letters. Catherine mentioned, moreover, that they had spoken at length about Manon and her children.[86] The note to her daughter reveals two salient aspects of women's transcolonial networks out of St. Louis: that women helped to maintain crucial transcolonial connections by hosting business associates; and that through these interactions, news traveled at least as much by word of mouth as by written correspondence. Madame Giard's hosting duties included visits from numerous family friends and associates, who regularly ferried letters back and forth. These contacts included *canadien* merchants like Mr. Quesnel, Mr. Orillat, and Jean-Philippe Leprohon, but also an increasing number of Scottish and English merchants such as Andrew Todd, Myer Michaels, and John Lyle. The ethnicity of Cerré's contacts reflected changes in Canada, where a number of British merchants had married into established *canadien* families as a way of accessing the western trade. Thus, Catherine Giard's work in hosting her husband's business associates helped maintain evolving transcolonial networks of the French river world.

Hosting their husband's associates and contacts was certainly crucial, but matriarchs in Upper Louisiana and Canada also kept in touch in what amounted to their own complex women's transcolonial network. Madame Giard and her daughters' frequent references to other women, usually elite merchants' wives, gives a tantalizing glimpse into this largely clandestine world. Regular instructions to pass along news and well wishes linked women in Upper Louisiana such as Madames Rigauche, Brazeau, St. Cire, and Madame Pélagie Kiersereau-Chouteau with those in Canada like Madames Quesnel, Orillat, and Panet.[87] Unfortunately, most detailed discussion within these circles took place through intermediaries and in private conversation, with few insights into what women were actually saying to each other. Still, the Giard-Cerré correspondence makes evident that these transcolonial women's networks were part of the social fabric of the broader French river world.

Conclusion

Catherine Giard and her daughters were central in establishing a French-creole transcolonial empire. Whether it was through intermarriage; the procurement and shipment of goods; managing slave labor and agricultural production for the southern grain trade; traveling the rivers of the continent; acting as surrogate parents for children abroad; hosting merchants and visitors; or corresponding among themselves and other elites, the Giard-Cerré women were intricately involved in French-creole networks anchored at colonial St. Louis but stretching as far as Quebec City and New Orleans and, by extension, the Atlantic and Caribbean. Much like their English-speaking counterparts in the Atlantic colonies, French-creole women in St. Louis influenced and shaped an emerging society and consumer culture.[88]

Notwithstanding tropes of isolation and self-sufficiency, which frontier colonial societies routinely inspire, the Giard-Cerré women looked decidedly east to the Atlantic. The consumption of Atlantic goods created expectations for what society could become, as well as constraints in terms of how people should live and interact. The extent to which French creoles in Upper Louisiana were free or "rogue" ultimately had to be balanced with how compelled they were to conform to notions of "good society" derived from a transcolonial and Atlantic consumer culture.[89] As architects, purveyors, and participants of transcolonial French-creole networks, Catherine Giard and her daughters were at the center of the struggle to define St. Louis, frontier society, and their connections to the world.

1. Names show up in the records with a number of different spellings—Dupuy/Dupuis, Durant/Durand, etc. Where possible PRDH standardized names have been used.

2. Marguerite Dupuy's statement, MHM, Litigation Collection, Dupuy v. Durant, St. Louis, 18 November 1778. Though there is little on either Leduc or Ducharme in the suit, it is likely that the two merchants were Pierre Leduc dit Souligny and Jean-Marie Ducharme, both *canadien* merchants from Montreal. For Leduc see: PRDH Individual 79956; "Pierre Leduc Souligny," SBHS, Voyageur Contracts Database. For Ducharme see: Foley and Rice, *The First Chouteaus*, 18; Primm, *Lion of the Valley*, 26; Armour, "DUCHARME," accessed October 31, 2017; PRDH Individual 161837.

3. Pierre Durant's rejoinder, MHM, Litigation Collection, Dupuy v. Durant, St. Louis, 21 November 1778; Testimonies of Augustin Monpetit, Joseph Poitevin, and Étienne Cardinal, MHM, Litigation Collection, Dupuy v. Durant, St. Louis, 24 November 1778.

4. Petition of Joseph Montpetit, Augustin Monpetit, Étienne Cardinal, and Joseph Desrocher, MHM, Litigation Collection, St. Louis, 30 November, 1778.

5. Podruchny, *Making the Voyageur World*, 6–9.

6. Englebert and St-Onge, "Paddling into History," 71–103.

7. Sleeper-Smith, "Women, Kin, and Catholicism," 423–52; Sleeper-Smith, *Indian Women and French Men*; Van Kirk, *"Many Tender Ties"*; Brown, *Strangers in Blood*; Marrero, "Women at the Crossroads," 159–85.

8. Englebert, "Beyond Borders," 54–68.

9. For a detailed explanation of how the term French creole has been employed here see: Gitlin, "From Private Stories to Public Memory," 3–16; Villerbu, "Introduction," 7–16.

10. Choquette, "'Ces Amazones Du Grand Dieu,'" 627–55; Noel, *Women in New France*; Noel, "'Nagging Wife' Revisited," 45–60; Noel, *Along a River*; Richter, "Widowhood in New France," 49–62; Savoie, "Women's Marital Difficulties," 473–85; Young, "'. . . Sauf Les Perils et Fortunes,'" 388–407; Ferland and Grenier, *Femmes, culture et pouvoir*; Grenier, *Marie-Catherine Peuvret*; Clark, *Masterless Mistresses*; Spear, *Race, Sex, and Social Order*.

11. Noel, *Along a River*, 15; Moogk, *La Nouvelle France*, 229.

12. Boyle, "Did She Generally Decide?," 775–89; Brown, *History as They Lived It*, 192; Cleary, *The World, the Flesh*, 136–41, 146–50.

13. Ekberg, *Stealing Indian Women*; Rushforth, *Bonds of Alliance*; Person, *Standing up for Indians*; Morrissey, "Kaskaskia Social Network," 103–46; White, *Wild Frenchmen and Frenchified Indians*; Foster, "Women in Early America," 2; The literature is voluminous, but for the shift in women's early American history, see: Sklar, *Catharine Beecher*; Norton, *Liberty's Daughters*; Kerber, *Women of the Republic*; Clinton, *Plantation Mistress*; Ulrich, *Good Wives*; Buel and Buel, *Way of Duty*; White, *Ar'n't I a Woman?*; Salmon, *Women and the Law*; Karlsen, *Shape of a Woman*; Brown, *Good Wives*; Berkin, *First Generations*; Cott, *Bonds of Womanhood*; Gordon-Reed, *Thomas Jefferson and Sally Hemings*; Allgor, *Parlor Politics*; Wellman, *Road to Seneca Falls*.

14. Burnett and Luebbering, *Immigrant Women*, 34.

15. Noel, *Along a River*; Young, "'. . . Sauf Les Perils et Fortunes'"; Choquette, *Frenchmen into Peasants*; Ferland and Grenier, *Femmes, culture et pouvoir*; Clark, *Masterless Mistresses*; Spear, *Race, Sex, and Social Order*.

16. Calloway, *Scratch of a Pen*.

17. Fausz, *Founding St. Louis*; Cleary, *The World, the Flesh*; Ekberg and Person, *St. Louis Rising*; Christian, *Before Lewis and Clark*; Thorne, *Many Hands of My Relations*.

18. Gitlin, *Bourgeois Frontier*.

19. Englebert, "Merchant Representatives," 63–82.

20. PRDH Individual 79595; KM 34:11:12:1.

21. Englebert, "Gabriel Cerré," 48–57.

22. Mathieu, Therrien-Fortier, and Lessard, "Mobilité et sédentarité," 223; Lessard, Mathieu, and Gouger, "Peuplement Colonisateur," 59; Vidal, "Les Implantations Française," 238–43; Englebert, "Beyond Borders," 64.

23. KM 38:3:20:3; KM 40:3:17:1; KM: 45:1:14:2; KM 45:7:29:1; KM 45:9:24:1.

24. KM 51:3:21:1; 52:3:19:1; KM 53:1:17:2.

25. Benton and Ross, "Empires and Legal Pluralism," 1–17; Kolish, *Nationalismes et conflits de droits*, chaps. 1–3; Morin, "Discovery and Assimilation," 583; Morin, Decroix, and Gilles, *Les Tribunaux et l'arbitrage*, 32–33; Fyson, *Magistrates, Police, and People*, 16; Baade, "Marriage Contracts," 1–92; Banner, "Written Law and Unwritten Norms," 33–80; Ekberg and Person, *St. Louis Rising*, 127–46; Brooks Sundberg, "Women and Property," 633–65.

26. Noel, *Along a River*, 14.

27. Gabriel Cerré Land Transfer, BANQ, Greffes de Notaires, P. Panet de Méru (1755–78), 31 July 1767; KM 69:06:12:1.

28. Little, *Many Captivities of Esther Wheelwright*, 5–8.

29. Faribault-Beauregard, *La vie aux Illinois au XVIIIe Siècle*, 14–15; Magnuson, *Education in New France*, 134–48; Gray, *Congrégation de Notre-Dame*, 9.

30. PRDH Family 41114; Morel, "Pierre—Louis Panet," accessed May 21, 2008.

31. Cerré to Mme P. L. Panet, AUM, Baby Collection, P0058, U2522, mf 4405, St. Louis, 28 May 1782.

32. PRDH Individual 220373; Tutelle ad hoc de Marie Anne Serré, fille mineure de Gabriel Serré et Catherine Giard absents aux Illinois, BANQ, CP601, S5, D2753, 11 August 1781.

33. Morel, "Pierre—Louis Panet."

34. Dame Cerré-Soulard à Mme. P. L. Panet, AUM, Baby Collection, P0058, U2545, St. Louis, 23 September 1796.

35. Gadoury, *La famille dans son intimité*, 77.

36. Dame Giard-Cerré à Mme P. L. Panet, AUM, Baby Collection, U4530, St. Louis, 17 June 1793.

37. Marriage contract of Thérèse Cerré and Auguste Chouteau, IGD, Drouin Collection, St. Louis, 26 September 1786. For a detailed rethinking of the founding of St. Louis see: Ames, *Auguste Chouteau's Journal: Memory*; Fausz, *Founding St. Louis*; Ekberg and Person, *St. Louis Rising*.

38. Marriage contract of Julie Cerré and Antoine Soulard, IGD, Drouin Collection, St. Louis, 17 November 1795. Furstenberg, *When the United States Spoke French*; Ekberg, *French Aristocrat in the American West*.

39. Knutson, "Soulard," 712.

40. Devine, *People Who Own Themselves*, 68.

41. Foley contends that most furs were shipped to Canada. Foley, *Genesis of Missouri*, 96, 314 n61.

42. Marriage contract of Paschal Cerré and Thérèse Louise Lami, IGD, Drouin Collection, St. Louis, 14 February, 1797.

43. Collot, *Journey in North America*, 2:201.

44. Belting, *Kaskaskia under the French Regime*, 51.

45. Inventory of assorted goods sent by Michaels, Lacroix, and Bleakley to Auguste Chouteau. MHM, The Chouteau Collection, Microfilm Reel 2 (00697), St. Louis & Michilimackinac, 10 July 1800.

46. Letter from Auguste Chouteau to P. L. Panet, MHM, The Chouteau Collection, Microfilm Reel 2 (00634), St. Louis, 10 May 1800.

47. de Finiels, *Account of Upper Louisiana*, 63.

48. Foley, *Genesis of Missouri*, 106.

49. Burnett and Luebbering, *Immigrant Women*, 33.

50. Cangany, *Frontier Seaport*, 64–65.

51. Alt, *Cahokia's Complexities*, 16–17; Morrissey, *Empire by Collaboration*, 14–38; Warren, *Worlds the Shawnees Made*, 41–54, 78–79.

52. Dame Giard-Cerré à Mme P. L. Panet, AUM, Baby Collection, U4530, St. Louis, 17 June 1793.

53. Julie Cerré à Mme P. L. Panet, AUM, Baby Collection, P0058, U2550, mf 4413, St. Louis, 3 June 1793.

54. Julie Cerré à Mme P. L. Panet, AUM, Baby Collection, P0058, U2551, mf 4413, St. Louis, 18 June 1793.

55. Mad. Cerré's Estate 1802, MHM, St. Louis Archives, St. Louis, 14 April 1802; McDermott, *Private Libraries*.

56. Heerman, "Beyond Plantations," 1–22; O'Malley, *Final Passages*; Rushforth, *Bonds of Alliance*; Ekberg, *Stealing Indian Women*; Brett Rushforth, "'A Little Flesh,'" 777–808.

57. Ekberg, *French Roots*, 150–56. Ekberg notes that nearly half grain-producing inhabitants of Upper Louisiana owned at least one slave, but that only Cerré owned more than fifteen between 1787 and 1791. Weight, "'Come Recently from Guinea,'" 26. Weight contends that Cerré had as many as eighty slaves after Marie-Thérèse's marriage to Auguste Chouteau. Unfortunately, no reference is provided. Also see: "Statistical Census," in Houck, *Spanish Regime in Missouri*, 2:373–78; Foley, *Genesis of Missouri*, 114–16. There were seventy free blacks in St. Louis according to the Spanish census of 1800. For a discussion on the distinction between slave society and a society with slaves see: Berlin, *Many Thousands Gone*.

58. "Statistical Census," in Houck, *Spanish Regime in Missouri*, 2:374.

59. Pierre v. Gabriel Chouteau, MSA, SLCC, November 1842, no. 125, 35–36, 177–79.

60. Cleary, *The World, the Flesh*, 133, 142–62; Ekberg, *Colonial Ste. Genevieve*, 223–25; Winch, *Clamorgans*, 40–69.

61. Palmer, *Intimate Bonds*, 3–16.

62. Cerré's granddaughter Amélie noted that slavery was a key distinction between the French in Canada and Illinois Country. Marcel Trudel and Brett Rushforth show that Black and Indigenous slaves were in Canada under the French regime. It is likely that Amélie was generalizing from her own family context, as there is no real evidence of Black slaves owned by the Cerré family in Canada. Faribault-Beauregard, *La vie aux Illinois*, 7; Trudel and d'Allaire, *Deux siècles d'esclavage*; Rushforth, *Bonds of Alliance*.

63. Weight, "'Come Recently from Guinea,'" 160–62.

64. Brasseaux, "Administration of Slave Regulations," 148; Sleeper-Smith, "Women, Kin, and Catholicism"; Person, *Standing up for Indians*; Morrissey, "Kaskaskia Social Network."

65. Faribault-Beauregard, *La vie aux Illinois*, 11.

66. Dame Giard-Cerré à Mme P. L. Panet, AUM, Baby Collection, U4537, St. Louis, 6 May 1800. Although there are many letters, this one epitomizes the grievances.

67. Corbett, *In Her Place*, 18–19.

68. Boyle, "Did She Generally Decide?"; Burnett and Luebbering, *Immigrant Women*, 34; Foley, *Genesis of Missouri*, 110.

69. Englebert, "Legacy of New France," 43.

70. Reda, *From Furs to Farms*, 33–34; Fausz, *Founding St. Louis*, 20.

71. Carl Ekberg indicates that women did not generally work the fields, but rather tended to the household garden. He also notes that the Giard-Cerré family became one of the largest grain producers of Upper Louisiana. He does not, however, broach the subject of women managing agricultural labor. Ekberg, *French Roots*, 139, 155.

72. "Statistical Census," in Houck, *Spanish Regime in Missouri*, 2:373–78.

73. Ekberg, "Flour Trade in French Colonial Louisiana," 261–82.

74. Cleary, *The World, the Flesh*, 48.

75. PRDH Individual 169084; PRDH Individual 169083; PRDH Marriage 299280; PRDH Individual 124145; PRDH Family 48692; Houck, *Spanish Regime in Missouri*, 1:186.

76. Devine, *People Who Own Themselves*, 67; Lewis, *Robidoux Chronicles*, 12; Thorne, *Many Hands of My Relations*, 89, 127; PRDH Family 26848; In actual fact, Marie-Josephe married twice at Montreal, first in 1783, and then again in 1788, three years after the death of her first husband. See: PRDH Individual 200526; PRDH Individual 201783.

77. Faribault-Beauregard, *La vie aux Illinois*, 14–15; Magnuson, *Education in New France*, 134–48. For a history of the school in question see: Gray, *Congrégation de Notre-Dame*.

78. Corbett, *In Her Place*, 9. For more on early education in St. Louis, see: Parks, "Introduction," 28; Hodes, *Beyond the Frontier*, 335; Hyde, *Empires, Nations, and Families*, 6, 27.

79. Gitlin, *Bourgeois Frontier*, 80, 98, 148.

80. Thérèse Chouteau à Mme P. L. Panet, AUM, Baby Collection, U2732, St. Louis, 15 June 1796.

81. Auguste Chouteau à sa soeur, AUM, Baby Collection, U2730, n.d.; MHM, The Chouteau Collection, Microfilm Reel 2 of 40, 00634.

82. Dame Giard-Cerré to Mme P. L. Panet, St. Louis, AUM, Baby Collection, U4535, 18 June 1799.

83. Faribault-Beauregard, *La vie aux Illinois au XVIIIe siècle*, 26–27.

84. P. L. Panet à sa femme, AUM, Baby Collection, U9311, Québec, 27 September 1790; Dame Panet à son mari, AUM, Baby Collection, U9350, St. Louis, 28 April 1791.

85. Dame Giard-Cerré à Mme P. L. Panet, AUM, Baby Collection, U4531, St. Louis, 11 March 1795.

86. Dame Giard-Cerré à Mme P. L. Panet, AUM, Baby Collection, U4533-1, St. Louis, 23 September 1796.

87. Dame Giard-Cerré à Mme P. L. Panet, AUM, Baby Collection, U4530, St. Louis, 17 June 1793; Dame Giard-Cerré à Mme P. L. Panet, AUM, Baby Collection, Université de Montréal, U4535, St. Louis, 18 June 1799.

88. Shammas, "How Self-Sufficient?," 247–72; Brewer and Porter, "Introduction," 1–15; McKendrick, Brewer, and Plumb, *Consumer Society*; Breen, "Empire of Goods," 467–99.

89. Clark, "Patrimony without Pater," 95–110; Dawdy, *Building the Devil's Empire*; Clark, *Masterless Mistresses*; White, "'Baser Commerce.'"

BIBLIOGRAPHY

Archives and Manuscripts

AUM. Archives de l'Université de Montréal. P58. Collection Louis-François-Georges Baby, 1602–1924 (Baby Collection). Montreal, Canada.

BANQ. Bibliothèque et Archives nationales du Québec. Montreal, Canada.

Collot, Victor. *A Journey in North America, Containing a Survey of the Countries Watered by the Mississippi, Ohio, Missouri, and Other Affluing Rivers . . .* 2 vols. Paris: Arthus Bertrand, 1826.

de Finiels, Nicolas. *An Account of Upper Louisiana*. Edited by Carl J. Ekberg and William E. Foley. Columbia: University of Missouri Press, 1989.

Houck, Louis, ed. *The Spanish Regime in Missouri: A Collection of Papers and Documents Relating to Upper Louisiana during the Dominion of Spain*. 2 vols. 2. Chicago: R. R. Donnelly & Sons, 1909.

IGD. Institut Généalogique Drouin. Drouin Collection. Montreal, Canada.

KM. Kaskaskia Manuscripts. Microfilm. Randolph County Court House. Chester IL.

MHM. Missouri History Museum Research Center. Litigation Collection. St. Louis MO.

MSA. Missouri State Archives. Office of the Circuit Clerk. Circuit Court Case Files (SLCC). St. Louis, http://digital.wustl.edu/c/ccr/.

PRDH. Programme de Recherche en Démographie Historique. Université de Montréal. Montreal, Canada. https://www.prdh-igd.com/fr/accueil.

SBHS. St-Boniface Historical Society. Voyageur Contracts Database. http://shsb .mb.ca/en/Voyageurs_database.

Published Works

Allgor, Catherine. *Parlor Politics: In Which the Ladies of Washington Help Build a City and a Government.* Charlottesville: University of Virginia Press, 2002.

Alt, Susan M. *Cahokia's Complexities: Ceremonies and Politics of the First Mississippian Farmers.* Tuscaloosa: University of Alabama Press, 2018.

Armour, David A. "DUCHARME, JEAN-MARIE." In *Dictionary of Canadian Biography*, Vol. 5, University of Toronto/Université Laval, 2003–, accessed October 31, 2017. http://www.biographi.ca/en/bio/ducharme_laurent_4E.html.

Baade, Hans W. "Marriage Contracts in and French and Spanish Louisiana: A Study in 'Notarial' Jurisprudence." *Tulane Law Review* 53, no. 1 (1979): 1–92.

Banner, Stuart. "Written Law and Unwritten Norms in Colonial St. Louis." *Law and History Review* 14, no. 1 (1996): 33–80.

Belting, Natalia Maree. *Kaskaskia under the French Regime.* Carbondale: University of Southern Illinois Press, 2003.

Benton, Lauren, and Richard J. Ross. "Empires and Legal Pluralism: Jurisdiction, Sovereignty, and Political Imagination in the Early Modern World." In *Legal Pluralism and Empires, 1500–1850,* edited by Lauren Benton and Richard J. Ross, 1–17. New York: New York University Press, 2013.

Berkin, Carol. *First Generations: Women in Colonial America.* New York: Hill and Wang, 1996.

Berlin, Ira. *Many Thousands Gone: The First Two Centuries of Slavery in North America.* Cambridge MA: Belknap Press, 1998.

Boyle, Susan C. "Did She Generally Decide? Women in Ste. Genevieve, 1750–1805." *William and Mary Quarterly* 44, no. 4 (1987): 775–89.

Brasseaux, Carl A. "The Administration of Slave Regulations in French Louisiana, 1724–1766," *Louisiana History* 21 (1980): 139–59.

Breen, T. H. "An Empire of Goods: The Anglicization of Colonial America, 1690–1776." *Journal of British Studies* 20, no. 4 (1986): 467–99.

Brewer, John, and Roy Porter. "Introduction." In *Consumption and the World of Goods,* edited by John Brewer and Roy Porter, 1–15. New York: Routledge, 1994.

Brooks Sundberg, Sara. "Women and Property in Early Louisiana: Legal Systems at Odds," *Journal of the Early Republic* 32, no. 4 (2012): 633–65.

Brown, Kathleen M. *Good Wives, Nasty Wenches, and Anxious Patriarchs: Gender, Race, and Power in Colonial Virginia.* Chapel Hill: University of North Carolina Press, 1996.

Brown, Jennifer S. H. *Strangers in Blood: Fur Trade Families in Indian Country.* Vancouver: University of British Columbia Press, 1980.

Brown, Margaret Kimball. *History as They Lived It: A Social History of Prairie Du Rocher, Ill.* Tucson: Patrice Press, 2005.

Buel, Joy Day, and Richard Buel Jr. *The Way of Duty: A Woman and Her Family in Revolutionary America.* New York: Norton, 1984.

Burnett, Robyn, and Ken Luebbering. *Immigrant Women in the Settlement of Missouri.* Columbia: University of Missouri Press, 2005.

Calloway, Colin G. *The Scratch of a Pen: 1763 and the Transformation of North America.* New York: Oxford University Press, 2006.

Cangany, Catherine. *Frontier Seaport: Detroit's Transformation into an Atlantic Entrepôt.* Chicago: University of Chicago Press, 2014.

Choquette, Leslie. "'Ces Amazones Du Grand Dieu': Women and Mission in Seventeenth Century Canada." *French Historical Studies* 17, no. 3 (1992): 627–55.

Clark, Emily. *Masterless Mistresses: The New Orleans Ursulines and the Development of a New World Society, 1727–1834.* Chapel Hill: University of North Carolina Press, 2007.

———. "Patrimony without Pater: The New Orleans Ursuline Community and the Creation of a Material Culture." In *French Colonial Louisiana and the Atlantic World,* edited by Bradley G. Bond, 95–110. Baton Rouge: Louisiana State University Press, 2005.

Cleary, Patricia. *The World, the Flesh, and the Devil: A History of Colonial St. Louis.* Columbia: University of Missouri Press, 2011.

Clinton, Catherine. *The Plantation Mistress: Woman's World in the Old South.* New York: Pantheon Books, 1982.

Corbett, Katharine T. *In Her Place: A Guide to St. Louis Women's History.* St. Louis: Missouri Historical Society Press, 1999.

Cott, Nancy F. *The Bonds of Womanhood: "Woman's Sphere" in New England, 1780–1835.* New Haven CT: Yale University Press, 1997.

Christian, Shirley. *Before Lewis and Clark: The Story of the Chouteaus, the French Dynasty That Ruled America's Frontier.* New York: Farrar, Straus and Giroux, 2004.

Dawdy, Shannon Lee. *Building the Devil's Empire: French Colonial New Orleans.* Chicago: University of Chicago Press, 2008.

Decroix, Arnaud, David Gilles, and Michel Morin. *Les tribunaux et l'arbitrage en Nouvelle-France et au Québec de 1740 à 1784*. Montréal: Éditions Thémis, 2012.

Devine, Heather. *The People Who Own Themselves: Aboriginal Ethnogenesis in a Canadian Family, 1660–1990*. Calgary: University of Calgary Press, 2004.

Ekberg, Carl J. *Colonial Ste. Genevieve: An Adventure on the Mississippi Frontier*. Tucson: Patrice Press, 1986.

———. "The Flour Trade in French Colonial Louisiana." *Louisiana History: The Journal of the Louisiana Historical Association* 37, no. 3 (1996): 261–82.

———. *A French Aristocrat in the American West: The Shattered Dreams of De Lassus de Luzières*. Columbia: University of Missouri Press, 2010.

———. *French Roots in the Illinois Country: The Mississippi Frontier in Colonial Times*. Urbana: University of Illinois Press, 1998.

———. *Stealing Indian Women: Native Slavery in the Illinois Country*. Urbana: University of Illinois Press, 2007.

Ekberg, Carl J., and Sharon K. Person. *St. Louis Rising: The French Regime of Louis St. Ange de Bellerive*. Urbana: University of Illinois Press, 2015.

Englebert, Robert. "Beyond Borders: Mental Mapping and the French River World in North America, 1763–1805." PhD diss., University of Ottawa, 2010.

———. "Gabriel Cerré: Marchand Canadien." In *Vivre La Conquête à Travers plus de 25 Parcours Individuels*, Vol. 2, edited by Gaston Deschênes and Denis Vaugeois, translated by Caroline Lavoie, 48–57. Québec: Septentrion, 2013.

———. "The Legacy of New France: Law and Social Cohesion between Quebec and the Illinois Country, 1763–1790." *French Colonial History* 17 (2017): 35–65.

———. "Merchant Representatives and the French River World, 1763–1803." *Michigan Historical Review* 34, no. 1 (2008): 63–82.

Englebert, Robert, and Nicole St-Onge, "Paddling into History: French-Canadian Voyageurs and the Creation of a Fur Trade World, 1730–1804." In *De Pierre-Esprit Radisson à Louis Riel: Voyageurs et Métis*, edited by Denis Combet, Gilles Lesage, and Luc Côté, 71–103. Winnipeg: Presses universitaires de Saint-Boniface, 2014.

Faribault-Beauregard, Marthe, ed. *La vie aux Illinois au XVIIIe Siècle: souvenirs inédits de Marie-Anne Cerré, un voyage de Montréal à Kamouraska en 1840*. Translated by Michel Thibault. Montréal: Archiv-Histo, 1987.

Fausz, J. Frederick. *Founding St. Louis: First City of the New West*. Charleston: History Press, 2011.

Ferland, Catherine, and Benoît Grenier, eds. *Femmes, culture et pouvoir: relectures de l'histoire au féminin, XVe–XXe siècles*. Québec: Presses de l'Université Laval, 2010.

Foley, William E. *The Genesis of Missouri: From Wilderness Outpost to Statehood.* Columbia: University of Missouri Press, 1989.

Foley, William E., and David Rice. *The First Chouteaus: River Barons of Early St. Louis.* Urbana: University of Illinois Press, 1983.

Foster, Thomas A. "Women in Early America: Crossing Boundaries, Rewriting Histories." In *Women in Early America,* edited by Thomas A. Foster, 1–6. New York: New York University Press, 2015.

Furstenberg, Francois. *When the United States Spoke French: Five Refugees Who Shaped a Nation.* New York: Penguin Press, 2014.

Fyson, Donald. *Magistrates, Police and People: Everyday Criminal Justice in Quebec and Lower Canada.* Toronto: University of Toronto Press, 2006.

Gadoury, Lorraine. *La famille dans son intimité: Échanges épistolaires au sein de l'élite canadinne du XVIIIe siècle.* Montréal: Éditions Hurtubise, 1998.

Gitlin, Jay. *The Bourgeois Frontier: French Towns, French Traders, and American Expansion.* New Haven CT: Yale University Press, 2010.

———. "From Private Stories to Public Memory: The Chouteau Descendants of St. Louis and the Production of History." In *Auguste Chouteau's Journal: Memory, Mythmaking, and History in the Heritage of New France,* edited by Gregory P. Ames, 3–16. Mercantile Library, St. Louis: University of Missouri St. Louis, 2010.

Gordon-Reed, Annette. *Thomas Jefferson and Sally Hemings: An American Controversy.* Williamsburg: University of Virginia Press, 1997.

Gray, Colleen. *The Congrégation de Notre-Dame, Superiors, and the Paradox of Power, 1693–1796.* Montreal: McGill-Queen's University Press, 2007.

Grenier, Benoît. *Marie-Catherine Peuvret, 1667–1739: veuve et seigneuresse en Nouvelle-France.* Sillery: Septentrion, 2005.

Heerman, M. Scott. "Beyond Plantations: Indian and African Slavery in the Illinois Country, 1720–1780." *Slavery and Abolition: A Journal of Slave and Post-Slave Studies,* March 10, 2017: 1–22.

Hodes, Frederick A. *Beyond the Frontier: A History of St. Louis to 1821.* Tucson: Patrice Press, 2004.

Hyde, Anne F. *Empires, Nations & Families: A History of the North American West, 1800–1860.* Lincoln: University of Nebraska Press, 2011.

Karlsen, Carol F. *The Devil in the Shape of a Woman: Witchcraft in Colonial New England.* New York: Norton, 1987.

Kerber, Linda K. *Women of the Republic: Intellect and Ideology in Revolutionary America.* Chapel Hill: University of North Carolina Press, 1980.

Knutson, Kaia A. "Soulard, Antoine Pierre (1766–1825)." In *Dictionary of Missouri Biography*, edited by Lawrence O. Christensen et al., 712. Columbia: University of Missouri Press, 1999.

Kolish, Evelyn. *Nationalismes et conflits de droits: le débat du droit privé au Québec, 1760–1840*. LaSalle: Hurtubise HMH, 1994.

Lessard, Rénald, Jacques Mathieu, and Lina Gouger. "Peuplement Colonisateur Au Pays des Illinois." In *Proceedings of the Annual Meeting of the French Colonial Historical Society, Ste. Genevieve 1986*, edited by Philip Boucher and Serge Courville, 57–68. Lanham MD: University Press of America, 1988.

Lewis, Hugh M. *Robidoux Chronicles: French-Indian Ethnoculture of the Trans-Mississippi West*. Victoria BC: Trafford, 2004.

Little, Ann M. *The Many Captivities of Esther Wheelwright*. New Haven CT: Yale University Press, 2016.

Magnuson, Roger. *Education in New France*. Montreal: McGill-Queen's University Press, 1992.

Marrero, Karen L. "Women at the Crossroads: Trade, Mobility, and Power in Early French America and Detroit." In *Women in Early America*, edited by Thomas A. Foster, 159–85. New York: New York University Press, 2015.

Mathieu, Jacques, Pauline Therrien-Fortier, and Rénald Lessard. "Mobilité et sédentarité: stratégies familiales en Nouvelle-France." *Recherches sociographiques* 28, nos. 2–3 (1987): 211–27.

McDermott, John Francis. *Private Libraries in Creole Saint Louis*. Baltimore: Johns Hopkins University Press, 1938.

McKendrick, Neil, John Brewer, and J. H. Plumb, *The Birth of a Consumer Society: The Commercialization of Eighteenth-Century England*. Bloomington: Indiana University Press, 1982.

Moogk, Peter N. *La Nouvelle France: The Making of French Canada—A Cultural History*. East Lansing: Michigan State University Press, 2000.

Morel, André. "Pierre—Louis Panet (1761–1812)." In *Dictionary of Canadian Biography*, Vol. 5, University of Toronto/Université Laval, 2003–, accessed May 21, 2008. http://www.biographi.ca/en/bio/panet_pierre_louis_1761_1812_5E.html.

Morin, Michel. "The Discovery and Assimilation of British Constitutional Law Principles in Quebec, 1764–1774." *The Dalhousie Law Journal* 36, no. 2 (2013): 581–616.

Morrissey, Robert Michael. *Empire by Collaboration: Indians, Colonists, and Governments in Colonial Illinois Country*. Philadelphia: University of Pennsylvania Press, 2015.

———. "Kaskaskia Social Network: Kinship and Assimilation in the French-Illinois Borderlands, 1695–1735." *William and Mary Quarterly* 70, no. 1 (2013): 103–46.

Noel, Jan. *Along a River: The First French-Canadian Women.* Toronto: University of Toronto Press, 2011.

———. "'Nagging Wife' Revisited: Women and the Fur Trade in New France." *French Colonial History* 7 (2006): 45–60.

———. *Women in New France.* Canadian Historical Association Historical Booklet, Vol. 59. Ottawa: Canadian Historical Association, 1998.

Norton, Mary Beth. *Liberty's Daughters: The Revolutionary Experience of American Women, 1750–1800.* Little, Brown, 1980.

O'Malley, Gregory E. *Final Passages: The Intercolonial Slave Trade of British America, 1619–1807.* Chapel Hill: University of North Carolina Press, 2014.

Palmer, Jennifer L. *Intimate Bonds: Family and Slavery in the French Atlantic.* Philadelphia: University of Pennsylvania Press, 2016.

Parks, Douglas R. "Introduction." In *A Fur Trader on the Upper Missouri: The Journal and Description of Jean-Baptiste Truteau, 1794–1796,* edited by Raymond J. DeMallie, Douglas R. Parks, and Robert Vézina, 1–75. Lincoln: University of Nebraska Press, 2017.

Person, Sharon. *Standing up for Indians: Baptism Registers as an Untapped Source for Multicultural Relations in St. Louis, 1766–1821.* Naperville IL: Center for French Colonial Studies, 2010.

Podruchny, Carolyn. *Making the Voyageur World: Travelers and Traders in the North American Fur Trade.* Toronto: University of Toronto Press, 2006.

Primm, James Neal. *Lion of the Valley: St. Louis, Missouri, 1764–1980.* St. Louis: Missouri History Museum Press, 1998.

Reda, John. *From Furs to Farms: The Transformation of the Mississippi Valley, 1762–1825.* DeKalb: Northern Illinois University Press, 2016.

Richter, Molly G. "Widowhood in New France: Consequences and Coping Strategies." *French Colonial History* 4 (2003): 49–62.

Rushforth, Brett. *Bonds of Alliance: Indigenous and Atlantic Slaveries in New France.* Chapel Hill: University of North Carolina Press, 2012.

———. "'A Little Flesh We Offer You': The Origins of Indian Slavery in New France." *William and Mary Quarterly* 60, no. 4 (2003): 777–808.

Salmon, Marylynn. *Women and the Law of Property in Early America.* Chapel Hill: University of North Carolina Press, 1986.

Savoie, Sylvie. "Women's Marital Difficulties: Requests of Separation in New France." *History of the Family* 3, no. 4 (1998): 473–85.

Shammas, Carole. "How Self-Sufficient Was Early America?" *Journal of Interdisciplinary History* 13, no. 2 (1982): 247–72.

Sklar, Kathryn Kish. *Catharine Beecher: A Study in American Domesticity*. New York: Norton, 1976.

Sleeper-Smith, Susan. *Indian Women and French Men: Rethinking Cultural Encounter in the Western Great Lakes*. Amherst: University of Massachusetts Press, 2001.

———. "Women, Kin, and Catholicism: New Perspectives on the Fur Trade." *Ethnohistory* 47, no. 2 (2000): 423–52.

Spear, Jennifer M. *Race, Sex, and Social Order in Early New Orleans*. Baltimore: Johns Hopkins University Press, 2009.

Thorne, Tanis C. *The Many Hands of My Relations: French and Indians on the Lower Missouri*. Columbia: University of Missouri Press, 1996.

Trudel, Marcel, and Micheline d'Allaire. *Deux siècles d'esclavage au Québec*. Montréal: Hurtubise, 2004.

Ulrich, Laurel. *Good Wives: Image and Reality in the Lives of Women in Northern New England, 1650–1750*. New York: Alfred A. Knopf, 1982.

Van Kirk, Sylvia. *"Many Tender Ties": Women in Fur-Trade Society, 1670–1870*. Winnipeg: Watson & Dwyer, 1980.

Vidal, Cécile. "Les implantations française au Pays des Illinois au XVIIIe siècle, 1699–1765." PhD diss., École des Hautes Études en Science Sociales (EHESS), Centre d'Études Nord-Américaines (CENA), 1995.

Villerbu, Tangi. "Introduction." In *Une Amérique Française, 1760–1860: Dynamiques du Corridor Créole*, edited by Guillaume Teasdale and Tangi Villerbu, 7–16. Paris: Les Indes savantes, 2015.

Warren, Stephen. *The Worlds the Shawnees Made: Migration and Violence in Early America*. Chapel Hill: University of North Carolina Press, 2014.

Weight, Donovan. "'Come Recently from Guinea': Control and Power in the African-Descended Illinois Country, 1719–1848." PhD diss., Southern Illinois University Carbondale, 2010.

Wellman, Judith. *The Road to Seneca Falls: Elizabeth Cady Stanton and the First Woman's Rights Convention*. Urbana: University of Illinois Press, 2004.

Winch, Julie. *The Clamorgans: One Family's History of Race in America*. New York: Hill and Wang, 2011.

White, Deborah Gray. *Ar'n't I a Woman? Female Slaves in the Plantation South*. New York: Norton, 1985.

White, Sophie. "'A Baser Commerce': Retailing, Class, and Gender in French Colonial New Orleans." *William and Mary Quarterly* 63, no. 3 (2006): 517–50.

———. *Wild Frenchmen and Frenchified Indians: Material Culture and Race in Colonial Louisiana.* Philadelphia: University of Pennsylvania Press, 2013.

Young, Kathryn. "'. . . Sauf les perils et fortunes de la mer': Merchant Women in New France and the French Transatlantic Trade, 1713–46." *Canadian Historical Review* 77, no. 3 (1996): 388–407.

3

THE CAPITAL OF ST. LOUIS

From Indian Trade to American Territory, 1764–1825

J. FREDERICK FAUSZ

In 1720 a London publication, entitled *Some Considerations on the Consequences of the French Settling Colonies on the Mississippi*, warned that the Anglo-American colonies would surely "suffer continual Incursions, Depredations, and Murders from the Savages on our Frontiers." Numerous French-allied Indian warriors were allegedly eager to launch such attacks due to the "cunning" persuasiveness of "the Jesuits." While such Protestant prejudice condemned Catholic *men of the cloth* for inciting murderous raids, it was actually *cloth men*—merchants, especially fur traders—who supported such violence by supplying Indian allies with imported fabrics, beads, utensils, and especially muskets.[1]

Virtually surrounding the thirteen English colonies in a broad arc of settlements extending from Canada and the Great Lakes to Louisiana and the Gulf Coast, the French exploited a vast collection of interethnic interest group alliances among multiple Indian communities. The 1744 *Carte de la Louisiane* map by Jacques-Nicolas Bellin revealed key Indian territories and major rivers. But no European place-names appeared in a blank space west of the Mississippi River and south of the Missouri River until French St. Louis emerged as the capital of multicultural commerce in 1764.[2]

That commercial success had its origins in France's catastrophic territorial losses in the Seven Years' War. Great Britain claimed Canada, Acadia, and other territories from the Atlantic Coast to the east bank of the Mississippi River, while Spain gained the West. King Louis XV also abandoned several hundred "French Illinois" residents—Creoles, Canadians, Algonquians, *metis*, and Africans, slave and free—who relied upon

FIG. 3. *Carte de la Louisiane et des pays voisins,* Jacques-Nicolas Bellin, Paris, 1757 version. Library of Congress, Geography and Map Division.

the military capital at Fort de Chartres, where a French commandant and his garrison provided defense, conducted Indian diplomacy, and helped regulate fur trading with multiple tribes. St. Louis inherited those varied functions in 1764, along with many nearby French-speaking civilians, when the west bank of the Mississippi came into its own because British troops were coming to Illinois.[3]

Those emigres built the new village of St. Louis across the river at a most strategic site. Its location on the Mississippi allowed easy access to the Missouri, Illinois, and Ohio Rivers, becoming an incomparable capital for commerce extending a thousand miles in every direction. Enhancing those natural advantages were indispensable human resources among the Osage Indians, who provided the economic prosperity and military security in early St. Louis. Long considered the "Masters of the Hunting Country" on the eastern prairie-plains, numerous mounted Osage warriors ranged some one hundred thousand square miles to harvest the furs of deer, beaver, bison, bear, and many smaller mammals. Adding considerable value to those raw harvests, Osage women expertly manufactured "bucks"—the softest, brain-tanned deer chamois most desired by Parisian women. The labor of both sexes for generations earned the Osages recognition as the "best of the Missouri nations for trade." Historian Kathleen DuVal concluded that the Osages were "far more successful than either France or Spain at building a mid-continental empire" encompassing key areas of Missouri, Kansas, Oklahoma, and Arkansas.[4]

The "Osages accounted for between 40 and 60 percent" of all furs obtained by St. Louisans in the 1770s, including 215,000 pounds of quality chamois. Such admirable productivity established those Indians as the "bankers" of the Missouri Valley, since their "bucks" served as the local currency in St. Louis for many decades. The fierce reputations of allied Osage warriors also deterred serious depredations against the small French capital from other Indians. By 1782 the Osages were receiving over 70,000 *pesos* worth of European presents from officials in New Orleans—more than double the annual cost of maintaining a garrison of white troops in St. Louis. According to anthropologist Patricia Galloway, the special French affinity for such indispensable Indian allies encouraged an "openness to people of other races and cultures."[5]

To preserve multicultural harmony and confirm their sensitivity to Indian interests, St. Louis residents limited the village boundaries for French housing and farming. Despite respectable harvests that contradicted their reputation for laziness, St. Louisans proudly embraced the derogatory nickname of *Pain Court* ("meager bread") for their town, revealing their prudent decision not to impinge upon Indian territories and animal habitats. The rarity of such admirable attitudes was the greatest legacy of eighteenth-century St. Louis, but catering to Indians became a liability after the U.S. invasion imposed an aggressive agenda of racial prejudice and Indian exclusion.[6]

In his 1974 historical novel, *Centennial*, James Michener wondered why, of all the American frontier towns founded in the 1760s and 70s, "St. Louis *alone* should grow into one of the world's great cities." His answer was *"Brains"*—thoughtful early colonists committed to peace and prosperity in league with essential Indian allies. The best known of those early leaders were Pierre Laclède (1729–78), a young, affluent, and highly cultured French businessman from the Pyrenees, who emigrated to New Orleans in 1755, and Captain Louis St. Ange de Bellerive (1702–74), a Montreal-born veteran of France's frontier army, who had never been to Europe. Their respective careers intersected at St. Louis, when superiors in New Orleans chose them to preserve and develop that young town as a key center of Indian diplomacy and trade.[7]

Laclède was the protégé of Gilbert Antoine de St. Maxent (1724–94), the leading New Orleans merchant who served Louis Billouart, Count Kerlerec, governor-general of Louisiana (1704–70), as the official supplier of diplomatic gifts to some forty southern tribes. Kerlerec and Maxent defended such "tribute to savages" as rewards for "generous" Indian service to the French over many generations. To cultivate key alliances with the Indians of southern Illinois, 1,200 miles upriver, Kerlerec in 1760 installed his brother-in-law, Major Pierre-Joseph Neyon de Villiers, as commandant of Fort de Chartres. St. Ange succeeded him as France's final commander in Illinois and surrendered the huge stone fortress to the British Black Watch regiment in 1764 before relocating his twenty troops to St. Louis.[8]

St. Ange and Laclède complemented one another in their respective roles of military and mercantile leadership in tiny St. Louis, surrounded by populous Native nations. Their contrasting ages, backgrounds, experiences, and expertise helped them cope with a variety of issues. St. Ange's Canadian family, with a combined 130 years of service at frontier forts, imparted an invaluable knowledge of Native American cultures, while Laclède was more familiar with affluent French elites on both sides of the Atlantic. Enhancing their diverse talents, the young businessman and the old soldier both lived in Madame Marie Chouteau's home, where their varied experiences must have impressed her eldest child, Auguste (Laclède's stepson). When St. Ange died in December 1774, Laclède served as the executor of his estate and purchased his sword.[9]

In the first decade of the St. Ange-Laclède era, St. Louis became a major center of fur trading and multitribal diplomacy. Licensed St. Louis merchants collected large annual fur harvests in allied Indian villages, paid for them with coveted European merchandise, and transported that valuable natural bounty to town. To lessen the likelihood of intertribal jealousy, St. Ange did not reveal the value or quantity of merchandise allotted to each tribe. He also determined that the "best way" to prevent Indians from plundering European products stored in St. Louis was "to take [those] things out to them."[10]

That experienced commander established other vital diplomatic precedents that made St. Louis a centrally located "Indian capital" where Native people of diverse cultures "could walk the white road" in the "clean earth" of a hospitable village not "dirtied" by bloodshed. Knowing that a "discontented tribe drags in its wake various other tribes allied to it," St. Ange avoided the "slightest affront" to any Indians—even entire tribes that stayed "for two weeks, eating us out of house and home." In 1769 he hosted twenty-two tribal delegations, and for the remainder of the eighteenth century, up to thirty-two tribes visited the "Indian capital" almost every year. Annual spring visits were focused on diplomacy, hospitality, and the distribution of official presents unrelated to fur *purchases*. During the conference season in 1770, "daily Indian canoes" arrived in St. Louis loaded with food and "trifles" to sell, while dozens of different Natives were "well satisfied" with European goods they purchased in the town's "shops and stores." In 1787 "not one" Indian "committed the slightest act of hostility," despite the consumption of 1,400 jugs of sugarcane brandy.[11]

Annual visits for business and pleasure over several decades made St. Louis the "most cosmopolitan place within a five-hundred mile radius" for peaceful multitribal gatherings. That was especially notable, considering that the town's tiny population in 1766 included only 118 mature male civilians among 257 free persons. St. Louisans considered the "affection" of Indians, developed through "familiar acquaintance" over many years, to be the most valuable contribution to preserving "public security." The "good union and friendship" with the Osages depended upon *"presents,"* which Native hunters were long "accustomed" to receiving "in great abundance." Laclède's warehouse in 1769 contained an extensive inventory of products valued at 41,000 livres—including 100 muskets, 2,000 pounds of powder, 4,000 pounds of lead, 10,000 European gunflints, and 150 tomahawks.[12]

In eighteenth-century St. Louis, the fur trade was popular and appealing as "an abundant mine [that] . . . promises treasures more valuable than those of Potosi." The annual wholesale value of St. Louis furs averaged more than $220,000 (half of the London retail price) from 1764 to 1803, with profit margins ranging between 27 and 80 percent. Between 1772 and 1775, St. Louis shipped 215,000 pounds of the finest ("dressed") deer leather and over 133,000 pounds of raw deerskins to New Orleans. The total volume of all furs exported in those four years was nearly 625,000 pounds, but many chamois "bucks" remained in St Louis to serve as the main currency. The dominant Osage portion averaged 50 to 60 percent of fur harvests most years. Those Indians were the "true bankers of this region," wrote a Parisian, since Osage "peltries are the bills placed in circulation, and their hunting provides security for the fictitious specie on which merchants base their business."[13]

When the first Spanish commandant arrived in 1770 to replace St. Ange, he reported that St. Louis had "no law, no faith, and no king." But he found a well-functioning and safe society surrounded by Indians, because French residents did have a "king"—the fur trade—which placed their town on admirable terms with most of its Native neighbors. The Spanish governor in New Orleans compared the vast wealth of the Missouri fur trade to Spain's historic gold and silver mines, declaring that St. Louis was "one of the most populous, extensive, well-managed, and respectable of all settlements that have been established." He praised the town as the most "modern settlement" in his domain, which was "very advantageous" in providing full employment, retaining the "affection of the natives," and preserving "Public Security."[14]

For centuries white intellectuals debated whether conquest, coercion, conversion, or commerce was the best way to persuade Indians to accept and protect European populations in early America. Intercultural commerce was the unanimous choice in St. Louis—and the only conceivable one, since the tiny French population in the 1700s was dwarfed by thousands of Indians with fierce reputations. French colonists throughout "Indian

America" understood that the traditions of trading led to the trading of traditions among different cultures, creating positive partnerships. No one appreciated the value of mutually beneficial Indian business partners more consistently than French fur traders, who were dependent on Native nations for their lives, as well as their livelihoods.[15]

Enlightenment reformers in the eighteenth century were trying to make amends for Spain's infamous "Black Legend" of cruel conquistadors in earlier eras. Liberal leniency was now the policy, as Spanish officials required regional commandants to overlook the occasional "perfidy of the Osages" and never respond with "cruel" policies. Generous gift giving to all Indians became the norm in St. Louis, since the "good union and friendship which reigns between us and the nations of the Mississippi" depended upon "presents," which for "many years past they have been accustomed." Thanks to Maxent, in 1770 the twelve principal Indian nations in Upper Louisiana received 56 percent of all gifts dispensed from New Orleans (an increase of 44 percent since 1762).[16]

Between 1770 and 1803, St. Louis officials spent an average of $13,500 on Indian presents each year. As the American Revolution raged east of the Mississippi, St. Louis maintained the "Friendship of Indian Populations" with gifts to 130 tribes as far away as Ohio. The St. Louis commandant in 1782 provided "proofs of . . . good friendship" with Indian allies (called the "ramparts" of defense).[17]

The fur trade was "the sole and universal" source of revenue—and multicultural goodwill—in late eighteenth-century St. Louis. When Laclède died in 1778, Indian commerce provided a livelihood for 67 percent of white men in town: twenty-two merchants, fourteen traders, eighty-four boatmen, twenty-four hunters, and a silversmith who made jewelry for the Indian trade. Adult males in other fields included forty-six farmers, twenty-three craftsmen, and one musician. The wealth of pelts also had a magnetic effect in encouraging immigration by 1780, with 63 percent of St. Louis men originating in Canada and 21 percent coming from "Illinois" (including those born in town). One man was born in Acadia, two came from Spain, and three were from New Orleans. But most surprising was the 13 percent of men who were born in France, with several affluent merchants having been recruited by Laclède himself. St. Louis appealed to French capitalists seeking to do well under Spanish commandants determined to do good, with profitable trade replacing punitive terror in a peaceful local landscape. Believing that "self-interest is the motive force of all men," old founders and new arrivals alike considered the city's Indian allies *essential* to the peace, prosperity, and protection of St. Louis.[18]

When St. Louis celebrated its twenty-fifth birthday in 1789, it became the oldest and largest French town in Upper Louisiana on its original site, containing a growing population of 1,168. Its elevated location prevented the flooding that devastated Ste. Genevieve in 1785. St. Louis also escaped the frequent Indian raids suffered by that rival town to the south.[19]

The most stunning landmark in St. Louis—now the "handsomest and genteelist village" in Upper Louisiana—was the magnificent mansion of Auguste Chouteau, comparable in size to George Washington's "Mount Vernon." Chouteau could afford such extravagance because he and half-brother Pierre operated their own profitable trading post—Fort Carondelet—at the Osage capital of Marais des Cygnes in far southwestern Missouri. Pierre Chouteau moved his entire family there, including young children, to prove how "tranquil" the "intractable" Osages had become once abundant merchandise removed their need to rob white settlers. "Osages trusted and respected" the Chouteau brothers—the son and stepson of Laclède—who "could think as they thought, speak as they spoke, and live as they lived," giving those Frenchmen "accredited ascendancy."[20]

Fort Carondelet—a colony of a colony of a colony—was an unqualified success in conciliatory diplomacy, providing materialistic rewards for all parties. The Chouteaus maintained their status as essential peacekeepers respected by both Osage and Spanish leaders for helping to avert a major frontier war. They were well rewarded for their "honor, activity, and zeal" in "the royal service"—receiving an eight-year monopoly (1794–1802) on 55 percent of the entire Missouri River fur trade. That was reputedly worth 96,000 livres per year, and some historians credit the Chouteau family with controlling 42 percent of *all trade* throughout Upper Louisiana in that period.[21]

The Chouteaus now had the capital to procure larger quantities of the best British merchandise to satisfy savvy Osage customers. They expanded their business into Canada by partnering with the North West Company of Montreal and merchants in Great Britain. Trade at the bustling fortress of Michilimackinac introduced those St. Louis merchants and their boat crews to other countries, cultures, and currencies. In 1794 alone, the London agent for the House of Chouteau purchased expensive merchandize for the Osages at Fort Carondelet that included dozens of the latest North West muskets, 10,000 European-knapped gunflints, 2,100 knives, 2,100 awls, 4,300 rings, 70,000 trade beads, 670 heavy virgin wool point blankets, and 200 pounds of vermilion pigment. Imports for French St. Louisans included 2,000 pounds of Canadian maple sugar, 30 gallons of rum, 27 gallons of Madeira wine, 50 pounds of chocolate, 30 pounds of Chinese tea, 108 pairs of Moroccan leather shoes for all ages, silk hose, and fancy fabrics from India, Ireland, England, Russia, and Holland.[22]

The 1790s represented the zenith of commercial success for French St. Louis, as the wealth of the world poured into the tiny town, now enlarged to 2,500 residents (a 78 percent increase). Osage hunters and hide preparers had created a thriving fur trade that made St. Louis the hub of a symbiotic regional economy with worldwide reach. Affluent Frenchmen in that capital city handled the sale of Indian furs to New Orleans, Montreal, Europe, and elsewhere, while a dozen farming communities fed a growing population. With fierce and mobile Osage warriors protecting St. Louis and its extensive periphery from enemies, the region prospered as never before. Spain's 1796 official census of Upper Louisiana recorded a regional economy that supported some 3,200 residents, who harvested 75,000 bushels of maize, 35,000 bushels of wheat, and 25,000 pounds of tobacco. They also raised 3,900 cattle and 600 horses, mined 219,000 pounds of lead, and produced 6,000 bushels of salt.[23]

The global commerce in furs during the 1790s stimulated even more affluent consumerism in St. Louis, as the old "Emporium of Trade" became increasingly famous as a "center of manners, urbanity, and elegance." The small city was "always remarkable for the degree of gentility among the better sort of its inhabitants," but its reputation grew in the late eighteenth century as increasing numbers of prominent immigrants from Paris and other European cities relocated to St. Louis. With excellent educations, expensive tastes, and enormous talents, those elite residents defied American frontier stereotypes of crude cabins, deficient diets, and scarce schooling as they made little St. Louis a city of "refinement, fashion" and even "fine arts."[24]

Such impressive productivity and cultural sophistication on a mixed-race frontier disproved Thomas Jefferson's biased belief that "primitive" Indian hunting "only afforded a precarious subsistence" and could never support a large, affluent society with global reach. Such erroneous and hateful criticism from that powerful U.S. official caused many Indian and European leaders in St. Louis to expect a bloody invasion by envious Anglo-Americans— condemned as "a plague of locusts."[25]

The most shocking event related to escalating violence, however, occurred in the summer of 1800, with U.S. citizens as victims, not perpetrators. The decapitated corpses of an American farmer and his young son were found along the Meramec River, not far from St. Louis, and Lieutenant Governor Charles de Hault Delassus was determined to solve those murders. He summoned two hundred Osages from the Chouteaus' Fort Carondelet to St. Louis to discuss the issue, but an Arkansas Osage offered an unconvincing confession as the murderer. The gathering was far more hospitable than hostile, with the governor focusing on entertainment and future goodwill rather than past problems. Delassus concluded the "murder parley" with generous gifts of lethal weaponry to the Osages, including 100 new British muskets, 100 pounds of gunpowder, 300 pounds of musket balls, 300 gunflints, 288 large knives, and 50 hatchets—all bought in Canada and loaned to the governor by Auguste Chouteau.[26]

That friendly, gift-filled parley represented a stark contrast from Anglo-American frontier "justice" involving "savage crime." But it was an accurate reflection of how eighteenth-century St. Louis, over decades, enjoyed an unprecedented degree of peace and prosperity through mutually beneficial commercial alliances with trusted business partners. "Crime" was redefined and largely ignored, since successive Spanish officials admitted that all they could do to stop Osage aggression was to "put on an angry face." If that did not yield results, it was "customary to give them some gifts greater than usual." In fact, official medals were "kept on hand to be given out if some good Indian has to be rewarded or some bad one cajoled."[27]

From 1764 to 1803, St. Louis was a successful, strategically located center of a *Sutler Trading Empire* focused on the *wares of peace* in a north-south Corridor of Indian Commerce between Canada and New Orleans, where French and Indian populations joined in multicultural cooperation to share profits from a lucrative fur trade. Different traditions of trading led to the trading of traditions between French and Indian partners, and studying "the other" produced enlightened frontier diplomats rewarded with peace and prosperity. In the late 1700s, French St. Louis prospered in a "civilized wilderness," where Indian traditions and an animal empire flourished *despite*—not because of—extensive farming by a growing population. In contrast, Anglo-American farmers in the *Settler Farming Empire* of the United States required the *absence* of Indians to cultivate expansive acreage in former tribal territories. The incessant demand for increasing acres to farm created an east-west Corridor of Indian Conquest that eliminated successive Native homelands through the inevitable *peace of wars*.[28]

It certainly seemed that the rapid pace of Native displacement by "Virginians" (the Indian name for *all* aggressive Americans) implied Anglo intentions to seize "the vast continent occupied by Indians." Between 1700 and 1800, the population of English-speaking America mushroomed from 250,000 to 5.5 million, while the Chesapeake alone grew from 97,000 to 1.2 million. In only a quarter century, the United States had 386,000 citizens living west of the Appalachians, with most of the 250,000 Kentuckians claiming Virginia as their birth state. Even before the Louisiana Purchase in 1803, some forty thousand U.S. citizens already lived west of the Mississippi. French and Indian allies feared such "Kaintucks" as violent and dangerous.[29]

The Louisiana Purchase made St. Louis ground zero for an explosive clash of diametrically opposed frontier cultures that would determine the future of America. At stake was whether Virginia's historic *settler colonialism* would cross the Mississippi River. Mere colonialism "requires an ongoing political relationship ... between colonizer and the colonized," with hostile invaders exploiting the lives and labors of invaded Natives. In contrast, settler colonialism "seeks an end or completion of the colonial project" via the *elimination* of a Native population and its *replacement* by ethnically different invaders. Ironically, such a process often produces a "democratic republic." Patrick Wolfe argued that since settler colonizers "come to stay," Indian dispossession has to result, since "only Natives can provide land" for invading strangers from another location.[30]

St. Louis was suddenly the new U.S. "center of our western operations," according to President Jefferson, who envisioned an ambitious "Empire of Liberty" across the West for all peoples *except* Indians. The president's goal was to expand and enhance settler colonialism, encouraging thousands of American citizens to migrate westward to make a living on former Indian lands once the Natives were driven off. To begin that process, Jefferson relied on his Virginia "gun-men" (his term): William Henry Harrison, William Clark, and Meriwether Lewis. They were veterans of George Washington's army that had defeated Indian "animals of prey" (his term) in Ohio during the 1790s. Many Virginia plantation owners, who were always seeking fresh lands, now became official U.S. "sovereigns of the country" west of the Mississippi, and did "not fear any nation."[31]

Critics called President Jefferson the "Cardinal Richelieu of southern land speculation," given his hunger for Indian lands. Virginians had been fighting "the tawny sons of the forest" in *terror-tories* since 1607, and Jefferson had many ancestors and current friends who were notable "Indian-fighters." His inflammatory rhetoric in the Declaration of Independence reflected his biases against "merciless Indian Savages, whose known rule of warfare is an undistinguished destruction of all ages, sexes, and conditions." The president's inaugural address in 1805 posed this question to U.S. citizens: "Is it not better that the opposite bank of the Mississippi should be settled by our own brethren and children than by strangers of another family?"[32]

Unfortunately, the boomtown reputation of St. Louis encouraged an unwanted immigration of militantly aggressive Americans—residents of "imperial Virginia," the "new Rome." Virginians accused French "Indian-lovers" of fathering "half-breeds" to gain power and controlled "Savages as if they were Machines . . . by making presents." Americans predicted that "the time is not far distant when the uncultivated wilds of the interior part of the continent, which is now only inhabited by the tawny sons of the forest and the howling beasts of prey, will be exchanged for the hardy votaries of agriculture, who will turn those *sterile wildernesses* into rich, cultivated and verdant fields." One U.S. official despised the "mongrel race of Indian savages and French papists" that had opposed Virginia's westward quest. Ignoring ample evidence to the contrary, a biased U.S. official in St. Louis wrote that "as long as we are Indian Traders . . . our settlements can never flourish. . . . I care not how soon the savage is left to traverse in solitude his own Deserts, until the approach of cultivation obliges him to retreat into more gloomy recesses."[33]

The first American commander governing St. Louis, however, had a more favorable impression. U.S. Army captain Amos Stoddard did not expect to find a French frontier town so "elevated and healthy," containing "about 200 houses, mostly very large and built of stone," and inhabited by "rich and hospitable" citizens. Many Americans were shocked to discover that St. Louisans lived "in a style equal to those in the large seaport towns" of the eastern United States, with "no want of education among them." Stoddard pledged that U.S. policies would lead to the "emancipation [of people] from the chains of ignorance and barbarity" so that "man shall no longer be the enemy of man." But he failed to credit previous generations of French and Spanish St. Louisans for having already *achieved* many of those goals in the "civilized wilderness" dominated by the Osages.[34]

The Lewis and Clark Expedition of 1804–6 was designed to plot the "future path of civilization" by which the West would "receive . . . the overflowing tide" of the U.S. population. That expedition ended the Osages' commercial prominence by discovering prime beaver pelts in the Rockies that devalued Missouri deerskins and other furs. The once-feared Osages also lost face in 1806 by obeying President Jefferson's order not to retaliate against Indian enemies who massacred thirty-four of their women and children and stole another sixty. U.S. troops retrieved some of those captives and derided Osage warriors as "a nation of Quakers," too peaceful to be feared. Their pride plummeted even more when three U.S. treaties dispossessed them of one hundred thousand square miles between 1808 and 1825.[35]

As their oldest Indian allies lost lands, livelihoods, and leverage, the Chouteaus were forced to develop *American* trading partners. After 1803 they had to reinvent themselves—downplaying their roles as Indian fathers while stressing their talents as *city fathers* who could provide invaluable local knowledge to new U.S. officials. Having long prospered with Indian partners who did not share a common race, ethnicity, religion, literacy, or knowledge of capitalism, the Chouteau brothers found it easier to work with American officials, given the greater compatibility of their European cultural roots. The wily Chouteaus earned "a place in the city they had created," wrote historian Jay Gitlin, by working with Americans to avoid "the marginalization that was the fate of other non-Anglo communities taken over by the United States."[36]

Racial prejudices continued to resonate with American officials. When the Osages lost their last Missouri lands in the 1825 Second Treaty of St. Louis, that document allocated twenty-seven acres on the tribe's new Kansas reservation to forty-two "half breeds" with *European surnames.* Receiving 640 acres per person were three generations of Osages fathered by French traders and interpreters named Chouteau, Chardon, Larine, Mongrain, Reneau, and St. Mitchelle—plus a few others with Spanish and English bloodlines.[37]

About the same time, Pierre Chouteau Sr. described visiting Indians, "a hundred and more at a time," who enjoyed the hospitality of St. Louis. Dozens of warriors "promenaded down our Main Street in Indian file," he wrote, led by bare-legged chiefs wearing a "United States uniform coat, with golden epaulettes, and military hat and plume." Despite the sweltering heat of a "scorching July sun," those Indians were draped in "Mackinaw blankets," proudly carrying "a flaming scarlet umbrella" in one hand and "a palm-leaf fan in the other."[38]

That was a comical spectacle with tragic overtones, misleading any white "parade"-watchers into confusing Native attachments to American *presents* with an acceptance of U.S. *policies* that had eliminated their homelands and eroded their traditional cultures. The polite hospitality of the personable William Clark, head of U.S. Indian affairs in St. Louis from 1807 to 1838, obscured the sinister duties of his office, and memories of fair treatment by

French and Spanish diplomats left many Indians vulnerable to *American* aggression. The tribal leaders who visited the western U.S. capital at St. Louis, hoping for concessions from the new white "sovereigns," differed substantially from previous generations of free Indian nations that had determined the destiny of Upper Louisiana for forty years.[39]

Tribal delegations came to town as government dependents with diminished power and declining populations to marvel at the allurements of a growing American city. Crowding into Clark's "Indian Museum," those descendants of once-powerful, proud, and free Native nations viewed portraits of previously deceived and/or defeated chiefs, while nearby file cabinets contained the treaties that documented territorial conquests of land-hungry American "gunmen" who "did not fear any nation," as President Jefferson had boasted. Only thirty years after the Louisiana Purchase, the vast majority of Missouri's Indigenous inhabitants had been replaced by U.S. "yeomen" (and their slaves), who occupied the Osages' "immense" and "beautiful" country that had made eighteenth-century St. Louis rich and famous.[40]

In the final analysis, the *monetary* capital that St. Louis fur traders had long accumulated could not compete with the awesome power of America's *political* capital in Washington, which mobilized a huge population intent on owning the virgin soils of Native America. The visiting Frenchman, Alexis de Tocqueville, criticized the destructive impact that U.S. territorial and legal expansion in the early nineteenth century had on Indian nations. Historian Jeffrey Ostler wrote that Tocqueville "identified what may be a particular genius of the American people: their ability to inflict catastrophic destruction all the while claiming to be benevolent."[41]

In the century following the Louisiana Purchase, three other distinct voices evaluated those controversial transformations. In 1807 Frenchman François Marie Perrin du Lac championed the Osages by writing that "wise governments ought to found the basis of all their proceedings on the interest or power of their neighbors." In 1920 historian Clarence W. Alvord supported the U.S. government's position: "The most important event in the history of the United States and one of the most momentous in the history of humanity" was "the occupation of the great Mississippi valley by men of *English* speech"! He asserted that the "few Gallic families" who became "mere castaways in the conquest of the west" greatly benefited U.S. democracy. "It may be that Fate demanded from them, as it did from the Indians," he wrote, "a sacrifice for the greater good."[42]

The final evaluation was expressed in an illustration by the noted Czech artist and designer, Alphonse Mucha. In 1903, exactly a century after the Louisiana Purchase challenged the admirable alliance between the Osages and French fur merchants of St. Louis, Mucha, then living in Paris, produced this beautiful advertising poster. Its text was all in French, and it appeared only on the trains and ships of France to encourage its citizens to attend the 1904 St. Louis World's Fair. Visiting that *Exposition Universelle and Internationale* would constitute a nostalgic pilgrimage to a major U.S. city famous for its enlightened French and exotic Indian co-founders.[43]

The poster portrays a striking and stylish young woman, symbolizing the civility and affluence, beauty and innocence, of colonial St. Louis. But she is not alone and tenderly holds the hand of an affectionate old Indian in the shadowy background. That weathered and gentle warrior symbolizes Native American pride and wisdom in helping to create and support the "Indian capital" of St. Louis, which his people and her people once shared in harmony, cooperation, and mutual success.

NOTES

1. *Some Considerations* (London, 1720), 26, 41.
2. Jacques-Nicolas Bellin, cartographer, *Carte de la Louisiane Cours du Mississippi et Pais Voisins* (Paris, 1744). See the modern map, "French World of Mid-America," in Gitlin, *Bourgeois Frontier*, xiv.
3. Ekberg, *French Roots*; M. J. Morgan, *Land of Big Rivers*; Morrissey, *Empire by Collaboration*, esp. 191–201; and Fausz, *Founding St. Louis*, 75–99.
4. DuVal, *Native Ground*, 116–22; also see 103–9. Other informative sources on the Osages include: Rollings, *The Osage*; Burns, *A History of the Osage People*; Din and Nasatir, *Imperial Osages*; Bailey, "Osage;" Edwards, *Osage Women and Empire*; Silverman, *Thundersticks*, 224–25; and Saunt, *West of the Revolution*, 180–82 and chap 7.

   Joseph Zitomersky observed that "The establishment of new French places generally presupposed the existence of Native settlements either in their near vicinity or in their more general area. The one does not seem to have developed

FIG. 4. *Exposition Universelle & Internationale de St. Louis (États-Unis) du 30 Avril au 30 Novembre 1904*, Alphonse Mucha. An evocation of St. Louis's past as an "Indian Capital" of the Midwest. St. Louis Art Museum.

without the other." *French Americans-Native Americans*, 381. Also see Fausz, *Founding St. Louis*, 83–95 and 215, n. 114 for geographical and ecological details about the site of St. Louis.

5. MPA, 5:296–97; see also 122–28, 130, 146–48, 155–58, and 278–80.

6. SMV, 4:110; DuVal, *Native Ground*, 115, 125–27; Rollings, *Osage*, 42–43.

7. Michener, *Centennial*, 29; Fausz, *Historic St. Louis*, 12–13. Pierre Laclède wrote his name in the Occitan-Gascon dialect of his native province of Bearn *without diacritical marks*, since residents did not consider themselves French. Attaching *Liguest* to his surname (meaning "willow tree" in the Béarnais dialect of his native province) functioned like the suffix "junior" in identifying him as a second son in his family who was entitled to income from the family's forest along the Aspe River in the Pyrenees. See Labarère, *Pierre de Laclède-Liguest* and Fausz, *Founding St. Louis*, 27–42. The most complete biography of St. Ange is Ekberg and Person's, *St. Louis Rising*, while Cleary, *The World, the Flesh*, and Foley and Rice, *The First Chouteaus* remain essential sources on the influential Chouteau family and "their" city under the French and Spanish.

8. Fausz, *Founding St. Louis*, 53–66; Conrad, "Kerlerec," 461; Coleman, *Gilbert Antoine*; MPA, 122, 125, 128–30, 146–49, 155–58, 278–80; Villiers du Terrage, *Last Years of French Louisiana*; and Dawdy, *Building the Devil's Empire*. For an overview of the city's Louisiana roots, see Fausz, "Founding St. Louis," 8–23.

9. Ekberg and Person, *St. Louis Rising*, x, 52, 104, 116–17, 120–25, 193–94. They contend that Laclède was both a fake aristocrat and a failed merchant, but they ignore his family's prominence in France (see note 7 above); how he afforded prime real estate in and around St. Louis; and St. Ange's apparent confidence in him. They observe how Laclède owned St. Ange's sword, arguing that a mere middle-class man lacking military rank "could never wear this emblem of aristocracy . . . either in France or its American colonies" (Ekberg and Person, 213). However, that biased view overlooks the fact that Laclède was a champion fencer in his college days in Toulouse, receiving a ceremonial sword as a royal prize, and completed military service in France and Louisiana. See Fausz, *Founding St. Louis*, 40–41.

10. Fausz, *Founding St. Louis*, 120.

11. SMV, 2:59, 298–99; 3:367; 4:110; SR, 1:5, 10–12, 22, 26, 39, 44–45, 78, 240–46, 268–69; SR, 2:307; DuVal, *Native Ground*, 105.

12. Fausz, *Founding of St. Louis*, 127–29. The census statistics for 1766 are found in Ekberg and Person, *St. Louis Rising*, app. A, 228–29. Note that St. Ange's twenty troops were not counted in the figure of 118 males.

13. SR, 1:69, 72, 83–107, 139; SMV, 2:312–13; and Fausz, *Founding St. Louis*, 150–51.

14. SR, 1:70–71, 77, 209; SM V, 3:184; Din and Nasatir, *Imperial Osages*, 121, 134–45, 205–6.

15. Fausz, *Founding St. Louis*, 15–24.

16. Weber, *Bárbaros*, 3–8, 47–51, 190–92, 214–18, 250.

17. The variety of complex and confusing multicultural relationships is summarized in Fausz, *Founding St. Louis*, 146–56.

18. My computations are derived from the militia rosters of November 1779 in McDermott, *Spanish in the Mississippi Valley*, 373–80. Alvord and Carter, *Trade and Politics*, 489, 630.

19. Fausz, *Founding St. Louis*, 22, 164–66, 230.

20. Fausz, *Founding St. Louis*, 171–74.

21. Fausz, *Founding St. Louis*, 174–76; Nasatir, *Before Lewis and Clark*.

22. Fausz, *Founding St. Louis*, 174–76; Chouteau Canadian inventories and invoices at the Missouri History Museum Archives; Phillips, *The Fur Trade*.

   The Chouteaus traded with most of the leading merchants and companies in Canada at a most propitious time, when the Montreal market desired 70 percent of furs other than beaver, many coming from Missouri. In only two coffee house auctions in that city in 1802–3, the Chouteaus sold:

   9,064 pounds of beaver
   758 raccoon skins
   668 otter pelts
   352 bison hides
   248 pounds of deerskin
   233 black bear skins
   21 fox skins
   33 bobcat skins

   Fausz, *Founding St. Louis*, 232–34.

23. Verified figures quoted in Finiels, *Upper Louisiana*, 77, footnote 129.

24. Finiels, *Upper Louisiana*, 120. Laclède set the stage for intellectualizing the frontier and attracting educated elites to St. Louis. He accumulated an impressive library of 215 volumes on a wide variety of subjects in only fourteen years. See the boxed insert describing his books in Fausz, *Historic St. Louis*, 27.

   Notable Europeans who emigrated to St. Louis in the 1700s included:
   Jacques Ceran de St. Vrain, merchant brother of a Spanish commandant
   Pierre Francois de Volsay, a decorated Paris-born military officer
   Father Pierre Joseph Didier, of the Abbey Church of St. Denis in Paris
   Louis Chauvet Dubreuil, merchant son of a La Rochelle attorney
   Sylvestre Labbadie, merchant from Tarbes, France

Marie Philippe Leduc, Parisian attorney

Dr. Claude Mercier, a physician and surgeon from France

Dr. Antoine Francois Saugrain, Paris doctor; anti-smallpox crusader

Antoine Soulard, French navy veteran and royal surveyor in Louisiana

Benito Vasquez, merchant from Galicia, Spain

Fausz, *Historic St. Louis*, 29.

25. Fausz, *Founding St. Louis*, 178–79.

26. SR, 2:301–12; Din and Nasatir, *Imperial Osages*, 310, 318–19; Fausz, *Founding St. Louis*, 179–81.

27. Regarding official leniency concerning other Osage crimes: in 1790, a disgusted Miami chief complained that his Osage enemies received only "caresses" from St. Louisans, even "when they steal, pillage and kill." Din and Nasatir, *Imperial Osages*, 81, 150–51, 267. Based on fears as well as profits, city leaders in the 1790s became increasingly committed to "preserving [Osage] friendship . . . at any cost." Fausz, *Founding St. Louis*, 169–71.

28. Fausz, *Founding St. Louis*, 189–94.

29. Fausz, *Founding St. Louis*, 186–87; Ostler, *Surviving Genocide*, 11, regarding the term, "Virginians." Also see the 1755 "Greater Virginia" map by John Mitchell in Fausz, *Historic St. Louis*, 32 and accompanying text in chap. 2.

30. Witgen, "A Nation of Settlers," 393; Spear, "Beyond the Native/Settler," quoting Patrick Wolfe, 432. Also see Greer, *Property and Dispossession*; Veracini, *Settler Colonialism*; Hixson, *American Settler Colonialism*. For more detailed information on the Osages and the American onslaught see Ostler's chapter, "West of the Mississippi," in *Surviving Genocide*.

31. Jefferson's "gun men" comment is found in Jackson, *Letters of the Lewis and Clark Expedition*, 1:281–82, while Washington's quote comes from Fausz, "'Engaged in Enterprises,'" 115–55. On Jefferson's appointees, see Owens, *Mr. Jefferson's Hammer* and Buckley, *William Clark*. Also see Fausz, *Historic St. Louis*, 30.

32. Useful overviews about the complexities of such a cultural transition in St. Louis include Gitlin, *Bourgeois Frontier*, chaps. 2–3, and Fausz, *Founding St. Louis*, 183–98.

33. St. Louis baptisms beginning in 1766 involved some eighty-seven French fathers or spouses linked to Indians from twenty-one tribes, and Osages were named in forty-seven baptisms, according to Person, *Standing Up for Indians*, 129–36. See also Thorne, *Many Hands of My Relations*, 93–99, 114–15; Gitlin, *Bourgeois Frontier*, 5–12; and Fausz, *Founding St. Louis*, 157–59.

34. Stoddard's description of St. Louis in 1804 is found in his *Sketches*, 219–20 and 460.

35. The "Quaker" quote is found in Pike, *Zebulon Montgomery Pike*, 2:530–31. Also see Fausz, "Becoming 'A Nation of Quakers,'" 28–39; "'Pacific Intentions,'" 120–43. Believing that the Indian trade in furs was trivial compared to providing farm lands for millions of their countrymen, Lewis and Clark took the first steps in integrating the West into the United States by advancing American democracy through Indian dispossession. New policies followed old patterns, as Lewis and Clark's colonial inheritance from the Past of the East became a national bequest to the Future of the West.

36. Gitlin, "'Avec bien du regret,'" 9. Chouteau, "Report on the Indian Trade," in *American State Papers*, 2:66.

37. Fausz, "Removal of the Osage Indians," 36–38.

38. The "Indian parade" is described in J. Thomas Scharf, *History of Saint Louis*, 2:182.

39. Fausz, *Historic St. Louis*, 38–40.

40. Fausz, *Historic St. Louis*, 42–48.

41. Ostler, *Surviving Genocide*, 2; also see 216–28. Osage population declined from 6,300 in 1805 to 3,500 in 1857 according to Ostler, 400.

42. Perrin du Lac, *Travels through the Two Louisianas*, 99–100; Alvord, *Illinois Country*, 365, 379.

43. Alphonse Mucha (1860–1939), *French Poster Advertising the St. Louis 1904 Exposition* (1903), color lithograph, 41⅜ x 29 inches, from the collection of the Saint Louis Art Museum 40:1969. Mucha rarely featured Native Americans in his commercial posters, the major exceptions being advertisements for Chocolat Masson in 1897 and Vin des Incas, 1897–99. See Ormiston, *Alphonse Mucha Masterworks* and Bade, *Mucha*.

BIBLIOGRAPHY

Primary Sources

Alvord, Clarence W., and Clarence Edwin Carter, eds. *Trade and Politics, 1767–1769*. Collections of the Illinois State Historical Library. Vol.16. Springfield: Trustees of the Illinois State Historical Library, 1920.

Finiels, Nicolas de. *An Account of Upper Louisiana by Nicholas de Finiels*. Edited by Carl J. Ekberg and William E. Foley. Columbia: University of Missouri Press, 1989.

Houck, Louis, ed. *The Spanish Regime in Missouri*. 2 vols. Chicago: R. R. Donnelley & Sons, 1909. (Cited as SR.)

Jackson, Donald, ed. *Letters of the Lewis and Clark Expedition, with Related Documents 1783–1854*. 2 vols. Urbana: University of Illinois, 1978.

Kinnaird, Louis, ed. *Spain in the Mississippi Valley.* 4 vols. Washington DC: U.S. Government Printing Office, 1946. (Cited as SMV.)

Lowrie, Walter, and Matthew St. Clair, eds. *American State Papers: Indian Affairs, 1789–1827.* 2 vols. Washington DC: Gales and Seaton, 1821–34.

Nasatir, A. P., ed. *Before Lewis and Clark: Documents Illustrating the History of Missouri, 1785–1804.* 2 vols. St. Louis MO: St. Louis Historical Documents Foundation, 1952.

Perrin du Lac. *Travels through the Two Louisianas and among the Savage Nations of the Missouri.* London: printed for Richard Phillips, 1807.

Pike, Zebulon Montgomery. *The Expeditions of Zebulon Montgomery Pike.* Edited by Elliott Coues. 2 vols. 1895. Reprint, Minneapolis MN: Ross and Haines, 1965.

Rowlands, Dunbar, Patricia K. Galloway, and A. G. Sanders, eds. and trans., *Mississippi Provincial Archives,* Vol. 5: *French Dominion, 1749–1763.* Baton Rouge: Louisiana State University Press, 1984. (Cited as MPA.)

Some Considerations on the Consequences of the French Settling Colonies on the Mississippi, with Respect to the Trade and Safety of the English Plantations in America and the West Indies. London: printed for J. Roberts, 1720. Reprint, Cincinnati: Historical and Philosophical Society of Ohio, 1928.

Stoddard, Amos. *Sketches, Historical and Descriptive, of Louisiana.* Philadelphia: Matthew Carey, 1812.

Secondary Sources

Alvord, Clarence, W. *The Illinois Country, 1673–1818.* Springfield: Illinois Centennial Commission, 1920.

Bade, Patrick, *Mucha.* New York: Parkstone, 2010.

Bailey, Garrick. "Osage." In *Handbook of North American Indians.* Vol. 13: *Plains, Part I,* edited by Raymond J. DeMallie, 476–94. Washington DC: Smithsonian Institution, 2001.

Buckley, Jay H. *William Clark, Indian Diplomat.* Norman: University of Oklahoma Press, 2008.

Burns, Louis F. *A History of the Osage People,* 2nd ed. Tuscaloosa: University of Alabama Press, 2004.

Cleary, Patricia. *The World, the Flesh, and the Devil: A History of Colonial St. Louis.* Columbia: University of Missouri Press, 2011.

Coleman, James Julian, Jr. *Gilbert Antoine de St. Maxent.* New Orleans: Pelican, 1968.

Conrad, Glenn R., ed. *A Dictionary of Louisiana Biography.* 2 vols. New Orleans: Louisiana Historical Association, 1988.

Dawdy, Shannon Lee. *Building the Devil's Empire: French Colonial New Orleans.* Chicago: University of Chicago Press, 2008.

Din, Gilbert C., and A. P. Nasatir. *The Imperial Osages: Spanish-Indian Diplomacy in the Mississippi Valley.* Norman: University of Oklahoma Press, 1983.

DuVal, Kathleen. *Native Ground: Indians and Colonists in the Heart of the Continent.* Philadelphia: University of Pennsylvania Press, 2006.

Edwards, Tai S. *Osage Women and Empire: Gender and Power.* Lawrence: University Press of Kansas, 2018.

Ekberg, Carl J. *French Roots in the Illinois Country: The Mississippi River Frontier in Colonial Times.* Urbana: University of Illinois Press, 1998.

Ekberg, Carl J., and Sharon K. Person, *St. Louis Rising: The French Regime of Louis St. Ange de Bellerive.* Urbana: University of Illinois Press, 2015.

Fausz, J. Frederick. "Becoming 'A Nation of Quakers': The Removal of the Osage Indians from Missouri." *Gateway Heritage* 21 (Summer 2000): 28–39.

———. "'Engaged in Enterprises Pregnant with Terror': George Washington's Formative Years Among the Indians." In *George Washington and the Virginia Backcountry,* edited by Warren R. Hofstra (Madison: Madison House, 1998)

———. *Founding St. Louis: First City of the New West.* Charleston SC: History Press, 2011.

———. "Founding St. Louis: A New French Frontier at the End of Empire." *Gateway: The Magazine of the Missouri History Museum* 29 (2009): 8–23.

———. *Historic St. Louis: 250 Years Exploring New Frontiers.* San Antonio: HPNbooks, 2014.

———. "'Pacific Intentions': Lewis and Clark and the Western Fur Trade." In *Lewis and Clark: Journey to Another America,* edited by Alan Taylor (St. Louis: OASIS Institute and Missouri Historical Society Press, 2003).

Foley, William E., and C. David Rice. *The First Chouteaus: River Barons of Early St. Louis.* Urbana: University of Illinois Press, 1983.

Gitlin, Jay. "'Avec bien du regret': The Americanization of Creole St. Louis." *Gateway Heritage Magazine* 9 (Spring 1989).

———. *The Bourgeois Frontier: French Towns, French Traders, and American Expansion.* New Haven CT: Yale University Press, 2010.

Greer, Allan. *Property and Dispossession: Natives, Empires, and Land in Early Modern North America.* Cambridge: Cambridge University Press, 2018.

Hixson, Walter L. *American Settler Colonialism: A History.* New York: Palgrave Macmillan, 2013.

Labarère, Lucien. *Pierre de Laclède-Liguest, 1729–1778: le fondateur de St. Louis, Missouri, 15 février 1764.* Ciboure: L. Labarère, 1984.

McDermott, John Francis, ed. *The Spanish in the Mississippi Valley, 1762–1804*. Urbana: University of Illinois Press, 1974.

Michener, James A. *Centennial*. New York: Random House, 1974.

Morgan, M. J. *Land of Big Rivers: French and Indian Illinois, 1699–1778*. Carbondale: Southern Illinois University Press, 2010.

Morrissey, Robert Michael. *Empire by Collaboration: Indians, Colonists, and Governments in Colonial Illinois History*. Philadelphia: University of Pennsylvania Press, 2015.

Ormiston, Rosalind. *Alphonse Mucha Masterworks*. London: Flame Tree Publishing, 2013.

Ostler, Jeffrey. *Surviving Genocide: Native Nations and the United States from the American Revolution to Bleeding Kansas*. New Haven CT: Yale University Press, 2019.

Owens, Robert H. *Mr. Jefferson's Hammer: William Henry Harrison and the Origins of American Indian Policy*. Norman: University of Oklahoma Press, 2007.

Person, Sharon. *Standing up for Indians: Baptism Registers as an Untapped Source for Multicultural Relations in St. Louis, 1766–1821*. St. Louis MO: Center for French Colonial Studies, 2010.

Phillips, Paul Chrisler. *The Fur Trade*. 2 vols. Norman: University of Oklahoma Press, 1961.

Rollings, Willlard H. *The Osage: An Ethnohistorical Study of Hegemony on the Prairie-Plains*. Columbia: University of Missouri Press, 1992.

Saunt, Claudio. *West of the Revolution: An Uncommon History of 1776*. New York: W. W. Norton, 2014.

Scharf, J. Thomas. *History of Saint Louis City and County from the Earliest Periods to the Present Day*. 2 vols. Philadelphia: Louis H. Everts, 1883.

Silverman, David J. *Thundersticks: Firearms and the Violent Transformation of Native America*. Cambridge MA: Harvard University Press, 2016.

Spear, Jennifer M. "Beyond the Native/Settler Divide in Early California." *William and Mary Quarterly* 76, no. 3 (2019): 427–34.

Thorne, Tanis C. *The Many Hands of My Relations: French and Indians on the Lower Missouri*. Columbia: University of Missouri Press, 1996.

Veracini, Lorenzo. *Settler Colonialism: A Theoretical Overview*. New York: Palgrave Macmillan, 2010.

Villiers du Terrage, Marc de. *The Last Years of French Louisiana*. Translated and edited by Carl Brasseaux and Glenn R. Conrad. Lafayette: Center for Louisiana Studies, University of Southwestern Louisiana, 1982.

Weber, David J. *Bárbaros: Spaniards and Their Savages in the Age of Enlightenment*. New Haven CT: Yale University Press, 2005.

Witgen, Michael. "A Nation of Settlers: The Early American Republic and the Colonization of the Northwest Territory," *William and Mary Quarterly* 76, no. 3 (July 2019), 391–98.

Zitomersky, Joseph. *French Americans-Native Americans in Eighteenth-Century French Colonial Louisiana: The Population Geography of the Illinois Indians, 1670s-1760s.* Lund, SE: Lund University Press, 1994.

4

FASHIONING IDENTITIES ON THE FRONTIER

Clothing, Culture, and Choice in Early St. Louis

PATRICIA CLEARY

What not to wear on the frontier? No doubt few residents of colonial St. Louis sat down and devoted a great deal of time to reflecting on how to dress; the sheer demands of building adequate shelter for people and animals, obtaining a sufficient and steady supply of food, and making a living in an outpost of empire occupied the bulk of their energy and effort. In the late 1700s, they were creating a community, and the survival of their experiment was far from guaranteed. But the fur trade was for many the *raison d'être* of the village, a chance to profit from the desire for Europeans at home in the metropole for fashions made from American animal skins—such as hats manufactured from beaver pelts and the increasingly important trade in deerskins—as well as an opportunity to tap into vast markets of Indigenous consumers. For these reasons, the region's residents did carefully consider fashion: whether as merchants hoping to capitalize on the consumer desires of potential Indian customers; or as Indigenous inhabitants and visitors to St. Louis who adopted, adapted, or spurned European items of dress and hairdos; or as traders who had to transport select goods they thought would sell well directly to Indian communities in the Missouri watershed; or as villagers themselves, free or enslaved, wearing clothes that might signal their wealth, status, or personal ties. In doing so, men and women in St. Louis and its surroundings drew on a range of available options for covering their bodies, styling their hair, and in some cases, ornamenting their skin. In the process, they constructed identities, imbuing fabric, footwear, dye, and hair with meanings—some subtle and some not—for others to observe, ponder, and interpret. In manipulating their appearance with dress and ornament, they conveyed various messages about their relationship to symbols of identity and power, in ways that for some suggested the desire to act and present themselves as consumers of imported luxury wares and for others reflected a rejection of the trappings of European material culture.

Clothing could make the man or woman, and as a result, the stakes of fashion were high. On the frontier, life and death, freedom and slavery could all be inherent in the details of dress. This piece explores what men and women in early St. Louis wore and how they modified their appearance, what their choices meant, how individuals across the social spectrum interpreted the meaning of others' sartorial selections, and when and why authorities found fashion on the frontier a source of concern. With regularity, dress provoked commentary, criticism, and controversy as the diverse inhabitants of this region acted with creativity, intent, and autonomy to construct identities for themselves that expressed their (occasionally shifting) cultural affiliations and aspirations. As Sophie White argued for the period under the French regime in Colonial Louisiana, Indians and Europeans "encountered and absorbed each other's goods," and dressing proved "a cultural act subject to interpretation by onlookers."[1] In St. Louis, founded in 1764 by French traders and farmers and administered by French and later Spanish officials, this process of creative adaptation and display continued, at times provoking official response. As participants in a world of goods, contemporaries were conversant in the cues that dress provided as to cultural affiliation and status. They observed others' dress and at times altered their own to make cultural and political points.

Clothing and personal appearance deeply interested and indeed preoccupied people in medieval and early modern Europe, as well as in North America.[2] The power of clothing to signal status and to disrupt others' notions of one's own standing made fashion a focus of legislation in many societies. For inhabitants of seventeenth-century New England, for example, sumptuary laws targeted those women—the haughty daughters of Zion—who chose to present themselves as of a higher social standing than they were through actions such as putting on lace collars, legally allowed only for members of the elite.[3] Or consider the Indian men and women who converted to Christianity in colonial Massachusetts, where one of the cultural costs of dwelling in a Praying Town was the loss of personal decision-making control over one's hairstyle. Long hair on men struck Puritans as an unseemly expression of pride and vanity. Praying Town Indians, reported minister John Eliot, had laws ordering that all Indian men who wore long locks would be fined; women who wore their hair loose or as men did would be fined as well.[4] Such legislation conveys how clearly hair styles and clothing choices were seen as intentional refusals to abide by approved customs, and violations provoked recourse on authorities' part to the apparatuses of control: social condemnation, law, fines, and punishment. Along with styles of wearing one's hair, the varieties of Native apparel across the continent, as well as other methods of body adornment, represent a vast and complex subject beyond the scope of this brief essay.

What we know about fashion and responses to it in colonial St. Louis, from its founding in the 1760s through its incorporation into the United States in 1804, rests on two main types of sources: artifacts and texts. The more immediately arresting visual evidence—whether in the form of images or objects—is slender. There are few portraits from the era, and there is very little in the way of items of clothing that have survived. One reason has to do with wealth. Relatively few people possessed the means to sit for a portrait, and the village had a paucity of professional artists. For merchants, obtaining a portrait during a visit to New Orleans was a rare opportunity to commission a likeness. Moreover, cloth and clothing were so valuable that people bequeathed these goods in their wills. With their own clothes or those they inherited, colonists creatively modified objects of dress repeatedly, literally wearing them out. The few items of dress that survive are therefore exceptional, special attire like wedding clothes that were valued enough to be preserved by a few contemporaries.

Though less striking on the surface than works of art or pieces of cloth-ing, abundant textual sources establish what colonists and Indigenous consumers had access to in terms of fashion. Mercantile records illuminate transatlantic trading patterns, with accounts listing in detail the quantities and kinds of trade goods men of commerce imported, indicating what pos-sibilities were available for the colonial and Indigenous markets. Another conduit for European goods reaching Indian consumers was through the government, as officials provided presents to visiting tribal delegations, often recording those items in careful detail in order to convince distant authorities how important, substantive, and expensive the requirements for this customary emollient to trade were. During their annual visits to St. Louis, members of dozens of local and more distant tribes expected to receive significant gifts of tribute. Such merchandise provided crucial support to diplomacy, facilitating trade and cementing alliances. Together, these sources illuminate the fashion options available in the village and its environs at the time, as well as their possible meanings. In addition, legal documents offer insight into what people actually had, with estate inventories revealing what wealthy colonists, in particular, owned, with page after page listing quantities of different fabrics and other fashionable items, suggestive of the rich and varied imported material culture available to those of means.[5]

The story of fashion in St. Louis has some clear French connections. The painstaking Illinois Country research of Carl Ekberg and Sharon Person has fundamentally and persuasively challenged early St. Louis histories that center upon Pierre Laclède as founder, documenting the key role of Louis St. Ange de Bellerive and the French colonial inhabitants of Kaskaskia, Cahokia, and other Illinois villages in shaping the city's earliest years.[6] They were long-time consumers of imported French wares and had been engaged for decades in trade with Indian peoples. When they moved across the Mississippi to settle in St. Louis, these francophone colonists brought with them their chattel and their goods, including fashions imported from France. Elite merchants like Laclède, Gabriel Cerré, and Charles Gratiot, hailing from as far afield as France, Montreal, and Switzerland, were an important part of the fashion equation.

Although Laclède's role as a founding figure has been appropriately downsized as a result of Ekberg and Person's excellent scholarship, he and his family nonetheless remain useful figures for thinking about commerce and consumer culture, in part because some of their portraits, possessions, and inventories have survived. Laclède himself was wellborn and grew up in a fairly grand house, today a comfortable and historic bed and breakfast, in Bedous, a tiny village nestled in the French Pyrenees.[7] Towering, snow-covered peaks shaded the narrow valley in which Bedous stands, a physical setting rather different from that of St. Louis, where the grandeur came not from mountains but from fast-moving, powerful rivers. In both locations, the settlements' positions provided critical proximity to trade routes: in the French case, to Spain, and in North America, to the Missouri River watershed, the Mississippi River with its many tributaries, the Great Lakes, New Orleans, and the Gulf of Mexico. For Laclède, growing to adulthood in France and receiving his formal education there meant that he had formative exposure to the consumer goods of his homeland, developing his sense of tasteful and appropriate wear in southwestern France. Eighteenth-century French men and women consumed a wide range of manufactured textiles, both imported and domestically produced, and also had access to news about fashion from other parts of Europe. Moreover, France enjoyed a long and rich cultural tradition in the fine and decorative arts. In the late seventeenth and early eighteenth century, France's reputation as a center of fashion, both in terms of style and innovative production and marketing, grew dramatically.[8] Paralleling that growth was the expansion in French ambitions for commercial domination in North America.

After leaving France to seek his fortune overseas in the 1750s, Laclède traveled to New Orleans, interacted there with merchants and inhabitants, free people and enslaved laborers, foreign-born residents and locals, no doubt observing their varied dress. Like many other Frenchmen, he sought a career in the fur trade: exchanging fashionable wares manufactured in Europe with Indian peoples who provided raw and processed furs and hides, the materials that would be transformed into finished goods—gloves and hats for example—for European consumers. There was a well-established and competitive mercantile community in North America, with French traders in Canada, Illinois, and New Orleans eagerly seeking to partake in or develop lucrative markets among French colonists and Indigenous consumers. In New Orleans, Laclède entered into a partnership with Gilbert Antoine de St. Maxent, a French military man and merchant, who, for distinguished service to the crown, received an exclusive patent from the Louisiana governor in 1763 to trade with Native Americans west of the Mississippi. As a representative of Maxent, Laclède and Company—in which he was a 25 percent owner—Laclède made his way north, up the Mississippi River, in late 1763. On the journey upriver with the ambitious trader was Auguste Chouteau, Laclède's fourteen-year-old companion and de facto stepson. Laclède had a long nonmarital liaison with Auguste's mother, Marie Thérèse Bourgeois Chouteau, and they had four children. Over the next several decades, the members of this family were key players in early St. Louis, prominent in commerce and linked, through marriage as well as nonmarital relationships, to other mercantile families and Indian allies.[9]

The point of this review of Laclède's movements is in part to call to mind the mobility of this era. European immigrants and colonists, aspiring farmers and traders alike, traveled hundreds and even thousands of miles, carrying with them the clothing habits of their birthplaces but at the same time being exposed in transit to new peoples and cultures with their own distinctive fashions. Indian peoples traveled long distances as well, moving along the vast network of waterways traversing North America. People, ideas, and goods were in motion in this era. In letters and journals, travelers made it clear that they found the sights they encountered—including differences in dress (how much of one's body was covered especially) and customs—worthy of commentary. In encountering juxtapositions of traditions, tastes, and objects, individuals observed each other's fashions, admired some of them, were appalled by others, and creatively adapted items that fulfilled their needs, desires, and pocketbooks.[10]

Once he had established himself in St. Louis, Laclède pursued his goal of making a fortune as a merchant in the fur trade. It was a reasonable path for pursuing wealth, for the region's Indians and colonists alike had long been eager consumers of imported wares. As the village grew, many St. Louisans set themselves up as traders and merchants. The prospect of exchanging furs for European goods drew scores of men of commerce to this location. In order to succeed, these men of commerce had to possess sophisticated knowledge of trade goods, tribes, and tastes. They imported a wide range of wares, with the luxury items typically among the first objects brought to new regions. Sumptuous fabrics and fashions visually reinforced the social status of those who could afford them and thus were highly sought after by members of local elites. Members of the lower orders were not expected to enjoy and display expensive clothing, and indeed in some places were legally prohibited from doing so; they, however, could aspire to participate in a world of consumption and acquire plainer fabrics or less refined objects. For traders with backgrounds and connections in Canada, Louisiana, Illinois, and France, fueling and meeting consumers' appetites enabled them to exploit a range of lucrative commercial opportunities.

With a less successful career than many, Laclède engaged in trade in St. Louis, the capital of Upper Louisiana (as the area was known), for nearly a decade and a half, corresponding with and visiting merchants in Lower Louisiana.[11] In 1777 he traveled to New Orleans for the last time, writing a letter to Auguste Chouteau, now a business partner, about what Chouteau should do if Laclède died during the voyage. Laclède's intimations of mortality were accurate, for in 1778 he fell ill, died, and was buried near the confluence of the Arkansas and Mississippi Rivers on the journey back to the village he had called home for fourteen years. In the inventory of Laclède's possessions, taken not long after his death, there is evidence of a wide range of imported items, offering testimony to both his sartorial preferences and his mercantile plans.[12] In Laclède's list of goods, the clothes included a blue silk suit lined with taffeta and edged with silver braid, a coat of crimson satin embroidered with gold, fine linen shirts, clothing adorned with silver buttons, and a pair of silver buckles—not exactly the attire one might associate with the hardscrabble circumstances of life on the frontier. Such items seem, on the surface, more suited to a French drawing room than to a fur merchant's warehouse or a tiny village of a few hundred farmers and traders perched on the banks of the Mississippi.

In addition to the personal items of dress that were clearly imported, whether as part of the goods Laclède brought with him when he emigrated in the 1750s or acquired during his sojourn in New Orleans or subsequent tenure in St. Louis, Laclède's inventory also revealed a global variety of imported fabrics destined for trade. Like other merchants in the region who thought big, Laclède over the years brought to St. Louis huge quantities of cotton goods: handkerchiefs (square pieces of cotton cloth) from southeast Asia—different parts of India; canvas cloth from Ireland

and Russia; Polish-style robes; textiles from Africa and central Europe; gingham from Manchester, England; and French fabrics and threads. Other merchants' inventories are replete with fashionable fabric as well; cloth had long been an important part of European exchanges with Indians. Describing a first consumer revolution, involving Indians purchasing large quantities of European wares, James Axtell categorized their interests in tools, clothing, decorations, and novelties, with cloth being the single best-selling item from the seventeenth century onward.[13]

Also included in Laclède's estate were personal grooming and adornment items destined for Indigenous consumers: 60 pounds of vermilion, a brilliant red pigment used for body decoration; 84 small mirrors; and 168 wooden combs. In the colonial era vermilion became a staple of transatlantic trade, with Indigenous consumers supplementing local red dyes—obtained from sources such as bloodroot, a flowering plant found in eastern North America, or ground ochre derived from iron ores—with the more brilliant European and Asian product.[14] A chemical compound, mercuric sulfide, vermilion results from grinding cinnabar, the ore in which mercury occurs. In his fascinating study of the pigment, Jean-François Lozier notes that though primarily associated with China, where cinnabar has been produced in significant quantities since prehistoric times, vermilion came from many sources in the early modern era, including Spain. In North America, a few geological deposits of mercuric sulfide were mined and processed by Indigenous peoples in California and the southwest precontact.[15] European exports of synthetic vermilion came via Dutch manufacturers, who began producing it in large quantities in the 1680s; after the mid-eighteenth century, the Asian vermilion trade began to expand.[16] For Indigenous peoples, vermilion was highly prized for multiple purposes, including as a cosmetic, for adorning the bodies of the dead or decorating grave offerings, as part of ornamentation applied before council meetings, and as a base for tattoo ink.[17]

A popular item of trade, mirrors were similarly desired by and widespread among Indigenous peoples in North America. In her recent analysis of the social lives of mirrors, Rebecca Shrum notes that as early as the 1660s over 30 percent Connecticut River Valley Indians owned mirrors, with nearly everyone having access to one.[18] Interestingly, southern New

FIG. 5. *Painting of an Indian woman*, Anna Maria Von Phul, 1818. Missouri History Museum, St. Louis.

England Native burial grounds also reveal some evidence of mirrors being included as funerary objects.[19] Some colonial observers accused Indian men of vanity, claiming they spent too much time admiring themselves in mirrors.[20] Such criticism served rhetorically to question the masculinity of Indian men, suggesting they were obsessed with mirrors in a way typically ascribed to vain European women; Shrum suggests the difference in mirror usage was one of visibility: that colonial men used them more often in private, while Indian men used them more openly, and often carried them on their persons.[21] Clearly mirrors played an important role in personal grooming. Their utility might be suggested by the Osage portraits painted by Charles Balthazar Julien Févret de Saint-Mémin, whose 1807 watercolor of a warrior shows a man with eyebrows and facial hair fully removed by plucking.[22] Beyond being tools for examining one's reflection, mirrors were put to many uses, including as part of preparations for a range of rituals. Before engaging in important diplomatic encounters or going to war, for example, Indian men applied a mixture of bear's grease, natural dyes, and imported verdigris and vermilion to their faces and bodies.[23] All of these goods—cloth, dyes, mirrors, combs—point to an appetite for imported manufactures among St. Louis's residents, as well as the traders who frequented the village but spent much of their time in Indian communities, and especially the Indians who engaged in the fur trade; imported dry goods had been present in the Illinois Country decades before.[24]

For the Indian participants in these networks of exchange, it is clear that they were deeply tied to European markets, experiencing the pull of the market in villages distant from colonial trading outposts. They provided the furs and animal skins that Europeans sought for their own fashions, including hats made from felted beaver pelts and gloves from deerskin leather, and in turn were active consumers of European fashionable manufactures. Such production depended upon the labor of many individuals. Among the Osage, for example, whose huge territory encompassed most of Missouri and significant parts of Kansas, Oklahoma, and Arkansas, and whom Frederick Fausz describes as the "co-founders" of St. Louis, men pursued hunting, while women processed animal skins, producing thousands of pounds annually of prepared deer and bison pelts.[25] This work took place in their distant villages, where French and métis voyageurs visited and wintered before transporting pelts to St. Louis for further shipping. Such encounters facilitated personal connections, and members of the Osage and the Chouteau family developed intimate relationships as well. As Kathleen DuVal argues, the Osages were "far more successful than either France or Spain at building a mid-continental empire,"[26] working to keep European goods out of their enemies' hands and to cultivate European connections to obtain the "cloth, axes, knives, beads, rum, needles for tattooing, and the guns and ammunition that fueled their expansion."[27] Such trading connections predated the settlement of St. Louis and continued after its founding, even growing, as members of the Osage established personal relationships with the Chouteau family and deepened their ties to power brokers.

Throughout the colonial period, as part of ongoing diplomatic negotiations with authorities, members of dozens of tribes came annually to St. Louis. The Osage were among many whose activities contributed to the success of the fur trading ventures of St. Louis's merchants.[28] In 1769 the French commandant Bellerive, who played a critical role in advising the new Spanish authorities regarding Indian affairs, compiled a report on the twenty-three Indian tribes who had been receiving presents in the Illinois district, "the same ones," he certified, "who are accustomed to come here to get presents."[29] The list reads as a demographic survey of local Indigenous groups and French familiarity with their territories. From the Kaskasias and Kaokias, all Illinois River region tribes, to the "Poutuatami" and "Ayooua [Iowas]" of the "river San Joseph and that of Ylinneses," and the Little and Big Osages "of the district of the Misuri River," St. Ange's account served as a reminder to the new Spanish government that Indians were present, numerous, and regular trading partners and visitors to St. Louis. Delegations from the Kickapoo, Sioux, and Kansa also made repeated treks to the village. Annual visitors as well, the Osage on occasion dramatically swelled the population of the tiny village, bringing as many as two hundred men on one occasion.[30] While visiting St. Louis to meet with government officials, Indigenous peoples obtained significant quantities of imported goods. Part of the impetus for authorities in these encounters lay with competition and perceptions of it. Knowledge of the English distributing presents "with a very liberal hand" prompted Spanish officials to demon-strate what their superiors sometimes thought of as excessive largesse to the representatives of the many tribes that frequented the village.[31] Their presence could not be ignored; in the month of May 1788, alone, govern-ment officials recorded 260 Indians belonging to the Iroquois, Shawnee, Chickasaw, Choctaw, Cherokee, and other nations in St. Louis. During these visits, officials presented Indigenous leaders with gifts of consumer wares as an emollient to peaceful relations; such presents were the primary source of goods obtained during Indians' St. Louis sojourns. At the same time, tribal members also conducted some commercial endeavors as well. During their brief stays in St. Louis, Indian peoples thus acquired objects of practical domestic value in daily life, such as metal cooking implements, and personal grooming items, such as mirrors and combs.

Indian visitors to St. Louis acquired large quantities of imported cloth; indeed, textiles constituted the bulk of goods imported into North America in this period. Regional variations in clothing styles, as well as a scarcity of direct information, make is difficult to ascertain how Indians near St. Louis adapted European fabrics into their dress. Elsewhere, in colonial New York, Timothy Shannon has found evidence of Native American men wearing European cloth in a distinctive "Indian fashion," not involving tight-fitting garments but based around the use of larger pieces of cloth draped more loosely as body coverings.[32] A few clues for Osage use of European fabrics emerge in Saint-Mémin's portraits: one warrior wears bands of cloth across his chest and knotted around his neck, another wears a European military jacket, and another appears with a blanket wrapped around his shoulders. Given the lack of clothing that has survived from the era, such images offer valuable, if fragmentary, evidence.

The visual evidence for eighteenth-century St. Louis is more abundant for colonists. Indeed, one of the most striking visual representations of dress in eighteenth-century St. Louis comes from the man who became responsible for helping to settle Laclède's estate and unravel his accounts with numerous partners and customers, Auguste Chouteau. In a portrait experts believe he may have commissioned while in New Orleans in 1781, Chouteau is depicted wearing a red wool coat trimmed with gold braid.[33]

FIG. 6. *Portrait of Auguste Chouteau,* 1815–50. Missouri History Museum, St. Louis.

The decorative elements of the single-breasted cutaway coat with tails include twenty-seven buttons, made out of wood and covered with metallic thread that was likely gold before it oxidized to gray.[34] The coat, the only one of its kind known to exist in the United States, calls to mind military apparel, particularly French and Spanish styles, but it was not, as far as we know, part of a uniform St. Louisans wore during the American Revolution, when their village came under attack in May 1780 by a combined British and Indian force. As an officer, Chouteau may have had some leeway in what he wore and so had the coat made in a manner that he thought suited a leader. Thus a New Orleans-born man, who grew to adulthood in St. Louis, donned a custom-made military-style jacket of French and Spanish influence in the midst of the American Revolution, a fashion choice that points to the multicultural diversity of the community as well as the multiple sources of its fashion influences.

Several years later, in 1786, Chouteau wed, and he and his bride celebrated their nuptials with sumptuous second-day wedding outfits, made of the finest imported fabrics available. The originals are now in tatters, too fragile to be removed from their boxes, but replicas are on display at the Missouri History Museum in St. Louis. In a pale green satin coat, with a light beige silk waistcoat, embroidered in green, rust, pink, yellow, and blue, Auguste Chouteau must have cut quite a figure. His teenage wife, Marie Thérèse Cerré Chouteau, roughly twenty years his junior, was the daughter of Jean-Gabriel Cerré, a Montreal-born merchant who had settled in Kaskaskia for a time, where Marie Thérèse was born, before moving to St. Louis in 1779. The bride would have been dazzling as well, in her pink and green silk taffeta gown. There is nothing rustic here, nothing that speaks to the distance the goods traveled, the remoteness of the settlement, or the conditions of life on the frontier, where unpaved streets might have easily sullied such fine dress. Rather, such ostentatious, expensive, and delicate outfits speak to the wealth, status, and European cultural affiliations of the elite young couple who wore them. Enormous armoires, a number of which survive in the collections of the Missouri History Museum, held shelves for storing such garments, as well as drawers for holding smaller decorative items. It is not surprising that these pieces of furniture are impressive and

FIG. 7. Second-day wedding garments of Auguste Chouteau and Marie Thérèse Cerré Chouteau, married September 22, 1786. Photographer unknown, ca. 1960. Missouri History Museum, St. Louis.

ornamented; the goods they contained were expensive and cherished. One of the surviving armoires produced in St. Louis in the eighteenth century, the only one attributable to a specific craftsman, was built by Jean Baptiste Ortes, a Frenchman who came to the village with Laclède in 1764. Trained as a carpenter in France, Ortes constructed the tall walnut cupboard with two matching doors, each with three inset panels. Another colonial armoire in Louis XV style, belonging to the Chouteau family, combines French and English elements in a hybrid form common to furniture from Canada and the Upper Mississippi Valley, though no other piece quite like it has survived.[35] Fashion on the frontier, whether of dress or furnishings it seems, reflected the mobility of goods, styles, and individuals.

The second-day wedding outfits aside, women in colonial St. Louis did not always dress as showily as did the teenage newlywed Madame Chouteau. The portrait of her mother-in-law, Marie Thérèse Bourgeois Chouteau, partner of Pierre Laclède and mother of Auguste and his half siblings, reflects a less ostentatious sensibility. With a white handkerchief covering her hair and a dark wrap, Madame Chouteau appears a sober figure, the only nod to fashionable display the band of green embroidery. A practical item in the collections of the Missouri History Museum, a tortoiseshell comb identified as Madame Chouteau's, suggests a hint of luxury and fashion consciousness in its gold ornamentation. Nods to a taste for fine hair implements aside, the tenacity of a plain Creole look for women—covered hair and dark dress—appears in portraits done of Marie Thérèse Cerré Chouteau and Madame Ortes, both on display at the Missouri History Museum, from well past the colonial period. These women came to adulthood during the colonial period and seemed to retain the style of the era. In the sober attire they sport, nothing appears that would be likely to invite attention or commentary. The portrait of Marie Thérèse Cerré Chouteau in particular seems to emphasize the sobriety of matronly attire; the pink and green silk she donned as a bride are a far reach from this somber outfit. Without exaggerating the significance of a few images, the very similar fashions of these three portraits invite speculation about the norms governing dress: To what extent did social expectations dictate adult women's attire? Or, did mature Creole women attempt to preserve

FIG. 8. *Portrait of Marie Thérèse Bourgeois Chouteau*, Francois M. Guyol de Guiran, ca. 1810. Missouri History Museum, St. Louis.

FIG. 9. *Portrait of Marie Thérèse Cerré Chouteau.* Missouri History Museum, St. Louis.

the clothing styles of the colonial era when their families had dominated the culture and commerce of the community?

In government records from the period, we see evidence of problems caused by dress in St. Louis, fashion crises that forced authorities to bring the power of their positions to bear on what people should or should not wear. One early ruler forced to deal with some of the clothing crises in the colonial village was Francisco Cruzat, who served as lieutenant governor in St. Louis in the 1770s and then again, after a few years' break, for much of the 1780s, acting as the representative of the Spanish crown for a significant part of St. Louis's colonial history. What people wore troubled him enough that he took official action on more than one occasion to control fashion and access to clothing.

Under Cruzat's authority were members of the Spanish garrison, men who found serving in Upper Louisiana far from easy. Homesick, lacking for feminine companionship, complaining often of ill health and harsh conditions, many sought to escape their soldiering duties through desertion, but their uniforms gave them away. To some unhappy soldiers' relief and to Cruzat's chagrin, there were villagers who did not ask too many questions and were ready to make money by supplying deserters with nonmilitary dress. The problem was serious enough that Cruzat ordered punishments for St. Louisans who aided runaway soldiers.[36] "Private persons" had aided and concealed deserters "by giving them clothes for disguising themselves, or by purchasing from them some part of their clothing." Those who had knowledge of deserters but failed to denounce them risked a government fine sufficient to the cost of replacing that soldier as well as an additional financial penalty for replacing the "garments and clothes of deserters."[37] Not all early residents had sufficient clothing to spare, and their lack of "civilized" dress raised other concerns. Earlier, one of the first priests in St. Louis, Father Bernard de Limpach had written to the governor that many of his flock were in such a miserable condition that they lacked funds to clothe themselves adequately and were forced to hide in the woods to conceal their nudity. Descriptions of European residents of Upper Louisiana that characterized colonists as clothing themselves like the Indians continued until the end of the century. As late as 1795, André Michaux, a French agent, described the French of the Kaskaskia Village, across the Mississippi from St. Louis, as living "in the manner of the savages," wearing no breeches.[38] The language of such remarks suggests that while some colonists indeed may have had poor or inadequate clothing, others chose to don Indian fashions, with men covering their legs less than European men typically did, for instance. The allusion may also have harkened to stereotypical colonial notions of Indigenous people as less clothed and therefore less civilized. As James Axtell argued, colonists' obsessions with Indigenous clothing and bodily coverage were tied to their goal of transforming Indians into Europeans, with personal appearance the overt symbol of cultural conversion and more clothing seen as a sign of greater civilization.[39]

Given the importance of cultivating appearances, it is not altogether surprising that an early visitor from the United States, Moses Austin, entered the village of St. Louis "with as large a retinue, and as much parade as possible." Leading his party from horseback, "clothed in a long blue mantle, lined with scarlet and embroidered with lace," Austin rode to the governor's residence, trailed by his servants, guides, and others.[40] Interested in the lead mines of Upper Louisiana, Austin sought economic opportunity in Spanish Territory. His ostentatious arrival in the village may have been designed to convey to officials there that he was a man of substance, a leader who could be trusted to develop whatever opportunities Spain was willing to grant to him.

Just as military association and economic aspiration, such as Austin's, could be apparent in dress, so too could cultural affiliation and political inclinations. In 1795 Manuel Gayoso de Lemos, then in command of the Spanish colonial district of Natchez, traveled to St. Louis. An appointee of Louisiana Governor Francisco Luis Héctor de Carondelet, Gayoso de Lemos visited the capital of Upper Louisiana to make an assessment of the settlement's position, prospects, and population, including the loyalties of its inhabitants. He was pleased to report that he saw no signs of disloyalty or anti-monarchical sentiment, including in dress. At an "Illuminating Assembly at Mr. Ch[o]uteau's house," he closely observed "the fashions of the Ladies." "I have not seen a single tricolor ribbon nor decoration that might betray the sentiments of their families," he declared. That is, no woman could be seen sporting a symbolic statement of support for France and its revolutionary regime. The one potential exception was the "tricolored dress" of Madame Robidoux. "But I attributed this to the poor taste of the lady," he wrote, "furthermore it was older than the French Revolution, and her husband and she are persons of good character."[41] In other words, while her eveningwear might have been an offense against the dictates of fashion, it was no crime against the state.

A more troubling situation emerged in August 1781, when Cruzat learned that some resident Indians and Africans had taken to dressing themselves differently—"in barbarous fashion." Adorning themselves with vermilion and feathers, they were "unrecognizable," he wrote. Cruzat's comments suggest that previously, these non-Europeans, both enslaved and free, had dressed like the European inhabitants of the village, the former presumably provided with clothing by their masters, but they suddenly began to doff such dress or add to it in unmistakably Indian ways. They were performing, intentionally he seemed to believe, Indianness. "Thus metamorphosed" by their altered costume, Cruzat declared, these men might be mistaken as enemies, particularly outside of the village's boundaries, and shot by alarmed colonists. Dress, then, could be a matter of life or death, with plumes and pigment signaling the potentially deadly difference between friend and foe. To avoid the possible fatalities that might spring from encounters rendered dangerous through dress, Cruzat prohibited all Indians and all Blacks in St. Louis from clothing "themselves in any other manner than according to our usage and custom," whether in the village, the surrounding fields, or the nearby woods.[42] In other words, he censored sartorial choices, insisting on attire reflecting assimilation and outlawing self-determination in dress.

Why did Indians and Africans who had dressed like the French and Spanish in their midst suddenly don Indian dress and ornamentation? Why were their actions so troubling? That summer, still reeling from a devastating British and Indian attack of the previous year, St. Louisans were troubled by a spate of fires—arson they believed—and the flight of numerous enslaved residents. Was a rebellion or an attack from within the village in the works? Disturbed by fires they labeled arson, officials noticed at the same time that non-European enslaved and free peoples in the village were adopting Indian fashions. By daubing vermilion onto their bodies or adding feathers to their outfits, these individuals were—intentionally, overtly, and through fashion—declaring themselves to be "other"; "other" than French, Spanish, or the enslaved laborers thereof; "other" as in Indian. To be Indian could mean that one was an ally and trading partner, but it could also mean that one was an enemy, a potentially lethal opponent as had been the warriors who nearly destroyed the village in 1780. Cultural borrowings regarding dress were practiced by Europeans as well.[43] When enslaved Indians and Africans took off European styles of clothing likely obtained from masters or partners and changed their appearance to empha-size their cultural distance from European colonists, those colonists grew alarmed. The limits to their control over the non-European members of the community, many of them enslaved, were exposed by the ease with which they could be challenged by something as simple—and as complicated—as claiming the fashions of a free and forceful people. In his study of vermil-ion, Lozier found evidence of colonial anxieties over "painted neighbors," whose use of the pigment made them indistinguishable from enemies.[44]

The point here is not only that Indian fashions could be deployed stra-tegically, but that St. Louis and its inhabitants were deeply connected to and conscious of the Indigenous inhabitants of the region. St. Louis was in Indian territory, its very existence as a center of the fur trade dependent on the tolerance on Indians' part of the villagers' presence as well as their willingness to engage in trade. Anyone strolling through the streets of St. Louis would have regularly and routinely seen numbers of Indians present in the village, whether as members of different tribes who visited the village annually, as enslaved members of the community (held illegally for many years after an early Spanish prohibition on Indian slavery), or as the legally married partners or unwed concubines of some of its European colonists.

This incident, which so troubled Cruzat and the village's colonists, also reminds us of the presence of Africans brought involuntarily to St. Louis, and their cohabitation and cultural interactions with both European col-onists and Indian peoples. Though there is little evidence to indicate the full range and substance of their relationships, it is clear Indigenous and African inhabitants resided in households together, socialized, and labored alongside each other. In this case, those who adopted Indian fashions were engaging in an act that may have suggested a desire to emphasize independence. An incident some years before, involving a runaway enslaved Indian woman from Kaskaskia who concealed her identity by covering her fashionable embroidered blouse and calico skirt with a man's striped shirt and baggy cotton culottes, similarly suggests that cross-dressing, whether culturally or in terms of gender, could serve as a useful means of disguise in the pursuit of independence.[45]

Official records reveal other crises in which a choice to display Indigenous fashions played a role. Take the case of Louis Mahas, an Indian man imprisoned in St. Louis for committing various seemingly unprovoked crimes over a period of years. In 1778 Mahas created resentment in the settlement when he shot and killed a cow in a villager's yard, the bullet barely missing an enslaved African woman standing nearby. On another occasion, he attacked a soldier from the Spanish garrison with a tomahawk. In yet another incident, while out hunting, he announced that he wanted to kill some Frenchmen. On returning to St. Louis the next day, Mahas went up the attic of his companion's dwelling and let down his braid, declaring that "for a long time [he had] dressed in the French way." With what seemed a very pointed rejection of the French and the life he was living, Mahas was reported as stating, "I'm going to dress myself as a warrior and do my hair." Mahas's purported declaration conveyed an understanding of what meanings such a change in hairstyle could signify—a cultural reassignment, a return to his cultural roots, a shift from comporting himself as a man of peace to presenting himself as a warrior—and his actions made his intentions clear. The religious and cultural significance of Indian men's hair varied dramatically according to tribe, with practices including cutting it in times of grief or wearing a long braid as a reflection of warrior status.[46] Reading the symbolism of his redone hair in ways that suggest their familiarity with the war rituals practiced by some tribes, villagers were alarmed, and within short order, Mahas was arrested and banished, managing, however, to escape from the prison before his sentence could be carried out. Removing the trappings of Frenchness and reclaiming Indianness may have signaled his rejection of customs he found oppressive or no longer of use.

Cross-cultural fashion was not always problematic in European eyes. Unlike Mahas, other Indian peoples continued to seek out and consume European clothing items and styles, willing participants in the vast network of transatlantic trade. Official records offer abundant evidence of Indians' consumption of manufactured wares and European fashions. To take just one example, a 1787 list of "presents for Indians" from the Spanish government included "lace-trimmed hats" for chiefs, dozens of striped shirts, eighty pounds of beads, seventy pounds of vermilion, and hundreds of combs.[47] Or consider the presents "given to the tribe of the Big Osages" by order of the lieutenant governor. During their stay in 1800—along with muskets, bullets, knives, and tobacco—the visitors to St. Louis received five yards of silk ribbon, four dozen mirrors, fifty white shirts, fifty blankets, limbourg cloth, and fifteen pounds of vermilion, all supplied to the government storekeeper by Auguste Chouteau.[48] Merchants' accounts reveal an active Indian market for silk ribbon, linen shirts, and French red and blue wool cloth. Acquiring and wearing such items however, did not fully "Frenchify" these Indians living in Indigenous communities far from St. Louis; no one mistook them for French.

What do we know about the clothing and fashion choices of Indian peoples who did not reside in the village? In 1804 an Osage delegation traveled from St. Louis to Washington DC, where a number of men sat for portraits by French artist Saint-Mémin.[49] The portrait of Pawhuska, *Cheveux Blancs*, or Chief White Hair, is striking in the sitter's creative combination of Indian and Euro-American fashions. His non-Indian objects of dress—the silver peace medal and armband, which were both manufactured for Indian consumers, and the blue officer's coat (part of an American military uniform)—all mark him as a chief. His severed auricle and the earring dangling from it, however, constitute unmistakably Indian styles of contemporary body modification and fashion. Two other portraits of Osage warriors, done by the same artist, present Osage men with a more Indigenous look. Both wore buckskin breeches (not visible here). The older man wears a blanket, possibly imported, draped around his shoulders. Both men wear beads in their ear ornaments that are likely Venetian.[50] The younger Osage man, in one of the most spectacular images

FIG. 10. *Payouska* (Pawhuska, ca. 1752–1832), Chief of the Great Osages, Charles Balthazar Julien Févret de Saint-Mémin, ca. 1806, black chalk and charcoal with stumping, white chalk, pastel, and graphite on pink prepared paper, 23 × 17⅛ inches, ID 1860.92. New-York Historical Society.

FIG. 11. *Unidentified Elder Osage Warrior*, Charles Balthazar Julien Févret de Saint-Mémin, ca. 1805–7, pencil, charcoal, 23 × 17 inches, ID 1860.94. New-York Historical Society.

FIG. 12. *Osage Warrior*, Charles Balthazar Julien Févret de Saint-Mémin, Washington DC, 1806–7, watercolor and graphite on paper, 1954.0019.003, museum purchase. Courtesy of Winterthur Museum.

FIG. 13. *Silhouette of Auguste Chouteau* (1749–1829), William Henry Brown (attributed), 1825–40. Missouri History Museum, St. Louis.

of Indians from this period, wears black cloth around his neck and chest that is likely European in origin, a silver armband manufactured for Indians, and brilliant pigments on his cheek, temple, chest, shoulder, and torso. The non-Indigenous goods do not detract from an overall impression of Native design and aesthetics; they were incorporated purposefully by Indian men. Combining cultural elements was not solely the practice of Indigenous peoples. For the métis residents of North America, their mixed-race heritage was reflected in their hybrid clothing styles; adopting and adapting elements of dress and self-presentation reflecting cultural background was the norm, with significant regional variations the result.[51]

Given the proximity and interactions of Indian and colonial peoples, it is not surprising that they borrowed from each other's material culture. St. Louis was in Indian country, its economy and topography reflecting that orientation and history. Contemporary Indian peoples were visible, essential participants in the fur trade; needed partners; and welcomed allies, who visited and cohabited with, as well as labored alongside and for, colonists. When Auguste Chouteau sent his nine-year-old son to be educated in Montreal, the homesick boy wrote in 1802 to request that his father send a few of his possessions, including his moccasins, which were ornamented with porcupine quills, and his bow and a quiver of arrows for exercising.[52] Beading and quill work were common decorative elements of moccasins. A silhouette of Auguste Chouteau, though from after the colonial period, shows a further example of this cultural borrowing, or cross-dressing. Wearing a top hat, likely made from a processed animal skin, and a knee-length coat, Auguste sports, as a close examination of his footwear makes clear, Indian-style moccasins. No one mistook Chouteau for Indian, yet his donning of items of Indigenous attire speaks to his intimate knowledge of Indian peoples and fashions. Particularly suited to covering rough terrain, elk or deerskin moccasins were worn by Indians and adopted by colonists who preferred them as footwear. So popular did they prove that non-Native manufacturing of moccasins developed in eighteenth-century Detroit.[53]

In St. Louis, an early description of local attire attests to the appeal of Indian fashions among European settlers. In 1811 Henry Marie Brackenridge characterized long-time inhabitants of St. Louis as "essentially Frenchmen" in their character while also noting that both men and women still wore older Indian-influenced styles of dress, including "mockasins, or the Indian sandals." Even at balls in St. Louis, where European-inspired fashionable elegance was the order of the day, one could "still see a few of both sexes in their ancient habiliments; capots, mockasins, blue handerchiefs on their heads, a pipe in the mouth, and the hair tied up in a long queue."[54] Cultural continuities and creative borrowing remained the order of the day. As Jay Gitlin notes, in the late 1810s, inhabitants sported both moccasins and Parisian fashions of the day, and both Indian and Creole women tinted their cheeks with either vermilion or rouge.[55]

So whose was the face of fashion in colonial St. Louis? Identities, like clothes, could seemingly be donned or shed, borrowed for a variety of reasons. What is clear is that in the first place clothing mattered, that it did more than cover the body. That obvious point invites us to consider the specifics of how and why clothing and styles made a difference to the residents of the region. In their efforts to control costume—whether their own or others—individuals and officials made it clear that dress was significant to them because of the wealth of information about identity, affiliations, aspirations, and intentions woven into it. A man's or a woman's choices about what (not) to wear could express an attitude or reflect an identity that others might find worrisome. Especially in new settlements like St. Louis, where residents frequently lacked background information about the people they encountered and indeed may have lacked the linguistic skills to converse with many of those whom they saw, clothing could be helpful in communicating one's social status and position, whether shoring up the position of the wealthy local elite or designating a person of color as a friend, a servant, or a trading partner. It is possible that in such fluid settings, one might also be more tempted to attempt to manipulate others' perceptions of identity through fashion choices. In colonial St. Louis—a predominantly French-speaking outpost of the Spanish empire, perched at the contact edge of European and Indigenous cultures, with residents and visitors of North American, European, and African origin—the clothing choices locals could make drew on imported and Indigenous sources, and were potentially problematic, particularly when they challenged European dominance.

Fashion conveyed multiple meanings, sometimes revealing elements of cultural cross-dressing or hybridization. At the same time, clothing crises offer insight into European powers' understanding of issues of identity and their attempts to legislate and dictate private behavior in the process of empire building. In St. Louis, the stakes could be very high, with some sartorial decisions tantamount to acts against the government: desertion and insurrection. Conspicuous consumption was less a problem than transgressive dress. Such incidents also can be suggestive, if not definitive, regarding the intentions of Indigenous and African inhabitants of the regions, individuals whose words were typically not recorded. Studying the material culture of the period thus offers an opportunity to access the histories of peoples often treated more as victims and less as actors and agents in their own right in the colonial era. Through their items of dress, individual men and women conveyed, both intentionally and not, ideas about their identity. Fashion was a central element in one's self-presentation, with fabrics, ornaments, hairstyles, and the methods of wearing them potential indicators of a person's status, cultural affiliation, or occupation. Perhaps most importantly, the consumption of fashionable wares tied the peoples of this region to vast webs of commerce that spanned Asia, Africa, Europe, and North America, a reminder that this tiny settlement on the banks of the Mississippi was truly a connected, global village.[56]

NOTES

1. White, *Wild Frenchmen*, 1–2.
2. Phillips, "English Sumptuary Laws," 22–42.
3. Fischer, "'Daughters of Zion,'" 27–50.
4. Eliot, *Day-Breaking*, 28.
5. Marriage record, Gaspard Roubieu and Marie Anne Bardet de la Ferme, October 28, 1777, MHSA.
6. Ekberg and Person, *St. Louis Rising*.
7. Cleary, *The World, the Flesh*.
8. Jones, "Repackaging Rousseau," 943; Sewall, "Empire of Fashion," 81–84.
9. Foley and Rice, *First Chouteaus*.

10. White, *Wild Frenchmen.*

11. Ekberg and Person, "Tracking Pierre Laclède," 153–66.

12. Inventory of the estate of Pierre Laclède, 1778, MHSA.

13. Axtell, *Natives and Newcomers,* 107–10.

14. Lozier, "Nicer Red," 45–46.

15. Lozier, "Nicer Red," 47.

16. Lozier, "Nicer Red," 50.

17. Lozier, "Nicer Red," 48.

18. Shrum, *In the Looking Glass,* 31.

19. Shrum, *In the Looking Glass,* 36–37.

20. Axtell, *Natives and Newcomers,* 116.

21. Shrum, *In the Looking Glass,* 113–15.

22. Osage Warrior, Courtesy Winterthur Museum.

23. Hanson, "Trade Mirrors," 1; Shannon, "Dressing for Success," 21.

24. Morrissey, *Empire by Collaboration,* 140.

25. Fausz, *Founding St. Louis,* 110; Payment, "'*Une femme en vaut deux,*'" 271, 281.

26. DuVal, *Native Ground,* 103.

27. DuVal, *Native Ground,* 109.

28. Fausz, *Founding St. Louis.*

29. St. Ange de Bellerive, "Report of the various tribes," May 2, 1769, in Houck, 1:44.

30. "Presents to the Osage Indians," Ramón de Lopez y Angulo, July 13, 1801, in Houck, 2:308–9.

31. Marquis of Casa-Calvo to Ramón de Lopez y Angulo, May 8, 1801, in Houck, 2:310.

32. Shannon, "Dressing for Success," 21.

33. Curator's notes and email with Shannon Meyer, Missouri History Museum Textile and Clothing Curator, January 2014; Moore and Haynes, *Lewis and Clark.*

34. Shannon Meyer, senior curator, Missouri History Museum, phone conversation, November 2017.

35. French colonial armoire from the Chouteau Family, 1920-053-0002, accessed July 8, 2019, http://collections.mohistory.org/resource/202657.

36. Cruzat, Ordinance of October 31, 1786, in Houck, 1:247–48.

37. Carroon, *Broadswords and Bayonets,* 83.

38. Michaux, "Travels into Kentucky, 1793–1796," in Thwaites, 3:70.

39. Axtell, *The European,* 57–58.

40. Houck, *History of Missouri,* 1:369; Schoolcraft, *Travels,* 241–42.

41. Liljegren, "Jacobinism in Spanish Louisiana, 1792–1797," 62–63, 85, 88, 89; Manuel Gayoso de Lemos to Francisco Luis Héctor de Carondelet, in Holmes, 269–70.

42. Cruzat, Ordinance of August 15, 1781, in Houck, 1:245.

43. Laxer, "Exchanges and Hybridities," 100.

44. Lozier, "Nicer Red," 53.

45. Ekberg, *Stealing Indian Women*, 142.

46. Doty, "Constitutional Law," 105–20.

47. Inventory of Presents for Indians, November 27, 1787, in Houck, 1:268–69.

48. List of Presents, September 6, 1800, in Houck, 2:310–11.

49. Miles, "Saint-Mémin's Portraits," 2–33.

50. Tim Shannon email, February 2014.

51. Calloway, *White People*, 136; Harrison, *Metis*, 29–31, 50–53, 66–72, 79, 86–89.

52. Foley and Rice, *First Chouteaus*, 187.

53. Cangany, "Fashioning Moccasins," 265–304; Ekberg and Person, "Tracking Pierre Laclède," 161.

54. Brackenridge, *Views of Louisiana*, 235, 240.

55. Gitlin, *Bourgeois Frontier*, 23.

56. The author wishes to acknowledge current and former staff Dennis Northcott, Shannon Meyer, and Anne Woodhouse of the Missouri Historical Society, St. Louis, Missouri, for their assistance, and Jay Gitlin and Bob Morrissey for their comments.

BIBLIOGRAPHY

Primary Sources

Brackenridge, Henry Marie. *Views of Louisiana; Containing Geographical, Statistical, and Historical Notices of America*. Baltimore MD: Schaeffer & Maund, 1817.

Carroon, Robert G., ed. *Broadswords and Bayonets: The Journals of the Expedition under the Command of Captain Thomas Stirling of the 42nd Regiment of Foot, Royal Highland Regiment (the Black Watch) to Occupy Fort Chartres in the Illinois Country, August 1765 to January 1766*. Chicago: Society of Colonial Wars in the State of Illinois, 1984.

Eliot, John. *The Day-Breaking If Not the Sun-Rising of the Gospel with the Indians in New-England*. London: Rich. Cotes, 1647.

Holmes, Jack D. L., trans. and ed. *Documentos Ineditos para la Historia de la Louisiana, 1792–1810*. Colección Chimalistac de Libros y Documentos Acerca de la Nueva España. Vol. 15. Madrid: Edición José Porrúa Turanzas, 1963.

Houck, Louis, ed. *The Spanish Regime in Missouri.* 2 vols. Chicago: R. R. Donnelley & Sons, 1909. Reprint, New York: Arno Press and *New York Times*, 1971.

MHSA. Missouri Historical Society Archives, St. Louis.

    Archivo General de Indias (microfilm)

    Chouteau Papers

SLA. St. Louis Archives, 1766–1804.

    Litigation Collection

Schoolcraft, Henry Rowe. *Travels in the Central Portions of the Mississippi Valley: Comprising Observations on Its Mineral Geography, Internal Resources, and Aboriginal Population.* New York: Collins and Hannay, 1825.

Thwaites, Reuben Gold, ed. *Early Western Travels, 1748–1846.* Vol. 3. Cleveland: Arthur H. Clark, 1904.

Secondary Sources

Axtell, James. *The European and the Indian: Essays in the Ethnohistory of Colonial North America.* New York: Oxford University Press, 1981.

———. *Natives and Newcomers: The Cultural Origins of North America.* New York: Oxford University Press, 2001.

Calloway, Colin G. *White People, Indians, and Highlanders: Tribal Peoples and Colonial Encounters in Scotland and America.* New York: Oxford University Press, 2008.

Cangany, Catherine. "Fashioning Moccasins: Detroit, the Manufacturing Frontier, and the Empire of Consumption, 1701–1835." *William & Mary Quarterly* 69, no. 2 (April 2012): 265–304.

Chartrand, René. "The Havana Regiment, 1769–1793." *Military Collector and Historian* 63, no. 3 (Fall 2011): 186–87.

Cleary, Patricia. *The World, the Flesh, and the Devil: A History of Colonial St. Louis.* Columbia: University of Missouri Press, 2011.

Doty, Peggy. "Constitutional Law: The Right to Wear a Traditional Indian Hair Style: Recognition of a Heritage." *American Indian Law Review* 4, no.1 (1976): 105–20.

DuVal, Kathleen. *The Native Ground: Indians and Colonists in the Heart of the Continent.* Philadelphia: University of Pennsylvania Press, 2007.

Ekberg, Carl J. *Stealing Indian Women: Native Slavery in the Illinois Country.* Chicago: University of Illinois Press, 2007.

Ekberg, Carl J., and Sharon Person. *St. Louis Rising: The French Regime of Louis St. Ange de Bellerive.* Urbana: University of Illinois Press, 2015.

———. "Tracking Pierre Laclède, 1763–66: A Trading Career Gone Wrong." *Missouri Historical Review* 108, no.3 (April 2014): 153–66.

Fausz, Frederick J. *Founding St. Louis: First City of the New West*. Charleston SC: History Press, 2011.

Fischer, Gayle Veronica. "'The Daughters of Zion are Haughty': Clothing and Sexual Oppression in Puritan New England." *Journal of Unconventional History* 3, no. 1 (1991): 27–50.

Foley, William E., and C. David Rice. *The First Chouteaus: River Barons of Early St. Louis*. Chicago: University of Illinois Press, 1983.

Gitlin, Jay. *The Bourgeois Frontier: French Towns, French Traders, and American Expansion*. New Haven CT: Yale University Press, 2010.

Hanson, Charles E., Jr. "Trade Mirrors." *Museum of the Fur Trade Quarterly* 22, no. 4 (December 1986): 1–11.

Harrison, Julia D. *Metis: People between Two Worlds*. Vancouver: Glenbow-Alberta Institute, 1985.

Houck, Louis. *A History of Missouri from the Earliest Explorations and Settlements until the Admission of the State into the Union*. 3 vols. Chicago: R. R. Donnelley & Sons, 1908.

Jones, Jennifer M. "Repackaging Rousseau: Femininity and Fashion in Old Regime France." *French Historical Studies* 18, no. 4 (1994): 939–68.

Laxer, Daniel R. "Exchanges and Hybridities: Red Leggings and Rubbaboos in the Fur Trade, 1600s-1800s." *Material Culture Review* 82–83 (Fall 2015/Spring 2016): 97–112.

Liljegren, Ernest R. "Jacobinism in Spanish Louisiana, 1792–1797." *Louisiana Historical Quarterly* 22 (January 1939): 47–97.

Lozier, Jean-François. "A Nicer Red: The Exchange and Use of Vermilion in Early America." *Eighteenth-Century Studies* 51, no. 1 (Fall 2017): 45–61.

Miles, Ellen G. "Saint-Mémin's Portraits of American Indians, 1804–1807." *American Art Journal* 20, no. 4 (1988): 3–33.

Moore, Robert J., Jr., and Michael Haynes. *Lewis and Clark, Tailor Made, Trail Worn: Army Life, Clothing, and Weapons of the Corps of Discovery*. Helena MT: Farcountry Press, 2003.

Morrissey, Robert Michael. *Empire by Collaboration: Indians, Colonists, and Governments in Colonial Illinois Country*. Philadelphia: University of Pennsylvania Press, 2015.

Payment, Diane P. "Une femme en vaut deux—'Strong Like Two People': Marie Fisher Gaudet of Fort Good Hope, Northwest Territories." In *Contours of a People: Metis Family, Mobility, and History*. New Directions in Native American Studies. Vol. 6, edited by Nicole St-Onge, Carolyn Podruchny, and Brenda Macdougall, 265–99. Norman: University of Oklahoma Press, 2012.

Phillips, Kim M. "Masculinities and the Medieval English Sumptuary Laws." *Gender and History* 19, no. 1 (April 2007): 22–42.

Sewall, William H. "The Empire of Fashion and the Rise of Capitalism in Eighteenth-Century France," *Past and Present* 206, no. 1 (February 2010): 81–120.

Shannon, Timothy J. "Dressing for Success on the Mohawk Frontier: Hendrick, William Johnson, and the Indian Fashion." *William and Mary Quarterly* 53, no. 1 (January 1996): 13–42.

Shrum, Rebecca K. *In the Looking Glass: Mirrors and Identity in Early America.* Baltimore: Johns Hopkins University Press, 2017.

St-Onge, Nicole, Carolyn Podruchny, and Brenda Macdougall, eds. *Contours of a People: Metis Family, Mobility, and History.* New Directions in Native American Studies. Vol. 6. Norman: University of Oklahoma Press, 2012.

White, Sophie. *Wild Frenchmen and Frenchified Indians: Material Culture and Race in Colonial Louisiana.* Philadelphia: University of Pennsylvania Press, 2012.

PART 2

St. Louis and New Orleans

A Regional Perspective

5

YOU ARE WHO YOU TRADE WITH

Why Antebellum St. Louis Industrialized and New Orleans Didn't

LAWRENCE N. POWELL

It has never been satisfactorily explained, much less attempted, why ante-bellum St. Louis industrialized and New Orleans never did. For nearly a century the links between these two river cities bordered on sibling intimacy. St. Louis was founded in 1764 by a New Orleans fur-trading firm. It was the place where trappers got outfitted before coming into the country and settled their debts with pelts and deerskins upon returning. When the Upper Mississippi Valley began swelling with settlers following the Louisiana Purchase, western produce—grains, packed meat, tobacco, bourbon, etc.—was the tie that bound. New Orleans was the big brother—the urban sibling with the developmental head start, the cultural capital of what Jay Gitlin has called the Creole Corridor. But as early 1840 St. Louis and New Orleans began parting economic ways, the former racing ahead as the antebellum era drew to a close. By 1880 St. Louis had surpassed New Orleans in almost every statistical category that mattered. The reason was plain: the Gateway City had laid a manufacturing foundation under its economy and the Crescent City had not. What explains New Orleans's failure to follow suit, how to account for the economic divergence?[1]

One thing is clear: you can't ascribe the divergence to cultural differences. Early on the two communities were practically demographic twins, their histories intertwined like threads in a carpet. The sorts of people who settled New Orleans also populated St. Louis. The waves of Irish and German immigration that flooded the Crescent City during the 1830s, '40s, and '50s also washed over the River City—and with comparable effects. Each town's power structure in the wake of the American takeover repelled efforts to overturn their legal system, to relegate them to second-class citizenship, to ban slavery and the slave trade, or to vacate eleventh-hour Spanish land grants. Eventually, both francophone establishments came to terms with the new order. For one, they had to. For another, they had become adept at pulling its political wires. "By 1815," writes Jay Gitlin of St. Louis's French-speaking elites, "they had taken the measure of republican government and made the transition from old regime clientage to American-style backroom deals." His words could be easily transposed to New Orleans.[2]

As for the supposed want of animal spirits among French settlers—the notion that the "innate" business conservatism of St. Louis was somehow owing to "the surviving French influence"—these fur merchants were scarcely novitiates in the religion of trade. They understood markets, kept abreast of price currents, monitored capital flows, and spent much of their waking hours catching up with business correspondence. They invested shrewdly. Even before the Louisiana Purchase had been negotiated, they were placing bets on the booming American economy, hoping to share in the bonanza that the Mississippi Valley, one of the greatest free-trade zones the world had ever seen, was holding forth to men willing to seize it.[3]

Simply put, New Orleans and St. Louis grew apart not because of cultural but because of institutional differences: one became the entrepôt of a plantation economy powered by compulsory labor; the other, the market center for freehold farms and small towns. It was a contrast of hinterlands: St. Louis's teemed with small and midsize commercial towns; New Orleans's was dominated by large estates worked by enslaved labor. In the trading ambit of St. Louis, small-scale urbanization had free rein. In New Orleans's hinterland, urbanization had been choked off. The feedback process that stimulated manufacturing and drew St. Louis into its orbit was largely missing in New Orleans.

This narrative of brotherly love devolving into sibling rivalry reflects geopolitical realignments in the last years of the antebellum period. Regional trade patterns shifted on their axes, and the ground of antebellum politics gave way under the sectionalizing shocks that preceded disunion. Border slave states like Missouri (whose slave population never much exceeded ten percent of the whole) became untethered from the Lower South. Historians have approached the subject from different angles, sometimes by drawing North-South comparisons, less frequently, by contrasting the South with the Midwest. But no one has narrowed the aperture to St. Louis and New Orleans, examining how they grew together before growing apart. Or, to put it somewhat differently, how St. Louis became the anchor of an urban region, while New Orleans became the American anomaly: the nation's only city system without an urban region.

Top Ten Cities

Both New Orleans and St. Louis emerged as top-ten American cities during the first half of the nineteenth century. Those decades, particularly the years 1840–60, witnessed the fastest rates of urbanization in U.S. history. Never again would towns and cities grow as rapidly as they did during that twenty-year run up to secession and war. Before 1840, New Orleans often set the pace. In the 1830s it was America's fastest growing city, vaulting from seventh to third place in total population, overtaking Boston and Philadelphia and closing hard on Baltimore (with which it was practically tied for second place) and New York. Just as explosive was the expansion of the port, which was soon vying with New York both in tonnage and the value of cargo. Steamboats were New Orleans's forte. Throughout the antebellum period New Orleans was the undisputed steamboat capital of western waters, outpacing all comers (save for St. Louis during the 1850s) in annual steamboat arrivals. Before canals and trunk rail lines pierced the Appalachian mountain barrier, western trade followed the river. Most of those waters flowed south, emptying into the Mississippi on its way to the Gulf. The town's location near the river's mouth gave it command of the valley's strategic narrows of commerce. New Orleans was the last stop on the river where exports from the landlocked trans-Appalachian West could be consolidated before transshipment to the Caribbean and the East Coast. For the city's merchants, making money was as easy as stretching their arms over the levee and raking it in.[4]

Commerce boomed. The earliest tinder was western produce, for New Orleans was a western town before it became a southern one. An impressive wholesale-trading complex arose focused on the traffic in western grains, salted meats, whiskey, tobacco, and lead. There were wholesale grocers, dry goods merchants, and commission merchants; to say nothing of legions of shipping agents, purchasing agents, and marine insurance agents; plus retailers of every size, shape, and variety. But by 1840, the city's economy fell under the thrall of cotton, its commerce dominated by a small oligarchy of cotton factors. Cotton factors were merchants extraordinaire, jacks of all trade. They saw that the planters' cotton was stored, insured, re-baled, and sold when the price was right. They served as their purchasing agents, ordering luxury imports for the Big House or cheap brogans for the slave quarters. They were bankers, suppliers of credit, and concierges for planters and their families during their extended stays *en ville*. Whatever commodity was riding high at the time, New Orleans could always count on filling its many hotels and boarding houses between November and May. It was a frenetic period in the town's commercial calendar, everyone chasing profit and pleasure with the same greedy intensity. In antebellum New Orleans money changed hands at warp speed. In 1837 Louisiana's banking system ranked third behind New York and Massachusetts, in no small part because of its tie-ins with such international bankers as the Baring Brothers in the City of London. There were some years when the volume of business paper—bills of exchange, promissory notes, accommodation paper, and banknotes—discounted by New Orleans banks and counting houses surpassed even that of Gotham.[5]

Hardly more than a village when New Orleans's population lunged forward following the Purchase, St. Louis shambled even to reach the 2,500-person threshold set by the U.S. Census to define an urban place. As late as 1840 its population was but one-sixth that of New Orleans's. By 1860 its census rank had almost pulled even with its big brother.

Sprawling across a gently sloping limestone ledge along the upper Mississippi, St. Louis rose to prominence on the strength of its location between the Missouri and Ohio Rivers. Above the town, the Mississippi's channel narrowed dangerously, its shallow riverbed a limestone razor to the hulls of large steamboats arriving from New Orleans, Louisville, and Cincinnati. Thus, St. Louis became to the Upper Mississippi Valley what New Orleans was to the lower delta: a break-of-bulk and consolidation point for commerce coming up and down the river. St. Louis rose to steamboat

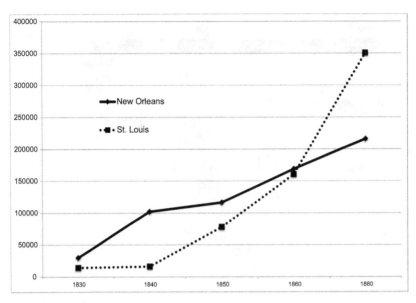

GRAPH I. New Orleans and St. Louis population growth, 1830–80. U.S. Census Bureau. Population 1830–80. Prepared by Social Explorer. Accessed September 25 09:43 a.m. CDT 2017.

prominence because it was where farmers and trappers exchanged grains and pelts for the products of the North and West. The New Orleans-descended Chouteaus certainly recognized steam power's possibilities. This first family of fur traders pounced on the new technology soon after the first steamboats put in at St. Louis. Steamboats gave them a head start on the competition for control of trading posts on the Missouri.[6]

St. Louis also turned to advantage its reciprocal trade and credit arrangements with New Orleans. That Deep South port was the preferred destination for commodities gathered by St. Louis merchants from the Upper Valley. It was where they purchased sugar and molasses for distribution to retailers near and far, financing those commodities with lines of credit made available through New Orleans's correspondent relationships with New York and London. It was on the strength of that relationship that St. Louis's jobbing business surged; by 1855 wholesale houses operating on or near the quay were said to have numbered in the hundreds. Population soared. St. Louis had even overtaken Louisville and Cincinnati

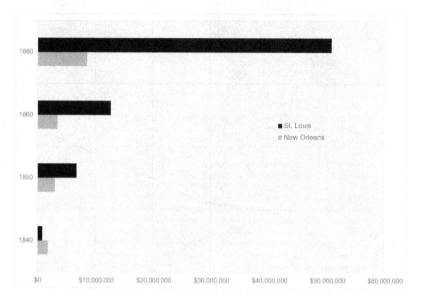

GRAPH 2. New Orleans and St. Louis manufacturing capital, 1840–80. U.S. Census Bureau. Population 1830–80. Prepared by Social Explorer. Accessed September 25 09:43 a.m. CDT 2017.

as a commercial emporium. "Just as once all roads led to Rome," wrote one historian in explanation of the town's meteoric rise, "so it may be said that all the river routes of the great interior converged on St. Louis." The city's ability to capitalize on its enviable location had a lot to do with its trade with New Orleans.[7]

But even as St. Louis was reaching demographic parity with New Orleans, it was surpassing its older sibling in another statistical category: manufacturing. By 1840 that disparity had become impossible to ignore. Twenty years on, it had hardened into a trend line. By then St. Louis's manufacturing workforce was twice the size of the Crescent City's; even starker was the discrepancy in manufacturing value-added (net output) between the two cities. In St. Louis a kind of self-reinforcing industrial expansion had gotten underway.[8]

It was evidenced in the explosion of small towns across St. Louis's hinterland. Many of them were aspirational, the imaginings of boosters

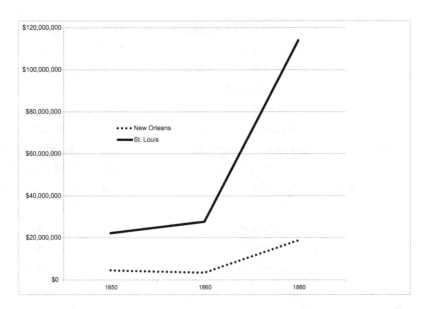

GRAPH 3. New Orleans and St. Louis value of manufactured products, 1850–80. U.S. Census Bureau. Industry and Manufacturing 1830–80. Prepared by Social Explorer. Accessed September 25 09:43 a.m. CDT 2017.

self-assured that their plats would become overnight sensations. Not a few evolved into loci of manufacturing start-ups. As Timothy R. Mahoney has explained, in his meticulous examination of St. Louis's hinterland: "Town economic development became the catalytic force in regional economic development."[9]

The dynamism nudged St. Louis from "a wholesaling-trading complex" to "the production of manufactured goods for domestic consumption." To the extent that you are who you trade with, the Gateway City is a prime example of micropolitan dynamism driving metropolitan development.[10]

St. Louis's Industrial Takeoff

It is hard to say who came first: squatters or speculators. After 1787, when federal surveyors began carving the Old Northwest into thousands of compact townships, speculators were among the earliest arrivals. Richard Wade surely had them in mind when he memorably observed that "The towns were the spearheads of the frontier," places that held the West for the advancing line of settlement. That colonizing phalanx had been advancing ever since Americans won their independence, driving indigenous people further west, if not against the wall. The spectacular land rushes occurred after the War of 1812—first in 1816–19, then in 1835–37, both manias irrigated by easy credit. As commonplace as barn raisings may have been, the platting of new towns was almost as frequent. Ambitious young men flocked to these places. Small farmers were single-minded about being within a wagon ride of market centers in order to exchange surpluses for store-bought comforts from Europe and the eastern seaboard.[11]

By the time of the Spanish cession in 1763, the French in Upper Louisiana had already established "a landscape of villages and urban places alongside Indian villages." This was the landscape the historian Richard White famously termed "Middle Ground"—a backcountry of mixed settlements of francophone trappers and traders who had smoothed the integration of Indians into an international market economy, producing in the process a new people of mixed ancestry (métis). By 1800 both French trappers and their métis kinfolk had formed satellite villages in St. Louis's surrounds. They blossomed into retirement communities where aging trappers took up farming. Soon other towns took root along the Mississippi and its tributaries. The region's growing lead business, centering around Galena, Illinois, was an early stimulus. Like most Midwestern towns, many of these places started as speculations, barren lots scratched onto a grid, coupled with a single make-or-break accessory—a wharf. Without one, packet boats would hardly bother putting these "paper" towns on their regular schedule. And without regular steamboat service, neither would settlers bother populating the neighborhood. Steamboats pumped life into these satellite villages and small-town promotions.[12]

This pell-mell urbanization began making itself felt in St. Louis in the 1830s and '40s. This was when American settlement penetrated the outer limits of the Prairie Peninsula—that wedge of grasslands and undulating hills extending from the Great Plains to eastern Indiana. Over the next two decades torrents of migrants swept over those prairies. They blanketed northern Illinois and southern Wisconsin, then spread over much of Iowa and Missouri, eventually dipping down toward Cairo, Illinois. The chief impetus was rising wheat prices, due principally to famine and crop failures in Europe and the British Isles, and later, in the 1850s, the Crimean War. Land was affordable (thanks to liberal public land policies) and credit easy. Soil quality was excellent, and drainage more than adequate. And the climate for growing grains—cool evenings and lots of rain, without the excessively sticky wetness of the Mississippi's sickly bottomlands—could hardly be improved upon. Then there were the many medium-size rivers capable of accommodating steamboat traffic. Everything came together just as St. Louis's demographic growth began its steep ascent. The two developments were not unconnected.[13]

The urbanization of St. Louis's hinterland occurred with startling suddenness. Where one day there was a rolling prairie dotted with stands of timber, the next day there was a clearing for a town. It has been estimated that in Illinois alone between 1835 and '37 more than five hundred of these places had been laid out, many of them platted by their founders. From inland townships deprived of waterways, roads speared across the plains toward the nearest river town—"tributaries on land," to use Mahoney's clever turn of phrase. A red-letter day was the arrival of sedentary merchants willing and able to offer store-bought merchandise on credit—which was usually all it took to undam a flood of grain and livestock from the surrounding countryside. The "circle of trade" was not large. In this self-replicating ecosystem the average distance between towns was a mere seven to ten miles. But these compact trading zones were dense, thickening each year with people and commerce. Thousands of young men looking for careers barged in, joined by artisans and craftsmen scouting for work and opportunity. The ease with which "the basic agrarian experience flowed into that of commercial small-urban enterprise," as Stanley Elkins and Eric McKitrick insightfully observed in their seminal article on Frederick Jackson Turner's frontier thesis, still beggars belief.[14]

It was nothing less than the thunder of a market revolution storming across the prairies. A leading sector was the milling of wheat into flour. Milling had been an industrializing trigger in the Mid-Atlantic region. It exhibited similar multiplier effects in St. Louis's hinterland. The wheat trade boosted demand for barrel making, cooperage, wagon-building, warehousing, and baking. Rising wheat income enabled urban and farming residents to purchase such consumer durables as cast-iron stoves. As towns grew in number and size, so did the market for bricks, lumber, and windows, even prefabricated doors and window sashes. Urban consumer demand was especially robust: an estimated three times greater than rural demand. However, farming income didn't stay hidden under the mattress. It bought cast-iron stoves and window sashes. Not to be overlooked was the demand for farm equipment, particularly laborsaving appliances, to compensate for chronic labor shortages at harvest time.

At first, most consumer and producer durables were fabricated in the East. By the time they reached western shelves transit costs had driven up the price considerably. That differential caught the eye of prairie-style Yankee tinkerers convinced they could fabricate reasonable knockoffs and spare parts less expensively. The inventors ranged across the artisanal spectrum—from wheelwrights and blacksmiths to carpenters and cabinet makers, or anyone, for that matter, who was mechanically inclined, handy at woodworking, and attuned to market signals. They lacked a term for what they were grabbing hold of, but modern economists have since come up with one: import substitution. Artisans conjured the opportunity into saleable merchandise, perhaps registering their innovations with the patent office. It was only a matter of time before their sorcery transmuted small workshops into incipient machine tool manufactures. The Midwest's industrial base sprouted from this soil. Competition spurred specialization, fostering more competition, which stimulated a virtuous circle of more inventions, more specialization, and more competition. By the 1850s the Prairie Peninsula was thrumming with hundreds of these small, urban, breeder reactors of entrepreneurialism.[15]

Fueling the chain reaction was "the fact that every town was a promotion." Whoever cast his lot with the town's fortunes knew that success turned on its prosperity (read: rising real estate values). The credo was uncomplicated: the "town must grow—it was vital to get people there and keep them there—it was of the essence to allure the man with money." Each understood his role: lawyers and politicians had to bring home the legislative bacon; newspaper editors must broadcast the town's virtues. Bonds were issued to build bridges and lay track. Schoolhouses went up far beyond the town's immediate need. In the vanguard of developmental change stood the town's merchants. As the fever of economic growth rose, they started thinking regionally. Being mere middlemen ceased to hold interest for them. They aspired to the loftier status of regional wholesalers. They envisaged their towns as grander places than mere transshipment points. Conversations turned to strategies of economic development. Why couldn't they become entrepôts the equal of St. Louis? Before long they were pooling their capital so as to upgrade the town's infrastructure, meanwhile investing in those small-scale manufacturing ventures launched by future-oriented artisans.[16]

Farmers close to the river were also recalibrating their economic strategies. Proximity to town had driven up land values. Soon, wheat cultivated on wet bottomlands couldn't compete with the superior grade gushing from the Prairie Peninsula. To maximize return on higher-priced acreage, river town farmers diversified. They planted and pruned orchards. They grew corn and raised hogs, because corn, unlike wheat, grew well under hot, wet conditions. As hog-raising spread—a seasonal and risky enterprise—so did pork packing. Many of the packers in places like Alton, Quincy, and Peoria had been general merchants who drew on commercial credit to supplement their own modest capital. "The transition from merchant to manufacturer, at least in the river towns, was gradual," observed Margaret Walsh. But in the early 1840s the transition went into overdrive. Cincinnati, the nation's central distributor of groceries, had long laid claim to the title as the Upper Mississippi Valley's Porkopolis. That reputation wouldn't last much longer.[17]

Economists call them agglomeration effects, the forces that were reconstituting the prairie's larger towns. The larger the town, the greater its allure for ambitious men drawn to communities where ideas and tech-savvy information (read: knowledge "spillovers") circulated fast and freely. In St. Louis, the largest town of all, the clustering was particularly far-reaching. The Gateway City's ability to amass larger workforces and centralize production—that is, achieve economies of scale, thus lowering per-unit costs and increasing returns—equipped it with insurmountable advantages over start-ups in smaller towns. This was the case with St. Louis's rivalry with Alton for the lead business. It was true of pork packing, due to ability of the city's packinghouses to draw on the swelling number of swine raised in nearby Missouri counties. Between 1843 and 1851 the number of hogs packed in St. Louis exploded from sixteen thousand to as many as two hundred thousand per year. There was also the matter of St. Louis's ability to exploit external economies available chiefly in large cities: the ability to turn a profit from the sale of waste products. It wasn't coincidental that St. Louis's packinghouses grew in tandem with soap and candle makers. Before long St. Louis was vying with Cincinnati for pork supremacy.

In time St. Louis would join the industrial age, with its forward- and backward- and final-destination-linkages, the output of one manufacturer functioning as the input of another, in townscapes buzzing with hot tips and new ideas.[18]

In 1854 an early St. Louis booster could marvel: "There are few branches of industry, few kinds of manufacturing, but what are now being carried forward successfully in St. Louis." He counted twenty flour mills, a large number of lumber and planning mills, twenty-five foundries, a bevy of engines and boiler manufacturers, numerous machine shops. There were stove-casting shops, plus an extensive locomotive building works, railroad car works, saddle and harness works, rope works and bagging factories, never mind "large quantities of furniture"—a consumer durable particularly sensitive to the density of market demand. There were shops that turned out "tin and sheet iron ware, carriages and wagons, and agricultural implements, *heretofore imported*" (italics added). Inexplicably overlooked was St. Louis's five-hundred-man tobacco factory, one of the nation's largest.[19]

As for the Chouteaus, the founding family of St. Louis, Americanization had treated them well. At one time their fur-trading empire was almost the equal of John Jacob Astor's. After 1810, however, it was slowly winding down. The penultimate stage was reached when the family segued into the "Indian business"—that brisk commerce in guaranteed annuities disbursed regularly by the U.S. government to Native Americans for the purchase of tribal lands. Next to blunt force, annuities were the most effective method for separating Indians from their lands. By the 1830s, when white settlers began overrunning the Prairie Peninsula, ratcheting up pressure for Indian removal, the Chouteaus stumbled on the cheerful prospect that "as much money [could be] made in supplying annuity goods as . . . in furs." The annuities could be spent only at government-approved trading posts, like those owned and operated by the Chouteaus. Furthermore, the profits were guaranteed by the government, as were the debts that Indian customers were encouraged to run up on credit. Thanks to those profits, the Chouteaus "entered the world of industrial capitalism with enthusiasm," stuffing their portfolios with railroad, mining, and banking stock, along with interests in the lead business and milling.[20]

By 1860 St. Louis's industrial workforce was approaching twelve thousand—twice that of New Orleans. For the Crescent City, that sobering data point was a harbinger of worse to come.[21]

The Unevenness of Southern Urbanization

That only eleven of America's 102 cities larger than ten thousand residents were in the South as of 1860 should cause little surprise to anyone passingly familiar with the literature on southern industrialization. But what many might find startling is the sectional imbalance in towns consisting of at least one thousand residents or more. In Missouri, Illinois, and Iowa—the core of St. Louis's hinterland at one time or another—the number of such places surged from 178 to 1,017 (a 471 percent increase) between 1850 and 1860; in Louisiana and Mississippi, the heartland of New Orleans's cotton and sugar country, the number of towns shambled from twenty to thirty during the same span of time.[22]

The difference was in kind, not just degree, a structural lopsidedness that spotlights the southern urban system's "*primate* character." In the cotton South, the city system was not an urban system at all. It consisted of a few cities and large towns, and little else. Southern cities perched on the periphery, usually on or near the seacoast, not in the center of a trading territory. They were frozen in utero, wholesale-trading complexes that failed to make the critical transition to manufacturing prior to the Civil War because they were tethered to an agrarian order that had scant need for what small towns and forwarding centers had to offer. Everything slave plantations required—commercial services such as marketing, shipping,

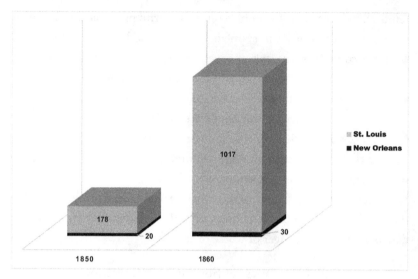

GRAPH 4. The urban systems of New Orleans and St. Louis (towns with at least one thousand inhabitants). U.S. Census Bureau. Population of Cities and Towns. 1850 and 1860. Includes Louisiana and Mississippi as well as Missouri, Illinois, and Iowa.

and insuring the crop; clothing for the slave quarters; luxury items for the Big House with luxury imports; plus ample credit to pay for it all—New Orleans's cotton factors-cum-commission merchants were able to furnish directly through connections with local bankers, brokers and wholesalers. In such an agrarian order, small towns were redundant.[23]

It is hard to sustain the once popular argument that the southern lag in urbanization derived from some profound agrarian antagonism to large towns and cities per se. True, the anti-urban slurs directed by southern nationalists against northern abolitionists were biting and hard to miss. And if you took them at their word you would think they would never be caught dead setting foot in such places. But several of these agrarian ideologues actually resided in the South's occasional cities, joined by many of the region's largest slaveholders for at least part of the year.[24]

It is even harder to blame differences in land surveying practices for the South's failure to keep pace with the Midwest's rapid urbanization. The Prairie Peninsula and the Old Southwest were settled practically contemporaneously, and in accord with the same Euclidean template. Public lands were parceled into six-mile-square townships, then subsequently subdivided into smaller sections. Each witnessed similar land rushes (usually following the removal of Indians from their ancient homelands), fueled by easy credit from wildcat banks that asked little more from the loan applicant than "an authentication of his great distress for money." As the date set for the land auction drew near, speculators streamed into both areas, the influx turning into flashfloods between 1830–37. And invariably, whether in Alabama or Illinois, the speculators discovered that squatters had gotten there first.[25]

But here is where the sectional parallel breaks down. In the Old Northwest squatters were able to hold their own against would-be land barons. Preemption laws gave them the right to buy, at prescribed minimum prices, land on which they had notionally made improvements. Territorial and state legislatures taxed unimproved land in order to discourage speculators from sitting on large tracts until prices rose. But in the Old Southwest it was slaveholding planters—"pioneers with means"—from the Chesapeake, Georgia, and the Carolinas, who gained the upper hand. With the help of their adult children, and overseers and hirelings, they claimed or scarfed up preemption rights, then deployed coffles of slaves to "improve" the land. They weren't above hiring thugs on occasion to drive off squatters brash enough to make a stand. Colluding on bids, and unburdened by high land taxes, large syndicates were able to resell public land at markups that only planters could afford. Against the methodical acquisitiveness of cotton planters, the little man had few defenses.

Jefferson's "empire of liberty," that vast wilderness west of the Appalachians envisioned by the third president as a yeoman's republic, went down like so many southern forests before axe-wielding bondsmen. Squatters retired to the backcountry, the sand barrens, and the piney woods. It was now settled fact that desirable areas for commercial agriculture—the loamy black belt of central Alabama and Mississippi, the rich alluvia of the Mississippi River and its tributaries—was roped off for the benefit of large growers of cotton and their enslaved workforce. Theirs would become the geopolitical heart of the storied cotton kingdom—a province ruled, dominated, and molded by slave plantations, with seldom a town beyond a post office crossroads worthy of the name.[26]

Naturally, there were some towns, a few of them major, like eighteenth-century Natchez and Baton Rouge, that evolved into important market hubs for assembling cotton from the surrounding countryside earmarked for New Orleans. As the cotton frontier penetrated deeper into the interior, newer towns emerged to perform similar functions. Still, on the lower Mississippi, there was nothing like the wharf-building frenzy of town promoters in the Upper Valley, each scrambling to get on the schedule of packet boats plying the waters between St. Louis and Galena. Downstream, it was large plantations that dominated steamboat commerce. It was individual planters, deploying slaves, who threw up makeshift landings, where itinerant steamboats nosed against the riverbank as enslaved deckhands wrestled cotton bales on board. There was no need to wagon their cotton to nearby towns for transshipment to New Orleans. Their cotton could be forwarded to New Orleans just as easily from repurposed riverbanks.[27]

There has been a recent outpouring of literature concerning capitalism and slavery, mostly to the effect that, contrary to an already-faltering school of interpretation, southern slavery *was* compatible with capitalism. Large cotton growers were good businessmen. Their plantations were profitable, earning better than satisfactory rates of return, not least because their owners stayed up-to-date with nineteenth-century best practices. A complex division of labor (often by age and gender) characterized large plantations, down to the management of labor time. That was one reason southern planters diversified into corn and livestock during downtimes in the cotton cycle. It maximized their return on labor (for slaves were capital goods). They were so successful at it, their estates became self-sufficient in foodstuffs. Basically, antebellum slave plantations resembled factories in the field, their small workshops populated with enslaved blacksmiths and wheelwrights, coopers and carpenters. On Louisiana's large sugar estates, the factory likeness was especially close. To quote Louisiana's Judah P. Benjamin, U.S. senator and future Confederate cabinet member, "a sugar plantation is incomplete without its workshop, that is, its sugar house. The owner is manufacturer as well as agriculturist, and the manufacture of sugar is one of great delicacy and difficulty." Confessedly, large cotton plantations lacked steam engines and other expensive technology. But in the way of organizational efficiency, they did not lag far behind.[28]

Yet for all their resemblance to nineteenth-century factories, antebellum cotton and sugar growers never galvanized a general industrialization—and, indeed, really couldn't. The compatibility that may have obtained between southern slavery and capitalism scarcely existed between slavery and industrialization—at least, not the kind of industrializing process that unspooled in the North and the Midwest. Marshaling examples of slaves working in mills, mines, foundries, and factories proves very little. This random collection of factories and mills never cohered into a southern manufacturing belt. The reason should be obvious: the impossibility of stimulating consumer demand in an economy where slave underconsumption was the norm and self-sufficiency in foodstuffs stymied the emergence of a local food industry grounded in milling and meatpacking. Nor was there much demand for laborsaving equipment, since it was easier to expand operations by purchasing additional slaves. Slave plantations had thrown too many guardrails around consumer and producer demand for a manufacturing breakthrough to occur.[29]

Yet it was in the way that plantation slavery choked off town development that the institution's stultifying effects on industrialization made themselves felt. The pall even fell over the backcountry, where, according to David Carlton, yeoman consumption levels were too depressed "to spark major town-based manufacturing." But the worst effects were felt in the cotton belt, where plantation slavery stunted the home market, not merely by enslaving half of it but by short-circuiting the development of towns. In the Old Northwest the town generated demand for consumer goods and producer durables, for infrastructural materials and agricultural equipment, for warehousing and transportation conveyances. A commercial food industry grew up to service small-town markets. But most of all, small towns in the fast-emerging manufacturing belt incubated an artisanal economy undaunted by competition with eastern and European imports.

Among the economic sins for which southern slavery might be taken to task, few were more developmentally injurious than the bondage of enslaved artisans to the undemanding needs of the plantation economy. Who knows what infant industry the inventive tinkering of African-descended craftsmen might have fostered in an unchained urban milieu like that of the Midwest?[30]

Thus, in New Orleans's hinterland there would be no sudden lurch from suspended to extraordinary animation such as occurred in that of St. Louis. Or downstream clustering of small urban manufacturers—agglomeration effects, to use the language of economics—of the kind that brought millers and meat packers, smelters and furniture makers together in large towns and cities because that's where you went to build to scale, join the conversation of change and innovation, and enjoy increasing returns.

It would be misleading to leave the impression that antebellum New Orleans was devoid of manufacturing. In 1860 there were scores of boot and shoemakers, hosts of cigar makers (mainly free men of color), and bakers by the dozens. There was a respectable machinery and steam engine sector and a few large iron foundries. Across the river the recently deceased John McDonogh, one of the largest property holders in the South, had operated a brick and lumber yard, at one time employing a hundred slaves, which supplied the city with building materials.[31]

New Orleans's largest manufacturing sector was men's clothing. That preeminence was due to Leon Godchaux, an Alsatian Jew, who won post-war fame as the sugar king of Louisiana. However, his first fortune had been made selling city duds to mariners eager to paint the town after months at sea. When he built his first department store on Canal Street, he established a garment factory and used the new technology of sewing machines to stock inventory. But the ready-made clothing market beyond metropolitan New Orleans was shallow. The market in cheap slave clothing, while admittedly wider, had been cornered by northern manufacturers. And that was the problem with New Orleans's minimalist industrial sector: the consumer market for what it produced was bound by the limits of the plantation. It is startling to learn that in 1860 New Orleans manufactured more macaroni and vermicelli than home hardware. As for lead, 99 percent of which had once flowed through the port on its way to the East, nary an ounce was transmuted into lead pipes, paint, or oil. For that matter, New Orleans scarcely traded with the South's other city systems either.

Just as astonishing, the nerve center of the Cotton Kingdom was bereft of textile mills.[32]

The First Shall Be Last

Even before the Old Union unraveled, an upstart on the malarial marshes of Lake Michigan had knocked New Orleans and St. Louis from their pedestals. The transportation revolution's latest phase—canals but especially railroads—had transformed Chicago into the colossus of the "Great West." By the 1850s trunk rail lines were breaching the Alleghenies, redirecting trade flows from a north-south to an east-west axis. Chicago's hard-charging business community completed the system by thrusting branch lines into Iowa and downstate Illinois, walking off with much of the grain and livestock trade that had formerly passed through the hands of merchants in St. Louis and New Orleans. It happened with jaw-dropping speed. New Orleans and St. Louis were caught napping, both succumbing to the "stupid fatalism" regarding the Mississippi's supposed superiority over artificial channels of trade. They had become victims of their own complacency.[33]

Yet not all declines are equal. New Orleans's postwar slump proved much more difficult to arrest, let alone reverse. Emancipation had upended the old plantation system, together with the cotton factorage system propping it up. Reconstruction rejectionism and racial backlash became the city's raison d'être, tourism and social exclusivity its stock in trade. By contrast, St. Louis merchants refused to become bogged down in the politics of race and resentment. There were markets to recover, new ones to conquer, and no time to waste accomplishing both. Drummers invaded the new Southwest, including Texas. They stormed into southern territory once dominated by New Orleans, capturing swaths of its customer base because St. Louis jobbers were willing to accept any order, no matter how small the transaction. New Orleans wholesalers thumbed their nose at transactions less than fifty dollars.[34]

Postwar St. Louis didn't stagnate like postwar New Orleans did. It grew and prospered, albeit in Chicago's shadow. It was hard to challenge the Windy City's command of a 1,600-mile water route to New York via the Erie Canal, especially after railroads and the Illinois and Michigan

Canal unlocked the promise of this richly productive region. Nonetheless, St. Louis thrived. Over the next two decades its population leapt forward while New Orleans's slowed to a crawl. During that same twenty-year span, New Orleans's industrial workforce remained stuck between five and six thousand; St. Louis's ballooned to forty thousand and was climbing fast. By now, the discrete regional industrial systems that had congealed on both sides of the Alleghenies were exchanging goods and services across each other's trading frontiers. Manufacturing belts once defined by geography were now melding into multiregional systems functioning as important cogs in a national market. Then came the discovery of Midwestern iron and coal deposits and the rise of heavy industry.[35]

The seminal period for this development was 1840 to 1860, when the Midwestern manufacturing belt first took shape. The Crescent City stood on the outside looking in. It was a missed opportunity that would echo through the next century of the city's growth and development.[36]

NOTES

For their helpful criticisms, the author wishes to thank Jason Berry, David Carlton, Jay Gitlin, Steven Hahn, Howard Hunter, Peter Kastor, Lance Hill, Patrick Maney, Scott Marler, Jonathan Pritchett, C. Peter Ripley, Michael Ross, Rebecca Scott, Randy Sparks, Michael Wayne, Charles Wellford, Gavin Wright, and the anonymous reviewers for the University of Nebraska Press.

1. Gitlin, *Bourgeois Frontier*, 1–2; Adler, *Yankee Merchants*, 13–42; Pred, *Urban Growth*; and Meyer, "American Manufacturing Belt," 145–74.
2. Gitlin, *Bourgeois Frontier*, 81. Also, Clark, *New Orleans*; Faber, *Land of Dreams*; and Kastor, *Nation's Crucible*.
3. Belcher, *Economic Rivalry*, 14–15; Gitlin, *Bourgeois Frontier*, 6–7, 14–16.
4. Hunter, *Steamboats*, 34–35, 644.
5. Marler, *Merchants' Capital*, 1–52; Woodman, *King Cotton*; Schermerhorn, *Business of Slavery*, 95–123; Green, *Finance and Economic Development*, especially 5n; and Kilbourne, *Louisiana Commercial Law*, 121.
6. Gitlin, *Bourgeois Frontier*, 21, 68; Belcher, *Economic Rivalry*, 26–31; Cronon, *Nature's Metropolis*, 106–9, 296–97.
7. Belcher, *Economic Rivalry*, 41–49 (48 for the quotation); Gitlin, *Bourgeois Frontier*, 13–14, 21, 68; Mahoney, *River Towns*, 213–14; and Adler, *Yankee Merchants*, 61–90.

8. Pred, *Urban Growth*, 8.

9. Mahoney, *River Towns*, 213.

10. Pred, *Urban Growth*, 8.

11. Wade, *Urban Frontier*, 1; Sellers, *Market Revolution*, 3–33; Hahn, *Nation without Borders*, 79–113; Elkins and McKitrick, "Turner's Frontier," 342.

12. Gitlin, *Bourgeois Frontier*, 10 (for the first quotation), 15–18; Mahoney, *River Towns*, 110–14. Also, White, *Middle Ground*.

13. Swierenga, *Pioneers and Profit*, 18–19; Mahoney, *River Towns*, 9–13, 49; Rohrbough, *Trans-Appalachian Frontier*, 455–91.

14. Mahoney, *River Towns*, 93, 128 (for the first quotation); Elkins and McKitrick, "Turner's Frontier," 333, 340–42 (the quotation is on 340).

15. Pred, *Urban Growth*, 5–6, 43; *Spatial Dynamics*, 77, 37, 87; Higgs, "American Inventiveness," 661–67; Mahoney, *River Towns*, 228, 233; Meyer, "American Manufacturing Belt," 149–50, 153. No studies have been undertaken of patent activity between 1840 and 1860. But insofar as inventions multiply in lockstep with urbanization and manufacturing, it's a reasonable assumption that there was a comparable uptick in patents (assuming they were filed) in the urban ecosystem described here.

16. Elkins and McKitrick, "Turner's Frontier" 342 (for the quotation); Mahoney, *River Towns*, 211–13, 228; and Wright, *Economic Development*, 74–75.

17. Mahoney, *River Towns*, 177–78, 197; Walsh, "Pork Packing," 710.

18. Mahoney, *River Towns*, 195–97, 231; Hogan, *City of St. Louis*, 13; Walsh, "Pork Packing," 702–17. For a sophisticated but highly readable explanation of how manufacturing "cores" grew in tandem with agricultural "peripheries," see Krugman, "Increasing Returns," 483–99; *Geography and Trade*.

19. Hogan, *City of St. Louis*, 13; Prim, *Lion of the Valley*, 63, 104. For a less roseate picture of St. Louis's manufacturing breakthrough, see Adler, *Yankee Merchants*, 87–90.

20. Gitlin, *Bourgeois Frontier*, 68–82, 128, 132, 135 (the quotations are on 69 and 81).

21. Meyer, "Industrial Retardation," 373.

22. Maps prepared by Gavin Wright highlighting population density per square mile and farm value per acreage capture the urban differential North and South in visually striking ways. See *Economic Development*, 64–65. Darrett B. Rutman and Anita H. Rutman sound notes of caution respecting the U.S. Census's accuracy concerning urban places. Because the census lumped townships and towns together, it is easy to overestimate urbanization in the Old Northwest. I've tried to correct for this by counting only places with a minimum of one thousand inhabitants. They are also correct regarding the undercounting of southern

towns, especially in an older state like Georgia. Still, few of those towns were more than places where small farmers rendezvoused to socialize and buy groceries. Even the Rutmans admit, "There is an ephemeral quality to many of these towns and villages." See their *Small Worlds*, 231–72 (the quotation is on 250).

23. Carlton, "Antebellum Southern Industrialization," 35–39 (the quotation is on 39); Smith, *Debating Slavery*. See also, Goldfield, *Region, Race, and Cities*.

24. Dorsett and Shaffer, "Was the Antebellum South Antiurban?," 93–100.

25. Quoted in Johnson, *River of Dark Dreams*, 39. See also, Rothman, *Slave Country*, 42–45, 168–70; Rohrbough, *Land Office Business*, 9, 102; and Swierenga, *Pioneers and Profits*.

26. Johnson, *River of Dark Dreams*, 37–40; Rothman, *Slave Country*, 45, 169–70, 185–86; and Rohrbough, *Land Office Business*, 102, 169–70, 184–85. Elkins and McKitrick drew this useful distinction between the town and cotton speculator: "There was an essential difference in type between this petty-urban speculator and the speculator who engrossed vast cotton lands and held them for a price rise. The distinction was between the monopolist and the promoter." In their "Turner's Frontier," 242.

27. Carlton, "Antebellum Southern Urbanization," 38; Gudmestad, *Steamboats*, 140–58.

28. The literature is expertly addressed and analyzed in Smith, *Debating Slavery*. Also, Starobin, *Industrial Slavery*, 19–20 (for the quotation); and Follett, *Sugar Masters*.

29. Smith, *Debating Slavery*, 61–70; Meyer, "Industrial Retardation," 369–71; Carlton, "American South," 169; Genovese, *Political Economy of Slavery*, 23–26; and Majewski, *House Dividing*.

30. Carlton, "American South," 165, 170; Meyer, "Industrial Retardation," 382–83; Wright, *Political Economy*, 109, 120; *Old South, New South*, 23–24.

31. *1860 Census of Manufacturing*, 199–200; Starobin, *Industrial Slavery*, 19.

32. Wall, "Leon Godchaux," 50–66. Also, Carlton, "Antebellum Southern Industrialization," 38–39; Marler, *Merchants' Capital*, 53–84.

33. The story is told brilliantly in Cronon, *Nature's Metropolis*, 296–308; see also Marler, *Merchants' Capital*, 40 and 47 (for the quotation, which comes from *DeBow's Review*); Belcher, *Economic Rivalry*, 55–61, 72–75, 100, 170, 188–93; and Mahoney, *River Towns*, 191, 218.

34. Belcher, *Economic Rivalry*, 112, 139–44; and Ross, "Resisting the New South," 61–63; Marler, *Merchants' Capital*, 217–20, 224–25.

35. Meyer, "American Manufacturing Belt," 145–47.

36. Meyer, "Industrial Retardation," 382–83; Coclanis, "The Paths before US," in Carlton and Coclanis, *The South, the Nation*, 12–23.

BIBLIOGRAPHY

Adler, Jeffrey S. *Yankee Merchants and the Making of the Urban West: The Rise and Fall of Antebellum St. Louis.* Cambridge: Cambridge University Press, 1991.

Belcher, Wyatt W. *The Economic Rivalry between St. Louis and Chicago, 1850–1880.* New York: Columbia University Press, 1947.

Carlton, David. "The American South and the American Manufacturing Belt." In *The South, the Nation, and the World: Perspectives on Southern Economic Development*, edited by David L. Carlton and Peter A. Coclanis, 163. Charlottesville: University of Virginia Press, 2003.

———. "Antebellum Southern Industrialization." In *The South, the Nation, and the World: Perspectives on Southern Economic Development*, edited by David L. Carlton and Peter A. Coclanis, 35–48. Charlottesville: University of Virginia Press, 2003.

Clark, John G. *New Orleans, 1718–1812: An Economic History.* Baton Rouge: Louisiana State University Press, 1970.

Cronon, William. *Nature's Metropolis: Chicago and the Great West.* New York: W. W. Norton, 1991.

Dorsett, Lyle W., and Arthur H. Shaffer. "Was the Antebellum South Antiurban? A Suggestion." *Journal of Southern History* 38, no. 1 (February 1972). 93–100.

Elkins, Stanley, and Eric McKitrick. "A Meaning for Turner's Frontier: Part I: Democracy in the Old Northwest." *Political Science Quarterly* 69, no. 3 (September 1954), 321–53.

Faber, Eberhard L. *Building the Land of Dreams: New Orleans and the Transformation of Early America.* Princeton: Princeton University Press, 2016.

Follett, Richard J. *The Sugar Masters: Planters and Slaves in Louisiana's Cane World, 1820–1860.* Baton Rouge: Louisiana State University Press, 2005.

Genovese, Eugene D. *The Political Economy of Slavery: Studies in the Economy and Society of the Slave South.* New York: Pantheon Books, 1965.

Gitlin, Jay. *The Bourgeois Frontier: French Towns, French Traders, and American Expansion.* New Haven CT: Yale University Press, 2010.

Goldfield, David R. *Region, Race, and Cities: Interpreting the Urban South.* Baton Rouge: Louisiana State University Press. 1997.

Green, George D. *Finance and Economic Development in the Old South: Louisiana Banking, 1804–1861.* Stanford CA: Stanford University Press, 1972.

Gudmestad, Robert H. *Steamboats and the Rise of the Cotton Kingdom.* Baton Rouge: Louisiana State University Press, 2011.

Hahn, Steven. *A Nation without Borders: The United States and Its World in an Age of Civil Wars, 1830–1910*. New York: Penguin Random House, 2016.

Higgs, Robert. "American Inventiveness, 1870–1920." *Journal of Political Economy* 79, no. 3 (May–June 1971), 661–67.

Hogan, John. *Thoughts about the City of St. Louis, Her Commerce and Manufacturers, Railroads, Etc.* St. Louis MO: Republican Steam Press, 1854.

Hunter, Louis C. *Steamboats on the Western Rivers: An Economic and Technological History*. Cambridge MA: Harvard University Press, 1949.

Johnson, Walter. *River of Dark Dreams: Slavery and Empire in the Cotton Kingdom.* Cambridge MA: Harvard University Press, 2013.

Kastor, Peter J. *The Nation's Crucible: The Louisiana Purchase and the Creation of America.* New Haven CT: Yale University Press, 2004.

Kilbourne, Richard H., Jr. *Louisiana Commercial Law: The Antebellum Period*. Baton Rouge: Publications Institute, Paul M. Hebert Law Center, Louisiana State University, 1980.

Krugman, Paul R. *Geography and Trade*. Cambridge MA: MIT Press, 1993.

———. "Increasing Returns and Economic Geography." *Journal of Political Economy* 99, no. 3 (June 1991), 483–99.

Mahoney, Timothy R. *River Towns in the Great West: The Structure of Provincial Urbanization in the American Midwest, 1820–1870*. Cambridge MA: Cambridge University Press, 1990.

———. "Urban History in a Regional Context: River Towns on the Upper Mississippi, 1840–1860." *Journal of American History* 72, no. 2 (September 1985), 318–39.

Majewski, John. *A House Dividing: Economic Development in Pennsylvania and Virginia before the Civil War*. Cambridge MA: Cambridge University Press, 2000.

Marler, Scott P. *The Merchants' Capital: New Orleans and the Political Economy of the Nineteenth-Century South*. Cambridge MA: Cambridge University Press, 2013.

Meyer, David R. "Emergence of the American Manufacturing Belt: An Interpretation." *Journal of Historical Geography* 9, no. 2 (April 1983), 145–74.

———. "The Industrial Retardation of Southern Cities, 1860–1880." *Explorations in Economic History* 25, no. 4 (October 1988).

Pred, Allan R. *The Spatial Dynamics of U.S. Urban-Industrial Growth, 1800–1914: Interpretive and Theoretical Essays*. Cambridge MA: MIT Press, 1966.

———. *Urban Growth and City-Systems in the United States, 1840–1860*. Cambridge MA: Harvard University Press, 1980.

Prim, James Neal. *Lion of the Valley: St Louis, Missouri, 1764–1980*. 3rd ed. St. Louis: Missouri Historical Society Press, 1998.

Rohrbough, Malcolm J. *The Land Office Business: The Settlement and Administration of American Public Lands, 1789–1837.* New York: Oxford University Press, 1968.

———. *Trans-Appalachian Frontier: People, Societies, and Institutions, 1775–1850.* 3rd ed. Bloomington: Indiana University Press, 2008.

Rothman, Adam. *Slave Country: American Expansion and the Origins of the Deep South.* Cambridge M A: Harvard University Press, 2005.

Rutman Darrett B. and Anita H. Rutman. *Small Worlds, Large Questions: Explorations in Early American Social History, 1600–1850.* Charlottesville: University Press of Virginia, 1994.

Schermerhorn, Calvin. *The Business of Slavery and the Rise of American Capitalism, 1815–1860.* New Haven CT: Yale University Press, 2015.

Sellers, Charles. *The Market Revolution: Jacksonian America, 1815–1846.* New York: Oxford University Press, 1991.

Smith, Mark. *Debating Slavery: Economy and Society in the Antebellum American South* Cambridge M A: Cambridge University Press, 1998.

Starobin, Robert S. *Industrial Slavery in the Old South.* New York: Oxford University Press, 1970.

Swierenga, Robert P. *Pioneers and Profits: Land Speculation on the Iowa Frontier.* Ames: Iowa State University Press, 1968.

U.S. Bureau of the Census. *1860 Census: Manufactures of the United States*, 199–200.

Wade, Richard C. *The Urban Frontier: The Rise of Western Cities, 1790–1830.* Cambridge M A: Harvard University Press, 1959.

Wall, Bennett H. "Leon Godchaux and the Godchaux Business Enterprises." *American Jewish Historical Quarterly* 66, no. 1 (September 1976).

Walsh, Margaret. "Pork Packing as a Leading Edge of Midwestern Industry, 1835–1875." *Agricultural History* 51, no. 4 (October 1977).

White, Richard. *The Middle Ground: Indians, Empires, and Republics in the Great Lakes Region, 1650–1815.* Cambridge M A: Cambridge University Press, 1991.

Woodman, Harold D. *King Cotton and His Retainers: Financing and Marketing the Cotton Crop of the South, 1800–1925.* Lexington: University of Kentucky Press, 1968.

Wright, Gavin. *Old South, New South: Revolutions in the Southern Economy since the Civil War.* New York: Basic Books, 1986.

———. *The Political Economy of the Cotton South: Households, Markets, and Wealth in the Nineteenth Century.* New York: W. W. Norton, 1978.

———. *Slavery and American Economic Development.* Walter Lynwood Fleming lectures in Southern History. Baton Rouge: Louisiana State University Press, 2006.

6

THE CREOLE FRONTIER

Free People of Color in St. Louis and along the
French Mississippi Corridor, 1800–1870

ANDREW N. WEGMANN

When Pelagie Rutgers died on February 24, 1867, she left a will that surprised no one. Her rather large estate of some $64,000 would be split between her surviving kin, several family friends, and a few designated charities. Likely born a slave around 1802, Rutgers never knew her father. She had twice married well, establishing filial bonds with some of the mainstays of St. Louis's colored aristocracy—most notably the Clamorgans, a mixed-race family tracing its lineage back to St. Louis's founding generation by way of New France.[1] By nearly all standards, she lived a comfortable life, as much the result of her own efforts as those of her husbands. The tenants of her thirteen rental properties, from which she collected more than $5,700 annually, were all white, and her own house contained more mahogany than pine. She owned a rosewood piano and table settings of "fine China" for twenty-four guests in the parlor and dining room. She had five bedrooms, all furnished, and even an "invalid chair" of mahogany and leather. She had mirrors and art, furs and rugs worth hundreds.[2]

Rutgers was also light skinned, a "mulatto" by state law and a "colored aristocrat" by social convention. As Cyprian Clamorgan, a relative by marriage and a fellow member of the elite, would have it, she was "brown-skinned [and] straight-haired . . . fine-looking and healthy."[3] She owed and dealt money to trusted colleagues, invested in businesses and property, hosted and attended fashionable dinners, drank from crystal, and carved out a place in high society—rarely known to the formerly enslaved—for herself and her only surviving daughter, Antoinette.[4] In many ways, she served as the matriarch of a remarkable community, one built, maintained, and supported by at least four generations of free people of color in the relatively young city of St. Louis, founded as a riverine trading post along the French frontier in 1763. This community differed, at least on the surface, from most other free colored communities in the expanding United States. Those names that appeared in Pelagie Rutgers's will and estate, attended her parties, celebrated her straight hair and brown skin, and sought, perhaps above all, to marry her daughter, were almost entirely French, mixed-race, and old. She owned property that neighbored the homes of Charlevilles, Clamorgans, Labadies, and Creviers—all names that appear on the rolls of St. Louis's first families. As far as one can tell, her first language was French, as it was for all with whom she most publicly interacted and lived. She was a devout Catholic who attended the same church as her neighbors, relatives, and business partners. She wove herself into a community that looked, spoke, worshipped, and profited like her.[5]

But Pelagie Rutgers conducted more than just social networks and wealthy friends. Her life, as captured in her 1867 will, served as a link between two similar communities along the same river rarely mentioned in the same sentence, much less read together as sections of the same cultural and historical story. Written into Rutgers's will are the lines of an economic, cultural, and familial map connecting St. Louis and its older, more Atlantic southern neighbor, Louisiana and its capital at New Orleans. The map, constructed over decades of individual movement and communal acceptance, brings St. Louis into a larger French American narrative, one that exposes shared roots along a stretch of the French Mississippi corridor previously seen more as a barrier rather than a conduit for exchange and cultural mobility.

Indeed, as far as the standard story is concerned, the free communities of color in St. Louis and Louisiana, even those who shared the "Creole" identity and the French language, might as well have flowed into two entirely different historical and national streams.[6] Until quite recently, the so-called free blacks of St. Louis fit the mold of any similar population in the antebellum United States. Oppressed, exploited, and left to fend for themselves as "slaves without masters," the "free Negroes" of previous narratives came directly out of slavery, worked for white men, lived in poverty, and fell victim to countless laws forbidding their very presence in certain parts of the state. Their names, naturally, were English in origin, and any individual who defied this universal order of things stood out as an obvious aberration and even a racist.[7]

The great exception in the larger American narrative was the city of New Orleans, that French-speaking port with a history all its own and a population unlike anything found in the proper United States. There, and in the rest of Louisiana, *les gens de couleur* stood entirely separate from the "free Negro" aggregate of their more northern compatriots. The key was that free blacks in New Orleans were not, as early scholars noted, really "black." They were "Creoles," "mulattoes," people so racially and culturally ambiguous that they defied any attempt at definition, even in the law. When a piece of legislation frowned them down, society rejected it, accepting these liminal men and women as part of a social system far removed from the active and respected racial binary of the encroaching "American" purview. They spoke French, prayed in Catholic churches, and had white parents who hailed from France and its empire. They owned slaves and property, sued white folks, defied the law constantly, and even ran profitable plantations. They could not possibly fit within the strict confines of the universally oppressed black masses wandering the American countryside and wasting away in the poverty of America's *real* cities.[8]

Even outside of New Orleans, free people of color became washed up in generalized communities of outsiders and others. Creoles disappeared and became "Black Cajuns," even though to be Creole is and was certainly not to be Cajun either in language, religion, or cultural identity. The further north one looked, the more generally "Negro" free people of color became, lumped yet again into the aggregated image of the oppressed, impoverished, culturally Anglo "blacks" of the rest of the country. Creoles, in more traditional scholarship, were urban people, so bizarre and singular that they could not exist outside of the circum-Caribbean meld of New Orleans and its abjectly un-American social order and outlook. Outside of that city, French speakers were Cajun or nonexistent and blackness became a quality of the enslaved, not the free, of any color or combination.[9]

Louisiana and Missouri, then, as well as their talismanic cities, though separated by a single state along the same river, according to this tradition, came from different worlds. Missouri did not secede as Louisiana did when civil war engulfed the nation. St. Louis, though just several hundred miles upriver from New Orleans and the Louisiana interior, served as a "gateway to the West," not a stopover to the South. It is almost as though historians had forgotten that St. Louis was there before the Crisis of 1820; that the Louisiana Purchase made St. Louis just as "American" as it did the rest of the massive Louisiana Territory; that the French first founded St. Louis, moving downriver rather than up; that as Congress debated the Tallmadge Amendment and negotiated the borders of slavery in connection to Missouri's admittance to the union, legal records and newspapers across the future state still bore the French language so seemingly "unique" to its Creole neighbor, then already a state for nearly a decade.[10]

Though somewhat indirectly, and certainly unknown to her, Pelagie Rutgers changed this. At the heart of her will, as well as the lifetime it reflected, lay the fact that Missouri and Louisiana were not so different, and they were very much parts of the same world. They existed along the same frontier that was once French and only became "American" as the United States pushed its known world westward to the Pacific. Their cultural histories and practices mirrored each other far more than most scholars have been willing to admit, and they exchanged far more than just products and profits within a system of riverine trade. Indeed, St. Louis and the French-speaking parts of Louisiana shared a soul and an identity, a sense of history and culture that transcended attempts at "Americanization" in any form and found its way into the lines and names drawn into Pelagie Rutgers's will and the community of which she served, in effect, as matriarch.

At the heart of this exchange sat the only community permanent and self-conscious enough to survive a shifting frontier with its culture still intact—the community variously called "Creoles," "colored aristocrats," and *gens de couleur* depending on the time, place, and perspective. It was this community that maintained a culture and identity in both St. Louis and Louisiana that defied expected practice in the antebellum decades. They went to the wrong churches, spoke the wrong language, and had skin that was a shade too dark. When they moved, they moved south or north, not west or east. Virginia was not theirs, just like Kentucky, Tennessee, or any other state outside the north-south corridor of the former French frontier. White entrepreneurs, homesteaders, and gold rushers were transients in town, pulling slaves along for weeks and months, not years and lifetimes.[11]

Working whites likewise found new jobs and skipped town, leaving the landed white gentry in place, but opening new spots in the ranks of the laboring classes. As a result, the francophone Creoles of color who owned land, kept skilled and professional jobs, and continued the same family lines and surnames the white gentry protected and sustained were among the most consistent inhabitants of their towns and areas. They had no need to leave; their lives, families, and histories were in St. Louis and Natchitoches and New Orleans and Red River. But their networks were wide and complex, and their family lines did not remain strictly in place. Nephews went to work with uncles down south; brothers visited sisters upriver and stayed for years. They did not always share names, but they did share language, parents, profits, and space. They had the most to lose from the encroaching "Americanization," so they stuck together, stayed in touch, and tracked each other down along political and cultural fault lines dug out generations and even centuries before.

Rutgers, to some degree, was exceptional in St. Louis. Even in her own community, few others had made their way from rags to riches as she had. Indeed, nearly all of her neighbors and business partners had recorded histories, lineages traceable several generations back, and deep roots in the local social and economic system, both white and of color.[12] She was extremely wealthy, enough so to meet public criticism from relatives and contemporaries for her sartorial tastes and spending habits. In his cheeky and brutally honest 1858 pamphlet, *The Colored Aristocracy of St. Louis*, Cyprian Clamorgan, after providing the only known physical description of Rutgers, quickly targeted what he saw as her "penurious" and "ambitious" character. "Mrs. R. is a member of the Catholic church," he wrote, "but is not noted for her piety; she worships the almighty dollar more than Almighty God." She likewise "makes a fine appearance in society, but exposes her ignorance when she attempts to converse," her noted illiteracy betraying her "good style."[13]

In truth, she *was* illiterate, and she *did*, in fact, live in a manner far more outwardly stylish than many of her contemporaries could afford. But there was more to Pelagie Rutgers and her life, family, and vision of herself and her community than Cyprian Clamorgan would have us believe. Indeed, Clamorgan was, at the time of *The Colored Aristocracy's* publication, on his way out of St. Louis headed for New Orleans where he would remain for more than a decade. Historian Julie Winch has already masterfully chronicled Clamorgan's sojourn to the south, but what perhaps Clamorgan did not know was that a striking number of those who appeared in his pamphlet also looked and sometimes moved south, finding business, family, and friends far beyond the borders of St. Louis but still within the corridor of similar-minded, similar-toned, and similar-speaking communities originally set in the French rather than the American western empire.[14]

Using Clamorgan as a guide, Pelagie Rutgers takes the form of a rabid capitalist, senseless in her ambition and dishonest in her appearance. She is wealthy, illiterate, proud, and connected only by marriage to the families others in their shared circle claimed by blood. On the surface, Clamorgan was right; Rutgers did not fit in. Though mixed-race like most others, she was not openly dedicated to the Catholic faith, as Clamorgan highlighted, and, perhaps worse, she had married Louis Rutgers, a descendent not of an ancient French family but a relatively youthful and wealthy Anglo-Dutch family.[15] Regardless of her native language—which was, in fact, French— she took on the public image of an agnostic ex-slave from the east, not a freeborn francophone Catholic from a family rooted in the north-south flow of the Mississippi River. She was, in Clamorgan's mind, from the wrong side of the wrong axis, representative of those who, by the 1850s, were transforming St. Louis into an American city people like the Clamorgans, Charlevilles, and Labadies, to name a few, did not recognize.[16]

But that was Cyprian Clamorgan, perhaps the most outspoken of his people but certainly not the most representative, and perhaps the last from his family in a position to make sense of the community's timeworn and complex connections up and down the French Mississippi corridor. The youngest son of white pioneer and St. Louis founder Jacques Clamorgan, Cyprian had two brothers, Louis and Henry, who survived to adulthood and whose names dot the probate records, wills, and business dealings of nearly everyone their brother included in his pamphlet on the colored aristocracy. They became symbols of the successful community of color that defined antebellum St. Louis and were emblematic of the growing urban centers across the nineteenth-century United States.[17] Cyprian, on the other hand, though serving as a distant, mainly silent partner in his brothers' luxurious bathhouse and barbershop, never stuck around for more than a few years at a time, skipping town for new lands and new opportunities whenever the fever of profit took him.[18] He wrote his take down for posterity, and that remains our best source for understanding who the men and women of St. Louis's most successful and socially "seen" colored families were. But perhaps his pamphlet's chief value is the reality behind the list and the realization that Cyprian Clamorgan was more an outsider than he let on in 1858.

The truth is that Pelagie Rutgers represented her community perfectly, and nearly everyone agreed. Though a Rutgers, she spoke French with her friends and actively sought to create a legacy for both herself and her daughter within that community. Upon her death, she left several hundred dollars to St. Vincent Catholic Church and left an additional sum of one hundred dollars for the creation of "the first Catholic Colored Orphan Asylum which may be established in the City of St. Louis."[19] She closely controlled her daughter's suitors. Indeed, in what can only suggest a conscious effort to erase her own slave past, she reportedly rejected Antoinette's proposed marriage to James P. Thomas, an extremely successful barber from Nashville, Tennessee, because he was dark skinned and slave born, going so far as to state in her will that the funds left to Antoinette were "for her sole and separate use and under her control."[20] The couple married in 1868, a year after Pelagie's death.[21]

Cyprian's brothers traded properties with Rutgers for nearly thirty years, exchanging thousands of dollars, providing each other mortgages, and representing each other in court on several occasions.[22] Louis and Jean-Baptiste Charleville, two scions of one of the oldest and wealthiest of St. Louis's colored families, cared for several of Rutgers's properties as her age advanced, exchanged those and other properties with the elderly matron over more than a decade, and forgave the substantial debt her estate owed them upon her death.[23] The same goes for hundreds of other examples involving dozens of other well-known and respected families, but space does not allow their inclusion here.

In the end, Henry and Louis Clamorgan's dedication to Pelagie Rutgers made sense. She was, in fact, the widow of their uncle, St. Eutrope Clamorgan, Pelagie's first husband. She helped raise them, to some degree, and had been an active part of both their lives since childhood.[24] The Charlevilles, though, shared a different bond with her, one that stretched well beyond the financial and familial connections that linked St. Louis's "colored aristocracy" within the limits of the city. This bond in particular evinced St. Louis's, and indeed these families', membership in the broader cultural community suggested and outlined in Rutgers's will, one far larger than the "colored aristocracy" in town and far older than any of its members realized. It brought together families, individuals, and identities dozens of years and hundreds of miles separated yet located within the same cultural corridor defined by a disappearing French past and a sense of survival buttressed by the Mississippi River and the exchange it brokered.

Pelagie Rutgers's will provided generously for family. Above all else, Antoinette Rutgers received more than $14,000 from her mother's estate. Nearly a third of Pelagie's real property fell to her "adopted son" Emanuel Griveaud, a white native of France who lived with Rutgers for more than ten years and later became a physician in St. Louis. Her "family friends" all received legacies of forgiven debts ranging from $200 to $1,100. In total, Rutgers forgave more than $5,000 in debts, paid off more than $12,000, and dispersed nearly $23,000 in standing cash and property with a single, shaky "X."[25]

One exception stood out, however. Neither a "family friend" nor an "adopted son," one "Charles Cotomie" received $300 in cash, his name listed not in the roll of forgiven debts but in the roll of family members.[26] Cotomie was not from St. Louis, though; and his name was not "Cotomie." The man listed as "Charles Cotomie of Red River, Louisiana," in Pelagie Rutgers's will was, in fact, Charles Coton-Maïs of Cloutierville, Louisiana, an area known for its wealthy, mixed-race, self-consciously francophone

Children of
Antoine Coton-Maïs
Born 1775
Kaskaskia, Illinois

With *Unknown Slave*

- Pelagie Rutgers**
  Née Pelagie Aillotte Baptiste
  Born 1802
  St. Louis, Missouri
  - With St. Eutrope Clamorgan
    Born 1799, Died 1824
    St. Louis, Missouri
    - Louise Clamorgan
      Born 1821
      St. Louis, Missouri
  - With Louis Rutgers
    Born 1800
    St. Louis, Missouri
    - Antoinette Rutgers
      Born 1837
      St. Louis, Missouri

With Marie Bellepeche
Born 1790
Illinois Country

- Lisette Coton-Maïs
  Born 1805
  Born St. Louis, Missouri, raised Île Brevelle,
  Louisiana
  - Married Louis Monette, *Île Brevelle*
- Desirée Coton-Maïs
  Born 1807
  Île Brevelle, Louisiana
  - Married Joseph Metoyer, *Île Brevelle*
- Adélaïde Coton-Maïs
  Born 1809
  Île Brevelle, Louisiana
- Antoinette Coton-Maïs
  Born 1810
  Île Brevelle, Louisiana
- Charles Coton-Maïs
  Born 1816
  Cloutierville, Louisiana
- Marie Coton-Maïs
  Born 1816
  Cloutierville, Louisiana
  - Married Louis Mullon, *Natchitoches,*
    Louisiana
- Arsène Coton-Maïs
  Born 1819
  Cloutierville, Louisiana

GENEALOGY I. Pelagie Rutgers family tree. The information in this chart came from a number of sources. See "Record of Marriage," February 2, 1826, Missouri Marriage Records, 1826, MSA; Probate Record of Pelagie Rutgers, #7,984, 1867, StLPC; Clamorgan, *The Colored Aristocracy*, 72–73; Van Ravenswaay, *St. Louis: An Informal History*, 115–16, 183–84; Winch, *The Clamorgans*, 129–30; Brasseaux, Fontenot, and Oubre, *Creoles of Color in the Bayou Country*, 108–14; Burton and Smith, *Colonial Natchitoches*, chap. 4; Mills, *The Forgotten People*, xxxv, 66–69, 72–75, 90–93, 116–18; and the Federal Censuses of 1840, 1850, and 1860. Chart by the author.

community, the largest and most successful in the state outside of New Orleans.[27] Coton-Maïs likewise shared more than just $300 in kind with the dying matriarch of St. Louis's colored aristocracy. Indeed, he shared with her a father as well as an entire family in Natchitoches Parish, Louisiana, where, after leaving young Pelagie and her mother in St. Louis, her father Antoine Coton-Maïs, a native of Kaskaskia, Illinois, settled down and started a new family.[28]

As far as we can tell, Charles and Pelagie were born at least fourteen years apart, and it took them at least that long to meet each other once they both walked the earth. We know almost nothing about Pelagie's birth. She lacks a birth certificate, and her probate record mentions nothing of her exact birthdate. If the less than enthusiastic Cyprian Clamorgan is to be believed, she was born a slave and purchased her freedom at some unknown date for three dollars. In 1820, when she married St. Eutrope Clamorgan, Cyprian and his brothers' uncle, she went by the name "Pélagie Antoine Baptiste" and was presumably already free.[29] In 1835 she received a "free Negro license," lived with her second husband, Louis, mended clothing for a living, and stood at five foot seven inches, a "light mulatto slim built."[30]

Charles Coton-Maïs was born 525 miles south, as the crow flies. The sixth child and only son of Antoine Coton-Maïs, Charles grew up in the small rural hamlet of Cloutierville, Louisiana, along the banks of the Cane River, a tributary of the Mississippi. This area, part of Natchitoches Parish in central Louisiana, was known for its community of mixed-race "Creoles," nearly all of whom were, according to historian Gary B. Mills, "a race apart from the blacks" of the region. As créoles, or "natives," of the area, Mills explains, the community as a whole maintained "an inherent pride in their French or Spanish heritage" and identified more "with the white rather than the black race."[31] The community to which Charles Coton-Maïs and his local sisters belonged was purely and proudly francophone and devoutly Catholic. They founded and worshipped at the oldest African-American Catholic churches in the South outside of New Orleans and worked diligently for generations to maintain a social, cultural, and political identity generally "unknown among nonwhites in North American society."[32] Historians have referred to them as a "third class," neither white nor black but something in between, more accepted and respected in society than those below them but shunned by "nature" from the rank above.[33]

The Creoles of color of Natchitoches and the Cane River shared a jarring number of similarities with their better-known contemporaries in New Orleans to the south and their distant neighbors (and family members) to the north in St. Louis. In all three places, Catholicism, the French language, and mixed ancestries bound them together and forced them apart from archival images of the "free Negro" constructed in the minds of America's white politicians, planters, and leaders.[34] And unlike other, more eastern parts of the South, where mixed-race families existed and used their English heritage and Protestant faiths to advance their specific causes, this riverine corridor of former French frontier spaces housed colored Creole communities that remained relevant and visible by moving between and engaging with each other.

Of Charles Coton-Maïs's seven sisters, five were born in or around Cloutierville, and six remained in the area for the majority of their lives. Two of the sisters were born in Missouri—the first, of course, Pelagie Rutgers (née Baptiste) and the second, Lisette Monette (née Coton-Maïs). The latter was born in or around 1805, making her just three or four years Pelagie's junior and more than ten years Charles's senior. By 1829 she had lived in Cloutierville for at least fifteen years, marrying the wealthy Creole planter Louis Monette on July 23 of that year.[35] They had six children of their own, all of whom married into other Creole families. Aménaïde married another Monette, her second cousin; Emélie married Engelbert Dubreuil, whose family had an equally wealthy and socially established branch in New Orleans; and Mélisaire married Firmin Rachal, a local planter with deep roots and a lot of land in the area.[36] All three women became integral parts of the community, standing in for their husbands when they were away and continuing the family businesses upon their husbands' deaths. They were all Catholic. They all spoke French. And they all made and maintained connections outside the Cane River valley and throughout the former French Mississippi territory.[37]

The Rachal clan in particular made the most of these connections, creating a web of commercial and familial relationships that spanned the entire length of their so-called Creole Corridor.[38] Mixed-race and free for generations, by the middle of the nineteenth century the Rachal family stood among the wealthiest and most expansive of Louisiana's Creole families. By 1810, along with the neighboring Metoyer, Lambre, Lecour, and Prudhomme clans, they owned more slaves and land than all other colored families in the Louisiana Purchase territories combined. Over the following decades, they expanded their lot, merged with fellow Creole clans (notably the Mullons, Lecours, and Metoyers), and reinforced the economic and filial ties that brought them vital privileges in the rapidly changing legal and social landscapes of antebellum Louisiana.[39]

By the time Charles Coton-Maïs came of age, he had two direct links to the Rachal clan. Both his niece Mélisaire Monette and his sister Adélaïde Jacquitte Coton-Maïs had married into the Rachal family by the 1840s. Though her husband died shortly after their marriage, Jacquitte, as Adélaïde was called, became a formidable representative of her in-laws and their interests. She bought and sold slaves, maintained several ferries crossing both the Cane and Red Rivers, and created valuable economic ties with a number of white planters in the area, most notably Charles Benoist, with whom she arranged accommodations for her widowed niece, Mélisaire, in exchange for the labor of two of her slaves.[40] She lived a long time, outliving all of her siblings and remarrying at least once. In 1863, at the age of about fifty-four, she married Antoine Lecour, a member of two of the oldest and wealthiest Creole families in the area—the Lecours, through his father, and the Metoyers, through his mother.[41] In so doing, Adélaïde became an in-law of her sister Désirée, who had married Antoine's uncle, Joseph François Metoyer, in 1827.[42]

The Rachal clan, and thus portions of the Coton-Maïs, Lecour, and Metoyer clans as well, did not restrict their threads of family and finance to the Natchitoches region. Indeed, at times they actively sought out partners from outside the community, a number of whom served as liaisons between the Cane River and other French towns within the greater Mississippi River Valley. Charles Coton-Maïs, of course, constructed one of these bridges between Cloutierville and St. Louis. But St. Louis itself also provided a number of emissaries to the Cane River region, several of whom remained active in both camps and provided valuable and sustained points of connection for families long separated by distance and time.

Louis Dunois Charleville came from elite white stock. Born free in 1804, the son of white merchant Louis Faro Charleville and *mulâtresse* Thérèse Adelaide Aubuchon, Charleville claimed maternal and paternal grandfathers who both founded St. Louis and stood as hallmarks of the city's landed gentry. He likewise married well, wedding young Louisa Julie Labadie on November 26, 1827.[43] Their marriage united two multiracial families with origins in the Illinois Country and New France and roots that ran deep in St. Louis's "colored aristocracy." Indeed, the Charlevilles and Labadies would marry again several times in the following decades and maintain social and business relationships that lasted well into the twentieth century. They lived beside each other, traded property and a few slaves, and posted bond for each other on dozens of occasions.[44] Alongside other "elite" mixed-race families like the Clamorgans, Creviers, and Aubuchons, the families first bound together that day in November 1827 created the St. Louis equivalent of the Cane River Creoles of color—a community of colored francophone families dedicated to each other and the wealth and privilege their French ancestries, family bonds, and respected surnames granted them in a newly "Americanized" Western frontier.

Not all of these families remained in place, however. Indeed, there were other places to go to achieve the same success and add to the family's economic and social networks. Louis Dunois Charleville knew Charles Coton-Maïs rather well. They lived next door to each other for at least eight years, and likely longer. Following Pelagie Rutgers's death, they exchanged receipts and payments and served as witnesses on deeds, bonds, and affidavits for months on end. They exchanged property at least one time and seemed, by all accounts, to be rather close in the greater St. Louis social scene.[45] Their connections, though, did not stop there.

Louis and Louisa Charleville had three children—two sons and one daughter. Their first two children, Louis Jr. and Louisa Adelaide, stayed in St. Louis, married well, and became standard-bearers of their shared community.[46] The youngest son, Joseph Louis, born in 1834, did much the same, but not in St. Louis. A river trader, Joseph Louis Charleville took to the cotton and cattle trades south of Missouri. Although he maintained an official residence in St. Louis, he spent long periods in Louisiana, serving as his father's agent and an "assistant postmaster" in none other than Natchitoches and Cloutierville as late as 1871, positions that would have required both standing in the community and a network of communications built along and across the Mississippi River Valley.[47]

In Cloutierville, Joseph Louis was not alone. Beyond the potential contacts provided by family friend Charles Coton-Maïs, who, by 1870, had lived in St. Louis for at least a decade, his cousin Jean-Baptiste Charleville, had lived in the Natchitoches area since the 1820s. Born in St. Louis in 1798, the *fils naturel* of Baptiste Charleville and an unknown free woman of color noted in one source as *"une sauvagesse native de la nation osage,"* Jean-Baptiste grew up in the same household as Joseph Louis's father, Louis Dunois, with whom he worked along the river as a porter and smalltime trader in the late 1810s.[48] In the early 1820s he left St. Louis for Cloutierville where he married fifteen-year-old planter's daughter Marie Aurore Rachal in 1825. The union made him one of Mélisaire Rachal's uncles, a claim Charles Coton-Maïs could also make, though with him it was through blood rather than marriage.[49]

It was from Jean-Baptiste and Marie Aurore that a clan of Creole Charlevilles sprouted up in Louisiana while another branch of the same family made its mark in the colored aristocracy of St. Louis. Both branches were prolific. In Cloutierville, Jean-Baptiste and Marie Aurore had ten children, eight of whom survived to adulthood. Although the surname was relatively new to the area, the Charlevilles were part of the Rachal clan that, as detailed above, was connected by marriage to nearly every other respected colored Creole family in central Louisiana. Indeed, though distant, it actually connected the Charlevilles to the Coton-Maïses and thus to the Rutgerses of St. Louis. The roots Jean-Baptiste set down in Louisiana, though, did not keep him from his hometown. He made his way to St. Louis relatively often, purchasing property and otherwise involving himself in the regular economic movement of the city's colored francophone community. He was present for Joseph Louis's baptism in 1835 and left several plots of land to Louis Dunois upon his death in 1853.[50]

The Relationship of Jean-Baptiste Charleville and Joseph Louis Charleville

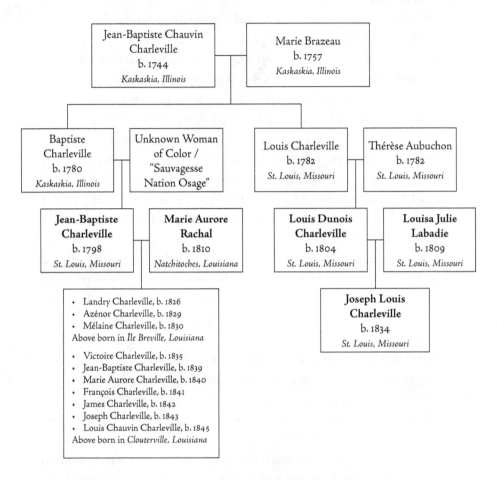

GENEALOGY 2. Although Jean-Baptiste Charleville was Joseph Louis Charleville's second cousin, their relationship likely mirrored that of an uncle and nephew, given their ages and Jean-Baptiste's relationship with Joseph Louis's father. See "Naissance," September 7, 1830, DROUIN; "Record of Marriage," January 27, 1848, Missouri Marriage Records, 1848, MSA; and "Obituary of Louisa Charleville," *St. Louis Post-Dispatch*, December 21, 1909; "Charleville, Joseph Louis," August 17, 1871, Natchitoches Parish LA, p. 510, Record of Appointment of Postmasters, 1832–1971, mf #28, NPCOC; and "Agent Joseph Charleville," May 1864, St. Louis MO, District 3, p. 197, IRS Tax Assessment List, mf #6, MHM. Chart by the author.

By the time Joseph Louis arrived in Cloutierville, he was no stranger to the area or its people. Indeed, he was part of the people—a mixed-race, francophone Catholic with the surname "Charleville." He belonged there even if he had never been and would not stay long. His family—though his immediate kin was gone—opened their arms to Joseph, taking him in and getting him involved in several business transactions that amounted to nearly two decades and thousands of dollars worth of sustained trade.[51] He worked particularly closely with his cousin Landry Charleville, the eldest of Jean-Baptiste and Marie Aurore's ten children. Landry spent several years in the 1830s at school in St. Louis, likely alongside his father, who spent much of that decade with Louis Dunois and his children in their shared hometown. Landry was the most entrenched of the Louisiana Charlevilles, having married Pauline Dupré, another wealthy, landed Creole, in 1850, and entering into a cattle trading and mercantile business with his father in-law.[52]

Given that Joseph's father had amassed a considerable estate doing just that in St. Louis, Landry and Joseph became fast friends and partners, buying and selling land, cattle, and crops up and down the Mississippi River with stunning frequency. Indeed, when Landry died in 1900, the oldest and longest lived of his generation, his estate required a probate record in a city he never actually called home—St. Louis, Missouri, where he maintained land, debts, and insurance policies exceeding $35,000 in value. Upon his death, Joseph Louis's probate looked much the same—a collection of receipts, deeds, and bonds transcending state borders but never leaving a single riverine corridor. And it was this corridor, this north-south axis, and the people and towns within it, and the way those people spoke, prayed, and reproduced, that allowed these Creoles to move seamlessly across spaces rarely seen, then or now, in the same light.

Pelagie Rutgers, perhaps unconsciously, then, drew a map in 1867. Though located purely in St. Louis, distributing money and land to known characters and names long connected to the new "Gateway to the West," her will and probate records outline the borders of a system more than a century in the making, linking New France to New Orleans, St. Louis to Cloutierville, white to nonwhite. It was not an "American" system, though the majority of its inhabitants fell under the laws and racial designations of the United States. This was a system defined and sustained by the seemingly "foreign," the "colored," the "French," Creoles and mulattoes, not Negroes and blacks. It was different, and, according to some, still is. But the lines of exchange—familial, financial, cultural, social—that made Creoles of Missourians and "colored aristocrats" of Louisianans in the mid-nineteenth century make the borders and lines often seen as "American" more porous and less defined today. Pelagie Rutgers, her brother Charles Coton-Maïs, his in-law Jean-Baptiste Charleville, and his cousin Joseph Louis Charleville all show us that St. Louis was not always American and that Louisiana was not always French, that "blackness" was not always the opposite of "whiteness," that established communities do not always become, and just as rarely remain, what others choose to call them.

The whole story is not told here. The story of the Rutgers, Charleville, Rachal, and Coton-Maïs clans serves only as a hint. Their connections were not public. They never celebrated each other. Rather, they simply lived. It made sense for Joseph Louis to go to Cloutierville and not New York, Nashville, or even New Orleans. Whatever his personal reasons, he belonged there, just as his father's neighbor, friend, and distant cousin Charles Coton-Maïs belonged in St. Louis with his older sister, the only one of his siblings who never made it down to Louisiana with the rest of the family. The Mississippi River, then, as well as its median city, did not always serve as a border between the East and the West, the known and the unknown, the American and the soon-to-be-American. It was, in many ways, a frontier that never closed, a corridor of exchange rooted in a north-south current that never cared or worried about what was coming from the east. St. Louis and Cloutierville, as well as all of francophone Missouri and Louisiana, were and remain critical parts of the same cultural, social, and racial narratives. To be "American" was to be anything—ill-defined and mixed, fluid and mobile, French and English, Native and Creole. Pelagie Rutgers and the map she drew in her will provide us a single example of what it meant to remain the same as everything else seemed to change, to look up and down when everything else looked side to side. That, in the end, is the story St. Louis requires and deserves.

1. Rutgers lacks a birth certificate or a record of birth. Indeed, beyond secondary sources, some contemporary to her lifetime, there is no direct evidence that she was born a slave, though it seems more likely than not. See note 2 below for the most standard reference to her slave origins. Born Pélagie Baptiste, she was free by 1820 when she married St. Eutrope Clamorgan, a free man of color from the famous Clamorgan clan who were descendants of Jacques Clamorgan, one of the first and most successful white traders in St. Louis. Pélagie Clamorgan then became Pelagie Rutgers when she married Louis Rutgers, the mixed-race son of Dutch trader Arend Rutgers, on February 2, 1826. Records of her appear under all three names, but the majority appear under the name "Rutgers." See "Record of Marriage," April 20, 1820, French Catholic Church Records, DROUIN; "Record of Marriage," February 2, 1826, Missouri Marriage Records, 1826, MSA; and Probate Record of Pelagie Rutgers, #7,984, 1867, StLPC.

2. "Inventory of Estate," Probate Record of Pelagie Rutgers, #7,984, StLPC. Cyprian Clamorgan, in his well-known pamphlet, *The Colored Aristocracy of St. Louis*, also mentions Pelagie Rutgers. Although he claims that she maintains a net worth of more the $500,000, he is correct in his description of her household furnishings, which he notes include "a piano worth two thousand dollars" she cannot play. See Clamorgan, *Colored Aristocracy*, 49.

3. Clamorgan, *Colored Aristocracy*, 48. In the 1860 census, one "Palach Louis Rutgers," aged sixty, appears with the "m" for "mulatto" scratched out and a total worth of $60,000. The household, which she heads, is surrounded by modest, laboring-class white families. The "Louis" clearly stands for her then-deceased husband, Louis Rutgers. See 1860 Census, St. Louis City, Ward 2, 105.

4. See "Certificate of Inventory," May 9, 1867; "Addendum to Bill from John Holmes," April 4, 1867; and "Account of Estate," March 20, 1869, all in Probate Record of Pelagie Rutgers, #7,984, StLPC. For additional information on her investments and social concerns, almost entirely focused on the Clamorgan clan, see Winch, *Clamorgans*, 129–30, 158–60. Pelagie had a daughter with St. Eutrope Clamorgan, her first husband, named Louise Clamorgan. This child, however, died in infancy. See Winch, *Clamorgans*, 71, 91–92.

5. On the so-called "colored aristocracy" of St. Louis, see Clamorgan, *Colored Aristocracy*, including Julie Winch's two informative essays within the volume; Winch, *Clamorgans*; Bellamy, "Free Blacks" 212–15; and, among others, Reichard, "Black and White," 12–15. On the earliest families of St. Louis, see, among others, Cleary, *The World, the Flesh*, as well as Winch, *Clamorgans*, chaps. 1 and

2. Some scattered details of Rutgers's dinners: see "Account of Estate," March 20, 1869, Probate Record of Pelagie Rutgers, #7,984, StlPC.

6. No single study of French North America includes both Louisiana and Missouri in the same discussion beyond a larger survey narrative. The best study of the French colonial frontier, which does, to some degree, place St. Louis and New Orleans at least within a common cultural and colonial corridor, is Gitlin, *Bourgeois Frontier*. Although Ira Berlin's *Slaves without Masters* provides general treatments of "free Negroes" in both Missouri and what he calls the "Gulf South," which includes Louisiana, he places them largely in contrast to each other and does not actively engage St. Louis's position on the Mississippi River or its French colonial origins.

7. This is not to say that such scholarship is a long way gone. Indeed, some of the more iconic studies of free populations of color from the 1970s have stood the test of time rather well and continue to inform newer works. However, it is important to note that the 1970s generally produced a wave of social and political histories that lumped free people of color into a single exploited mass, treating communities and individuals outside that mass as aberrations and beside the point. See Reichard, "Black and White"; Bellamy, "Free Blacks"; Jordan, *Black over White*, part 4; Berlin, *Slaves without Masters*, prologue, chaps. 1, 8, and 9; Genovese, *Roll, Jordan, Roll*, part 2; and, among many others, Frederickson, *Black Image*, chaps. 1 and 2.

8. This image and its reverse—Louisiana as a proud and capable outsider more Caribbean and/or Atlantic in nature than American—remains active today. Until very recently, New Orleans and Louisiana have both existed outside the American social, racial, cultural, and even economic narratives (the latter to a lesser extent than the others). For New Orleans and Louisiana as unique and disconnected, see Berlin, *Slaves without Masters*, chap. 4; Jordan, *Black over White*, part 4: chap. 6; Powell, *Accidental City*; Blassingame, *Black New Orleans*, specifically chap. 1; Kein, *Creole*; Hirsch and Logsdon, *Creole New Orleans*; and, among many others, the most well read but least scholarly, Garvey and Widmer, *Beautiful Crescent*. For more recent scholarship that weaves New Orleans and Louisiana more deeply into the North American colonial and national narratives, see Fernandez, *From Chaos to Continuity*; Englebert and Wegmann, *French Connections*, intro.; Vidal, *Louisiana*; Vidal, *Caribbean New Orleans*; Faber, *Building the Land of Dreams*; and, among others, Wegmann, *An American Color*.

9. The two fundamental and tragically underappreciated exceptions to this narrative are Brasseaux, Oubre, and Fontenot, *Creoles of Color*, particularly chaps. 1,

2, and 4, and Mills, *Forgotten People*. Most other studies of Louisiana's cultural and social history outside of New Orleans either focus entirely on the Acadians (Cajuns), a group that has received extraordinarily valuable attention in recent years, or place the state within the agricultural standard of the South, focusing more on the use and practice of slavery in the "Cotton Belt" of the northern parishes and ignoring the rather large population of French-speaking non-Cajuns, a large portion of which was of African descent and identified as Creole and French far more than African or American.

10. On the early history of St. Louis and the "Americanized" treatments of the city, see Cleary, *The World, the Flesh*, chapters 1, 4, and 6; Winch, *The Clamorgans*, chapters 1 and 2; Gitlin, *The Bourgeois Frontier*, chapter 2, 3, and 5; Van Ravenswaay, *Saint Louis: An Informal History of the City and its People*, parts I and II; and Arenson, *The Great Heart of the Republic*, introduction and chapter 1.

11. Several recent studies have noted the consistency and rootedness of African-descended communities in the shadow of more transient European populations in colonial North America. See Dawdy, *Building the Devil's Empire*, introduction, chap. 3, and conclusion; Winch, *Clamorgans*, chaps. 1 and 2; Hall, *Africans in Colonial Louisiana*; Spear, *Race, Sex, and Social Order*, chaps. 3, 4, and 5; Ekberg and Person, *St. Louis Rising*, chaps. 8 and 9; and White, *Wild Frenchmen*, chaps. 4, 6, and 7.

12. As mentioned above, Rutgers owned several properties that bordered those owned by other members of the "colored aristocracy," and nearly all of these men (and the majority were, indeed, men) had roots in the local community stretching back to the city's founding. Louis Charleville, for example, who owned no fewer than three properties bordering at least one of Rutgers's, came from the Chauvin dit Charleville clan of Upper New France. Louis's grandfather, in fact, was none other than Jean-Baptiste Chauvin Charleville, one of the white founders of St. Louis and a major French trader in the Kaskaskia region of New France. Mixed-race members of the Aubuchon family, another major white player in the founding of the town, also neighbored Rutgers, as did members of the Labadie and Clamorgan clans. See "Letters Testimentary [*sic*] Granted to Peter Chouteau, Sr., as Executor of the Last Will of the Widow Charleville," March 27, 1826, Chouteau Collections, MHM; "Certificate of Inventory," May 9, 1867, Probate Record of Pelagie Rutgers, #7,984, StLPC; and Winch, *Clamorgans*, chaps. 1 and 2.

13. Clamorgan, *Colored Aristocracy*, 49.

14. Julie Winch's work on the Clamorgan family is absolutely critical to any understanding of the free community of color in St. Louis and stands as a masterpiece

of social and racial history. On Cyprian Clamorgan's time in New Orleans and Louisiana, see Winch, *Clamorgans*, 177–93 and chap. 12. On what historians have now termed the "Creole Corridor," stretching from the French-speaking parts on Canada, down the Mississippi River to New Orleans, encompassing lower Illinois, St. Louis, and Ste.-Geneviève, to name a few, see Gitlin, *Bourgeois Frontier*, chap. 2. On the free people of color generally and the fluidity of movement along the Mississippi River, see Buchanan, *Black Life*, chap. 3.

15. On the Rutgers family, see note 1. Also see Julie Winch's annotations in Clamorgan, *Colored Aristocracy*, 72–73; Van Ravenswaay, *St. Louis*, 115–16, 183–84; Winch, *Clamorgans*, 129–30; and Probate Record of Arend Rutgers, #1,313, StLPC.

16. On the surprisingly rapid transformation of St. Louis into a quintessentially Western "American" city, see Arenson, *Great Heart of the Republic*, particularly introduction, chap. 1, and chap. 5. For more on Cyprian Clamorgan's views, see Julie Winch, "The Clamorgans of St. Louis," in Clamorgan, *Colored Aristocracy*, 21–36; and Clamorgan, *Colored Aristocracy*, 45–48.

17. This subject has received immense academic coverage in the past twenty or so years. The first, and perhaps most iconic work, is Curry, *Free Black*. Other more recent studies include Landers, *Against the Odds*; Koger, *Black Slaveowners*; Horton and Horton, *In Hope of Liberty*; Nash, *Forging Freedom*; Phillips, *Freedom's Port*; and, among many others, Myers, *Forging Freedom*.

18. On Cyprian Clamorgan's forays in other towns, see Winch, *Clamorgans*, 146–51, 173–96, and 303–20.

19. See Will, February 15, 1867, Probate Record of Pelagie Rutgers, #7,984, StLPC.

20. See Schweninger, *Tennessee Slave*, 11–12, 101–4; and Clamorgan, *Colored Aristocracy*, 49. For Pelagie's will, see Will, February 15, 1867, Probate Record of Pelagie Rutgers, #7,984, StLPC.

21. See Schweninger, *Tennessee Slave*, 11–12; Winch, *Clamorgans*, 158–59; and "Record of Marriage," February 11, 1868, MSA.

22. For just a few of these exchanges, see St. Louis County Deed Books, #155, 279; #237, 26; #238, 460, 462; #239, 271, 286, 301, 448, 455; #240, 115, 209; #246, 258, 299, 474, 503, 665, all at StLCC. For an incomplete but impressive list of several of Rutgers's exchanges, see Winch, "Annotations," in Clamorgan, *Colored Aristocracy*, 72.

23. See St. Louis County Deed Book, D.3, 101; E.3., 62; I.3., 435; M3., 243; V.3., 196; X.3., 264, 265; C.4., 157; D.4., 181; E.4., 403; and V.4., 509, to name a few, all at StLCC. Also see "Account of Estate," n.d., Probate Record of Pelagie Rutgers, #7,984, StLPC; "Accounts Due," March 25, 1853, Probate Record of

Louis Clamorgan, #3,685, StLPC; and "Affidavit of Executor Concerning Claims of Heirs," November 12, 1881, Probate Record of Louis D. Charleville, #3,202, NPPC.

24. See Winch, *Clamorgans*, 90–93. Also see "Affidavit of Assessors," May 8, 1867, Probate Record of Pelagie Rutgers, #7,984, StLPC; and "Affidavit of Heirs," March 11, 1853, Probate Record of Louis Clamorgan, #3,865, StLPC.

25. See Will, February 15, 1867; "Account of Heirs," March 12, 1867; "Account of Estate," n.d.; "Account of Estate," March 20, 1867; and various receipts signed between March 1867 and August 1869, all in Probate Record of Pelagie Rutgers, #7,984, StLPC.

26. See Will, February 15, 1867; "Note," February 24, 1870; and "Settlement of Estate," March 31, 1870, all in Probate Record of Pelagie Rutgers, #7,984, StLPC. Julie Winch briefly mentions this man in her annotations to Clamorgan's *Colored Aristocracy*, but misspells his name as "Charles Cahomie" and, understandably, provides no additional information on him. See Winch, "Annotations," in Clamorgan, *Colored Aristocracy*, 71–72.

27. Although the Creoles of color of Natchitoches Parish, Louisiana, have all but entirely escaped academic coverage, finding brief and inconsequential reference in just a handful of articles, one remarkable study remains invaluable on the subject, Gary B. Mills's 1977 classic history of the Metoyer family, *The Forgotten People*. For a glancing but still valuable treatments of Creoles in this central western area of Louisiana, see Brasseaux, Fontenot, and Oubre, *Creoles of Color*, 108–14, and Burton and Smith, *Colonial Natchitoches*, chap. 4. The more general history of this area is lively captured in Leeper, *Louisiana Place Names*, 68–69, and Boren and Davis, *Kate Chopin Reconsidered*, introduction.

28. Antoine Coton-Maïs was a classic river trader in late New France, born in Kaskaskia just before the French and Indian War. For select portions of his probate record, see Mills, *Professional Genealogy*, 303–7. Also see "Affidavit of Matthew Mullon," December 15, 1882, Probate Record of Charles Coton-mais, #12,825, StLPC and "Baptisme," October 19, 1821, French Catholic Church Records, DROUIN.

29. See Clamorgan, *Colored Aristocracy*, 48; Winch, *Clamorgans*, 91; and "Record of Marriage," April 20, 1820, French Catholic Church Records, Drouin Collection. It is curious that Clamorgan, in *Colored Aristocracy*, did not mention that Rutgers was his uncle's widow, instead noting only that she had been married to Louis Rutgers and that "previous to her marriage she was a slave, and purchased herself for the sum of three dollars."

30. St. Louis County Free Negro Licenses, December 15, 1835, Book 1, p. 458, Dexter Tiffany Collection, MHM.

31. Mills, *Forgotten People*, xiv.

32. Mills, *Forgotten People*, xiv.

33. The vast majority of scholarship focusing on "Creoles of color," or alternatively *gens de couleur*, deal almost entirely with the community found in New Orleans. Some relatively minor exceptions exist, however. For both approaches, see Mills, *Forgotten People*; Dormon, *Creoles of Color*; Weiss, "Introduction," in Shapiro, *Creole Echoes*, xxiii–xxxix; Thompson, *Exiles at Home*; Hangar, *Bounded Lives, Bounded Places*; and, among others, Wegmann, "Blood of a Negro," 204–25.

34. For more on the idea of the "image archive," see Spear, *Race, Sex, and Social Order*, 2–3; Peabody, "'Born to Slavery,'" 113–26; and Wegmann, *An American Color*, chaps. 3 and 4.

35. See 1860 Federal Census, Natchitoches LA, p. 51 and "Affidavit," August 12, 1854, *Chevalier v. Metoyer*, District Court Records, #4,668, Natchitoches Parish Records, NPCOC.

36. See "Affidavit of Matthew Mullon," December 15, 1882, Probate Record of Charles Cotonmais, #12,825, StLPC and 1850 Federal Census, Natchitoches Parish LA, p. 70.

37. See "Affidavit of Heirs," August 27, 1877; "Affidavit of Matthew Mullon," December 15, 1882; and "Report of Administrator," January 20, 1883, all in Probate Record of Charles Cotonmais, #12,825, StLPC. Also see 1850 Federal Census, Natchitoches Parish LA, p. 70; 1860 Federal Census, Natchitoches Parish LA, p. 53; Mills, *Forgotten People*, 72–74 (family trees); and Burton and Smith, *Colonial Natchitoches*, 75–76, 99–101.

38. On the Creole Corridor, see note 11. The term was coined by Jay Gitlin in his book, *Bourgeois Frontier*, and has since become widely accepted as a descriptor for the riverine valley(s) stretching from Québec to New Orleans, the Mississippi River serving as the largest and most central avenue of the cultural region.

39. See Mills, *Forgotten People*, xxxv, 66–69, 72–75, 90–93, 116–18. Also see "Affidavit of Matthew Mullon," December 15, 1882, Probate Record of Charles Cotonmais, #12,825, StLPC.

40. See 1850 Federal Census, Slave Schedules, Natchitoches Parish LA, p. 933; Jacquitte Rachal to Charles Benoist, Series 1, Robert DeBlieux Collection, Watson Memorial Library, Northwestern State University; Bills of Exchange, Box M-30, Benoist-Charleville Papers, MHM; and Mills, *Forgotten People*, 117.

41. See "Record of Marriage," July 25, 1863, Natchitoches Parish Marriage Records, NPCOC.

42. See "Record of Marriage," April 26, 1827, Register 6, #114, St. Francis Catholic Church, Natchitoches LA. Also see Mills, *Forgotten People*, 72, for a brief family tree that links Joseph François Metoyer to several other branches of the Metoyer family, and "Affidavit of Matthew Mullon," December 15, 1882, Probate Record of Charles Cotonmais, #12,825, STLPC, for an explanation of Coton-Maïs's heirs, complete with a list of his siblings, their spouses, and their descendants.

43. See "Letters Testimentary [*sic*] Granted to Peter Chouteau, Sr., as Executor of the Last Will of the Widow Charleville," March 27, 1826, Chouteau Collections, MHM; "Le Mariage de Louis Charleville et Louise Julie Labbadie," November 26, 1827, French Catholic Church Records, DROUIN; and 1840 Federal Census, St. Louis City MO, 35.

44. The connections between the Charlevilles and Labadieson the whole are relatively well documented. See Winch, "Annotations," in Clamorgan, *Colored Aristocracy*, 88–90; Winch, *Clamorgans*, 160–61; Wong, *Neither Fugitive nor Free*, 177–78; and Greene, Kremer, and Holland, *Missouri's Black Heritage*, 70–71. Also see St. Louis County Free Negro Licenses, Books 1–3, Dexter Tiffany Collection, MHM and St. Louis County Deed, Books E.3, #62; I.3, #435; S.3, #201, 244; X.3, #234, 235; A.4, #159, among many others, all at STLCC.

45. See "Note of Exchange," June 29, 1880; "Receipt," September 24, 1877; and "Bond," August 27, 1877, in Probate Record of Charles Coton-Maïs, #12,825, STLPC. Also see "Account of Estate," n.d.; "Account of Estate," March 20, 1869; "Receipt," April 12, 1869; "Settlement of Estate," March 31, 1870; "Note," February 21, 1869; and "Note," March 2, 1861, in Probate Record of Pelagie Rutgers, #7,984, STLPC.

46. See 1860, 1870, and 1880 Federal Censuses, all Ward 4, St. Louis, MO, pp. 46, 108, 4; 1900 Federal Census, District 155, Ward 10, St. Louis, MO, p. 20; "Naissance," September 7, 1830, DROUIN; "Record of Marriage," January 27, 1848, Missouri Marriage Records, 1848, MSA; and "Obituary of Louisa Charleville," *St. Louis Post-Dispatch*, December 21, 1909.

47. See "Charleville, Joseph Louis," August 17, 1871, Natchitoches Parish LA, p. 510, Record of Appointment of Postmasters, 1832–1971, mf #28, NPCOC and "Agent Joseph Charleville," May 1864, St. Louis, MO, District 3, p. 197, IRS Tax Assessment List, mf #6, MHM.

48. See "Baptisme," August 24, 1798, Drouin Collection; "Letters Testimentary [*sic*] Franted to Peter Chouteau, Sr., as Executor of the Last Will of the Widow Charleville," March 27, 1826, Chouteau Collections, MHM; "J. B. Charleville & Co.," May 1866, Louisiana, District 9, p. 73, IRS Tax Assessment List, mf #1, New Orleans Public Library; "Affidavit of Heirs," December 11, 1853, Probate

Record of J. B. Charleville, #16,853, NPPC; "Affidavit of Power of Attorney," November 28, 1881, Probate Record of Louis D. Charleville, #3,202, NPPC; and "Statement of Claim," June 9, 1900, Probate Record of Landry Charleville, #26,469, StLPC.

49. See 1850 Federal Census, Natchitoches LA, p. 119; and 1870 Federal Census, Ward 10, Natchitoches LA p. 7.

50. See "Baptisme," December 20, 1834, Drouin Collection; "Affidavit of Heirs," December 11, 1853; "Settlement of Estate," March 19, 1854; Probate Record of J. B. Charleville, #16,853, NPPC; and "Inventory," October 12, 1881, Probate Record of Louis D. Charleville, #3,202, NPPC.

51. See Probate Record of Landry Charleville, #26,469, StLPC.

52. See Probate Record of Landry Charleville, #26,469, StLPC; 1870 Federal Census, Ward 10, Natchitoches LA p. 7; "Natchitoches Parish," *Biographical and Historical Memoirs of Northwest Louisiana* (Nashville TN: Southern Publishing, 1890), 333–34.

BIBLIOGRAPHY

Archives and Manuscripts

DROUIN. French Catholic Church Records. St.-Louis Marriages, 1781–1826, Drouin Collection, Institut Généalogique, Montréal QB.

MHM. Missouri History Museum Library and Research Center, St. Louis MO.

MSA. Missouri State Archives, Jefferson City MO.

New Orleans Public Library, Louisiana Collection, New Orleans LA.

NPCOC. Natchitoches Parish Clerk of Court Office, Natchitoches LA.

NPPC. Natchitoches Parish Probate Court. State Archives of Louisiana, Baton Rouge LA.

Robert DeBlieux Collection. Watson Memorial Library, Special Collections, Northwestern State University, Evanston IL.

St. Francis Catholic Church Archives, Natchitoches LA.

STLCC. St. Louis County Deed Books. St. Louis Circuit Court, St. Louis MO.

STLPC. St. Louis City Probate Records. St. Louis City Probate Court, St. Louis MO.

Published Works

Arenson, Adam. *The Great Heart of the Republic: St. Louis and the Cultural Civil War*. Cambridge MA: Harvard University Press, 2011.

Bellamy, Donnie D. "Free Blacks in Missouri, 1820–1860." *Missouri Historical Review* 67, no. 2 (January 1973): 198–226.

Berlin, Ira. *Slaves without Masters: The Free Negro in the Antebellum South*. New York: Pantheon Books, 1974.

Blassingame, John W. *Black New Orleans, 1860–1880*. Chicago: University of Chicago Press, 1971.

Boren, Lynda S., and Sara deSaussure Davis, eds. *Kate Chopin Reconsidered: Beyond the Bayou*. Baton Rouge: Louisiana State University Press, 1999.

Brasseaux, Carl A., Claude F. Oubre, and Keith Fontenot. *Creoles of Color in the Bayou Country*. Jackson: University Press of Mississippi, 1994.

Buchanan, Thomas C. *Black Life on the Mississippi: Slaves, Free Blacks, and the Western Steamboat World*. Chapel Hill: University of North Carolina Press, 2004.

Burton, H. Sophie, and F. Todd Smith. *Colonial Natchitoches: A Creole Community on the Louisiana-Texas Frontier*. College Station: Texas A&M University Press, 2008.

Clamorgan, Cyprian. *The Colored Aristocracy of St. Louis*. Edited by Julie Winch. Columbia: University of Missouri Press, 1999.

Cleary, Patricia. *The World, the Flesh, and the Devil: A History of Colonial St. Louis*. Columbia: University of Missouri Press, 2011.

Curry, Leonard P. *The Free Black in Urban America, 1800–1850*. Chicago: University of Chicago Press, 1981.

Dawdy, Shannon. *Building the Devil's Empire: French Colonial New Orleans*. Chicago: University of Chicago Press, 2008.

Dormon, James H., ed. *Creoles of Color of the Gulf South*. Knoxville: University of Tennessee Press, 1996.

Ekberg, Carol J., and Sharon K. Person. *St. Louis Rising: The French Regime of Louis St. Ange de Bellerive*. Urbana: University of Illinois Press, 2015.

Englebert, Robert, and Andrew N. Wegmann, eds. *French Connections: Cultural Mobility in North America and the Atlantic World, 1600–1875*. Baton Rouge: Louisiana State University Press, 2020.

Faber, Eberhard L. *Building the Land of Dreams: New Orleans and the Transformation of Early America*. Princeton NJ: Princeton University Press, 2016.

Fernandez, Mark F. *From Chaos to Continuity: The Evolution of Louisiana's Judicial System, 1712–1862*. Baton Rouge: Louisiana State University Press, 2001.

Frederickson, George M. *The Black Image in the White Mind: The Debate on Afro-American Character and Destiny, 1817–1914*. New York: Harper Row, 1971.

Garvey, Joan B., and Mary Lou Widmer. *Beautiful Crescent: A History of New Orleans*. Gretna LA: Pelican, 2013.

Genovese, Eugene D. *Roll, Jordan, Roll: The World the Slaves Made*. New York: Vintage Books, 1974.

Gitlin, Jay. *The Bourgeois Frontier: French Towns, French Traders, and American Expansion*. New Haven CT: Yale University Press, 2009.

Greene, Lorenzo J., Gary R. Kremer, and Antonio F. Holland. *Missouri's Black Heritage*. Columbia: University of Missouri Press, 1980.

Hall, Gwendolyn Midlo. *Africans in Colonial Louisiana: The Development of the Afro-Creole Culture in the Eighteenth Century*. Baton Rouge: Louisiana State University Press, 1992.

Hangar, Kimberly S. *Bounded Lives, Bounded Places: Free Black Society in Colonial New Orleans, 1769–1802*. Durham NC: Duke University Press, 1997.

Hirsch, Arnold R., and Joseph Logsdon, eds. *Creole New Orleans: Race and Americanization*. Baton Rouge: Louisiana State University Press, 1992.

Horton, James Oliver, and Lois E. Horton. *In Hope of Liberty: Culture, Community, and Protest among Northern Free Blacks, 1700–1860*. New York: Oxford University Press, 1998.

Jordan, Winthrop D. *Black over White: American Attitudes toward the Negro, 1550–1812*. Chapel Hill: University of North Carolina Press, 1968.

Kein, Sybil, ed. *Creole: The History and Legacy of Louisiana's Free People of Color*. Baton Rouge: Louisiana State University Press, 2000.

Koger, Larry. *Black Slaveowners: Free Black Slave Masters in South Carolina, 1790–1860*. Jefferson NC: McFarland, 1985.

Landers, Jane G., ed. *Against the Odds: Free Blacks in the Slave Societies of the Americas*. London: Frank Cass, 1996.

Leeper, Clare D'Artois. *Louisiana Place Names: Popular, Unusual, and Forgotten Stories of Towns, Cities, Plantations, Bayous, and Even Some Cemeteries*. Baton Rouge: Louisiana State University Press, 2012.

Mills, Elizabeth Shown, ed. *Professional Genealogy: A Manual for Researchers, Writers, Editors, Lecturers, and Librarians*. Baltimore MD: Genealogical Publishing, 2001.

Mills, Gary B. *The Forgotten People: Cane River's Creoles of Color*. Baton Rouge: Louisiana State University Press, 1977.

Myers, Amrita Chakrabarti. *Forging Freedom: Black Women and the Pursuit of Liberty in Antebellum Charleston*. Chapel Hill: University of North Carolina Press, 2011.

Nash, Gary B. *Forging Freedom: The Formation of Philadelphia's Black Community, 1720–1840*. Cambridge MA: Harvard University Press, 1991.

Peabody, Sue. "'A Nation Born to Slavery': Missionaries and Racial Discourse in Seventeenth-Century French Antilles." *Journal of Social History* 38, no. 1 (Autumn 2004): 113–26.

Phillips, Christopher. *Freedom's Port: The African American Community of Baltimore, 1790–1860*. Urbana: University of Illinois Press, 1997.

Powell, Lawrence N. *The Accidental City: Improvising New Orleans*. Cambridge MA: Harvard University Press, 2012.

Reichard, Maximilian. "Black and White on the Urban Frontier: The St. Louis Community in Transition, 1800–1830." *Missouri Historical Society Bulletin* 33, no. 4 (October 1976): 3–17.

Schweninger, Loren, ed. *From Tennessee Slave to St. Louis Entrepreneur: The Autobiography of James Thomas*. Columbia: University of Missouri Press, 1984.

Spear, Jennifer M. *Race, Sex, and Social Order in the Early New Orleans*. Baltimore MD: Johns Hopkins University Press, 2007.

Thompson, Shirley Elizabeth. *Exiles at Home: The Struggle to Become American in Creole New Orleans*. Cambridge MA: Harvard University Press, 2009.

Van Ravenswaay, Charles. *Saint Louis: An Informal History of the City and its People, 1764–1865*. St. Louis: Missouri Historical Society Press, 1991.

Vidal, Cécile. *Caribbean New Orleans: Empire, Race, and the Making of a Slave Society*. Chapel Hill: University of North Carolina Press, 2019.

Vidal, Cécile, ed. *Louisiana: Crossroads of the Atlantic World*. Philadelphia: University of Pennsylvania Press, 2014.

Wegmann, Andrew N. *An American Color: Race and Identity in New Orleans and the Atlantic World*. Athens: University of Georgia Press, 2021.

———. "The Vitriolic Blood of a Negro: The Development of Racial Identity and Creole Elitism in New Spain and Spanish Louisiana, 1763–1803." *Journal of Transatlantic Studies* 13, no. 2 (Summer 2015): 204–25.

Weiss, M. Lynn. "Introduction." In *Creole Echoes: The Francophone Poetry of Nineteenth-Century Louisiana*, edited and translated by Norman R. Shapiro, xxiii–xxxix. Urbana: University of Illinois Press, 2004.

White, Sophie. *Wild Frenchmen and Frenchified Indians: Material Culture and Race in Colonial Louisiana*. Philadelphia: University of Pennsylvania Press, 2012.

Winch, Julie. *The Clamorgans: One Family's History of Race in America*. New York: Hill & Wang, 2011.

Wong, Edlie L. *Neither Fugitive nor Free: Atlantic Slavery, Freedom Suits, and the Legal Culture of Travel*. New York: New York University Press, 2009.

PART 3

Visualizing Place

New Sources and Resources for
Telling the Story of St. Louis

7

VISUALIZING EARLY ST. LOUIS

ROBERT J. MOORE JR.

The Problem

Like the rings of a tree or the lines found in sedimentary layers of rock, every city has a physical history in its succession of built structures and landscapes. Using new tools available to us through computer imaging technology, and relying upon historic photographs, archival records, maps, and other sources, we now have the ability to recreate landscapes and structures of the past with a fidelity that can inform and envelop the viewer. These three-dimensional "worlds" are not like artistic recreations of the past in that they are based on actual distances and measurements for the landscapes and structures they depict. The idea of mapping and "restoring" a vision of the past presents many fascinating possibilities in various contexts. An authentic image of a vanished historic landscape, like the present project, might be one. Another might be the study of decay or regeneration within a neighborhood, or studies in the contrasts of rich and poor, hierarchies of structures and neighborhoods, and arrangements of habitations on the landscape. Knowing more about the environment in which people once lived can tell us a great deal about who those people were and what their culture and lifestyle were like. Computer technology offers an opportunity to try portraying space as well as volumes within the space, various points of view, perspective, distances, exact measurements, and proximity of structures to one another during early periods of our urban heritage. The possibilities for the application of this type of technology are vast. In the present case it was used to recreate a completely vanished landscape of early St. Louis and all of its associated structures.

Some cities are fortunate and have been able to preserve a few of their earliest buildings, or at least their original street grid. For others, like St. Louis, it is very difficult to discern the city's original physical appearance by looking at the contemporary streetscape or even by trying to match modern features with historic maps. No original structures dating to the first forty years of the city's history survive within the modern street grid. With so much lost or unknown physical information, the application of 3-D drawing technology seemed like a custom-made tool for twenty-first-century observers to try to visualize colonial St. Louis.

St. Louis was founded in 1764 on the Mississippi River. A now-vanished, thirty- to forty-foot-tall river bluff protected the colonial town from flood-waters. Like most French and Spanish towns founded along bodies of water, St. Louis was centered on its river landing (at today's Market Street) and spread nine to ten blocks in both directions parallel to the shoreline. The town was long and narrow, advancing inland only three blocks. Today, the 1764 street grid and its accompanying fifty-block area, which contained the colonial-era village of St. Louis for over forty years, is in the heart of what is now downtown St. Louis.[1]

The Jefferson National Expansion Memorial project of the 1930s was centered on Market Street and the colonial town, replacing the original street grid with parkland. Creation of the park resulted in the demolition of nearly every structure on thirty-seven of the original fifty blocks. From 1963 to 1965 the Gateway Arch was constructed within the park, symbolizing St. Louis's role in the westward expansion of the United States during the nineteenth century. But the wanton demolition of the 1930s to make way for the Arch did not destroy any of St. Louis's colonial fabric, which was already long gone. The last French colonial structure within the town's original street grid was torn down in 1875 and, like all the previous buildings of its kind, was replaced with warehouses and factory structures. Today St. Louis has a large riverfront park that was preceded by several successive generations of commercial buildings of brick, cast iron, and concrete that obliterated the original French town by the mid-nineteenth century.

The problem for those who are now interested in understanding the physical nature of the original colonial town is that of visualization. But now there are sophisticated ways to solve that problem. In order to do so, an overlay must be placed on modern-day maps or satellite images to form any conception of where the colonial street grid and its structures once stood. Over the years, many attempts have been made to use historical evidence from personal reminiscences, maps, and early daguerreotypes to "fill in the blanks" and create an artistic visualization of the early St. Louis village. Several works of art, mostly conjectural bird's-eye views, have been created using these scattered pieces of evidence, some being far more successful than others.[2]

In attempting to create a visual aid to make all of this information understandable, computer technology and architectural drawing programs have opened new avenues to the historian and historical architect eager to learn more about a city's past. The old axiom is that "a picture is worth a thousand words," yet historians are often either content with using only words or do not have the means to use images as part of the story they tell.

As I worked to create a 3-D computer model of early St. Louis with as much accuracy as possible, I found that a large body of primary sources as well as an interesting array of secondary sources existed that could be tapped to render an accurate model, one that is acceptable even to purists.

History: Losing the Past and Twentieth-Century Attempts to Recreate It

In the year 1875, the L. D. Bienvenue house was torn down. Originally built by Louis Delisle Bienvenue in 1786 and measuring twenty by twenty-five feet, it was of *poteaux en terre* (posts in the earth) construction. This was the last surviving French colonial house in St. Louis and was photographed at least three times before it was demolished. The razing of this structure obliterated the last physical vestige of colonial St. Louis. The demolition was just the final blow in a process that lasted for nearly sixty years, wherein the old timber and stone French colonial infrastructure was replaced with American-style buildings of brick and cast iron. Warehouses, factories, and other commercial structures were essential additions to the thriving port of St. Louis during the mid-nineteenth century, and the old wooden houses of the early trading post were casualties of the demands of progress.

FIG. 14. A depiction of a vertical log house in St. Louis, ca. 1780, with surrounding galerie. This is the house owned by Dr. Auguste Conde, built in 1766 at the northwest corner of Second and Elm Streets. Image created by Bob Moore.

In addition, a devastating fire in 1849 burned out large swaths of surviving wooden buildings.[3]

The late nineteenth century brought further changes to the riverfront. Railroads supplanted riverboats as the main movers of cargo and people. Barge tows took the place of steamboats, and the harbor left the mile-long levee, instead stretching out eighteen miles along the shores of the Mississippi River. Although several businesses continued in the riverfront district, a slow, steady decline in the importance of the area took place between 1880 and 1930. By 1933 the landscape where St. Louis was born was no longer an integral part of the city, which turned its back on the river. Only a few isolated buildings dating to the early American period, including the Old Rock House of 1818, remained to remind passersby of the early history of the town.

In anticipation of what became the 1904 World's Fair, Pierre Chouteau III (1849–1910) wanted to recreate part of the village co-founded by his great-great-grandfather Pierre Laclède. Chouteau commissioned sketches from artist Clarence Hoblitzelle, who pieced together memories and descriptions of the long-vanished structures provided by long-term residents. The original plan, never realized, was to tear down the riverfront buildings and recreate portions of the French town, or certain significant houses, for the fair.[4]

The idea of mixing preservation with historic recreations surfaced once more in the 1930s, when Charles Peterson, founder of the Historic American Buildings Survey, and others passionately interested in French Colonial heritage formulated plans for the new Jefferson National Expansion Memorial federal project on the riverfront. They advocated preserving the original orthogonal grid of streets as laid out by Laclède and Chouteau in 1764. Their "Plan 8009" would have honored the history of the site by collecting important structural aspects of the buildings and displaying them in a museum of American architecture. A second museum would have been devoted to St. Louis's importance in the fur trade. Representative examples of the best surviving structures—the Old Rock House (1818), the National-Scotts Hotel (1846), and the second Merchant's Exchange Building (1875), among others—would have been left standing on their original sites. Replicas of colonial-era buildings might have been constructed under this plan, and studies were made of surviving records of several important structures for this purpose.[5]

Other research was conducted by historians and architects on the period of colonial St. Louis, some of which resulted in dioramas and other museum exhibits, a historic base map for the park area pinpointing the locations of historic structures, and a translation to English of portions of the city's land-deed books and real estate records originally written in French and Spanish.[6]

The Tabula Rasa of Modernism

Local boosters of Jefferson National Expansion Memorial insisted that all of the old buildings in the district be razed, leaving a blank tablet upon which to create the memorial to westward expansion. The two exceptions were the Old Rock House and the Old Cathedral, which the plan allowed to survive in situ. The Rock House was "restored" by being torn down to its foundations and rebuilt (with some of the original material) to look as it probably did in 1818 when it was new, stripping away over 120 years of its history in the process.

The submissions for the architectural competition of 1947 for Jefferson National Expansion Memorial negated the past and emphasized modernity. Although the competition booklet, authored by St. Louis architect Louis LaBeaume, preserved some of the idealism of Peterson and his cohorts by stating that submissions might include "the possible re-erection and reproduction of a few typical SMALL BUILDINGS, such as stood in Old St. Louis in earlier days," the main thrust of the design problem and hope for the site was a memorial in the modernist architectural idiom of the era. The competition booklet included a measured drawing of a French colonial house as encouragement to the competing architects, while the design advisor, George Howe of Philadelphia, and all seven of the architects and experts on the jury prized the work of Le Corbusier, Mies van der Rohe, and Frank Lloyd Wright. At least two of them, Howe and Richard Neutra, were themselves well-known practitioners in the modernist idiom. City boosters who pushed the memorial concept—and sponsored the architectural competition—wanted something new, shining, and special that signaled to visitors that St. Louis was a modern, progressive city, not hidebound or excessively rooted in the past. The ironic fact that nearly every historic building was torn down with a view to building modernist structures, and that reproduction historic structures were to be a sideshow—incidental to the design—was not lost on the then-small historic preservation community.

The winning design for the memorial, by Eero Saarinen, included not only the Gateway Arch but also the historic houses. Saarinen's planned "Historic Village" included a cluster of colonial houses and another part of the grounds featured a grouping of early nineteenth-century row houses. These historic replicas were never built, however, for several reasons. First, the National Park Service generally frowned upon reproductions, and the competition booklet's goals did not always mesh with those of the Park Service. Also, the idea of reproduction historic structures was less and less appealing to architect Saarinen as the years went by between when his design was chosen in 1948 and the final planning of the memorial in the late 1950s and 1960s.

FIG. 15. The little village of French houses planned by Eero Saarinen appears on the 1948 model of the Gateway Arch plan, exhibited in the museum at the Gateway Arch. Photograph by Bob Moore.

As the Gateway Arch rose over the St. Louis riverfront in the 1960s, many of the dwindling remnants of St. Louis's past, of any era, fell to the wrecker's ball. Outside of a handful of structures in the area north of the Arch grounds called Laclède's Landing, the only pre-1849 buildings to survive in the downtown area were the Old Cathedral (1834) and the Old Courthouse (1839–62). Even the Old Rock House was torn down and put into storage, removed forever from its original site.

The dearth of actual surviving structures to be seen today throughout the city only adds to the intrigue and mystery about what the St. Louis of the past looked like. It is almost as though one city was built successively atop another. Each of these successive cityscapes added another layer to the built legacy of the town, but each razed and erased what came before. There were so many layers, and so many erasures between the colonial period and the present: Could the early French village be recreated?

Methodology

In order to drill back in time through the various layers of habitation, a lot of documentary evidence needed to be located in order to make a computer recreation of the early town. Computer technologies like SketchUp that provide 3-D renderings of structures and landscapes are ordinarily used to augment the work of designers to present better visualizations to their clients, for, let's say, a new house or a kitchen remodeling project. I wondered, as a historian, what sort of application this software might have in visualizing a more epic and accurate view of the vanished past. If enough information could be gathered to create a convincing and somewhat accurate representation of early St. Louis, would it be worth the time and effort to plot out an entire town, consisting of a landscape, 50 square blocks, and over 200 buildings? This was what I set out to do over a decade ago.

The search for documentary evidence of early St. Louis took a long period of time. The process began with primary source documentation found in the Livres Terrien, lists kept by the governing authorities of St. Louis of original property concessions. Another collection known as the St. Louis Recorded Archives contained transcriptions of official documents generated in early St. Louis including property sales, wills, and deeds. Many of the land deeds in the Recorded Archives included information about the subject property. These included house dimensions, materials (masonry or vertical log), roofing materials, additions to the house, and outbuildings such as barns, wells, chicken houses, beehive ovens, and sheds. The early records also included block sizes and street widths. In addition, using the writings and quoted primary source documentation in works by Frederic Billon, J. Thomas Scharf, Charles Peterson, and others, I was able to begin to envision the town three dimensionally. The most helpful find was of a cache of old city maps and the book of "Brown's Surveys," intensive surveys made beginning in 1818 of each plot of land in the colonial district of St. Louis down to ¼ inch, all in English measure.[7]

The first order of business was to lay down a landscape for the town to rest upon. For this task there were maps to be consulted as well as the physical remains of the landscape as it stands today. Early maps clearly show the street layout of the town. They include the Guy Dufossat map of

1767;[8] a map of the town's fortifications by Lieutenant Governor Manuel Pérez sent to Spain in 1787;[9] an engraved map of the Illinois Country by Agent-General Georges Henri Victor Collot, 1796; as well as the sketch map probably drawn by Collot's adjutant, Charles Warin;[10] the Nicolas de Finiels Map of the Middle Mississippi River Valley, 1797–98;[11] and the so-called Chouteau Map, of unknown date but possibly made as early as 1781. The last map no longer exists, but has been copied many times and used in so many subsequent engravings and images that it has become the best-known map image of the colonial town.[12] There are also two maps probably made by surveyor Antoine Soulard around the year 1804.[13]

Information from these manuscript maps was used in conjunction with a 1948 map prepared by the National Park Service of the vicinity of the Jefferson National Expansion Memorial.[14] This map has topographical lines denoting changes in elevation. Although many aspects of the landscape had changed since 1764, most notably the excavation and elimination of the original river bluff, the topographical lines still gave some indication of the unchanged undulations of the landscape after it had been stripped of nineteenth-century buildings and before the Gateway Arch landscape supplanted it, burying the original topography under eighteen feet of fill in some places. In the end the single most helpful piece of information was the Joseph Brown surveys of 1818, which when drawn out in the computer a block at a time actually allowed the gentle curve of the town's streets and land plots to unfold naturally.

The greater St. Louis village area of the late eighteenth century consisted of four major parts: the riverfront and its thirty-to-forty-foot limestone bluff; the town grid, placed on a slightly east-west ascending plain, with a steep declination between modern-day Clark and Spruce streets dividing the town into upper and lower areas; the common fields stretching for over a mile westward from modern Fourth Street to Jefferson Avenue; and the Mill Creek, with its mill and large millpond to the southwest of the town. All of these features were modeled first, using a variety of map sources, primarily a selection of accurate nineteenth-century maps with street grids.[15]

Using the maps and the block descriptions, as well as the c. 1818 survey book of each St. Louis block by Joseph C. Brown, the pattern of streets could be laid over the computer-simulated landscape. Most blocks in early St. Louis measured 240 by 300 French feet, which translates to 255 feet 9 inches by 319 feet 9 inches in English measure. In all cases the older system of French measures had to be converted to English measures for use in the 3-D drawing program, which only accommodated metric or English measures. St. Louis's blocks were smaller in size than those in other nearby French towns, where 300 by 300 feet was more common, with even larger block sizes in Ste. Genevieve and New Orleans. St. Louis preserved the concept of the New Orleans layout with an east-west spine of larger blocks centered on the river landing dividing the long, narrow town layout at the center. In St. Louis these central blocks measured 300 by 300 French feet (or 319 feet 9 inches on a side in English measure). The streets of the town were laid out in principal or "main streets" running north and south and cross streets running east and west. The north-south streets were thirty-six French feet wide, the east-west cross streets thirty French feet wide. Almost all of this street system has been obliterated by the Jefferson National Expansion Memorial save for a few streets to the north and to the south of the park boundaries. The surviving streets have been significantly narrowed by the addition of sidewalks in the nineteenth century. When the sidewalks were constructed they were taken from the streets and not from the land within the established blocks.[16] When the entire town was platted as shown in the early maps, the landscape was complete and it was time to add the structures.

Tantalizingly few clues remain as to what St. Louis's housing stock looked like during the colonial period. However, we have the measurements of the footprint of each structure from a survey printed in J. Thomas Scharf's *History of St. Louis City and County* in 1883 and the deeds in the St. Louis Recorded Archives.[17] Extra information included in some of the deeds states that the house size is measured "not including the gallerie," so that these measurements were strictly for the interior floor plan of the structures and did not include porches or additions which they called "*apentis*."[18] House types could be conjectured from remaining evidence in the standing structures of Ste. Genevieve, Missouri; Cahokia and Dupo, Illinois; and other sources.[19] The Holy Family Church in Cahokia, Illinois, has almost the same dimensions and employed the same construction techniques as the colonial-era church in St. Louis. It served as an ideal model on which to base the depiction of the village's sole house of worship.

The placement of the structures on the blocks was influenced by several factors. First, deeds in the St. Louis Recorded Archives sometimes mentioned exact distances of a house or a building from a property line. Second, tradition placed houses close to the street corners at the outside edges of the blocks, allowing more space for gardens, fruit trees, and outbuildings in the back. Third, the deeds sometimes alluded to the orientation of a house by using the word "front" to denote the dimension of the side of the house facing the main street. For example, in a deed for Joseph Robidoux to Alexis Marié from January 8, 1782, "a house of posts in the ground, covered with shingles, floored above and below, forty feet deep by twenty front" indicated that the long side of the house faced the side street. In many cases, when the houses were platted, this made eminent sense as these houses most often were built on a hill and constructed so that their short sides were on the declivity.[20]

Sorting out which deeds in the Recorded Archives went with which blocks in the colonial town was a very time-consuming process, one which could only be solved by creating a spreadsheet with a row for each quarter block. The block numbering system employed by the Americans after 1804 was not in use during the colonial period, so properties can only be understood by references in the deeds to neighboring landmarks—the river; the first, second, or third main street; or adjacent property owners. None of the streets had proper names, although the street parallel with and closest to the Mississippi was sometimes called Royal Street (*Rue Royale*) or simply Main Street (*La Rue Principale*), while the second street was known as Church Street (*Rue d'Eglise*), and the third, Barn Street (*Rue des Granges*). None of the cross streets had names that were used in the deeds. Properties changed hands frequently, and very few properties were held by one person or family for the entire forty-year colonial period.

Early maps showed the actual placement of the houses, some with more fidelity to scale than others. The earliest known illustration of St. Louis was an engraving that appeared on an 1817 banknote, followed a year later by the charming watercolors of Anna Maria Von Phul, who provided scenes of everyday life with sketches of the *habitants* in their working clothes.[21] Although some French period buildings can be seen in these images, they provide just a faint hint of what the town looked like during the colonial period. A source of informed artwork can be found in the drawings made by Charles Heberer under the supervision of Frederic Billon in 1886 for inclusion in Billon's book on colonial-era St. Louis. Billon first came to St. Louis as a boy in 1818, and saw the remnants of colonial St. Louis firsthand. It is assumed, therefore, that Heberer's illustrations conformed to the, by then, nearly seventy-year-old memories of Billon.[22] Some of the French period buildings survived into the age of photography, and the daguerreotypes taken with great foresight by Thomas Easterly in the 1840s and 1850s provide us with a glimpse of their appearance.[23]

Another tremendous source of information is the book by James B. Musick, *St. Louis as a Fortified Town*, published in 1941. It provides detailed information on the defensive structures in St. Louis built after 1780. These included five masonry towers, a bastion, and a demilune, as well as a log blockhouse.[24] Particularly helpful in the effort to model these structures was a manuscript map hand drawn by Caleb Lewis Beck, later engraved for his *Gazetteer*, a full size copy of which is in the collections of the Missouri History Museum.[25] This map features Beck's pictorial representations of each of the defensive features of the town, despite the fact that nearly all of these features had been razed a few years prior to the map's publication.

Modeling

To create the model, I used what was at the time a freeware program, Google SketchUp. Although SketchUp is often used to draw single structures, it is rarely if ever used to recreate an entire town, building by building. In 1804 St. Louis included 161 private residences, at least 17 barns, 11 military structures, 6 mills, 11 stores, and several shops, warehouses, and the church and its rectory. Altogether, this constituted about 208 large structures of all types in the town. In addition there were smaller structures mentioned in real estate records and inventories of property such as sheds, detached kitchens, chicken coops, wells, bake ovens, workshops, privies, and slave cabins.

Visual information including six structures photographed by Thomas Easterly and those drawn by Heberer and Hoblitzelle enabled the recreation of about twenty-six of the colonial-era buildings based on visual information, as well as all of the town's fortifications and Roy's wind-powered mill. This is not a large number—26 houses out of 161. For the remainder, existing examples of French colonial houses, outbuildings, and other resources had to be used. Some purists may say that too many structures in the model are conjectural, and this may be a valid criticism. Unfortunately, unless more material is discovered, we will never be able to illustrate the town without a great deal of conjecture about details. At least we can be sure about the number of the buildings, the size of their footprints, and their locations in the town. And as long as we use the authentic types of structures that were built by colonial residents in the Mississippi River Valley in this period, I feel that we are being true to the essence of the quest to visualize what the town looked like.

One great advantage to the SketchUp program is that structures can be moved about easily, altered completely, or even removed entirely if corrections need to be made. If more information becomes available about an individual structure, it can be updated. I am constantly updating the model as I discover new bits of information that change the look of it in any way.

Once the baseline model of St. Louis in 1804 was created to a rigorous set of standards, the year-by-year charts and lists in the Scharf book (augmented by primary source documentation in the real estate records) could be used to create a specific and separate model for each year of the colonial period. Saving the model of 1804 St. Louis under the name 1803 to create a new, second model, I could subtract the structures that were built in 1804. I followed this procedure going back in time to the founding date, 1764.[26]

But Scharf, who collaborated with Billon on this information, did not stop in 1804. The two men compiled a list of all of the structures built subsequently to 1804, going up to 1821. Once the computer models of 1764–1804 were completed, I added buildings to the 1804 model and created subsequent models for each year leading up to 1821.[27]

FIG. 16. (*top*) This rendering depicts the home of Jeanette Forchet, a free person of color in the St. Louis community. Forchet purchased the property in 1765 and had the house built by the following year. She lived at the same location, the southwest corner of Second and Elm Streets, throughout the colonial period. Image created by Bob Moore.

FIG. 17. (*bottom*) Wealthier St. Louis fur traders had separate structures built on their property in which to conduct business. This scene depicts the Labadie store at the northeast corner of Chestnut and Main Streets. The stone store measured 36 × 32 feet and was built in 1785. The adjacent Labadie house was built in 1778. Image created by Bob Moore.

FIG. 18. This rendering depicts the home of Catherine Crepeau Togard, which was a small poteau en terre house built in 1771 and measuring 17 × 14 French feet. The house was located near the western boundary of the town at the southwest corner of Third and Market Streets, and the Fort San Carlos tower can be seen in the background. Image created by Bob Moore.

The acid test of the entire project was the use of St. Louis's first city directory of 1821 as a check to see how accurate the resulting 1821 model was. I scanned the entire directory, then reordered the names by street address or block location. Allowing for a few discrepancies, the 1821 model was surprisingly accurate and matched very closely with the city directory regarding how many structures were on each block and their proximity to one another.

Applications

To what uses could historical models of early St. Louis or other cities be put? Technologies that are just emerging will be useful in bringing aspects of computer models to the public in a variety of ways. The advent of 3-D printers means that individual houses from the colonial town could be created as stand-alone physical models, which could then be placed within a created model landscape, creating the town as a scale model. This was done in the new Arch museum with a model of six blocks of the St. Louis riverfront as it looked in 1852, at HO scale.[28] With technology constantly improving, 3-D renderings will look more realistic, processors will improve, RAM memory and capacities of video cards will expand. This means that the current computer models will look dated in a few years, but the software that created them is easily adaptable to technological advancements and can be updated. The research is complete, and the placement of the structures and the relative measurements will not change.

The first major public use of the model is in a computer-generated "flyover" simulation for the new museum beneath the Gateway Arch. Converted from SketchUp to the computer-gaming program Unity, the model was augmented with sunlight effects, shadows, realistic vegetation, and textures of wood and stone on the structures that make the program look nearly photographic and very realistic. Visitors to the museum can take a virtual tour of the colonial town, giving them an unprecedented and realistic glimpse of the past.

Virtual walking tours in real-life environments using this technology are already possible. This means that while holding a device such as a smart phone or iPad and looking at the screen, or by wearing a virtual reality helmet or goggles, an image of the past—in this case from the computer model—can be superimposed upon the real-life image of the landscape in front of you. When you take a step forward, the model moves on the screen. If you look to your left or right, you see what is on that portion of the model. Of all the new technology, perhaps this type of program, called "augmented reality," has the most brilliantly futuristic ring to it. Augmented reality works in two ways based either on geolocation, using GPS; compass; and other sensors in a mobile device, or vision, using sensors to track the visual features of real-world objects. No matter how it works, it provides the greatest sense of "being there." It will be exciting when this technology can actually be used in conjunction with the colonial St. Louis model on the Arch grounds. This will mean that while walking on the grounds, the viewer will see not only the real world around them but also the added layer of augmented reality, which will give them the sense of walking through the streets of colonial St. Louis.

An exciting archaeological find by Michael Meyer and his team of Missouri Department of Transportation archaeologists of the remains of several colonial houses just south of the Arch grounds points out the importance of possessing detailed information and spatial renderings of the early town. Certainly the findings of the exact size of the Louis Beaudoin house and its outbuildings—as discovered in the archaeological dig—can be added to the computer-generated models to update them and make them as accurate as possible.

Implications for the Study of Early St. Louis

When using the computer models, other things begin to become apparent that maps and 2-D renderings simply do not emphasize. For instance, the disparity between the huge size of the houses of the fur barons (Auguste Chouteau's measured ninety-five by fifty-five feet) and a home of a man like Louis Beaudoin, for example (fifteen by eighteen feet), that graphically show the wealth disparities in the early town. Auguste Chouteau's house was actually one of the very largest private residences in all of North America during that period.[29] Evidence in wills and inventories of the period indicates that even some of the poorest St. Louisans were doing well in terms of amassing material possessions. This means that house size was not necessarily an indicator of relative poverty or wealth. However, Auguste and Pierre Chouteau's houses were much larger than any others in the village and probably the largest of the Louisiana plantation-style houses built during the colonial era. The presence of these homes highlighted St. Louis's affluence and importance, and this can be seen more clearly in the environment of a 3-D computer model than in a 2-D rendering.

The models also help demonstrate how the French town, with its generous quarter-block lots, was subdivided into town lots by the Americans after 1804. With subdivisions made of narrow frontage lots, St. Louis began to look like Philadelphia or Baltimore, with row houses built side by side. Thus, American St. Louis became a completely different place in ambiance and infrastructure than the French town had been.

Hopefully, 3-D computer modeling of early St. Louis and other cities will lead to more specific and accurate renderings and further research. Historians will have new tools to help reimagine the past and analyze the factors that influenced the changes in the landscape and the rise of urban areas. The computer models have helped bring to fruition the early dreams of Pierre Chouteau III and Charles Peterson, providing a vision of what was lost. Hard research and new technological tools beckon us forward along new pathways in an attempt to visualize and understand the fascinating colonial town that became the city of St. Louis.

NOTES

1. Peterson, *Colonial St. Louis*; Kornwolf, *Architecture and Town Planning*.
2. Some of the most accurate and successful of these were created by Norbury L. Wayman in the 1960s; see his book, *Pictorial History*.
3. Lowic, *Architectural Heritage*.
4. The drawings of Clarence Hoblitzelle are in the collections of the Missouri History Museum.
5. Peterson, Oral History interview; "Description and Explanation."
6. These materials are preserved in the JNEMA.
7. Brown, "Surveys." This massive survey, the first to record the corners and lines of the blocks and streets, was begun about the year 1815 by Joseph C. Brown, U.S. deputy surveyor. It includes a separate page on each block of land with accurate survey lines and measurements recorded for that block to within ¼ inch.
8. Biblioteca National de España.
9. Archivo General de Las Indias, Seville.
10. Carte No. 7, Service Historique de la Marine, Vincennes, France.
11. Archives de la Marine, Chateau, Vincennes, France.
12. See Document F, which accompanied the report of August 2, 1841 to the St. Louis Land Office; the "Papin Map," made sometime after 1854, Missouri History Museum; *Edwards's Great West and Her Commercial Metropolis*, 1860; Engraving of the "Chouteau Map" by Charles Juehne for *Campbell's Gazetteer of Missouri*, 1874, Missouri History Museum; and the plat map drawn for Frederick Billon's *Annals of St. Louis*. Details surrounding the "Chouteau Map" are explored in Gilman and Jaycox, "Chouteau Map Re-Examined."
13. U.S. Army Corps of Engineers, National Archives.
14. "Topographical Survey Map," U.S. Army Corps of Engineers Sept. 1948, JNEMA.
15. Mill Creek and the millpond were studied in great detail in Henry, "Sequent Occupance," which includes several excellent maps.
16. This unpublished research on block sizes and street widths is my own and involved close examination of satellite images combined with actual measurements on the ground, not only in St. Louis but also in St. Charles, Carondelet, and Ste. Genevieve.

17. Scharf, *History of St. Louis*, 1:142–48.

18. See, for example, Zenon Trudeau approving the agreement between Charles Tayon, Jean Pierre, and Pierre Joseph Didier, March 29, 1796, STLRA, I, no.1:163–64, #1433. In another instance, the earlier measure of a house in 1787 without galleries can be subtracted from the measure provided in a 1796 sale noting that it measures the house including the galleries, thus providing the exact width of the galleries; see Alexis Marie to Bonaventura Collell, August 13, 1788, STLRA, I, no.1:126, #480; and Bonaventura Collell to Gabriel Cerré, June 5, 1796, STLRA, I, no.1:127–29, # 675, Bonaventura Collell to Gabriel Cerré, June 5, 1796.

19. Several books were helpful in this effort, as were invaluable consultations with Jesse Francis, the foremost authority on the restoration and construction of French Colonial structures today. See Peterson *Colonial St. Louis* and Francis and Luer, *Vanishing French Heritage*.

20. STLRA, 2, no. 2:228, # 336.

21. The banknote is owned by the St. Louis Money Museum, Washington University, Kemper Art Gallery; the Anna Maria Von Phul watercolors are in the collections of the Missouri History Museum; see also Van Ravenswaay, "Anna Maria von Phul."

22. Billon, *Annals of St. Louis*.

23. The largest collection of original Easterly daguerreotypes is found in the Missouri History Museum. Kilgo, *Likeness and Landscape* reproduces the daguerreotypes on high quality paper and allows the opportunity for close study of the images.

24. Each of these was a defensive structure based on the general theories and designs of Sebastien de Vauban (1633–1707), a French military engineer. The towers resembled cylindrical Norman windmills. A bastion was ordinarily a pointed projection extending outward from the wall of a fortification that allowed defenders to fire along the wall at attacking forces trying to breach their defenses; a demilune was a half-moon shaped stand-alone fortification; and a blockhouse was a small two story structure meant, like the watchtowers, to provide an elevated position to watch for enemy movements and a gun platform for muskets and cannon.

25. Beck, *Gazetteer*, 1823.

26. Scharf, *History of St. Louis*, 1:145–48.

27. Scharf, *History of St. Louis*, 1:148–56.

28. HO scale is a modeling scale popular with model railroaders. It utilizes a ratio of 87 inches (8 feet, 3 inches) in the real world scaled down to 1 inch in a model.

29. The scale of architecture in all of North America was small during the colonial era. Robert "King" Carter's plantation house in Virginia, begun in 1720,

which may have been the largest private house in British North America at the time, measured only 40 × 90 feet. In 1786, when George Washington finished enlarging the small house he had inherited at Mount Vernon and the present mansion stood complete with its two-story portico, it measured 45 × 96 feet. When Jefferson's enlargements and modifications of Monticello were essentially complete in 1806, he had created a home measuring 97 × 110 feet. These were two of the largest private residences in North America. Auguste Chouteau's rebuilding of the Maxent, Laclède and Company house in 1789 resulted in the largest structure in early St. Louis. Wild, *Valley of the Mississippi*, 28–31, stated that this incarnation of the house measured 55 × 95 feet. This house was close in scale to both Mount Vernon and Monticello. Kornwolf, *Architecture and Town Planning*, for further information on "King" Carter's home, Mount Vernon, and Monticello; and the measured drawings of each in the Historic American Buildings Survey collection, Library of Congress.

BIBLIOGRAPHY

Archives and Manuscripts

Archives de la Marine, Chateau, Vincennes, France.

Archives Service Historique de la Marine, Vincennes, France.

Biblioteca National de España.

Brown, Joseph C. "Surveys in the Old Town of St. Louis," Book A, c. 1815–18, Division of Geology and Land Survey, Missouri Department of Natural Resources, Rolla MO.

Henry, Virginia Anne, "The Sequent Occupance of Mill Creek Valley," Ph.D. diss., Washington University Department of Geography, June 1947, Washington University in St. Louis Archives.

Hoblitzelle, Clarence, architectural drawings, Missouri Historical Society Archives, St. Louis MO.

JNEMA. Peterson, Charles E. "A Description and Explanation of 'Plan 8009' for the Jefferson National Expansion Memorial." St. Louis MO, October 1937, Jefferson National Expansion Memorial Archives.

JNEMA. U.S. Army Corps of Engineers, Topographical Survey Map, Jefferson National Expansion Memorial, Sept. 1948, Jefferson National Expansion Memorial Archives.

Peterson, Charles E. Oral History Interview, October 22, 1994, conducted by Bob Moore, Historian, Jefferson National Expansion Memorial, St. Louis MO.

St. Louis Recorded Archives, Jefferson National Expansion Memorial, St. Louis MO.

Published Works

Beck, Lewis C. *A Gazetteer of the States of Illinois and Missouri: Containing a General View of each State, a General View of Their Counties, and a Particular Description of Their Towns, Villages, Rivers, &c., &c.: With a Map, and Other Engravings.* Albany NY: Charles R. and George Webster, 1823.

Billon, Frederic Louis. *Annals of St. Louis in Its Early Days under the French and Spanish Dominations, 1764–1804.* St. Louis MO, 1886.

Edwards, Richard. *Edwards's Great West and Her Commercial Metropolis,* 1860. St. Louis MO: Published at the office of "Edwards monthly," 1860.

Francis, Jesse W., and Jack Richard Luer. *Vanishing French Heritage: A Complete Study of the Vertical Log Homes of the Illinois Country.* St. Louis MO: Independent, 2014.

Gilman, Carolyn, and Emily Troxell Jaycox. "The Chouteau Map Re-Examined: A Quest in Progress." *Gateway* 29 (2009): 25–37.

Kilgo, Dolores Ann. *Likeness and Landscape: Thomas M. Easterly and the Art of the Daguerreotype.* St. Louis: Missouri Historical Society, 1994.

Kornwolf, James D., and Geogiana Kornwolf. *Architecture and Town Planning in Colonial North America.* 3 vols. Baltimore: Johns Hopkins University Press, 2002.

Lowic, Lawrence. *The Architectural Heritage of St. Louis, 1803–1891: From the Louisiana Purchase to the Wainwright Building.* St. Louis MO: Washington University Gallery of Art, 1982.

Peterson, Charles E. *Colonial St. Louis: Building a Creole Capital.* Tucson AZ: Patrice Press, 1992.

Scharf, J. Thomas. *History of St. Louis City and County from the Earliest Periods to the Present Day: Including Biographical Sketches of Representative Men.* Philadelphia: Louis H. Everts, 1883.

Van Ravenswaay, Charles. "Anna Maria von Phul." *Bulletin of the Missouri Historical Society* 10, no. 3 (April 1954): 367–84.

Wayman, Norbury L. *A Pictorial History of St. Louis.* St. Louis MO: Boatman's National Bank, 1968.

Wild, John Caspar. *Valley of the Mississippi Illustrated in a Series of Views, 1841–1842.* Facsimile of the original, Andesite Press, 2015.

FIG. 19. *Pierre-Clément de Laussat,* 1904, collotype, by Goupil & Cie. The illustration was included in Alcée Fortier's 1904 *History of Louisiana* and is based on a portrait owned by Laussat's descendants. Courtesy of the Historic New Orleans Collection, gift of Mr. Thomas N. Lennox, 1991.34.21.

8

THE VIEW FROM UPPER LOUISIANA

*Pierre-Clément de Laussat's Concerns
and Contacts, 1803–1804*

JOHN H. LAWRENCE

In the spring of 1803, Pierre-Clément de Laussat (1756–1835), French colonial prefect, arrived in New Orleans to prepare Louisiana for a second colonial administration by France (the first one had lasted from 1699–1762). He could not know then that before the end of the year, he would be the last French official in the colony. The narrative of his tenure in Louisiana and the struggles he faced in accommodating his original mission and the later mission that occurred because of Louisiana's sale to the United States, are chronicled in his personal papers (over six hundred manuscript documents and printed items) housed at The Historic New Orleans Collection. These include his own writings, reports from others, printed proclamations, along with transferred documents and correspondence with the ever-present Spanish officials—that he accumulated between March 1803 and the spring of the following year.

These personal papers traveled with him to additional colonial posts and remained in his care until retirement in France and death in 1835. Some 140 years after that, those documents were acquired by The Historic New Orleans Collection, where they are today, available to those who have an interest in the waning days of French government in Louisiana in all its complexity, and the patience to confront what is a strong contender for the worst penmanship in Louisiana's colonial past.

Several documents among this trove keenly indicate Laussat's interest in and need to grasp the economic, cultural, and diplomatic conditions in Upper Louisiana, anchored by the towns of St. Louis, Ste. Genevieve, and New Madrid. His desire to learn about these areas from their influential

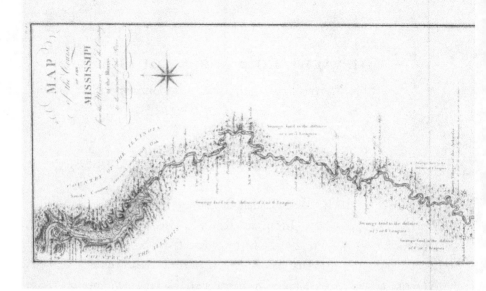

FIG. 20. *Map of the Course of the Mississippi from the Missouri and the Country of the Illinois to the Mouth of this River*, 1805 (published 1826 Victor), engraving, by Georges Henri Collot. This general map of the middle and lower Mississippi River course is from *A Journey in North America, Containing a Survey of the Countries Watered by the Mississippi, Ohio, Missouri, and Other Affluing Rivers; with Exact Observations on the Course and Soundings of These Rivers; and on the Towns, Villages, Hamlets, and Farms of that Part of the New World . . .* by Collot. Courtesy of the Historic New Orleans Collection, bequest of Richard Koch, 1971.59.

residents was both obvious and necessary. Some of those who provided that information are identified in the considerable personal archive of materials. Others remain shrouded in anonymity or speculation.

But the Laussat archives are an indispensable new source for understanding the regional and imperial contexts—as a province of Louisiana, and as part of a complex set of French colonial institutions and processes—in which early St. Louis grew. The papers are a window not only into Laussat's thinking, role, actions, and responsibility as colonial prefect in establishing his directives and command decisions, but also his ignorance and uncertainty about many matters where he sought counsel. They give us insight into several key aspects of colonial governance and the political

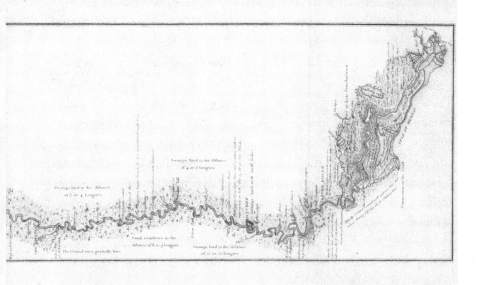

context of the early city: the constant struggle between Laussat and those he perceived as intractable Spanish officials in New Orleans, the pressure he received from planters in Lower Louisiana regarding their interests, the rumors about the pending sale of Louisiana, and the difficulties of planning to manage a fractious boom town when he had no formal authority, to name a few issues.

Three main documents among Laussat's papers shed new light on early St. Louis and other settlements of Upper Louisiana, and are the focus of this essay. Collectively, these new sources provide a more complete picture of the region (though hardly comprehensive), revealing not only evidence of early St. Louis, but also insight into the ways colonial knowledge was gathered by people like Laussat who meant to govern the colony from a distance. Two are letters from known correspondents—Jean-Pierre Chouteau and Michel Amoureux. The other is an intriguing completed questionnaire, but the respondent (or respondents) to the questions is yet undiscovered. Reading between the lines of these and other documents in the archive, one begins to understand the difficulty—if not the absolute folly—of trying to manage a sprawling colony from France or even New Orleans.

Laussat's administration was France's second stab at running Louisiana, but the charade of a remote central government—even mediated through the colonial prefect—just couldn't do the job. The "in country" intelligence of the residents whom Laussat sought out, and who shared their ideas with him, suggest a necessary disconnect between official policy and local solutions. Though the prefect was in communication with specific people—usually prominent ones in their realm—the unrecorded voices and thoughts of voyageurs, women, fortune seekers, Indigenous people, and others generally "lost" to the historical record certainly offered valuable counsel to the person at the top. This is important context to remember as we read these exciting new sources and contemplate the information that did circulate within the colonial administration, and also the information that did not.

When on March 26, 1803, the forty-six-year-old Laussat, French colonial prefect in Louisiana, wrote in his journal, "All Louisianans are Frenchmen at heart!" his exclamation was anticipatory and prospective rather than experiential, as it was his first day in New Orleans. Laussat had been sent to French Louisiana's capital, New Orleans, with the prospect of preparing the colony for reset of French rule, after a hiatus of over three decades during which Louisiana had been under Spanish authority.[1]

New Orleans was established in 1718 and had been colonial Louisiana's capital under France and then Spain since 1722. As the major (though still small) population center in a colony whose initial claims stretched from the Appalachian to the Rocky Mountains, and from the Gulf of Mexico to the Great Lakes, it had commanded more relative interest—however minimal that was in absolute terms—from the respective crowns than any other settlement in the colony. But it was still a relatively out of the way place, at the fringe of France's northern island colonies in the Caribbean; and from 1762 under Spain, nothing so much as a bad fit for an established New World empire. Success—or at least growth—for Louisiana required a vibrant capital and demanded both colonists and capital. It received neither in sufficient quantities from its colonial landlords, yet New Orleans had slowly grown throughout the eighteenth century.

But Louisiana was more than just its capital city. Even reduced dramatically from its initial colonial dimension as claimed by France at the close of the seventeenth century, the colony was still enormously vast, and St. Louis, a growing city nearing forty years of existence at the time of Laussat's arrival, was an important element of any colonial or imperial strategy that France might have for its second tenancy in Louisiana.[2] The prefect knew that nodes of informed, locally respected, trustworthy, and Francophile residents would be crucial to the success of his mission: to reinvigorate French presence and control of Louisiana as a component of retaking governance of the lucrative sugar colony of St. Domingue. At the time of Laussat's arrival, France's holding in western Hispaniola was in the final throes of a decade-long revolution that would ultimately result in the formation of a new nation, Haiti.[3] Early St. Louis—and Laussat's priorities for its colonial administration—need to be understood in the context of these larger imperial ambitions.

Laussat had no real grasp of who Louisiana's citizens were, his contacts being limited to those who had assisted his ship, *Surveillant*, in its passage from Balize at the mouth of the river, to the port.[4] It would be to his advantage to find out quickly what he could of the colony that stretched hundreds of miles north from the Gulf and west from the Mississippi River. Its population of colonists, though weighted toward the lower valley, was sprinkled in settlements spaced along the river's western bank between New Orleans and St. Louis, and to a lesser degree, further west of the Mississippi but still near the Gulf Coast, toward Spanish territories. As the Mississippi sprinted or strolled (depending on the season) past St. Louis, Ste. Genevieve, Natchez, Baton Rouge, and New Orleans to the Gulf of Mexico, it served as both a boundary and conduit. In the first role, it physically marked the departing Spanish and incoming French interests in North America from those of the United States; in the second role, the Mississippi facilitated trade, commerce, and information exchange, which often benefited individual colonists much more than any proclaimed and authorized national agendas.

But if the river provided a hard marker for separating lands to the east, there was no such feature that defined the western boundary of Louisiana that France had secured from Spain. Indeed, in 1803, the land area that bore the name had a western boundary that was yet to be determined, and cartographic efforts to define Louisiana's boundaries were speculative for decades.[5] The final drawing of Louisiana's western boundary would be of little consequence to France and to Laussat. Before the calendar changed from 1803 to 1804, Louisiana would become part of the United States. Though the usual reasoning given for the United States acquiring Louisiana was for the control of the river and the commerce at its principal port of New Orleans, the exploration and mapping of the Purchase's northern and western reaches were critical in the expansion of the United States, and the role of St. Louis as a launching point for these efforts, essential.

Within this expansive colony, major European-implemented settlements were dotted throughout the modern state of Louisiana (in Natchitoches, New Iberia, and the so-called German Coast[6] between New Orleans and the still-Spanish settlements at Baton Rouge, and Pointe Coupée), as well as further upstream in the aforementioned Illinois country.[7] Laussat needed on-the-ground intelligence from all of those areas if he was to fulfill his role in preparing Louisiana—by administration still a province of Spain—for the military governorship of General Claude Perrin Victor.[8] According to the larger imperial vision, Victor's mission would be to press Louisiana into the service of supplying St. Domingue, France's island colony in the final throes of revolution, so as to reestablish its economy derived from slave-based sugar production and its attendant revenue for the French treasury.[9]

In his memoirs, Laussat does not indicate that he personally traveled outside of New Orleans much beyond a distance that could be covered in a day or two on horseback, coach, or simple watercraft. Excursions to the German Coast upriver from New Orleans but not as far as Baton Rouge seem to be the limit of his travels outside of the city. The arrival of the steamboat, which would facilitate more rapid travel and communication throughout the Mississippi Valley during the nineteenth century, was still nearly a decade away. Not uncommon for those in his position, Laussat relied on a network of counselors—both near the capital of New Orleans, in the southwestern hinterlands along Bayou Teche west of the Atchafalaya River, and in Upper Louisiana, the so-called Illinois Country—whose reputations and accomplishments in their own districts and areas of expertise made them trusted sources for information about all aspects of Louisiana.

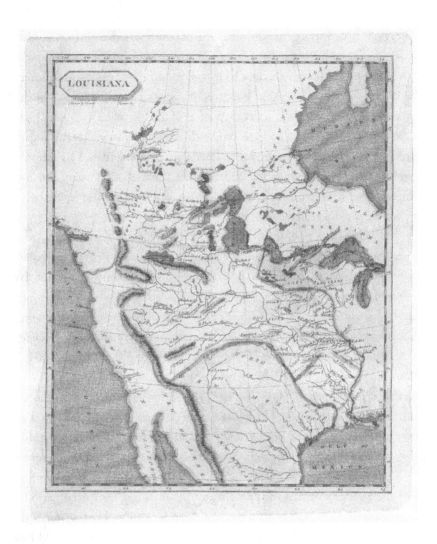

FIG. 21. *Louisiana,* from *A New and Elegant General Atlas, Comprising All the New Discoveries, to the Present Time,* 1805, by Samuel Lewis. Lewis's cartographic information was based on work done by St. Louis surveyor Antoine Soulard. Lewis and Aaron Arrowsmith were the publishers of the atlas. The engraving was by Henry S. Tanner. Courtesy of the Historic New Orleans Collection, 1974.74.2.

This knowledge was general—deeper in some areas than others—and covered geography and natural bounty, fortifications, Indigenous inhabitants, prospects for commercial development, and relationships with other nations or their colonies that bordered it. Laussat counted among such men Jean-Noël Destrehan, a Creole planter of the German Coast who had been educated in France and was one of the region's most successful sugar producers. Another confidant, Julien Poydras, a planter and merchant from the Pointe Coupée area near Baton Rouge, had arrived in Louisiana during the early years of Spanish rule and had managed to succeed spectacularly in numerous and varied commercial endeavors.[10]

Still another fount of information was James Pitot, born in the French port city of Nantes. Prior to his arrival in New Orleans in 1796 his New World experience was in St. Domingue but he fled the colony's revolution to return to France. From there, Pitot went to Philadelphia where he became an American citizen. Laussat credits Pitot with providing information on Louisiana in an extensive memoir by the latter—*Observations sur la Colonie de la Louisiane*—which covered the years 1795–1802.[11] Laussat also mentions Pitot bringing from France a copy of Pierre-Louis Berquin-Duvallon's *Vue du colonie espagnole du Mississippi*, a scathing account of the author's time in Louisiana that had been published in Paris in 1803.[12] But by the point that occurred in April of 1804, Laussat's official duties were behind him, and his interest in the publication must have been purely academic.

The counsel of these future leaders of Louisiana (Destrehan would become heavily involved in the politics of the coming territorial period, Poydras would head the constitutional convention of 1811 that transformed the Territory of Orleans to the state of Louisiana, and Pitot would be American New Orleans's first elected mayor), through both formal channels and in visits during the prefect's tenure, must have shaped his political thinking as he planned for an administration that lasted but twenty days near the end of 1803.[13]

But if he had trusted advisors close at hand in Lower Louisiana, the same was not true for the entire colony. Louisiana's size and its picket line of settlements along the Mississippi forced Laussat to rely on the intelligence of others not so closely situated to New Orleans for information regarding

Louisiana's upper section and sparsely inhabited western posts. He was, nominally, the center of French power in the colony, but communication with those of lesser (though regionally important) statures at the edges created an asymmetrical dynamic of power. It would seem that the regional leaders had more to gain in their relationship to Laussat than did he from them, and in any event he was simply further from them, in space and in familiarity, than some of his other advisors. And yet it is an important reminder about the nature of imperial power that these distant sources of information, intelligence and counsel were all Laussat had, all he could rely on for shaping his understanding of what was happening, and what needed to happen, in the colony.

Laussat's sources of information in Upper Louisiana, the so-called Illinois Country (or le pays Illinois), included members of pioneering French families like the Chouteau and Amoureux clans, Jean-Pierre Chouteau and Michel Amoureux. Their insights were indeed well-informed, based on long experience living in the region; both Jean-Pierre and Michel had multiple generations of family members in Upper Louisiana. Their insights were also informed by experience holding prominent and influential positions in their respective geographic regions and economic circles.[14] At the same time, these men had concerns far different than the cohort of wealthy planters who were in a better position to have Laussat's ear on matters important to their interests. They offered a fresh and valuable kind of intelligence to Laussat.

In addition to Jean-Pierre and Michel's reports, another source of Laussat's intelligence from Upper Louisiana was different but no less valuable: several completed questionnaires solicited by Laussat that survive among his papers. The one concerning Upper Louisiana is the longest (some twenty-two pages) and quite detailed in its information. The respondent is unidentified.[15] The questionnaire is obviously part of a group that Laussat ordered. For instance, another questionnaire seeks information about Louisiana in general, containing notably three pages of intelligence devoted to the posts at Attakapas and Opelousas, areas south and west of New Orleans.[16] Other documents received and presumably solicited by Laussat serve the same function as questionnaires, though their forms are different:

an account of the Ouachita post (present northeast Louisiana); notes on a trip made by one Citizen Paillette from Natchitoches (present central Louisiana) to the Colorado River in Texas; and a series of lists ranging from the gifts given annually to Indian tribes and eighty-four villages inhabited by Native Americans in the region, to lists of naval stores and documents relative to establishing the custom house in New Orleans.[17] Together these represent a fascinating archive into what was known about the region, as well as a window into the phenomenon of information gathering itself.

Laussat was no different from his contemporaries in using these methods to gain intelligence, especially where it concerned places quite distant from his residence. Spanish officials, in their early administration of Louisiana following the Seven Years' War, relied on an extensive *Memoria* from Francisco Bouligny, a former resident of the colony. Thomas Jefferson was forever soliciting expert advice of all types about Louisiana (both prior to and following acquisition by the United States) and the information he sought through questionnaires and reports is extremely similar to those documents of corresponding purpose in the Laussat Papers.[18]

So what did these sources tell Laussat—and what can they tell us— about early St. Louis? The earliest of the letters to Laussat from Upper Louisiana is one of five manuscript pages, dated July 12, 1803,[19] not quite four months after his arrival, and is from Jean Pierre Chouteau (1758–1849) written at St. Louis des Illinois.[20] Perhaps no one in Upper Louisiana could offer a better ear to the ground than the Chouteaus and extended family. The commercial and social networks they represented and their insight concerning matters cultural, social, economic, and martial were equaled by few others.[21] In his opening paragraph, Chouteau writes that his letter is "To prove to you how much I desire to fulfill the promises that I had the honor of making to you when I was in the capital, I am writing you in haste to take advantage of the postal courier who is departing just now. I arrived in this country after a crossing of fifty-six days, I did not experience, in the course of this long voyage, any difficulties, apart from those which are necessarily inherent to these sorts of voyages."[22]

René Auguste Chouteau met with Laussat fairly soon after the latter's arrival in Louisiana, and Laussat's journal entry of April 24, 1803, confirms an encounter between the two in New Orleans.[23] Laussat doesn't mention if Jean Pierre Chouteau (Auguste's younger half brother) was part of that meeting as well, though Pierre's letter could have been written upon Auguste's return to Upper Louisiana and a debriefing about the latter's meeting with the prefect.

The letter goes on to say that in the course of his travel to St. Louis numerous *chalans* (a type of flat-bottomed boat) were observed, including one with troops bound for Fort de la Roche and others with "flour, salted meat, and whiskey" that were destined for Natchez and New Orleans.[24]

This type of intelligence was useful to Laussat, but in addition to the tactical observational powers of Chouteau, Laussat was undoubtedly interested in what one of St. Louis's leading citizens thought about the larger issues of Upper Louisiana—his strategic thinking—and how the local's take on things could assist the administration of the colony. Chouteau gives Laussat a sense of the commercial networks in Upper Louisiana by writing:

The English merchants who have made a habit of trading in this country, to the detriment of the Capital, left a few days ago for Michilimakinac, which is the warehouse for the merchants of Canada, there they deliver their pelts and stock up on trade goods [with which] to return here in the course of August and September, which is a good time to provision the various posts that trade with the Indians. It is not necessary, Monsieur, for me to tell you that this commerce is absolutely damaging to that of our Capital and that the only means of preventing it, to my way of thinking, is that New Orleans should furnish merchandise at a reasonable price, suitable for the Indian trade, and that the government should take the measures necessary for stopping the influx of English goods into this country, through the routes of the Illinois River, and the Wisconsin, in which case, instead of the Capital's enjoying, as it did this year, some 160 thousand pounds [in trade], it would be more than 400 thousand pounds, and if we add the profit from the trade on the right bank of the Mississippi, which to us is not well known, starting above the Missouri up to the St. Pierre River, and beyond, where the English have been the only traders for many years.[25]

One may infer certain self-interest in Chouteau's remarks given his role in the commerce of the area and as a member of one St. Louis's founding families, but the core of his sentiment seems to be directed to advocating a stronger French presence in Upper Louisiana rather than advancing a narrow agenda of personal enrichment. Chouteau's mention of the English merchants and their Canadian headquarters underscores both the porosity of national borders in the St. Louis area (where, unlike at New Orleans, the waterway separated international interests) and the vacuum left by a somewhat weak and far-flung Spanish administration in Upper Louisiana that allowed such circumventions to persist.[26] Chouteau saw a thriving St. Louis area not only beneficial to himself but to French Louisiana. Implicit in his assessment is an open trade with both the neighboring United States and British Canada.

Continuing with the larger economic promise of the area, Chouteau goes on to discuss the agricultural potential, mentioning specifically a report on the cultivation of hemp that the late Pierre Laclède had written and given to Spanish governor Bernardo de Galvez, and that there are many minable ores in the area, whose extraction is limited by a lack of those experienced in mineralogy:[27]

I can at this moment give you only a poor idea of this pelt trade, as well as [of] commerce in this country, in its agricultural aspects, which has infinite possibilities for growth, thanks to the bounty and the richness of its soil, which produces wheat in abundance. Hemp here is of superior quality, according to the repeated experiments of the Jesuits settled afore-time in Kaskaskias, and the late [d.1778] Mr. Pierre Laclève [Laclède] Liqueste [Liguest] whose great genius left no doubt about it. He clearly demonstrated in a memoir concerning its cultivation, which he gave to Don Bernardo de Galvez, governor of this province at that time, that the hemp of this country had one-seventh greater strength than that from Russia, the quality being equal.[28] We have a quantity of mineable graphite iron, and probably others [i.e., ores], which are not known due to the lack of anyone capable of the practice of mineralogy. [A]dd to that flax, salted meats, butter, cheese and other items without number that [our] industriousness could introduce to this vast & rich country, which lacks nothing in order to become one of the most productive on the Globe, [and] that a large population, the mildness of its climate and the salubrity of its waters have greatly blessed.[29]

One may infer that the writer is suggesting that for the last quarter century under Spain (Galvez was Louisiana's Spanish governor at the time of the American Revolution) a lack of material and official support was holding back progress in the colony. The resources for success were present if only officials would recognize that and prioritize those elements needed for development—funding, expert talent, and colonists. This is not unlike the opinion expressed in James Pitot's *Observations sur la colonie de la Louisiane*, with which Laussat was familiar.

Before closing, Chouteau gives his recipient more to think about, including benchmarking some agricultural practices by the Americans, their neighbors across the Mississippi in present Illinois:

I will close saying that by all appearances the harvest is not a bad one, and better in this part of the country than in the other, where they only sow autumn wheat, and the year has not been favorable for this wheat. It is however the best and the only one that can be cultivated here in order to produce good flour[;] because the sort which is sown in the spring is never as good [and doesn't produce as fine a flour.] The Americans know all about this difference, and in this we would do well to imitate them.

The American side of the river is being quickly populated and it appears that this government is trying to augment this population; they recently sent two hundred troops to protect them [i.e., the population] against incursions by the Indians, who commit, from time to time, a few acts of barbarism; they plan to build a fort around four leagues above the Missouri, across from one of our settlements called the Sioux Portage.[30] They had the emplacement reconnoitered by officers of the troops who are stationed here; it is said that they found the site very favorable for the building of a fort.[31]

The "acts of barbarism" and "incursions" by the Indians in the letter were perhaps more a concern in the upper valley than near New Orleans.

Though the lower Mississippi Valley had experienced armed conflict with Native peoples during the eighteenth century, hostilities near the city had ceased by 1800, due to a concerted effort in Spanish Louisiana to maintain alliances with Native nations that could assist in stemming American and British interests in the area.[32]

On August 4, 1803, barely three weeks after Chouteau's letter was posted, a M. Amoureux (Michel Amoureux)[33] wrote to Laussat from New Madrid, noting that his five-page letter was routed via St. Louis des Illinois. Unlike Chouteau's letter, there is no indication that Amoureux was following up on a personal meeting with the prefect, but was simply offering assistance and perhaps lobbying a bit to have New Madrid recognized as the primary French settlement in Upper Louisiana. He begins his letter:

> The desire to be useful in public affairs causes me to take the liberty of sharing with you several observations touching on this part of Upper Louisiana.
>
> It has been announced that the French government has decided that New Madrid will be the administrative center of the settlements, [both] civilian and military, of Upper Louisiana: it is certain that by its location, being only fifteen leagues below the mouth of the Ohio, this outpost deserves that preference over all those which are above that confluence....[34] Travel on the river is practicable at all times of the year between New Orleans and New Madrid; whereas, even in mild winters, navigation above the latter outpost is entirely interrupted. Merchant boats ordinarily go up the river from New Orleans to New Madrid in 45 to 50 days; and it takes them 15 days, in clement seasons, to go from there up to St. Louis. Between New Madrid and St. Louis there is a much-used trail, by means of which one can make it from one to the other in 4 to 5 days, as do often the captains of boats bound for the upper outposts, when they arrive at this one. The boats that go up and down the Mississippi usually stop at New Madrid, either to trade here, or to rest their crews: there is moreover a constant parade of Indians from different nations, who come to exchange the kills from their hunts for European merchandise.[35]

Amoureux's promoting New Madrid as the de facto capital of Upper Louisiana is grounded in practical observations and undoubtedly some self-interest. Trade was critical to the region both in a local sense and in the literal downstream effects that such trade had to the development of French interests in New Orleans and the distribution of goods and commodities from Upper Louisiana to the rest of the United States and overseas markets. Amoureux points out the advantages of the New Madrid site as ingredients for success: the location of the settlement near the confluence of two great rivers, the convenience of the site for water traffic to stop, the year round navigability of the waterways at that point, the exchange with the Indian nations in the region, and the significantly shorter distance from New Orleans. Amoureux's implication is that such advantages are not present to the same degree—if at all—at St. Louis.[36]

The letter continues with pointed remarks on agriculture and farming, though there is no recorded reaction to them by Laussat found in his personal papers:

> The emigrants from the United States are in general good farmers; but they are not as hard working, not as diligent, not as disciplined as the Germans; it is the latter especially who would quickly make agriculture flourish in a country like this one: German farmers generally do not use any slaves, and it has been seen that, in those [states] of the United States where slavery is permitted, the few Germans who have slaves are less prosperous than those who haven't any. The introduction of slavery, especially in a temperate climate, is a great evil; the most noticeable [evil], that slavery produces here, is to make the free people indolent and lazy: as for the other problems it causes, you know them much better than I could describe them.[37]

After continuing at length on additional topics ranging from the abundance of natural resources—especially timber—and proposing the establishment of a customs house based on the potential of the trade in the area, to the need for more soldiers at New Madrid, and neglect of Upper Louisiana by the Spanish, Amoureux closes with the inadequacy of his own knowledge when compared to others:

There are individuals here much more learned, who could provide more in depth and satisfying information concerning the various topics that I have attempted to discuss: such a one above all is Mr. Henri Peyroux, current commandant of this outpost, a man who is educated, admirable, and a good Frenchman, capable, I believe, of putting aside all thoughts of personal interest when it is a matter of considering the public's interest.[38]

As for me and my family, comprised of my wife and my four children, we would like to return to France, where we have a few properties; but whatever misfortune fate may have in store for us, my wishes shall always be for a prosperous France, and to be able to contribute to that prosperity.[39]

Though Amoureux's future plans did not involve remaining in the territory, his willingness to offer the experience and knowledge of his time in Louisiana reflects his great affection for France. His sentiment embodies Laussat's declaration, "All Louisianans are Frenchmen at heart."

A third document among Laussat's papers pertaining principally to Upper Louisiana is critical for the understanding of the two previously mentioned. It is a longish one—a questionnaire with responses—covering some twenty-two pages, and unlike the others, not dated. Given the information supplied by both Chouteau (apparently solicited by Laussat) and Amoureux (who seems to have volunteered information), and the time it would have taken for responses to get between St. Louis, Ste. Genevieve, Cape Girardeau, New Madrid, and other settlements in Upper Louisiana and New Orleans, the questionnaire suggests it was written either shortly after Laussat's arrival in Louisiana (he entered the river at the Balize on March 20, 1803) or possibly (like his memoir of late 1802 on the importance of the Floridas to French presence in the region) drafted in anticipation of his administration.[40] The specific information (especially that provided by Chouteau) mirrors many queries posed by the questionnaire.

By way of example, question one asks for detailed information on the fortifications around settlements near St. Louis; question eleven elicits a response about outfitting and transporting a detachment of soldiers and auxiliary staff from New Orleans to the Illinois country while the reply to question fourteen indicates a route that such a force might take: New Orleans to Concordia (opposite Natchez) to the Arkansas Post, to Esperanza [modern Hopefield, Arkansas, opposite Memphis], and from there to New Madrid, Ste. Geneviève, and St. Louis, always hewing to the western (right) bank of the Mississippi.[41] Questions fifteen and sixteen are about the weather in winter; the responses indicate that good lodging for the troops is the only consideration in winter, and that it (the season) lasts about four months. The range of temperatures in the Illinois country on the Réaumur scale[42] ranged from negative ten to negative twelve in winter (approximately ten degrees Fahrenheit) to twenty-five to thirty (near one hundred degrees Fahrenheit) in summer. The seventeenth question concerned the numbers and names of Native American nations in the area. The response indicates total populations and numbers of warriors for the Osage, Ponca, Missouri, and Sioux, among others. The next question further explores the subject of Native Americans by asking if the government provides gifts to the leaders of the nations. The response indicates that the practice initiated by the French in the early eighteenth century continued under Spain.[43]

Fur trade is addressed in question nineteen, with the tabulation of different types of furs and skins making up the response.[44] Communication with Canada by mail, through Philadelphia, according to question twenty-one, occurs every two to three months, depending on the season.[45] In a question that relates to number eleven (equipping an expedition) the time of travel on the Mississippi for such a group is estimated for different times of the year, with the advice being given that summer travel might be prolonged due to the seasonal illnesses on the river.

Laussat's very detailed report to Minister of the Navy and Colonies, Denis Decrès, drafted April 15, 1803, on the expenses needed to conduct an Upper Louisiana (i.e., le pays Illinois) expedition, could hardly have been as minutely detailed as it is without his having information provided by respondents to the questionnaire, a circumstance that suggest the document was circulated earlier in his administration rather than later. Underscoring, perhaps, an interest in furthering his network of contacts, question twenty-five posed in Laussat's query asked who the principal landowners in Upper

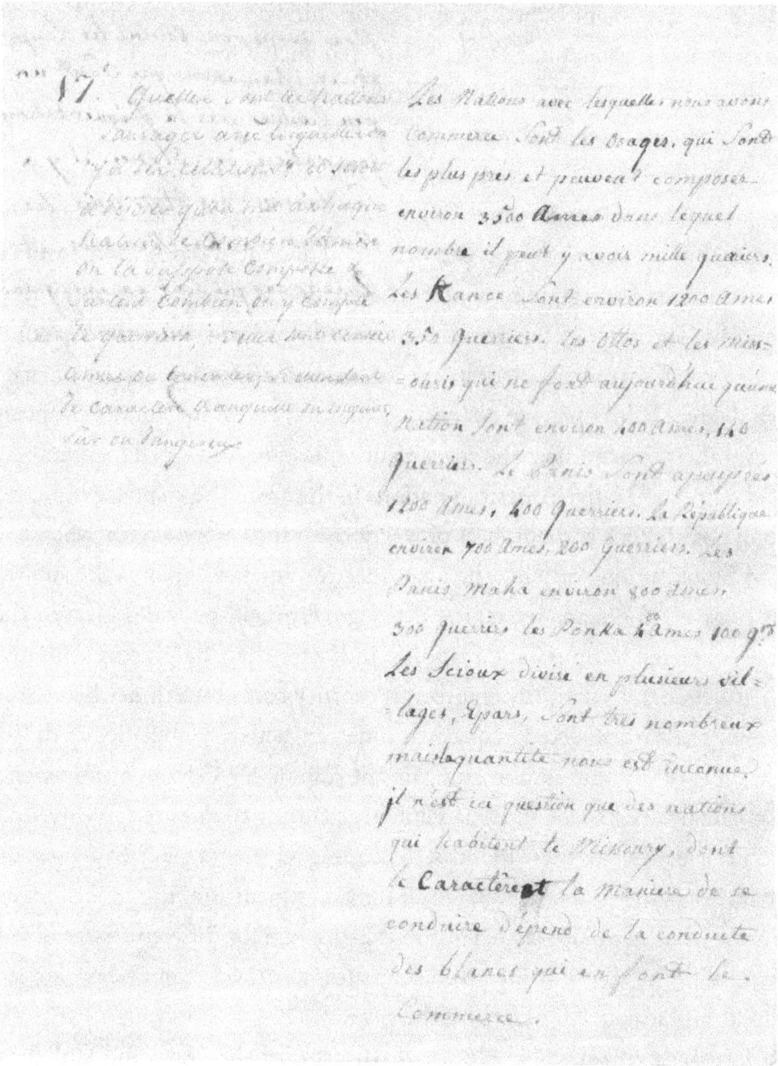

No 17.

Les Nations avec lesquelles nous avons commerce sont les Osages, qui sont les plus près et peuvent composer environ 3500 Ames dans lequel nombre il peut y avoir mille guerriers. Les Kance sont environ 1200 Ames 350 guerriers. les Ottos et les Missouris qui ne font aujourd'hui qu'une nation sont environ 400 Ames, 140 guerriers. Le Panis sont à peu près 1200 Ames, 400 guerriers. La République environ 700 Ames, 200 guerriers. Les Panis Maha environ 800 Ames, 300 guerriers les Ponka 400 Ames 100 grs Les Scioux divisé en plusieurs villages, épars, sont très nombreux mais la quantité nous est inconnue. il n'est ici question que des nations qui habitent le Missoury, dont le Caractère et la manière de se conduire dépend de la conduite des blancs qui en font le commerce.

FIG. 22. *Questionnaire about the Illinois Region,* [1803], manuscript, by an unknown compiler. This is question seventeen of twenty-six contained in the document, seeking information about Native American groups in Louisiana. In the first page of two, the respondent records the names of the groups (Osage, Ponca, and Sioux, for example) and estimates the overall population of each and the number of warriors. Courtesy of the Historic New Orleans Collection, Pierre-Clément de Laussat Papers, MSS 125.417.

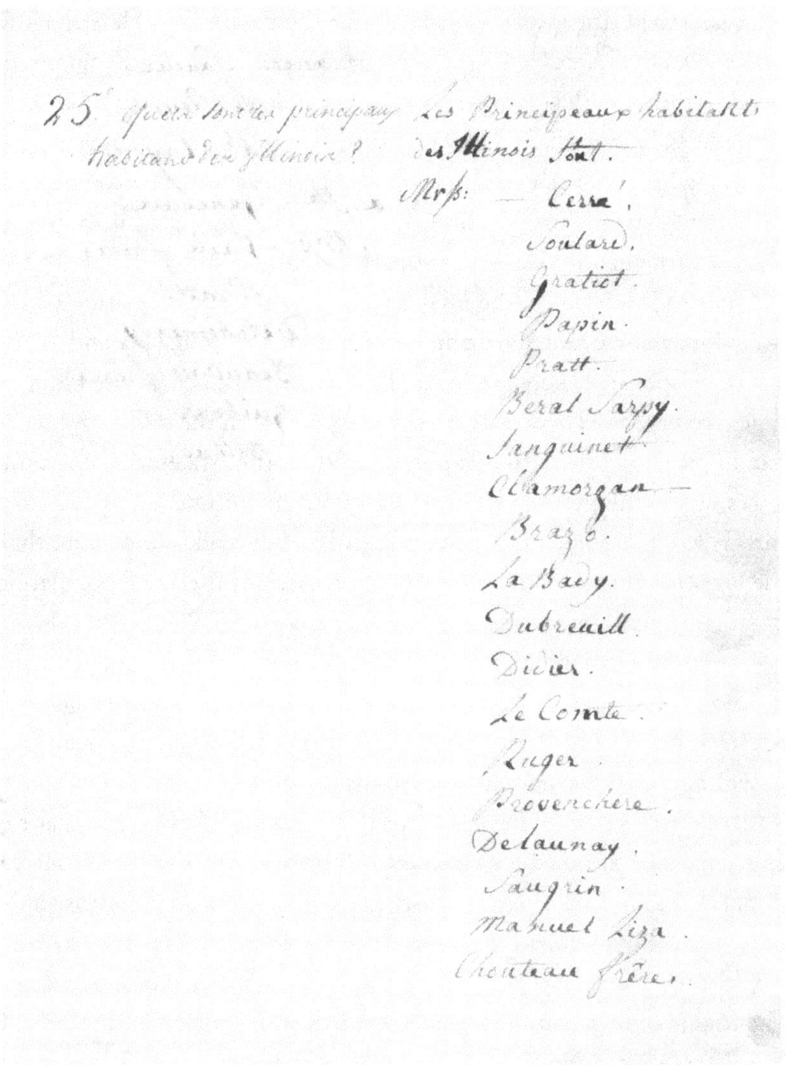

25 quels sont les principaux   Les Principeaux habitants
habitans des Illinois?   des Illinois sont.

                     Mrs: — Cerré.
                              Soulard.
                              Gratiot.
                              Papin.
                              Pratt.
                              Beral Sarpy.
                              Sanguinet.
                              Clamorgan —
                              Brazo.
                              La Bady.
                              Dubreuill.
                              Didier.
                              Le Comte.
                              Luger.
                              Provenchere.
                              Delaunay.
                              Saugrin.
                              Manuel Liza.
                              Chouteau frère.

FIG. 23. *Questionnaire about the Illinois Region*, [1803], manuscript, by an unknown compiler. This is question twenty-five of twenty-six contained in the document, seeking information about the principal families of the Illinois Country that is Upper Louisiana. In the first of two pages, shown here, the respondent recorded the names of twenty-nine individuals, including members of the Vallé and Chouteau families. Courtesy of the Historic New Orleans Collection, Pierre-Clément de Laussat Papers, MSS 125.417.

Louisiana were. The response reads: "In the Illinois are: Mr./Messrs.: [Jean Gabriel] Cerré, [Antoine Pierre] Soulard, [Charles]Gratiot, Papin, Pratt, Beral Sarpy, [Charles] Sanguinet,[Jacques] Clamorgan, Brazo, La Bady [Labadie?], Dubreuill, Didier, Le Comte, Ruger [Rutgers], Provenchère, Delaunay, Saugrin, Manuel Liza [sic], Chouteau brothers, François Saucier, Le Sieur, Charles Tayon. In St. Geneviève: Mr./Messrs.: Vallé brothers, Pratt, Detchemendy, Beauvais brothers, [Louis] Bolduc."

Question twenty-six, the final one, inquired about the nature of the skilled workforce and slave population in Upper Louisiana and elicits a short response: "There are in the Illinois no workmen of any kind, all types are needed. There are very few Negroes given the difficulties we've had in procuring them to this point." Of this latter statement: if Amoureux's observation on the effect of slaves on agricultural enterprise cited earlier was widespread rather than singular, then philosophy more than the logistics of procurement might be a reason for the small population of enslaved Africans.

The so-far anonymous identity of the respondent(s) to the questionnaire is a puzzle.[46] The detailed information in both Chouteau's and Amoureux's letters appears to be in different hands from each other, and from that providing the responses to the questions.

This document with its numerous questions and detailed responses is emblematic of the need for knowledge of geography, customs, resources, populations, and the financial costs needed to make an enterprise supported at the highest level of government viable. Answers to its questions would aid any central government or local administration in strategic and financial planning, and the verbal, rounded, and intellectual character of the information could augment or supplant the sparse and often speculative cartographic data that existed about Louisiana's central, northern, and western regions. Accurately detailed maps of anything west of Mississippi's course were yet to be published in this era, and knowledge of the region was often based on maps many decades old, or which existed only in manuscript form.[47] The commonly held assumptions of a water route to the Pacific—a northwest passage—as well as the myth of a great mountain of salt west of the Mississippi had yet to be disproved.[48] Had Laussat had the luxury of more time in office, things might have been different. The detailed information he sought from corners of the realm he had not visited were a start. Who knows what intelligence more time, more questionnaires, more contacts and reports could have produced?

A great unknown of the Louisiana colony was its western reaches: its geographical features, its natural bounty of animals and minerals, and the character of its non-European populations. That the United States almost immediately launched expeditions to the west and northwest to answer such questions following acquisition of Louisiana underscores just how sorely needed such information was in terms of national policy as well as scientific inquiry.[49] A report that Laussat might have produced had his vision for Louisiana held would be published nearly a decade after his departure. *Sketches Historical and Descriptive of Louisiana* (1812) was compiled by Amos Stoddard, United States commandant at St. Louis following a January 1804 ceremony in Upper Louisiana that transferred possession to the United States.[50] But whatever use to which Laussat would have put the information in these three documents will remain speculative. The French government had changed its mind about Louisiana.

Laussat's role as prefect reached its apex on November 30, 1803, when Spanish authorities formally transferred the governance of Louisiana to him.[51] As French authority in the colony, he dissolved the Spanish governing council and formed his own; he accepted the archives transferred by Spain as well as official buildings and watercraft; he appointed a collector of customs; made provisions for public safety; and executed or put into motion the myriad details of governmental machinery that would be necessary for a French colonial post. Twenty days later, in a parallel transaction, Laussat signed Louisiana over to the American commissioners, William C. C. Claiborne and James J. Wilkinson. All of these actions—in letters, decrees, drafts, and proclamations—are accounted for in the Laussat Papers. On April 21, 1804, just over a year after his arrival in Louisiana and his official duties there completed, Laussat boarded a ship for his next post in Martinique.[52]

Laussat's outsized importance in the closing days of French Louisiana is a matter of circumstance rather than planning. Remember, it was his role not to be the governor himself but to prepare Louisiana for a military governor who never arrived. The revolution in St. Domingue and the creation of Haiti saw to that. Another circumstance was the timing of his arrival in the colony. Louisiana had not yet been formally transferred from Spain to France, and Laussat's ability to effect immediate change was hampered by practical concerns and diplomatic protocols. He had neither official levers of power to manipulate, nor a military force to project his authority. He had been in Louisiana less than six weeks before his government sold Louisiana—scuttling the imperative of his mission—to the United States.

The capstone of Laussat's official duties as colonial prefect are perhaps embodied in a letter sent to him by William C. C. Claiborne and James Wilkinson, United States commissioners for the transfer of Louisiana, dated January 16, 1804. Claiborne and Wilkinson refer to the five letters from His Most Catholic Majesty (Charles IV of Spain) that Laussat had directed to the Spanish commandants in Upper Louisiana along with five from Laussat himself to the commanders at the posts of St. Louis, New Madrid, Ste. Genevieve, New Bourbon (south of Ste. Genevieve), and Cape Girardeau. Additional letters to Captain Amos Stoddard of the United States, and also to "Peter" Chouteau, merchant at St. Louis, are referenced as well. All of these letters addressed the change of possession of Louisiana from France to the United States.[53] With this action and its consequences, Laussat's official need to communicate with the leaders and citizens of Upper Louisiana came to an end, and his future posts in Martinique, Antwerp, and Guiana left him far from the place that France had hoped would be part of another North American empire.

Laussat's memoirs give a vision for Louisiana in all of its vastness and promise that, although fulfilled in time, was never realized in his brief administrative tenure. After learning in a communication received on August 18, 1803, of Louisiana's cession to the United States, the rumors that had been circulating among the population—and at which he initially scoffed—were finally confirmed. Another rumor, that he would be appointed France's minister to the United States, proved to be just a rumor.

In his *Memoirs*, Laussat writes poignantly and not without some bitterness of his time in Louisiana:

Personally, I had hoped to spend six or eight years in an administration that would have at least doubled the population and agriculture of the country, and tripled or quadrupled its trade, thus leaving behind a lasting and honorable memorial. . . . All that is vanished, leaving me only the regret of a year of idleness, of a useless migration by my family to the New World, and of many expenses, troubles, and fruitless inconveniences.[54]

Laussat's quest for information about all of Louisiana, and not just its capital city, underscored a strategic vision that he promoted for the colony. His papers are an invaluable window into the imperial context in which St. Louis took shape, and the processes by which imperialists tried—with various degrees of success and failure—to guide the early city. Laussat never saw the fulfillment of the promise for Louisiana—Lower or Upper—that he envisioned, promoted, and believed in. Perhaps his regret would vanish if he were to visit St. Louis today.

NOTES

I am most grateful to my colleague Howard Margot not only for applying his knowledge of the language anomalies of the French of this era, but also for his patience and diligence in making sense of these documents, both in transcription and translation, so that they may be referenced in this essay.

1. The larger story of Laussat's diplomatic background is given in Laussat, *Mémoires sur ma vie*. For an edited translation focusing on Laussat's time in Louisiana see Pastwa, *Memoirs of my Life*.

2. France's initial claim to Louisiana (essentially the drainage of the Mississippi River system) was made by René-Robert Cavalier, Sieur de La Salle in 1682. The 1697 Treaty of Ryswick ended the Nine Years War and validated the French claim to Louisiana in European eyes, and opened the possibility of colonization. This process began in earnest at the start of the eighteenth century, along the Gulf Coast in present Alabama and Mississippi. New Orleans was established in 1718 and became the capital in 1722. With the French loss of Louisiana in the Seven Years War concluded in 1763 (the colony had been placed in the protective custody of Bourbon-ruled Spain the year before), the portion of Louisiana east of the Mississippi was subsumed into the British colonies in North America. The Mississippi River became Louisiana's new eastern boundary, and the settlement of St. Louis, situated at the confluence of the Mississippi and Missouri Rivers, became the key location for controlling Upper Louisiana.

3. Part of the French plan for reestablishing control over St. Domingue was to have a newly reacquired Louisiana serve as a provisioning colony for the sugar-producing giant. For an overview on the connection between the Haitian Revolution and Louisiana, see Powell, *Accidental City*, 317–19.

4. See Kukla, *Guide*. Laussat's journals, personal papers from his Louisiana sojourn, and related documents have been housed at The Historic New Orleans Collection since 1975. References to specific Laussat documents are based on this work. *Guide* will enable the reader to identify individual original documents in the Pierre-Clément de Laussat Papers.

5. Adams-Onis Treaty or Transcontinental Treaty of 1819, Article 3, as published in Rodriguez, *Encyclopedia*, 442.

6. The German Coast acquired its name early in the French settlement of the lower Mississippi because, beginning in the early 1720s, it was populated with settlers from German-speaking regions of Europe.

7. These settlements had all been established in the eighteenth century: St. Louis (1764); Ste. Genevieve (1735); New Madrid (1789), and Cape Girardeau (1793).

8. Rodriguez, *Encyclopedia*, 345. See the entry on Claude Perrin Victor, for a summary of his intended duties in Louisiana.

9. By the time Laussat left Louisiana in early 1804, Haiti, the new nation born from the French colony of St. Domingue in western Hispaniola, had declared its independence.

10. Planter Jean Noël Destrehan (1754–1823) and Julien Poydras (1746–1824) were wealthy and influential Louisiana residents in the closing years of colonial rule and during the territorial and early statehood period. Both served on the convention to draft Louisiana's first state constitution (1811). Poydras was the convention's chair.

11. See Pitot, "Observations," THNOC. An English translation, Pitot, *Observations*, is available. Pierre-Clément de Laussat Papers, THNOC, MSS 125.424 is a document compiled by James C. Pitot with information specifically supplied by Joseph Xavier de Pontalba (1754–1834). It delineates the character and quantities of exports from the Mississippi Valley through New Orleans. Pitot (1761–1831) was a French-born businessman, politician, jurist, and mayor of New Orleans (1804–5).

12. Berquin-Duvallon, *Colonie espagnole*.

13. Bernard Xavier Philippe de Marigny de Mandeville (1785–1868) lived on a large plantation just downriver from today's French Quarter. Marigny offered his home for Laussat's use while he, Marigny, was away. Pastwa, *Memoirs*, 17.

14. Pierre-Clément de Laussat Papers, THNOC, MSS 125.449 In this document, Laussat lists the Spanish commandants of several posts in Upper Louisiana, including Francois Vallé, Louis Lorimier, Charles and Pierre Dehault Delassus and Pierre Lavallé. It is possible that some of these could have provided the information in Laussat's questionnaire pertaining to the Illinois country.

15. Pierre-Clément de Laussat Papers, THNOC, MSS 125.417.

16. Pierre-Clément de Laussat Papers, THNOC, MSS 125.415. Like the document describing the Illinois Country, those providing answers to questions about the Attakapas and Opelousas posts are anonymously done. But a description of the Attakapas Post by Phelippe [sic] Duffoslange is among the Laussat Papers.

17. Pierre-Clément de Laussat Papers, THNOC, MSS 125.410, MSS 125.413, MSS 125.414, MSS 125.415, MSS 125.416, MSS 125.418, MSS 125.419, MSS 125.421, and MSS 125.425.

18. Francisco Bouligny's (1736—1800) *memoria* of 1776 is a wide-ranging assessment of Louisiana's character at the onset of Spanish governance. See Din, *Memoria*. Jefferson's solicitation of advice from respected members of the Lower Mississippi Valley (e.g., William Dunbar of Natchez) is already happening before the end of the eighteenth century. See http://jeffersonswest.unl.edu/archive/view_doc.php?id=jef.00131, accessed February 13, 2018. I am grateful to Peter J. Kastor, coeditor of this volume, in directing me to the questionnaires prepared by Jefferson in the course of determining information about Louisiana.

19. Laussat's writing, especially his official correspondence, uses the French Republican calendar that organized the years into ten temporal units rather than the standard twelve months of approximately thirty days each. For the modern reader, the dates are given in the Gregorian calendar.

20. Jean Pierre Chouteau (1758–1849), usually called Pierre, was the younger half-brother of Rene Auguste Chouteau (1749?–1825) usually referred to as Auguste. The latter, with his foster father Pierre Laclède Liguest, founded St. Louis in 1764.

21. Another possible source of intelligence regarding Upper Louisiana for Laussat would have been the descendants of François Vallé (1716–83), especially his son François Vallé II (1758–1804) operating from Ste. Genevieve with an extensive network of economic and political influence. For more on this topic, see Ekberg, *François Vallé*, 149, 248.

22. Pierre-Clément de Laussat Papers, THNOC, MSS 125.204.

23. Pastwa, *Memoirs*, 22.

24. For those interested in specific French terms of the period, a useful resource is Edwards Kariouk *Creole Lexicon*.

25. The St. Pierre, or Minnesota River, is a tributary of the Mississippi. Its headwaters are in southwestern Minnesota near the South Dakota border and Big Stone Lake. It flows southeast to Mankato, then northeast where it enters the Mississippi near Minneapolis and St. Paul.

26. For a discussion of Spanish administration in Upper Louisiana at the close of the eighteenth century, see Din, "Empires Too Far," 261–92.

27. Pierre Laclède Liguest was one of the founders of St. Louis in 1764, at the start of Spain's governance of Louisiana; Galvez was Spanish Governor of Louisiana during the American Revolution.

28. The author has been unable to locate the report that Chouteau mentions here. Laclède did apparently ship a quantity of hemp (15 quintals or about 1500 pounds) to New Orleans in 1775, during Governor Bernardo de Galvez's administration of Louisiana, drawing considerable interest in the prospect of mass cultivation. But the (slave) labor requirements, whether from using Native Americans or importing enslaved Africans to Upper Louisiana, were too difficult to meet. A brief discussion of this proposal appears in Primm, *Lion of the Valley*, 28.

29. See Pitot, *Observations*, 165–80 for a schedule of tariffs of 1796 imposed by Spain following the 1795 Treaty of San Lorenzo. In addition to hemp, import duties on a number of other items mentioned by Chouteau are on the schedule of tariffs, including beef, cured buffalo, ham, and salt pork (meat), flour (from "Kentucky and the Ohio country"), and iron.

30. It is not clear from Chouteau's context if he is describing the American-side buildup as what he can observe directly from his location on the west bank of the Mississippi or imparting information received about activity beyond that. The east bank of the river would have seen increased activity a few months after this letter was sent as a result of the Corps of Discovery expedition gearing up. Chouteau believes that the Americans are planning to build a fort opposite Portage des Sioux on the west bank, but there is no evidence that this was ever accomplished.

31. Chouteau's praise for the Americans must have grated on Laussat, who never really seemed to get along with that population in New Orleans. Sister Agnes-Josephine Pastwa suggests that this diplomatic shortcoming of Laussat's may have been why he never replaced Louis André Pichon as the French minister to the United States. Pastwa, *Memoirs*, 129–30, n32, n35.

32. There are a number of documents in the Laussat Papers that address Native Americans throughout the Louisiana colony. See, for example, Pierre-Clément de Laussat Papers, THNOC, MSS 125.42, .47, .418, .419.

33. Michel Amoureux of France (1748?–1832), was a landowner and judge in Upper Louisiana at the beginning of the nineteenth century. See Jackson, *Letters*, 413. A note briefly describes Michel Amoureux who fled revolutionary France to the United States and made his way to the Louisiana Territory in 1803, settling in New Madrid. He later moved to Ste. Genevieve.

34. Amoureux doesn't provide the source of this announcement, which may have been a rumor or wishful thinking.

35. Pierre-Clément de Laussat Papers, THNOC, MSS 125.234.

36. It is interesting to think about how New Madrid would have developed had Louisiana remained French. With the acquisition by the United States, St. Louis would take on greater importance in the early territorial period as the mobilizing point for the Lewis and Clark expedition along the Missouri River, and others that emanated from or near that point.

37. Note the difference between this sentiment, and that of planters in Lower Louisiana, who urged Laussat to embrace and expand slavery unreservedly. See, for example, Faber, "Passion of the Prefect," 268–69. African slavery, though not unknown in Upper Louisiana was not the basis for the agricultural economy that it was in the lower valley. When Laussat finally gets official authority at the end of November 1803, he bends to the will of the planter class centered around New Orleans by reinstituting Louisiana's Code Noir of 1724 on December 17, just three days prior to transferring Louisiana to the United States commissioners. Pastwa, *Memoirs*, 87; Pierre-Clément de Laussat Papers, THNOC, MSS 125.379.

38. Henri Peyroux de la Coudrenière (1743–18??) was an important official in Spanish Louisiana whose career was beset by missteps and minor scandals. He arrived in 1784, accompanying a group of Acadians who were settling in the colony. He was appointed commandant of Ste. Genevieve in 1787, and served in that capacity until 1793. Peyroux also served as commandant of New Madrid by appointment of Gayoso de Lemos, serving until 1803. Nasatir, *Before Lewis and Clark*, 598, n.5.

39. Amoureux died in Ste. Genevieve in 1832. His wife Perine Janvier Amoureux died in 1845 and is buried in Memorial Cemetery in Ste. Genevieve.

40. Pierre-Clément de Laussat Papers, THNOC, MSS 125.417.

41. The left (eastern) bank of the Mississippi River was for most of the river's length the dividing line between French Louisiana and the United States. This condition changed as the river approached New Orleans. By treaties, the "Isle d'Orleans" (New Orleans and its immediate area), though on the east bank of the Mississippi, was part of French Louisiana.

42. This scale was established in 1730 by the French naturalist René-Antoine Ferchault de Réaumur (1683–1757). The scale set the freezing point of water at zero and the boiling point at eighty.

43. Pierre-Clément de Laussat Papers, THNOC, MSS 125.42, .47, .151, .409, .419.

44. The respondent to this question lists quantities of furs and hides from the Missouri trade. Deerskins (eighty thousand) are ten times greater than the next type: beaver pelts (eight thousand). Bearskins and wildcat hides are each reported at two thousand. Otters are at five hundred. Pitot, *Observations*, 68. Pitot notes that under Spain, the fur trade was not enlarged, but only maintained as a way for military commanders in Upper Louisiana to enrich themselves. Pitot, *Observations*, 165–80. The activity of the fur trade is indicated in the list of tariffs. Among the identified dutiable products are "sheepskin, dressed; calfskin; tanned leathers; rawhides." Other furs are not specifically mentioned as peltry, though some are mentioned as finished goods. The respondent to the questionnaire may be hinting that under France, this economic component of the colony could be more fully exploited.

45. The need for communication to Canada was likely influenced by both commercial and familial connections between St. Louis and other settlements in Upper Louisiana and the former New France. New Orleans and Lower Louisiana exhibited more ties and direct communication with French colonies in the Caribbean, especially St. Domingue. Laussat notes this in his journal. Pastwa, *Memoirs*, 55.

46. The completed questionnaire could be the work of a single individual or a collaboration. Laussat's journal is silent on the subject. It is possible that Nicolas de Finiels authored or contributed responses to the questions, as he provided Laussat with a detailed account of Upper Louisiana in 1803. This manuscript is now housed in the Louisa H. Bowen University Archives and Special Collections at Southern Illinois University Edwardsville. For a translation of this document, see Ekberg and Foley, *Account of Upper Louisiana*. Additional plausible respondents to the questionnaire suggested to this author include Antoine Pierre Soulard, King's Surveyor of Upper Louisiana and/or Lieutenant Governor Charles Dehault Delassus.

47. For example, the map of Louisiana accompanying Antoine-Simone Le Page du Pratz's *Histoire de la Louisiane* (1763) and the map of Baron de Lahontan (1703) showing the fictional "Riviere Longue" as part of the presumed Northwest Passage. Manuscript maps often provided detailed and current information to a smaller audience than printed maps. For example, Laussat commissioned

a very accurate map of the region from surveyor-engineer Nicolas de Finiels, now housed in the map division of the Services Historique de la Marine, in the Chateau des Vincennes on the eastern outskirts of Paris. Though the focus of this map is the central valley of the Mississippi River, it does show a small section of the Missouri. In another example, a manuscript map of the Missouri River prepared by James Mackay and used by Lewis and Clark on their trek to the Pacific Ocean, beginning in 1804, is an extremely detailed item. The original is in the Library of Congress. A discussion of Mackay and this map may be found in Danisi and Wood "Lewis and Clark's Route Map," 53–72.

48. The importance of geographic ignorance in eighteenth century North America, and how it affected the planning and decision-making of the French for western Louisiana is addressed in Mapp, *Elusive West*, 148, 149, 361.

49. Within months of the Louisiana Purchase the Lewis and Clark Expedition from St. Louis along the Missouri River and to the Pacific Ocean began (1804–6). Three other expeditions: Hunter-Dunbar on the Ouachita River (1804–5); Custis-Freeman, or Red River Expedition, (1806); and Pike (1806–7) reconnoitered other western reaches of the Louisiana Purchase territory. Lewis and Clark and Pike began their expeditions from or near St. Louis.

50. Stoddard, *Sketches*.

51. Pierre-Clément de Laussat Papers, THNOC, MSS 125.321. The procès-verbal transferring Louisiana to France under the terms of the Treaty of San Ildefonso (1800) was signed by Manuel de Salcedo, el marqués de Casa Calvo and Andrés López Armesto for Spain, and Laussat and Joseph Daugerot for France.

52. Pastwa, *Memoirs*, 106. Laussat traveled on the ship *Natchez*, under the alias of Pierre Lanthois, in the event the *Natchez* was seized by the British—at war with France—on its way to Martinique.

53. See note 14 for the listing of these officials.

54. Pastwa, *Memoirs*, 56–57.

BIBLIOGRAPHY

Archives

THNOC. The Pierre-Clément de Laussat Papers, MSS 125. The Historic New Orleans Collection, New Orleans LA. Public Permalink: http://hnoc.minisisinc.com/thnoc/catalog/3/121.

THNOC. Report by James C. Pitot, "Observations sur la Colonie de la Louisiane de 1796 à 1802" 75–251-L.1. The Historic New Orleans Collection, New Orleans LA. Public Permalink: http://hnoc.minisisinc.com/thnoc/catalog/3/411.

Published Works

Berquin-Duvallon, Pierre-Louis, ed. *Vue de la colonie espagnole du Mississipi: ou des provinces de Louisiane el Floride Occidentale* . . . Paris: Imprimerie expeditive, 1803.

Center for Digital Research in the Humanities. "Letter from Thomas Jefferson to William Dunbar," *Envisaging the West: Thomas Jefferson and the Roots of Lewis and Clark*. Accessed February 13, 2018. http://jeffersonswest.unl.edu/archive /view_doc.php?id=jef.00131.

Danisi, Thomas C., and W. Raymond Wood. "Lewis and Clark's Route Map: James MacKay's Map of the Missouri River." *Western Historical Quarterly* 35, no. 1 (Spring 2004): 53–72.

Din, Gilbert C. "Empires Too Far: The Demographic Limitations of Three Imperial Powers in the Eighteenth-Century Mississippi Valley." *Louisiana History: Journal of the Louisiana Historical Association* 50, no. 3 (Summer 2009): 261–92. Accessed: February 13, 2018. http://www.jstor.org/stable/40646271.

———, ed., trans. *Louisiana in 1776: a Memoria of Francisco Bouligny*. New Orleans: [J. D. L. Holmes ?], 1977.

Edwards, Jay Dearborn, and Nicolas Kariouk Pequet du Bellay de Verton, *A Creole Lexicon*. Baton Rouge: Louisiana State University Press, 2004.

Ekberg, Carl J. *François Vallé and His World: Upper Louisiana before Lewis and Clark*. Columbia: University of Missouri Press, 2002.

Ekberg, Carl J., and William E. Foley. *An Account of Upper Louisiana*. Columbia: University of Missouri Press, 1989.

Faber, Eberhard L. *Building the Land of Dreams: New Orleans and the Transformation of Early America*. Princeton: Princeton University Press, 2015.

———. "The Passion of the Prefect: Pierre Clément De Laussat, 1803 New Orleans, and the Bonapartist Louisiana That Never Was." *Louisiana History: Journal of the Louisiana Historical Association* 54, no. 3 (2013): 261–91. http://www.jstor .org/stable/24396395.

Jackson, Donald, ed. *Letters of the Lewis and Clark Expedition*. 2nd ed. Urbana: University of Illinois Press, 1978.

Kastor, Peter J. *The Nation's Crucible: The Louisiana Purchase and the Creation of America*. New Haven CT: Yale University Press, 2004.

Kukla, Jon. *A Wilderness So Immense: The Louisiana Purchase and the Destiny of America*. University Park PA: Penn State University Press, 2003.

———, ed. *A Guide to the Papers of Pierre Clément Laussat*. New Orleans: Historic New Orleans Collection, 1993.

Laussat, Pierre-Clément de. *Mémoires sur ma vie: a mon fils, pendant les années 1803 et suivantes* . . . Pau: É. Vignancour, 1831.

Mapp, Paul. *The Elusive West and the Contest for Empire: 1713–1763*. Chapel Hill: University of North Carolina Press, for Omohundro Institute for Early American History and Culture, 2011.

Nasatir, A. P., ed. *Before Lewis and Clark: Documents Illustrating the History of the Missouri, 1785–1804*. Norman: University of Oklahoma Press, 2002.

Pastwa, M. Bernarda, Sister. *Memoirs of My Life*. Baton Rouge: Louisiana State University Press, 1977.

Pitot, James C. *Observations on the Colony of Louisiana from 1796 to 1802*. Baton Rouge: Louisiana State University Press, for the Historic New Orleans Collection, 1979.

Powell, Lawrence N. *The Accidental City, Improvising New Orleans*. Cambridge MA: Harvard University Press, 2012.

Primm, James Neal. *Lion of the Valley: St. Louis, Missouri, 1764–1980*. 3rd ed. St. Louis: Missouri Historical Society Press, 1998.

Rodriguez, Junius P., ed. *The Louisiana Purchase: A Historical and Geographical Encyclopedia* Santa Barbara CA: ABC-CLIO, 2002.

Stoddard, Amos. *Sketches Historical and Descriptive of Louisiana*. Philadelphia: Matthew Carey, 1812.

PART 4

*Maintaining the French
Connection of St. Louis*

9

LOUIS CORTAMBERT AND *L'ESPRIT* FRANÇAIS IN ST. LOUIS IN 1854

ANNE JUNEAU CRAVER

Most scholars and St. Louisans think that the French disappeared from St. Louis after the signing of the Louisiana Purchase in 1803.[1] Nothing could be further from the truth. The French community continued to thrive economically, socially, and culturally for years afterward.[2] Proof of their existence can be seen on the pages of the *Revue de l'Ouest*, the most successful French newspaper in St. Louis, which made its debut on January 7, 1854.

Louis Cortambert, journalist and one of its founders, outlined the role of this newspaper in his opening remarks as editor-in-chief: "The *Revue* . . . only wishes to be inspired by a true French spirit to work, for its part, to broaden its influence on the New World, to rally, if possible, members of the great French family in the West and to advance with them on the road to social progress."[3] No doubt, this "French spirit" for Cortambert was synonymous with the American notion of progress as represented by the West. From his early days as a journalist, Cortambert understood the powerful role that a newspaper could play as "the" source of communication in the development of a community, not just locally but on a national scale.[4]

After a short, biographical introduction on Louis Cortambert, we will examine his philosophy and this "French spirit," which provides insight into the politics and life of the French community in St. Louis in 1854. Finally, a detailed map of St. Louis French businesses, in 1854, who advertised on the last two pages of the *Revue* reveals a broad range of activities,[5] which demonstrate without a doubt that this French community was "alive and well and living in St. Louis at this time."[6]

Louis Richard Cortambert: Journalist, Editor, Freethinker

Louis Richard Cortambert was born on April 23, 1809,[7] in the city of Dompierre-les-Ormes in the province of the Saône-et-Loire (Burgundy Region of France) to Dr. Richard Anne Cortambert, physician, and his wife, Louise Henriette Delaistre. His brother, Eugène Cortambert, was a well-known geographer.

Cortambert came to the United States in the 1830s as a young man and after extensive travel, decided to make St. Louis his home in 1840. No doubt a certain young woman, Susanne Chouteau,[8] who would become his wife, influenced his decision. Susanne was the daughter of Auguste-Pierre Chouteau and Sophie Labbadie.[9]

In 1841 Louis married Susanne, and with this union[10] instantly became a member of the founding family of St. Louis—very conservative and Catholic.[11] Louis became French vice-consul but, in 1851, in one of his first acts as a rebel, resigned in protest against the coup d'état staged by Louis-Napoleon, who reclaimed his uncle's throne as emperor of France, giving himself the title of Napoleon III.

On December 16, 1852, Cortambert's brother-in-law Dr. Nicolas DeMenil[12] introduced an "Act to Incorporate" in the Missouri legislature in order to establish a business under the name of "La Société Littéraire de St. Louis" or "The French Literary Company of St. Louis."[13] This act, which took effect on February 22, 1853, provided the necessary capital for the publication of a St. Louis newspaper in French, *La Revue de l'Ouest*.[14] Cortambert, who is named in the act as one of the members of "The French Literary Company,"[15] contributed articles from the very beginning and became the editor-in-chief of *La Revue de l'Ouest* on February 11, 1854.

Thanks to Alexander DeMenil, Dr. DeMenil's son, we have the following personal description of Cortambert: "I remember him from my boyhood as a tall, ordinarily built, solemn, dignified man [. . .] generally dressed in black. He always seemed to be in a meditative mood, even while on the streets. He was a handsome man, but his solemnity repelled in spite of his courteousness."[16]

According to DeMenil, Louis Cortambert's philosophy was much like Thoreau's: "He even undertook to duplicate Thoreau's Walden experience,

FIG. 24. Louis Cortambert, 1809–81. Courtesy of John F. McDermott V.

but Walden near Highland, Illionois, was a thing very different than Walden near Concord, and the malaria of the Illinois Bottoms soon ended the experiment."[17] DeMenil went on to describe Cortambert as an early abolitionist, whose "pen was not for sale."[18] As a humanist, he advocated for the "fraternité de l'homme" or "the brotherhood of man."

In 1864, a year before the end of the Civil War, Louis Cortambert is found living in Bloomfield, New Jersey, with a new wife, Melanie Racine, and a son, Louis Cortambert Jr.[19] He is now editor-in-chief of the *Messager Franco-Américain*, another French newspaper, published in New York City. He died on March 28, 1881, at the age of seventy-two, at his home in Bloomfield, New Jersey.

It should also be noted that Cortambert was a prolific writer and gave many lectures in French throughout the United States and Canada. Among his many works, the most important are *Voyage au Pays des Osages* (a firsthand account of his life among the Osage Indians), published in Paris in 1837,[20] and *Histoire de la Guerre Civile Américaine* (Paris, 1867) co-written with Mr. de Tranaltos, publisher of the *Messager Franco-Américain* (1860–83).[21]

Revue de l'Ouest: Success at Last!

On Saturday, January 7, 1854, when the *Revue de l'Ouest* or *Review of the West* appeared for the first time, the city of St. Louis had around 78,000 inhabitants.[22] Thanks to the invention of the steamboat and telegraph, the newspaper boasts on its first page that it will be able to give "news of Europe several days before the French newspapers of New York."[23] A yearly subscription cost two dollars and fifty cents.

The first page is the editorial page, and at the top of the second column we find a prediction for the city of St. Louis: "The French population is still small in the West. We are therefore obliged to begin at a modest pace. But since the city of St. Louis is evidently destined to become at the end of a few years a tremendous city, one of the first, if not the first center of business in the United States, it is likely that the French population will have at least the same growth as in New York."[24]

Next, *la Revue* speaks directly to the French population of St. Louis,[25] who are still worried simultaneously about the political situation in France (the despotic regime of Louis Napoleon Bonaparte) and the United States (the debate about the Kansas-Nebraska Act and the "Know-Nothing" political party) that threatened to divide the country:[26]

> The goal of this publication is to reunite as much as possible, in the same communion of ideas, sentiments, souvenirs, interests, the French dispersed in the West so far from native soil. A great number will never see it again. . . . The title of American is admittedly a very strong compensation to him. But where is the French man who ever stops feeling his heart beat intensely while remembering his native land?[27]

Although Cortambert, himself a recent arrival from France, may have over-estimated the nostalgia for France felt by the French Creoles in Missouri and the surrounding areas, it is likely that the French community continued to feel that the hyphenated identity of being French and North American was an uneasy one. In spite of the Louisiana Purchase in 1803, the French community continued to exercise economic, political, and cultural influences on the development of St. Louis and its increasing hinterland to the west and north. It is not clear, however, how anxious the local Creoles felt about their nativist neighbors and the various forces arrayed against the maintenance of francophone culture and language.[28]

Nevertheless, gauging the temperature of the local French community was not what Cortambert had in mind for his journalistic mission. He fancied himself a man of ideas.[29] Adjectives such as "radical," "liberal," and "freethinker" describe Cortambert. His philosophy glorified the virtues of "liberté de la pensée," which is exactly the title of his editorial of February 18, 1854.[30] His philosophy reflected the Age of Enlightenment, or Age of Reason, in eighteenth century France: namely, the revolt against the authority of tradition and knowledge through science.

Cortambert was in constant opposition to authority. According to certain critics, he was anti-Catholic.[31] However, in reality, he was against all established religions; instead he promoted *spiritualisme* and defended *socialisme*.[32] Not surprisingly, the old French families of St. Louis, the mercantile elite,

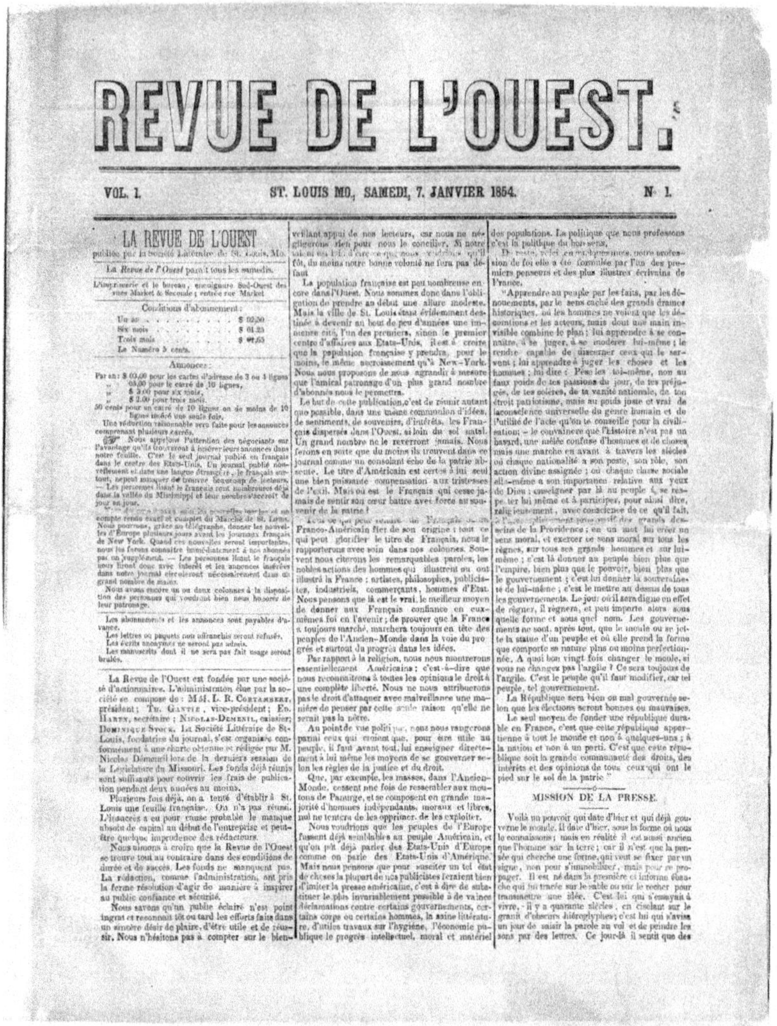

REVUE DE L'OUEST.

VOL. 1. ST. LOUIS MO, SAMEDI, 7 JANVIER 1854. N° 1.

LA REVUE DE L'OUEST

MISSION DE LA PRESSE.

FIG. 25. *Revue de l'Ouest*, January 7, 1854. Front page of the first issue of the *Revue de l'Ouest*. Courtesy of the St. Louis Mercantile Library.

and others were alarmed by his politics. Some readers called his newspaper "Red Republican."[33] In an editorial on March 11, Cortambert tried to calm them: "A republic always militant, that's what you call a red republic. You cry out devoutly, 'Oh! God save us from a Red Republic!' as if your republic didn't have its '76 and wasn't also a red republic!"[34]

According to Cortambert, "There are not two kinds of republics; the only true kind of republic there is and can ever be is a government of freedom and progress."[35] But he tried to further clarify his argument: "But there is the republic at peace as in America and the republic of war as it is in Europe. Here, in America, the republic shines peacefully on the horizon of reason; there, it is veiled by the dark clouds of despotism."[36]

Halfway through the first year of publication, Cortambert who, in his new role of editor, had proclaimed the goal of the *Revue* to be "inspired by a true French spirit" became concerned about the current lack of French influence in America:

> What has become of the French spirit? This is what people are asking with some concern. . . . Everything is not lost, however. It can still be found: on the banks of the St. Lawrence as on those of the Mississippi, it has maintained its gentle and refined style, its expressive agility; there again our language sets itself apart by its careful word choice and quick wit. But in the final analysis the French spirit runs the risk of evaporating over such an extensive [territory].[37]

Even though Cortambert never stopped arguing for an "esprit français" that would maintain a strong "French presence" in St. Louis and nationally, he gradually realized over time that his adopted city of St. Louis was becoming more and more American as time passed. Ironically, Cortambert's success rested not in his strident and thought-provoking editorials, but in his creation of this newspaper that provided a discursive focus or signpost for the French people in St. Louis.

As Benedict Anderson observed, "an imagined community" that is, a socially constructed community imagined by the people who believe that they belong to such a community; could exist in part, because the very act of reading the newspaper has placed them in virtual proximity.[38]

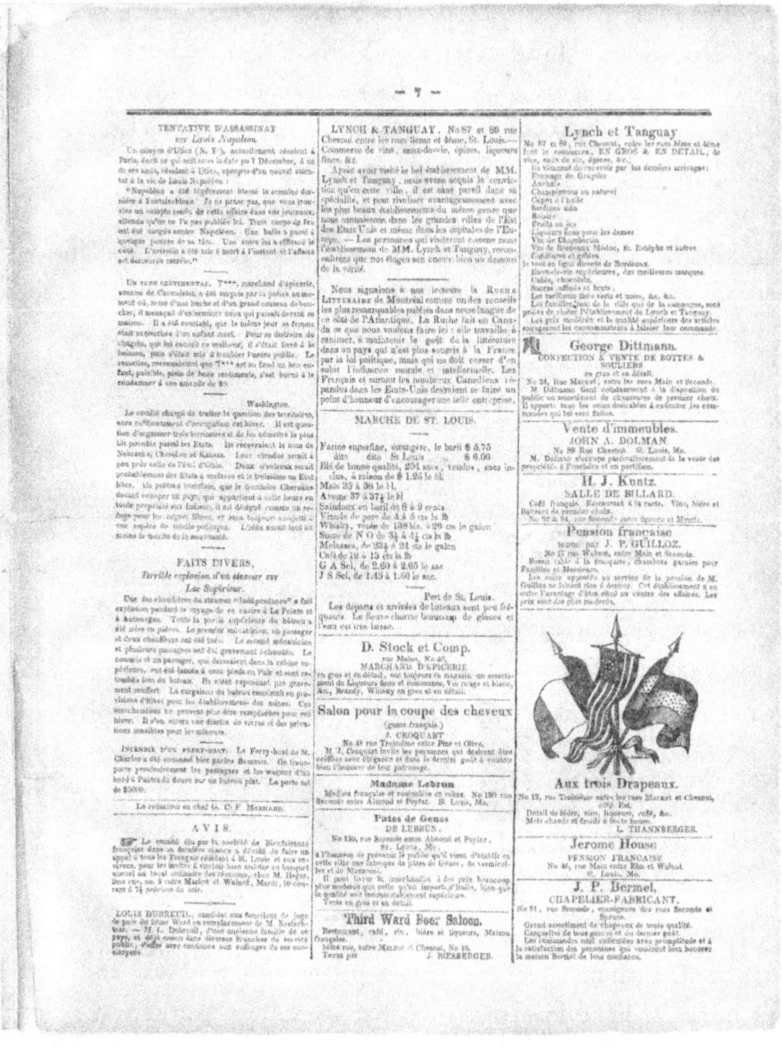

— 7 —

TENTATIVE D'ASSASSINAT
sur Louis Napoleon.

Un citoyen d'Utica (N. Y.), actuellement résident à Paris, écrit ce qui suit sous la date du 7 Décembre, à un de ses amis, résidant à Utica, apropos d'un nouvel attentat à la vie de Louis Napoléon :

"Napoléon a été légèrement blessé la semaine dernière à Fontainebleau. *Je ne pense pas,* que vous trouviez un compte rendu de cette affaire dans vos journaux, attendu qu'on ne l'a pas publiée ici. Trois coups de feu ont été tirés contre Napoléon. Une balle a passé à quelque pouces de sa tête. Une autre lui a effleuré le côté. L'assassin a été mis à mort à l'instant et l'affaire est demeurée secrète."

UN TERM SENTIMENTAL. T***, marchand d'épicerie, avenue de Carondelet, a été surpris par la police au moment où, armé d'une hache et d'un grand couteau de boucher, il menaçait d'exterminer ceux qui passait devant sa maison. Il a été constaté, que le même jour sa femme était accouchée d'un enfant mort. Pour se distraire du chagrin, que lui causait ce malheur, il s'était livré à la boisson, puis s'était mis à troubler l'ordre public. Le recorder, reconnaissant que T*** est au fond un bon enfant, paisible, plein de bons sentiments, s'est borné à le condamner à une amende de $5.

Washington.

Le comité chargé de traiter la question des territoires, aura suffisamment d'occupation cet hiver. Il est question d'organiser trois territoires et de les admettre le plus tôt possible parmi les Etats. Ils recevraient le nom de Nebraska, Cherokee et Kansas. Leur étendue serait à peu près celle de l'état d'Ohio. Deux d'entreeux serait probablement des Etats à esclaves et le troisième un Etat libre. On prétend toutefois, que le territoire Cherokee devant occuper un pays, qui appartient à cette heure en toute propriété aux Indiens, il est désigné comme un refuge pour les nègres libres, et sera toujours assujetti à une espèce de tutelle politique. L'idée aurait tout au moins le mérite de la nouveauté.

FAITS DIVERS.
Terrible explosion d'un steamer sur Lac Supérieur.

Une des chaudières du steamer "Indépendance" a fait explosion pendant le voyage de ce navire à La Pointe et à Autonagan. Toute la partie supérieure du bâteau a été mise en pièces. Le premier mécanicien, un passager et deux chauffeurs ont été tués. Le second mécanicien et plusieurs passagers ont été gravement échaudés. Le commis et un passager, qui dormaient dans la cabine supérieure, ont été lancés à cent pieds en l'air et sont retombés loin du bateau. Ils n'ont cependant pas gravement souffert. La cargaison du bateau consistait en provisions d'hiver pour les établissements des mines. Ces marchandises ne peuvent plus être remplacées pour cet hiver. Il s'en suivra une disette de vivres et des privations sensibles pour les mineurs.

INCENDIE D'UN FERRY-BOAT. Le Ferry-boat de St. Charles a été consumé hier par les flammes. On transporte provisoirement les passagers et les wagons d'un bord à l'autre du fleuve sur un bateau plat. La perte est de $5000.

Le redacteur en chef G. C. F. MORHARD.

AVIS.

☞ Le comité élu par la société de Bienfaisance française dans sa dernière séance a décidé de faire un appel à tous les Français résidant à St. Louis et aux environs, pour les inviter à vouloir bien assister au banquet annuel au local ordinaire des réunions, chez M. Heger, 2me rue, no. 8 entre Market et Walnut, Mardi, 10 courant à 7½ précises du soir.

LOUIS DUBREUIL, candidat aux fonctions de juge de paix du 2ème Ward en remplacement de M. Kretschmar. — M. L. Dubreuil, d'une ancienne famille de ce pays, et déjà connu dans diverses branches du service public, s'offre avec confiance aux suffrages de ses concitoyens.

LYNCH & TANGUAY. No 87 et 89 rue Chesnut entre les rues 3eme et 4ème, St. Louis.— Commerce de vins, eaux-de-vie, épices, liqueurs fines, &c.

Après avoir visité le bel établissement de MM. Lynch et Tanguay, nous avons acquis la conviction qu'en cette ville, il est sans pareil dans sa spécialité, et peut rivaliser avantageusement avec les plus beaux établissements du même genre que nous connaissons dans les grandes villes de l'Est des Etats Unis et même dans les capitales de l'Europe. — Les personnes qui visiteront comme nous l'établissement de MM. Lynch et Tanguay, reconnaîtront que nos éloges sont encore bien au dessous de la vérité.

Nous signalons à nos lecteurs la RUCHE LITTERAIRE de Montréal comme un des recueils les plus remarquables publiés dans notre langue de ce côté de l'Atlantique. La Ruche fait en Canada ce que nous voulons faire ici : elle travaille à ranimer, à maintenir le goût de la littérature dans un pays qui n'est plus soumis à la France par la loi politique, mais qui ne doit cesser d'en subir l'influence morale et intellectuelle. Les Français et surtout les nombreux Canadiens répandus dans les Etats-Unis devraient se faire un point d'honneur d'encourager une telle entreprise.

MARCHE DE ST. LOUIS.

Farine superfine, étrangère, le baril $ 5.75
dito dito St Louis „ $ 6.00
Blé de bonne qualité, 204 sacs, vendus, sacs inclus, à raison de $ 1.25 le bl.
Mais 35 à 36 le bl.
Avoine 37 à 37½ le bl
Saindoux en baril de 8 à 9 cents
Viande de porc de 4 à 5 cts la lb
Whisky, vente de 138 bls. à 29 cts le galon
Sucre de N O de 3¼ à 4¼ cts la lb
Melasses, de 23½ à 24 cts le galon
Café de 12 à 13 cts la lb
G A Sel, de 2.60 à 2.65 le sac
J S Sel, de 1.45 à 1.60 le sac.

Port de St. Louis.

Les départs et arrivées de bateaux sont peu fréquents. Le fleuve charrie beaucoup de glaces et l'eau est très basse.

D. Stock et Comp.
rue Main, No 40,
MARCHANDS D'EPICERIE
en gros et en détail, ont toujours en magasin un assortiment de Liqueurs fines et communes, Vin rouge et blanc, &c., Brandy, Whisky en gros et en détail.

Salon pour la coupe des cheveux
(genre français.)
J. CROQUART
No 48 rue Troisième entre Pine et Olive.
M. J. Croquart invite les personnes qui désirent être coiffées avec élégance et dans le dernier goût à vouloir bien l'honorer de leur patronage.

Madame Lebrun
Modiste française et couturière en robes. No 130 rue Seconde entre Almond et Poplar. St. Louis, Mo.

Pates de Genes
DE LEBRUN.
No 130, rue Seconde entre Almond et Poplar,
St. Louis, Mo.
a l'honneur de prévenir le public qu'il vient d'établir en cette ville une fabrique de pâtes de Gênes, de vermicelles et de Macaroni.
Il peut livrer la marchandise à des prix beaucoup plus moderés que celle qu'on importe d'Italie, bien que la qualité soit incontestablement supérieure.
Vente en gros et en détail.

Third Ward Beer Saloon.
Restaurant, café, vin, bière et liqueurs, Maison française.
3ème rue, entre Market et Chesnut, No 18.
Tenu par J. ROSSBERGER.

Lynch et Tanguay
No 87 et 89, rue Chesnut, entre les rues 3ème et 4ème font le commerce, EN GROS & EN DETAIL, de vins, eaux de vie, épices, &c.
Ils viennent de recevoir par les derniers arrivages :
Fromage de Gruyère
Anchois
Champignons au naturel
Cèpes à l'huile
Sardines dito
Raisins
Fruits au jus
Liqueurs fines pour les dames
Vin de Chambertin
Vin de Bordeaux Médoc, St. Estèphe et autres
Confitures et gelées
le tout en ligne directe de Bordeaux.
Eaux-de-vie supérieures, des meilleures marques.
Cafés, chocolats.
Sucres raffinés et bruts,
Les meilleurs thés verts et noirs, &c. &c.
Les familles, tant de la ville que de la campagne, sont priées de visiter l'établissement de Lynch et Tanguay.
Les prix modérés et la qualité supérieure des articles engageront les consommateurs à laisser leur commande.

George Dittmann.
CONFECTION & VENTE DE BOTTES & SOULIERS
en gros et en détail.
No 24, Rue Market, entre les rues Main et Seconde.
M. Dittmann tient constamment à la disposition du public un assortiment de chaussures de premier choix. Il apporte tous les soins desirables à exécuter les commandes qui lui sont faites.

Vente d'immeubles.
JOHN A. DOLMAN.
No 89 Rue Chesnut. St. Louis, Mo.
M. Dolman s'occupe particulièrement de la vente des propriétés à l'enchère et en partition.

H. J. Kuntz.
SALLE DE BILLARD.
Café français. Restaurant à la carte. Vins, bière et liqueurs de premier choix.
No 92 & 94, rue Seconde entre Spruce et Myrtle.

Pension française
tenue par J. P. GUILLOZ.
No 17 rue Walnut, entre Main et Seconde.
Bonne table à la française, chambres garnies pour Familles et Messieurs.
Les soins apportés au service de la pension de M. Guilloz ne laissent rien à desirer. Cet établissement a en outre l'avantage d'être situé au centre des affaires. Les prix sont des plus moderés.

Aux trois Drapeaux.
No 13, rue Troisième entre les rues Market et Chesnut, côté Est.
Détail de bière, vins, liqueurs, café, &c.
Mets chauds et froids à toute heure.
L. THANNBERGER.

Jerome House
PENSION FRANCAISE
No 46, rue Main entre Elm et Walnut.
St. Louis, Mo.

J. P. Bermel,
CHAPELIER-FABRICANT.
No 91, rue Seconde, encoignure des rues Seconde et Spruce.
Grand assortiment de chapeaux de toute qualité.
Casquettes de tous genres et du dernier goût.
Les commandes sont exécutées avec promptitude et à la satisfaction des personnes qui voudront bien honorer la maison Bermel de leur confiance.

FIGS. 26 & 27. *Revue de l'Ouest,* January 7, 1854. St. Louis French business advertisements were found on the last two pages of the *Revue de l'Ouest.* Courtesy of the St. Louis Mercantile Library.

No doubt the French Creole community of St. Louis thought of themselves already as a community before Cortambert's arrival. However, the *Revue de l'Ouest* reinforced that probable reality and provided historians with tangible evidence of this French Creole community that many thought had disappeared or become totally assimilated.

The best tangible evidence of this St. Louis French community can be found by perusing the *Revue de l'Ouest* advertisements. Through these advertisements we can discover the habits, taste preferences, and unique qualities of the St. Louis French Creole community. Indeed, commerce and shopping have always been indispensable aspects of our social and cultural lives.

Through the Eyes of *La Revue de l'Ouest*: Commerce and Community in French St. Louis in 1854

The great variety of French business advertisements in the *Revue de l'Ouest*, always found on the last two pages, seven and eight, of each edition,[39] reveal a vibrant French community that was still thriving in St. Louis in 1854. The majority of the French businesses were centrally located on Main, Second, Third, and Fourth Streets, a location that today is either part of or nearby the grounds of the St. Louis Arch.[40] Please refer to the map of St. Louis in 1854 (see fig. 28), in which a selection of French businesses is numbered 1 to 25. Corresponding numbers can be found in the key.

Some advertisements announce products that St. Louis has always been known for, such as shoes, boots, hats, and pasta. But then we find: "Urban et Levigneur" who sold "Chocolat français et espagnol: Cacao préparé— chocolat à la vanille—chocolat de santé—chocolat ferrugineux."[41] Other advertisements reinforce images of what it is to be "French."[42]

For instance, Monsieur Vitrey on Third Street, between Poplar and Plum, was a French baker proudly selling "Family and Fancy Breads."[43] Of course, the French cannot have bread without wine that can be found at Lynch & Tanguay.[44] A tailor, Monsieur Clerk advertises that he is a "cutter from the leading house in Paris."[45] Monsieur Croquart is giving "French-style" haircuts.[46]

A glimpse into St. Louis's political past is seen by way of a restaurant's name, "Aux trois drapeaux" or "At the Sign of the Three Flags," a restaurant that recalls the three countries that had controlled St. Louis in its history: France, Spain, and the United States.

Reflections of the French as promoters of the arts and education can be seen in the advertisements of a "French & English School for Young Ladies" (Number 15), a Professor of Music, Auguste Buchel (Number 19) and a French painter, L. H. Routier (Number 23).[47]

The French had always been known, unlike their fellow Anglo-Americans, for their hotels and hospitality, especially to their compatriots. If you had just arrived on the riverfront seeking lodging, a "French Boarding House: Managed by P. Guilloz" (Number 24) would be available to you.[48] "La Société Française de Bienfaisance" was a French benevolent society organized by French leaders at this time to help new French arrivals to St. Louis. Many announcements about this society and requests for monetary help to aid new French arrivals in St. Louis were found in the *Revue*. No longer called "benevolent," this society, however, still exists and is called "La Société Française de St. Louis" or "The French Society of St. Louis." This society holds meetings in French on the first Friday of every month to continue the promotion of French culture and language in St. Louis.[49]

It is interesting to note, in this busy metropolis of St. Louis in 1854, the presence of several French doctors, lawyers, and even a midwife who advertise in the *Revue*: C. de Montreville Médecin-Dentiste (doctor-dentist), A. P. et P. B. Garesché: Avocats français (French attorneys), Marie Weiss de Strasbourg: "sage femme" from Strasbourg, France, advertises that she is located near St. Mary's Church: "3rd St. South, no. 197 between Mulberry and Lombard."[50]

Due to the increase in its population and businesses, St. Louis in 1854 was experiencing an exciting time of new building and expansion. Only five years earlier, St. Louis confronted a dual challenge of a cholera epidemic and a devastating fire, thereafter known as the "Great Fire of 1849," that destroyed fifteen blocks and twenty-three steamboats.[51] St. Louisans were still rebuilding in 1854 and planning for the city's future.[52]

ST. LOUIS 1854
FRENCH BUSINESSES

Mississippi River

©2014 ANNE CRAVER

FIG. 28. Map of Saint Louis French businesses in 1854. Copyright 2014 by Anne Juneau Craver.

A Selection of French Business Advertisements in the *Revue de l'Ouest* (1854)

1. **BUREAU DE LA PRESSE ET DE *LA REVUE DE L'OUEST***
   No. 48, encoignure des rues Market et Seconde: *No. 48 corner of Market & Second Sts.* Imprimerie anglaise, allemande et française: *Press and Office of* Revue de l'Ouest: *An English, German and French Printing Company.*

2. **RESTAURANT AUX TROIS DRAPEAUX: AT
   THE THREE FLAGS RESTAURANT**
   No. 13, rue Troisième entre les rues Market et Chestnut, côté Est: *No. 13 Third St. between Market and Chestnut, on the East side.*

3. **MADAME PARIS: MARCHANDE DE MODES: MILLINER**
   No. 93, rue Market entre 3ème et 4ème: *No. 93 Market St. between 3rd and 4th.*

4. **C.N. VITREY: BOULANGER FRANÇAIS: FRENCH BAKER**
   No. 139, rue 3ème entre Poplar et Plum: *No. 139 3rd St. between Poplar and Plum.* Pain de famille et de fantasie: *Family and Fancy Breads.*

5. **M. CLERK: TAILLEUR DE PARIS: TAILOR FROM PARIS**
   Coupeur de la première maison de Paris: *Cutter from the leading house in Paris.* Rue 3ème entre Pine et Olive: *3rd St. between Pine & Olive.*

6. LYNCH & TANGUAY: COMMERCE DE VINS, EAUX-DE-VIES, EPICES, LIQUEURS FINES: EN GROS ET EN DETAIL: SELLING WINES, BRANDIES, SPICES, FINE LIQUEURS: WHOLESALE OR RETAIL
No. 87 & 89 rue Chestnut entre les rues 3ème et 4ème: *No. 87 & 89 Chestnut St. between 3rd and 4th Sts.*

7. J. CROQUART: SALON POUR LA COUPE DE CHEVEUX (GENRE FRANÇAIS): SALON FOR HAIRCUTS (FRENCH STYLE)
No. 48, rue Troisième entre Pine et Olive: *No. 48 Third St. between Pine & Olive.*

8. MADAME LEBRUN: MODISTE FRANÇAISE ET COUTURIERE EN ROBES: FRENCH MILLINER AND DRESSMAKER
No. 130, rue Seconde entre Almond et Poplar: *No. 130 Second St. between Almond and Poplar*

9. GEORGE DITTMANN: CONFECTION ET VENTE DE BOTTES ET DE SOULIERS EN GROS ET EN DETAIL: MANUFACTURE AND SALE OF BOOTS AND SHOES WHOLESALE AND RETAIL
No. 24, rue Market entre les rues Main et Seconde: *No. 24 Market St. between Main and Second.*

10. DE LEBRUN: PATES DE GENES: PASTA FROM GENOA
No. 130, rue Seconde entre Almond et Poplar: *No. 130 Second between Almond and Poplar.* Pâtes de Gênes, de Vermicelles et de Macaroni: *Pasta from Genoa, Vermicelli and Macaroni.*

11. C. DE MONTREVILLE: MEDECIN—DENTISTE: DOCTOR—DENTIST
Domicile et bureau: No., 61, rue Quatrième, vis-à-vis le Planters House: *Home and office: No. 61 Fourth St., next to the Planters House Hotel.*

12. URBAN ET LEVIGNEUR: CHOCOLAT FRANÇAIS ET ESPAGNOL: FRENCH AND SPANISH CHOCOLATE
No. 105, rue Seconde entre Spruce et Almond: *No. 105 Second St. between Spruce & Almond.* Cacao préparé—chocolat à la vanille—chocolat de santé—chocolat ferrugineux: *Prepared Cocoa—Vanilla Flavored Chocolate—Healthy Chocolate—Iron-Fortified Chocolate.*

13. A.P. ET P.B. GARESCHE: AVOCATS FRANÇAIS: FRENCH ATTORNEYS
Bureau: 49 rue Chestnut entre les rues Seconde et Troisième: *Office: 49 Chestnut St. between Second & Third.*

14. MADAME MOREL: ROBES, MANTELETS, MANTILLES: DRESSES, CAPES, MANTILLAS
150, Market entre 5 et 6ème rues, à côté du Théâtre des Variétés: *150 Market between 5th & 6th Sts., next to the Variety Theatre.*

15. INSTITUTION FRANÇAISE ET ANGLAISE POUR DEMOISELLES: FRENCH AND ENGLISH SCHOOL FOR YOUNG LADIES
Sous la direction de Mrs. Clarke et M. et Mme Boileau: *Under the direction of Mrs. Clarke and Mr. & Mrs. Boileau.* Encoignure sud-ouest de Pine et 7ème: *SW corner of Pine and 7th Street.*

16. DE SOEDING, FRERES: GRAND ASSORTIMENT D'OUTILS ET DE
QUINCAILLERIE: GREAT SELECTION OF TOOLS AND HARDWARE
No. 65, rue Seconde entre Spruce et Myrtle: *No. 65 Second St. between Spruce
and Myrtle.*

17. LIBRAIRIE ETRANGERE ET CABINET DE LECTURE DE FRANÇAIS
CHEZ ED BUHLER: FOREIGN LANGUAGE BOOKSTORE
AND FRENCH READING ROOM AT ED BUHLER'S
No. 31, rue Troisième entre Chestnut et Pine: *No. 31 Third St. between Chestnut
and Pine.*

18. M. WALTER: DOCTEUR EN MEDICINE: MEDICAL DOCTOR
104, Market, 1ère porte au-dessus de la 4ème rue (upstairs): *104 Market, 1st
door above 4th St. (upstairs).* Le docteur Walter se charge de guérir les cancers
et les fistules: *Dr. Walter takes care of curing cancers and fistulas.*

19. AUGUSTE BUCHEL: PROFESSEUR DE MUSIQUE: MUSIC PROFESSOR
Donne des lecons sur le forte piano au magasin de musique de Fritz et Derlethe,
rue Market entre Main et 2ème: *Gives lessons on a fortepiano at the Fritz and
Derlethe Music Store, Market St. between Main and 2nd.*

20. LEWIS V. BOGY & EUGENE MILTENBERGER:
MAISON DE BANQUE: BANKING HOUSE
Encoignure sud-est de Main et Olive: *Banking House: Southeast corner of Main
and Olive.*

21. PECHMANN & GAUCHE: IMPORTEURS DE PORCELAINE
FRANÇAISE, DE FAYENCE ET VERRERIE: IMPORTERS OF
FRENCH PORCELAIN, FAIENCE AND GLASSWARE
No. 8 & 10 rue Main: *No. 8 & 10 Main St.*

22. JACOB BLATTNER: OPTICIEN, FABRICANT D'INSTRUMENTS DE
PHYSIQUE ET DE MATHEMATIQUES: OPTICIAN, MANUFACTURER
OF INSTRUMENTS FOR PHYSICS AND MATHEMATICS
43, Rue Seconde entre Pine et Chestnut: *43 Second St. between Pine and Chestnut.*

23. L.H. ROUTIER: PEINTRE FRANÇAIS: FRENCH PAINTER
No. 96, Poplar St. Des tableaux à vendre, des leçons en peintre et en dessin:
Some paintings for sale, some lessons in painting and design.

24. PENSION FRANÇAISE: TENUE PAR P. GUILLOZ: FRENCH
BOARDING HOUSE: MANAGEDBY P. GUILLOZ
No. 17, rue Walnut, entre Main et Seconde: *No. 17 Walnut St. between Main &
Second.* Bonne table à la française, chambres garnies pour familles et messieurs.
Les prix sont des plus modérés: *Fine French dining, furnished rooms for families
and gentlemen. Affordable prices.*

25. MARIE WEISS DE STRASBOURG: SAGE-FEMME: MIDWIFE
3ème rue sud no. 197 entre Mulberry et Lombard près de l'église Ste. Marie: *3rd
St. South no. 197 between Mulberry and Lombard, near St. Mary's Church (founded
in 1843 as a German parish; now known as St. Mary of Victories; 744 S. 3rd St.).*

Even though the city continued to have a visible and audible French presence at this time, Irish, German, and New England immigrants were arriving daily. With these immigrants came beliefs, habits, and affiliations that threatened the *ordre établi* of the old French families. Increasingly, St. Louis was becoming a city of strangers and less a city known for its French culture and leaders.[53]

No doubt the genteel, old French families watched in horror on August 7, 1854, as one of the worst riots in the city's history erupted between the Protestant Nativists and the Irish Catholics on the day of the election between U.S. representative Thomas Hart Benton (the former U.S. senator), Democrat, running for reelection and the former mayor of St. Louis, Luther Kennett, supported by the Know Nothing Party.[54] The *Revue* gave a full account of this tragedy while concentrating on the plight of two French victims caught, unfortunately, in the brawl: a French woman, a recent arrival, whose place of business on the riverfront was destroyed at a cost of $1,000 (around $30,000 today) and a French Canadian, a sailor who was working nearby and was killed instantly by a stray bullet to his chest.[55]

In spite of these tumultuous times, full of uncertainty and doubt for the St. Louis French community, Louis Cortambert tried to breathe life back into it by reminding this French Creole community of the "esprit français" that could lead St. Louis and the United States on the road to social progress. The elite St. Louis French community, however, was more interested in maintaining the gentle way of life that they had always known, instead of confronting difficult social issues such as slavery and the daily arrival of immigrants.[56]

As the city exploded with activity, the exclusive inner circle of this French Creole community kept more and more to themselves, entertaining at home, educating their daughters in the study of French language and literature, music and the arts.[57] The sons of these French families, no longer leaders of St. Louis, went on, however, to Ivy League schools, and their education abroad was *de rigueur*.[58] No longer serving as elected officials of the city or state, French businessmen still controlled banking, invested in railroads, and made many important decisions that shaped the direction of the city of St. Louis.

Even though Cortambert was unable to conquer the old French families in St. Louis with his rallying cry of an "esprit français," he, undoubtedly, inspired his nephew, Alexander DeMenil to write a history of the literature of the Louisiana Territory and other states in which he highlighted "French authors" and spoke of his admiration for Kate Chopin, a native St. Louisan and Creole herself, whose novels and short stories were reflections of her own life experiences in the Louisiana bayou.[59] With the publication of this book, de Menil tried his best to keep the flame alive for regional French literature into the next century.

In 1861, unfortunately, the weekly publication of the *Revue de l'Ouest* was interrupted by the outbreak of the Civil War.[60] Just before the war, due to threats of bodily harm and being burnt alive, Cortambert, an abolitionist, decided to leave St. Louis for Hancock County, Illinois. After settling in Illinois, Cortambert, still in fear of his life, sent his partner, Melanie Racine, with his materials for publication tucked into the back of the dress of his son, Louis Cortambert Jr. Evidently, Melanie could "ride like the wind" on horseback, and delivered his editorials to the *Revue* in time for publication.[61] He then moved with his family to Montreal, Canada. He gave several lectures at the Institut Canadien de Montréal between November 1863 and January 1864.[62] In 1864 Cortambert and his family moved to Hoboken, New Jersey, where Cortambert took the ferry to New York City to work as an editor at the *Messager Franco-Américain* newspaper (1860–83). Cortambert and his family later relocated to Bloomfield, New Jersey, where Melanie died on November 28, 1880, at the age of fifty-three, and Cortambert died exactly four months later on March 28, 1881, at the age of seventy-two.[63]

Through our examination of *La Revue de l'Ouest* and its editor, Louis Cortambert, we can readily see that St. Louis continued to be a very viable part of French North America. Cortambert's connections from St. Louis to Montreal to New York and elsewhere kept the "esprit français" alive through his work as a journalist.[64]

It is interesting to note that Cortambert could live a life as *en français* in St. Louis and then move comfortably within the liberal and progressive circle of the Institut Canadien de Montréal, suggesting that the French community in 1854, though small, was still viable and had changed, as all communities change over time. Even though *La Revue* might not have reflected the social and political views of its readership, it connected local francophones to a liberal world of ideas that was far removed from the old fur-trade days, both in St. Louis and Montreal.

In fact, despite the suspension of the *Revue de l'Ouest* due to the Civil War, French newspapers continued to be published in St. Louis: *Le Courrier de St. Louis* (1866), *La Tribune Française* (1866–70s), *La République* (1876–77, editor: Honoré Beaugrand, who became the mayor of Montreal in 1885), *Le Patriote* (1877–81, suspended due to a fire; then 1885–87; later called *Le Patriote et le Phare des Lacs Réunis* for speakers of French from Alsace-Lorraine), *Le Journal Français de St. Louis* (1893).[65] Beaugrand was a liberal francophone journalist from Franco-New England who moved to St. Louis in 1876 to launch a French newspaper called *La République*. Unfortunately, *La République* was not successful, and Beaugrand returned to the East Coast briefly before moving to Montreal, where he became quite successful as the owner of a progressive newspaper, *La Patrie* (1879–97), and most importantly, as mayor of Montreal in 1885. Beaugrand's return visits to St. Louis and French-Canadian news were often the subject of St. Louis newspapers in English, which again showed the importance of St. Louis on the map of French North America even at the end of the nineteenth century.[66]

Cortambert worked his whole life as a journalist to unite the French community around a newspaper such as the *Revue de l'Ouest*. From the advertisements found in *La Revue de l'Ouest*, we discovered that the French did not disappear or become totally assimilated after the signing of the Louisiana Purchase in 1803. They remained a vital part of St. Louis and its economy albeit at a distance from the immigrants arriving on a daily basis—especially the German population. The French moved further north or south of the city in order to avoid the increasing numbers of Germans and their breweries in the heart of the city.[67] The French strove to maintain the "esprit français" within their own families even though they realized that the city of St. Louis was becoming increasingly more American. A visitor to St. Louis might have to look a little harder to find it, but Cortambert would be proud to know that this "esprit français" lives on in St. Louis today.[68]

1. St. Louis "was French in name only" according to some scholars. Williams, *State of Missouri*, 246.

2. The French community was located primarily on 1st, 2nd, and 3rd Streets, a neighborhood that began a long period of deconstruction, starting in the 1930s and lasting through the 1950s, due to the construction of the Jefferson National Expansion Memorial and its famous arch, known as the "Gateway to the West."

3. The word "esprit," in French, means "spirit," as in English, but in addition to this similar meaning, it can mean in the French language: the "mind" (intellect), "wit," or "finesse." "*La Revue* . . . manifeste seulement le désir de s'inspirer du véritable esprit français, de travailler pour sa part à en étendre l'influence sur le Nouveau Monde, et de rallier; s'il est possible; les membres de la grande famille française toujours dans l'Ouest et de s'avancer avec eux la voie du progrès social." *La Revue de l'Ouest*, numéro 6, le 11 février 1854.

4. "Speakers of the huge variety of Frenches, Englishes, or Spanishes, who might find it difficult or even impossible to understand one another in conversation, became capable of comprehending one another via print and paper." See Anderson, *Imagined Communities*, 44.

5. McLuhan notes: "The historians and archeologists will one day discover that the ads of our time are the richest and most faithful daily reflections than any society ever made of its entire range of activities." McLuhan, *Understanding Media*, 232.

6. I borrow from the musical revue of Brel's songs, *Jacques Brel is Alive and Well.*

7. Louis Cortambert's birth year is often erroneously cited as 1808.

8. Susanne Chouteau (1815–79) was born on April 23, the same day as her husband.

9. Pierre Laclède, cofounder of the city of St. Louis, is her great-grandfather.

10. Louis and Susanne had three, maybe four, children together. Their eldest daughter, Louise, was the only one who survived.

11. Ekberg and Person, "Laclède-Chouteau Legend," 1–7. These authors challenge the belief that Pierre Laclède and Auguste Chouteau were the true cofounders of the city of St. Louis.

12. Dr. Nicolas DeMenil was married to Susanne's sister, Emilie Chouteau.

13. *Act to incorporate*, 209–11: "said company shall have full power and authority to publish a daily newspaper, weekly, semi-weekly, or monthly in the French language or French and English languages in whole or in part of it, in the city or county of St. Louis." The law requiring corporations to file with the Missouri

secretary of state did not come into effect until 1866. Before 1866, corporations were created by an act of the state legislature. In addition to incorporation, the legislature handled many legal matters, such as probate, divorce, and name changes, now handled by the courts. The power granted to the general assembly for incorporation is directly related to English common law. See Stockard's *Treatise of the Corporation Laws*, 2. The state was not subsidizing the company by granting it the limited liability of a corporation. The board of directors and stockholders of the French Literary Company provided the necessary funds.

14. *Act to incorporate*, 209: "Capital stock of said company shall be ten thousand dollars, divided into shares of twenty five dollars each, with the privilege of increasing the same to twenty thousand dollars with the consent of two thirds of the stockholders which shall be in addition to the real estate, which said company is authorized to hold." Between 1808 (when Joseph Charless brought the first printing press to St. Louis) and 1854, other attempts to establish a French press failed. Cortambert played a role in some of these attempts. For instance, in 1840, *Le Telegraphe*, a French newspaper of four pages, appeared, whose publishers are listed as "M. Vergnes, L. Cortambert et Cie." None of these early newspapers survived due to a lack of subscribers and necessary funds.

15. *Act to incorporate*, 209: "Be it enacted by the general assembly of the State of Missouri as follows: That N. Nicolas Demirril [*sic*], Theodore Gautil [*sic*], Louis R. Cortambert and Domerrick [*sic*] Stock and such other persons as may hereinafter become associated with them ... are hereby incorporated ... by the name and style of 'The French Literary Company.'"

16. DeMenil, "Century of Missouri Literature," 82.

17. DeMenil, "Cortambert, Louis Richard," 489.

18. DeMenil, "Cortambert," 489.

19. Susanne Chouteau Cortambert died in 1879. When Melanie Racine Cortambert died on November 28, 1880, her death certificate described her as "married." I have been unable to obtain a marriage certificate between Louis Cortambert and Melanie Racine.

20. This book, *Voyage aux pays des Osages*, was translated into English by Mrs. Max Myer in 1963. Myer and Chapman, "Land of the Osages," 198–229.

21. Cortambert and Tranaltos, *Histoire de la Guerre Civile*.

22. By 1860 the city's population had increased to 161,000. According to Richard Edward, the *Revue de l'Ouest* had a circulation of 2,500 in 1860. See Edwards and Hopewell, *Great West*, 166. Only one year of *La Revue de l'Ouest*, January 7, 1854, until December 30, 1854, exists in digital or paper format. My search continues for the other years.

23. "Nous pourrons, grâce au télégraphe, donner les nouvelles d'Europe plusieurs jours avant les journaux français de New York." *Revue de l'Ouest*, numéro 1, le 7 janvier 1854, 1.

24. "La population française est peu nombreuse encore dans l'Ouest. Nous sommes donc dans l'obligation de prendre au début une allure modeste. Mais la ville de St. Louis étant évidemment destinée à devenir au bout de peu d'années une immense cité, l'un des premiers, sinon le premier centre d'affaires aux Etats-Unis, il est à croire que la population française y prendra, pour le moins, le même accroissement qu'à New York." *Revue de l'Ouest*, numéro 1, le 7 janvier 1854, 1.

25. By "French population" here I mean those people born in France, Creoles (those born in the United States with French roots), and French-Canadians.

26. Louis Napoleon Bonaparte's coup d'état of December 2, 1851, marked the beginning of an authoritarian empire (1852–60) in France. Cortambert resigned as vice-consul of France due to this coup. France and Great Britain declared war on the tsar (the Crimean War) on March 27, 1854. In the United States, the Kansas-Nebraska Act, adopted on May 30, 1854, allowed local settlers to decide about the introduction of slavery into Kansas and Nebraska. This act announced the end of the Missouri Compromise (1820). It led to horrible violence in the territories and contributed to the divide between the North and the South, announcing, according to some, the coming of the Civil War (1861–65). During the 1850s, the political party, "Know Nothing" (also known as the "Native American Party" or the "American Party") was an anti-Catholic, anti-immigration (particularly, anti-Catholic immigration) movement in the guise of a secret society. When a member was asked about his activities he replied: "I know nothing." The Know Nothings insisted on the election of only "native-born" Americans (i.e., white, Protestant men born in the United States).

27. "Le but de cette publication c'est de réunir autant que possible, dans la même communion d'idées, de sentiments, de souvenirs, d'intérêts les Français dispersés dans l'Ouest si loin du sol natal. Un grand nombre ne le reverront jamais . . . Le titre d'Américain est certes à lui seul une bien puissante compensation. Mais où est le Français qui cesse jamais de sentir son cœur battre avec force au souvenir de la patrie." *Revue de l'Ouest*, numéro 1, le 7 janvier 1854, 1.

28. Gitlin, *Bourgeois Frontier*, 139–56.

29. Cortambert warned of an "intellectual vassalage." "If one doesn't work on his own ideas and is obliged to borrow them, this person submits to the thought of another and alienates his own independence." "Celui qui ne travaille pas ses idées . . . qui néglige de penser pour son propre compte . . . Il emprunte des idées, c'est-à-dire, en définitive, qu'il se soumet à la pensée d'un autre, aliène

son indépendance et reconnaît son vasselage intellectuel." *Revue de l'Ouest*, numéro 1, le 28 janvier 1854, 1.

30. Louis Cortambert, "Liberté de la pensée," *Revue de l'Ouest*, numéro 7, le 18 février 1854, 1.

31. Robert A. Bakewell, editor of a St. Louis conservative Catholic newspaper, *Shepherd of the Valley*, frequently lambasted Cortambert for his anti-Catholic views: "There are some things, however, that we can affirm in regard to the *Revue de l'Ouest* . . . that it loses no opportunity to sneer at the sacred truths of the Catholic religion." *Shepherd of the Valley* 4, no. 30, April 29, 1854, 2.

32. Spiritualists believed in communication with the dead that makes for some interesting stories published in the *Revue de l'Ouest*.

33. This label of "Red Republican" was used by de Menil to describe the *Revue de l'Ouest*: "The *Revue* at once became red-Republican and anti-Catholic." de Menil, "French Newspapers." Historian Charles Van Ravenswaay wrote: "Even dignified Louis Richard Cortambert [. . .] developed Red Republican and anti-Catholic views when he became editor of the St. Louis *La Revue de l'Ouest*." Ravenswaay, "Years of Turmoil," 308.

34. ". . . la république toujours militante, voilà ce que vous appelez la république rouge . . . et vous écriez dévotement: "Oh, que Dieu nous garde de la république rouge!" comme si votre république n'avait pas eu son '76 et n'avait pas été aussi une république rouge." Louis Cortambert, "La République Rouge," *Revue de l'Ouest*, numéro 10, le 11 mars 1854, 1.

35. "Il n'y pas deux espèces de républiques; la seule véritable n'est et ne peut être que le régime de la liberté et du progrès." Cortambert, "La République Rouge," 1.

36. "Mais il y a la république en paix comme en Amérique, et la république en guerre comme en Europe. Ici elle rayonne tranquillement sur l'horizon de l'intelligence; là-bas, elle est voilée par les funèbres nuages du despotisme." Cortambert, "La République Rouge," 1.

37. "Que devient l'esprit français? Voilà ce que les gens demandent avec une certaine inquiétude. [. . .] Tout n'est pas perdu cependant. La physionomie n'est point effacée: sur les rives de St. Laurent comme sur celles du Mississippi, elle a conservé son type doux et fin, son expressive mobilité; là encore notre idiome se distingue par sa tournure lente et son trait rapide. Mais enfin l'esprit français court risque de s'évaporer sur une si grande étendue [. . .]." Louis Cortambert, "L'Esprit français en Amérique," *Revue de l'Ouest*, numéro 25, le 24 juin 1854, 1.

38. Anderson, *Imagined Communities*, 44.

39. In addition to 2,500 subscribers and funds provided by the board of directors and stockholders of the French Literary Company, these paid advertisements, no

doubt, contributed to the *Revue's* success. Cortambert knew Emile de Girardin (1802–81), journalist, politician, and publisher of *La Presse* in Paris (1836), an inexpensive newspaper (aka a "penny press") whose success relied heavily on paid advertising. Cortambert wrote an editorial on de Girardin on May 13, 1854, praising his skill as a liberal journalist confronting the tyrannical rule of Louis-Napoleon.

40. Unfortunately there were no federal laws in place to protect the archeological and historical artifacts that were found during the razing of buildings and warehouses at the time of the building of the Arch, Gateway to the West. These artifacts of this French community are sadly and permanently lost.

41. French and Spanish Chocolate, "Prepared Cocoa," "Vanilla-flavored Chocolate," "Healthy Chocolate," and "Iron-fortified Chocolate." "French chocolate" was a "combination of cocoa nibs (pieces of cocoa separated from the husks of cacao beans), sugar and vanilla"; "Spanish chocolate" was a "combination of cacao from Curaçao, cinnamon, cloves, sugar and almonds"; "Vanilla-flavored chocolate" was a combination of cacao from Caracas, cinnamon, cloves and vanilla from Mexico. See Grivetti and Shapiro, "Appendix I," 781. In the eighteenth and nineteenth centuries, chocolate, known as the "food of the gods," was used medicinally to treat everything from headaches, digestion, and hangovers to cholera, smallpox, and asthma. Grivetti and Shapiro, "Appendix I," 67–88. Pharmacists in nineteenth-century France, such as Jean-Antoine Brutus Ménier, immediately saw chocolate as a means to sell their drugs, especially bitter-tasting drugs that were hard to swallow. All kinds of medicine in the form of chocolate bars were sold at this time to a trusting public without any warning as to their potentially dangerous contents. See "La pharmacie et le chocolat" at Pharmaciemontgargan.com/la pharmacie-et-le-chocolat. "Healthy chocolate," also known as "homeopathic chocolate," surprisingly sometimes had no trace of cocoa. In 1850 Colmet d'Aage, a pharmacist, became known for his "iron-fortified chocolate" in Paris. This "iron-fortified" chocolate contained "limaille de fer porphyrisée" or "finely ground iron filings." Iron-fortified chocolate was advertised as a health benefit to women, children, and the elderly. The benefits of "iron-fortified" chocolate is currently in the news today. See Pastore and Muizeniece-Brasava, "Fortified Chocolate Snacks," 111–15.

42. Roland Barthes argues that the media drains images of real meaning to create myths (i.e., iconic stereotypes used as capitalist commodities to fulfill consumer desires). See Barthes, *Mythologies*, 223–28. The repetitive reading of these "advertisements" in each issue of the *Revue* also creates "that remarkable

confidence of community in anonymity which is the hallmark of modern nations." Anderson, *Imagined Communities*, 35.

43. C. N. Vitrey: Boulanger français: Pain de famille et de fantaisie: French Baker: Family and Fancy Breads.

44. Lynch & Tanguay: Commerce de vins, eaux-de-vies, épices, liqueurs fines: en gros et en détail: Selling wines, brandies, spices, fine liqueurs: wholesale or retail.

45. M. Clerk: Tailleur de Paris: Tailor from Paris: Coupeur de la première maison de Paris: Cutter from the leading house in Paris.

46. J. Croquart: Salon pour la coupe de cheveux (genre français): Salon for Haircuts (French style).

47. "Institution française et anglaise pour demoiselles"; "Auguste Buchel: Professeur de Musique"; "L. H. Routier: Peintre français."

48. "Pension française: Tenue par P. Guilloz."

49. A "Mr. X" wrote to *La Tribune Française* (a continuation of *La Revue de l'Ouest* by George Morhard, first editor of *La Revue*) in the December 20, 1866, issue about the Société Française de Bienfaisance's missing funds: "I would be curious to know what happened to the Société Française de Bienfaisance capital of a few hundred dollars. [...] Maybe we can create an office for the benefit of French immigrants." "Je serais curieux de savoir qu'il est devenu son capital qui était de quelques centaines de dollars. [...] On pourrait peut-être aussi établir un bureau français au profit des immigrants d'origine française." *La Tribune Française*, le 20 décembre 1866, vol. 1, no. 8, 4.

50. The attorney, Peter Bauduy Garesché's (1822–68) two daughters, Katherine "Kitty" Milligan Garesché (1850–1940) and Lydia "Lily" Johnston Stanislaus Garesché (1856–1932), entered the Order of the Sacred Heart. Peter Garesché's wife, Juliette McLane (1826–85), also entered the Convent of the Sacred Heart after his death and the death of their other children, Virginia and John. In 1887 Kitty Garesché and another Sacred Heart Academy schoolmate, Elise "Liza" Miltenberger (1848–1929) founded the Convent of the Sacred Heart in San Francisco, California. Both Kitty Garesché and Liza Miltenberger were close friends of their former schoolmate, the celebrated author Kate Chopin (1850–1904). Both Miltenberger and Chopin were daughters of old St. Louis French families. Marie Weiss advertises that she is located between 3rd St. South no. 197 between Mulberry and Lombard near St. Mary's Church. St. Mary's was originally founded as the first German Catholic parish in St. Louis in 1843. It is currently called St. Mary's of Victories. Hungarian families or those people

of Hungarian ancestry gather there every Sunday for a mass in Latin at 9:00 a.m. and a mass in English and Hungarian at 11a.m.

51. The explosion of the "White Cloud" steamboat that immediately destroyed twenty-three other steamboats and 430 buildings created the worst fire St. Louis had ever known, the "Great Fire of 1849." The Asiatic cholera that first reached St. Louis from Europe in 1832 was considered an epidemic in St. Louis by 1849. It killed one out of eleven St. Louisans or 6 percent of the population. Bellefontaine (1849) and Calvary (1854) cemeteries were founded in north St. Louis during this time to bury cholera victims far from the center of St. Louis. *La Revue de l'Ouest* was still announcing deaths from cholera on July 7, 1854: "The city mortality rose to 470; almost double from the previous week of 254: 470 deaths: 207 cases of cholera and 206 children under the age of 5." *La Revue de l'Ouest*, le 7 juillet 1854, 3–4. Suddenly, on August 12, there was finally a drop in the number of cholera deaths: "310 deaths: 55 cholera." *La Revue de l'Ouest*, le 12 août 1854, 3.

52. In the *Revue*'s "Chronique Locale/Local News" section on December 23, 1854, we read: "The City council has voted in favor of the expansion of St. Louis from the southern end of the mouth of the River des Peres to the northern boundary of the Gingras River and will extend on the Western side to 660 ft beyond Grand Ave. With this new district, the city will be almost 12 miles long and 2½ miles wide." "Le conseil de la ville s'est prononcé pour le projet de l'extension qui donnerait à St. Louis pour extrémité sud l'embouchure de la Rivière des Pères, pour limite au nord la Rivière à Gingras et qui l'entendrait du côté de l'ouest jusqu'à une ligne située à 660 pieds au-delà de Grand Avenue. Dans cette nouvelle circonscription, la ville aurait près de 12 miles de long et plus de 2½ de large." *La Revue de l'Ouest*, le 23 décembre 1854, 4.

53. John How, a Pennsylvanian by birth, defeated Charles Chouteau for mayor of St. Louis in 1853. Mayor How served two one-year terms, 1853–55, and then sat out a year before defeating John B. Carson of the Know Nothing Party in the election of 1856. Bernard Pratte, born in St. Louis immediately after the ratification of the Louisiana Purchase in 1804, was the eighth mayor of St. Louis, in 1844–46. Pratte was the last politician with French roots who ran the city of St. Louis. Jay Gitlin points out that the decline of the visible francophone communities happened from the 1840s in St. Louis and Detroit whereas New Orleans suffered this same decline in the 1860s and 1870s. Gitlin, *Bourgeois Frontier*, 169.

54. According to the *Revue*, about fifteen people died and the Irish neighborhood was completely decimated. It is interesting to note that the *Revue* took a neutral

stance as to who started the fight: "As there are different versions of the source of the fight, it is difficult to say exactly from which side came the first violent attack." "Comme il y a différentes versions sur l'origine de la querelle, il est difficile de dire au juste de quel côté vinrent les premières violences." The pro-Benton mayor, John How, finally brought the city to order after firing the police and calling upon citizens of St. Louis to act as a volunteer police force. *Revue de l'Ouest*, le 12 août 1854, vol. 1, no. 33, 3–4. Although the *Revue* does not mention it, the St. Louis Old Cathedral was almost destroyed by the Know Nothing Party during this riot of 1845.

55. *Revue de l'Ouest*, le 12 août 1854, vol. 1, no. 33, 3. Cortambert reminded this French woman that the city of St. Louis was responsible for the payment of all damages caused by the riot.

56. To this day, although no longer recognizable by French last names or speaking French, there is still an "inner circle" of a French community in St. Louis who are all related to one another. These French Americans can still trace their ancestry to Auguste Chouteau and Pierre Laclède. Within the francophone community of St. Louis, there were non-elite French families working as farmers or in other small businesses in Florissant, Missouri (north of the city of St. Louis), or Carondelet, Missouri (south of the city of St. Louis), and vice versa, outside of St. Louis in Ste Geneviève, Missouri, and Old Mines, Missouri, there were prominent French families that started out in humble professions such as farmers or miners but learned that they "could not rely on their good names and connections alone [. . .] [who] adapted to the new world order and triumphed," such as the Vallé family. "French surnames attached themselves to a host of enterprises, including the Vallé lead mines, the Menard and Vallé mercantile business, the Bolduc trading establishments, the Bogy copper mines and the Rozier stores and banks." See Stepenoff, *From French Community*, 140. Also Crist, *They Was Frenchmans*. No doubt, further research needs to be done on class divisions and other types of divisions (rural/urban; Ste Geneviève/St. Louis) that existed within the broader francophone communities in Missouri.

57. The St. Louis French community used to live south of today's St. Louis Arch. Their homes backed up to one another, which made it easy to visit. These residential homes were in walking distance to the Old Cathedral.

58. One such Frenchman born in St. Louis was Mayor Bernard Pratte Jr.'s son, Bernard Pratte, who graduated from Yale University in 1846.

59. de Menil, *Literature of the Louisiana Territory*.

60. After the war, the *Revue* was resurrected as *La Tribune Française*. *La Tribune Française*, "formerly *La Revue de l'Ouest*," appears on the front page of this

newspaper. The first issue appeared on October 22, 1866, published by G. Morhard, first editor of *La Revue de l'Ouest*. It was suspended in the 1870s.

61. I obtained this information thanks to an account of this story written by Isa Cortambert, Louis Cortambert Jr.'s wife. The distance between St. Louis, Missouri, and Hancock County, Illinois, is 172.8 miles. It is a three-hour drive or a four-day ride on horseback. However, given Melanie's ability, she probably made it to St. Louis in less than four days. *La Revue de l'Ouest* was published weekly on Saturdays.

62. See Lamonde, *Gens de Parole*, 156–57.

63. As mentioned before, Louis Cortambert's birth year is often erroneously cited as 1808, when in fact, he was born in 1809. Therefore his death certificate mistakenly gives his age as seventy-three when he actually is seventy-two years old at his death. He would have been seventy-three on April 23. According to their death certificates, Melanie died of paralysis due to her anasarca, which caused severe swelling, and Cortambert died of pneumonia.

64. Cortambert's father, Dr. Richard Cortambert, came to New Orleans, Louisiana, in 1820, became a U.S. citizen in 1830, and most likely died of cholera in 1832. Cortambert's first voyage to the United States was to settle his father's estate in 1832. He, no doubt, had many contacts in New Orleans. Cortambert was the agent in St. Louis for *La Ruche littéraire et politique* (*The Literary and Political Beehive*), a literary and political magazine published in Montréal from 1853–55. Cortambert lived and worked in Montreal from 1863–64 and worked in New York City for the *Messager Franco-Américain* from 1864 until his death in 1881.

65. The exact year for the suspension of *La Revue de l'Ouest* is not known. Some issues could have been published during the war. However, given the fact that Cortambert moved to Montreal in 1863, it is doubtful that the *Revue* continued much longer after that year.

66. Just as an example, articles about Honoré Beaugrand, or "Henri" Beaugrand as he was known to St. Louisans, appeared in four consecutive months from September to December 1885 in the *St. Louis Post-Dispatch*. See "Henri Beaugrand: Montreal's Courageous Mayor Well Known in St. Louis," *St. Louis Post-Dispatch*, September 30, 1885, 8; "Montreal's Mayor Seeking Rest in New York City," *St. Louis Post-Dispatch*, October 22, 1885, 1; "A Poor Legacy, The Editor and Manager of Le Monde Indicted for Libeling Mayor Beaugrand," *St. Louis Post-Dispatch*, November 18, 1885, 7; "Montreal's Mayor: M. Henri Beaugrand, the Hero of the Recent Small-Pox Riots," *St. Louis Post-Dispatch*, December 7, 1885, 2.

67. German immigrants started arriving in St. Louis in the 1840s. "The German-born population of St. Louis zoomed from 22,340 in 1850 to 50,510 in 1860. Native-born Germans made up about a quarter of the city's population but declined afterwards." See Merkel, *Beer, Brats, and Baseball*, xiii. "By 1860 there were forty breweries in St. Louis producing 200,000 barrels annually." See Herbst, Roussin, and Kious, *St. Louis Brews*, xiii.

68. This "esprit français" can be found in many French organizations in St. Louis: Alliance Française de St. Louis, La Société Française de St. Louis, Les Amis, the St. Louis-Lyon Sister Cities Organization, and the countless St. Louisans who are proud of their French heritage and continue to promote French culture and language. See the essay in this volume by Lionel Cuillé.

BIBLIOGRAPHY

An Act to incorporate the French Literary Company, Act of February 22, 1853. In *Missouri Laws*, 209–11. Jefferson City MO: James Lusk, 1853.

Anderson, Benedict. *Imagined Communities: Reflections on the Origin and Spread of Nationalism*. New York: Verso, 2006.

Brel, Jacques. *Jacques Brel Is Alive and Well, and Living in Paris*. Music and lyrics by Jacques Brel. Translated by Eric Blau and Mort Shuman. Village Gate Theater, Greenwich Village NY, January 22, 1968.

Cortambert, Louis, and F. de Tranaltos. *Histoire de la Guerre Civile Américaine (1860–1865)*, 2 tomes. Paris: Editeur Amyot, 1865.

———. *Voyage aux pays des Osages*, Paris: Chez Arhus-Bertrand Librairie, 1837.

Crist, Helen Valle. *They Was Frenchmans: The Vallée Family Legacy*. Brea CA: Creative Continuum, 2003.

DeMenil, Alexander. "A Century of Missouri Literature." *Missouri Historical Review* 15, no. 1 (October 1920): 82–83.

———. "Cortambert, Louis Richard." In *Encyclopedia of the History of St. Louis*. Vol. 1. William Hyde and Howard L. Conard, eds. New York: Southern History, 1899.

Edwards, Richard, and Menra Hopewell MD. *The Great West and Her Commercial Metropolis*. St. Louis MO: Published at the office of "Edwards's Monthly," 1860.

Ekberg, Carl J., and Sharon K. Person. "Beyond the Laclède-Chouteau Legend." In *St. Louis Rising: The French Regime of Louis St. Ange de Bellerive*, 1–7. Urbana: University of Illinois Press, 2015.

Gitlin, Jay. "'Avec bien du regret': The Americanization of Creole St. Louis and French Detroit." In *The Bourgeois Frontier: French Towns, French Traders, and American Expansion*, 139–55. New Haven CT: Yale University Press, 2010.

————. "'La Confédération Perdue': The Legacy of Francophone Culture in Mid-America." In *The Bourgeois Frontier: French Towns, French Traders, and American Expansion*, 156–83. New Haven CT: Yale University Press, 2010.

Grivetti, Louis E., and Howard Y. Shapiro, eds. "Appendix 1." *Chocolate: History, Culture, and Heritage*. Hoboken NJ: John Wiley & Sons, 2009.

Herbst, Henry, Don Roussin, and Kevin Kious, *St. Louis Brews: 200 Years of Brewing in St. Louis, 1809–2009*. St. Louis MO: Reedy Press, 2009.

Lamonde, Yvan. *Gens de Parole: Conférences publiques, essais et débats à l'Institut Canadien de Montréal 1845–1871*. Quebec: Les Editions du Boréal, 1990.

Merkel, Jim. *Beer, Brats, and Baseball: St. Louis Germans*. St. Louis MO: Reedy Press, 2012.

Myer, Mrs. Max, trans., and Carl H. Chapman, ed. "Journey to the Land of the Osages by Louis Cortambert." *Bulletin of the Missouri Historical Society*, 19 (April 1963): 198–229.

McLuhan, Marshall. *Understanding Media: The Extensions of Man*. New York: McGraw-Hill, 1964.

Pastore, Dace, and Sandra Muizeniece-Brasava. "Fortified Chocolate Snacks with Increased Level of Iron." 22nd Annual International Scientific Conference: Research for Rural Development, Latvia University of Agriculture, 1 (2016): 111–15.

La pharmacie et le chocolat, at www.pharmaciemontgargan.com/la-pharmacie-et -le-chocolat.

Stepenoff, Bonnie. *From French Community to Missouri Town: Ste. Geneviève in the Nineteenth Century*. Columbia: University of Missouri Press, 2006.

Stockard, F. T. *A Treatise of the Corporation Laws of the State of Missouri*. St. Louis MO: Thomas Law Book Company, 1929.

Van Ravenswaay, Charles. "Years of Turmoil, Years of Growth: St. Louis in the 1850s." *Missouri Historical Society Bulletin* (July 1967): 303–24.

Williams, Walter, ed. "St. Louis." In *The State of Missouri: An Autobiography*, 243–62. Columbia: Press of E. W. Stephens, 1904.

10

THE FRENCH PRESENCE IN ST. LOUIS TODAY

LIONEL CUILLÉ

What does the French presence in St. Louis mean today? Evidence of a French past can be found on the landscape, in the the the names of neighborhoods (Creve Coeur, Des Peres) and streets (Gravois), with original French names recently added to downtown street signs by Les Amis, an organization dedicated to preserving the city and region's French heritage.[1] But how many St. Louisians know that Union Station was inspired by the fortifications of Carcassonne, or City Hall by the Paris Hotel de Ville? Lets go further: if we were to question the passerby in our magnificent Forest Park, how many would even know who St. Louis (IX) was, or that his conquering statue in front of the Art museum (SLAM), with the handle of his sword brandished in the form of a cross, raises the ghost of the Crusades? As for Pierre Laclède, who still recognizes his statue behind the rosebushes in front of City Hall? A vestige, a term from the Latin through French that means a *footprint*, is all that remains of Laclède's Landing, the site of the former French village whose foundations were obliterated in order to build the Arch and museum dedicated to the Lewis and Clark expedition.[2] Indeed, the Arch and the Jefferson National Expansion Memorial rewrite the French story along the Creole Corridor, replacing it with a different narrative: the conquest of the West.[3]

And yet the francophone community in St. Louis manifests itself through a dense and active network. This essay will provide a panorama of French St. Louis today based upon questionnaires to businesses and associations, and interviews with local actors of the Francophile life between 2013 and 2017. My aim is to show that the community extends well beyond the activities of the more traditional Francophile associations and is particularly visible and active in social networks.

It might be noted that I am writing mostly from the perspective that many francophone cultural organizations in the history of St. Louis, but not all, have always adopted: the perspective that says "French" culture is "metropolitan French culture." Surely an alternative viewpoint about the location of "Frenchness" is well represented in discussions about French national identity both in France itself and abroad. Indeed, many Quebecois have long contested the idea that French culture signifies culture produced in France. At the Second Biennial on the French Language in Quebec City in 1967, Moroccan journalist Ben Ziane, Olympe Bhêly-Quenum from Dahomey, and representatives from Quebec demanded steps to decolonize speech. As one reporter covering the event observed, francophones from outside the metropole made it clear that French was no longer the "exclusive property of the French in France."[4]

As I suggest below, the situation in St. Louis reinforces this turn. From Haitians, to Senegalese, to Vietnamese and other populations tied to the French empire and speaking the French language, certain members of St. Louis's immigrant population have over the years redefined a "French" history in St. Louis that is much more various. In truth, the older eighteenth-century story—the French heritage story of the Creole Corridor—was itself diverse, shaped and contested by a variety of peoples. Importantly, it was a story made in North America—a local francophone story that defies the imperialist bias of Lord Durham who felt, referring to Lower Canada in his 1839 *Report*, that culture (literature and history) could only be produced in Europe. The great Alexis de Tocqueville suffered from a similar bias seen from a different angle. In his view, the French in America stopped being French the more American they became.[5] These various distortions and biases show just how difficult it is to both assess and reinvigorate the French presence in contemporary St. Louis where it is necessary to nurture useful intersections between a fading, but deeply rooted, regional French North American heritage; a continuing economic and cultural connection to metropolitan France; a variety of global francophone immigrant communities; and a neighboring Canadian state with a vital public life and culture in French. The potential is great; the harvesting of such intersections is a complex task. This essay can, and I hope will, provide a usable portrait of contemporary French St. Louis.

The French Community: A Disappearing Vestige

Having French ancestors in St. Louis continues to determine a certain cultural affiliation and social prominence. Robbie Pratte, the new director of Museum Operations in Ste. Genevieve, reminds me that the French presence extends beyond St. Louis: "As a resident in Ste. Genevieve, originally from the Bonne Terre-Old Mines area, and a descendant of Jean-Baptiste Sebastien Pratte, the French presence is *in my blood*, quite literally. As a child I would play in the woods and encounter sink holes from the closed lead mines." Local festivals are held not far from where he grew up (Old Mines Parish), and Robbie emphasizes that "Paw Paw French," a dialect of French once spoken throughout eastern Missouri, is still spoken. This dialect, also known as "Illinois Country French" or "Missouri French," was once used across a wide area ranging from Vincennes, Indiana, through Illinois, to the Missouri Ozarks, including Old Mines, Ste. Genevieve, and Potosi. The late Elizabeth Gentry Sayad, the founder of Les Amis (the French Creole preservationist organization of the Mid-Mississippi River Valley), made clear that their members are proud of their family tree: "Descendants of many old French families are still very active in our French Creole activities, like the members of the Chouteau and Desloges families." According to the *American Community Survey*, there are 153,420 Missourians of French ancestry; and while this figure does not measure the level of French proficiency, it does account for 10,932 speaking French at home.[6]

Beyond the descendants of the original French families in the area, there are also more recent French immigrants or expatriates. They constitute only a very small part of the constantly shifting ethnic, linguistic, and cultural landscape shaped by immigration: the waves of German and Irish newcomers in the middle of the nineteenth century, followed by the Italian, Lebanese, Syrian, and Greek immigrants—not to mention the large community of Bosnians (seventy thousand as of 2013). All have enriched our town's identity. In comparison, there are only 548 French-born Missourians in the

St. Louis metro area; and only 93 French nationals who live in St. Louis, according to the Consulate of Chicago's 2012 census.[7] According to Denis Quenelle, cultural attaché, these figures must be taken with caution, since French expatriates are not necessarily recorded in the consular registers. Some *candidats à l'émigration* no longer want to deal with their government, a trend confirmed by the very low participation rate in voting in French elections among expatriates living in North America (usually below 20 percent).[8] This very small presence of expats is confirmed by Caroline Achard and her husband Frédéric who founded the association St. Louis Accueil to welcome French expatriates: "Our compatriots are very few in St. Louis compared to New York City or Miami, where it is not uncommon to hear French spoken." Their association organizes a monthly picnic in a park from April to October that "typically brings together between ten and thirty French-speaking families." Another indicator is the French immersion school (SLLIS), created by Rhonda Broussard in 2009, which has not enrolled students whose parents are from francophone countries in 2017. According to Meghan Hill, head of the French section: " It seems as though St. Louis was a hub of French culture at one time, and that French language and culture have been on the decline. Those born in France or French expatriates constitute a *barely visible* minority." This perception is shared by Isabelle Heidbreder, director of the Alliance Française of St. Louis (AFSTL), founded in 1904 and offering French classes since 1964. According to Heidbreder, the French and Francophile community at large in St. Louis is dwindling: "The older generations had more of a sense of community, community involvement, sharing and giving. They belonged to French organizations that they were committed to and with whom they celebrated the highlights of French life together (La fête des rois, Mardi Gras, le 14 juillet, la Fête de St Louis, le 11 novembre). Today in all organizations there is a decrease in membership involvement, and it is getting harder and harder to attract younger people."

As for the descendants of the *coureurs des bois*, who would go back and forth along the Creole Corridor, they are not visiting the *poteaux en terre* houses in Ste. Genevieve, despite the town's prospect of being recognized as a Historical National Park.[9] According to Robbie Pratte, these historic vertical log structures, historical houses, are only visited by "40 French visitors a year from Canada and France combined, though more so from Canada."

Economic and Cultural Life

However, the French presence in St. Louis cannot be measured by the number of French citizens enrolled on the consular lists (*listes consulaires*). Not surprisingly, the French presence in St. Louis today is driven by commerce and economic forces that drew traders and *voyageurs* to St. Louis in the eighteenth century. France is highly ranked in terms of its investments in Missouri, where it creates approximately eight thousand jobs: fifteen businesses with French mother companies are implanted in the region, consisting primarily of international construction companies such as Lafarge or Bouygues, large industrial corporations such as Decaux Aviation, and insurance companies (Axa).[10] Fur trading may no longer be a viable undertaking for French-speaking entrepreneurs, but there are modern businesses that choose to promote their French cultural heritage. When I called Occitane's store—offering the "sun-drenched countryside of the south of France—an American employee answered the phone with a French 'Bonjour!'" The name of our local French culinary school (*L'école culinaire* written with an "accent aigu" and pronounced *à la française* when advertising on local airwaves), also provides an example of cultural affiliation or cachet. And restaurants or bakeries of course are still particularly prized by the Francophile population: the owner and pastry chef of La Bonne Bouchée, Olivier Leguet, for example, decorated his establishment like a Parisian bistro. Leguet was trained in France.

The French businesses located in St. Louis, however, were not drawn to the area by the beauty of the site praised by Chouteau, nor have they come to honor the memory of Louis IX. Located in the suburb of Hazelwood, the Biomérieux company is named after Marcel Mérieux, who first studied biology under Louis Pasteur and developed the first anti-tetanus sera. It is today a world leader in the field of in vitro diagnostics. When I interviewed Human Resource director Denis Brossard (January 14, 2014), he was not even aware that St. Louis was Lyon's *sister city*. He explained that the company had not been attracted by the fiscal advantages offered by the Missouri chamber of commerce but rather by a strictly economic opportunity: the 1988 purchase of one of McDonnel Douglas's subsidiary companies that had invented a medical sequencing procedure compatible with Biomérieux's service strategy. Seen from the outside, nothing indicates that the company is French; in fact, the building is topped by a gigantic American flag. According to Brossard, however, the employees of the St. Louis site are aware of the company's French identity for decisions are made on a daily basis in consultation with headquarters back in France. Curiously, he perceived no discrepancies between the French and American business cultures, though he regrets to confess that his compatriots "systematically arrive half an hour late to meetings whereas the St. Louisans' punctuality is irreproachable." Contrary to the popular belief that the French are opposed to professional mobility, however, Denis Brossard notes that those from the Lyon headquarters are more interested in coming to St. Louis than the St. Louisians are in transferring to Lyon. Of the 7 out of 630 employees who are French, all of them are executives and are therefore among the highly qualified entrepreneurs who constitute the new Laclèdes of the global world. Rare are the French who today choose to venture along the banks of the Mississippi without being decorated with the *diplômes* that have replaced the former titles of nobility.

It is also thanks to the prestige of its culture that France continues to shine in St. Louis. For Simon Kelly, curator at the St. Louis Art Museum (SLAM), not only has the institution partnered with the French Regional and American Museum Exchange consortium (FRAME), but also with related exhibitions associated with French culture, which still have a tremendous appeal for the St. Louisians.[11] Another annual *rendez-vous* of all Francophiles is the St. Louis International Film Festival, which presents around fifteen highly acclaimed francophone films, including animated films with original subtitles—a great way to expose young children to the French language. The Classic French Film Festival, funded by the Jane M. and Bruce P. Robert Charitable Foundation, shows additional French movies in March.

But what is most remarkable in St. Louis is the number of groups and associations dedicated to French language and culture: l'Alliance Française, la Société Française, Les Amis, St. Louis-Lyon Sister Cities, le Centre Francophone, which is now renamed French ConneXions at Washington University in St Louis. This does not even include the groups that have emerged spontaneously on social networks to create spaces of conversation in French (the Coin Français, the Amicale, South French Table). These groups celebrate French traditions, and their members frequently belong to several societies at once.

Past and Present: Educating about French Language and Culture

Missouri French might be spoken by fewer than thirty people in Old Mines, southwest of St. Louis, but this heritage remains important through various initiatives.[12] One of the most spectacular educational successes for the French presence is Rhonda Broussard's creation of the St. Louis Language Immersion School (SLLIS) in 2009. Teaching the curriculum required by the state of Missouri in the target languages (French, Spanish, Mandarin), the school clearly intends to serve an inclusive population comprised of at least 50 percent African American students, and 50 percent students who qualify for the National School Lunch Program. In creating this school, Rhonda Broussard not only developed new exchanges by recruiting native speakers as French teachers and interns, she also extended the francophone community to include children from the inner city. According to Meghan Hill, the young and energetic current principal: "Educating our students is a great way to share the French heritage of St. Louis and to help create a sense of community pride about it."

Energizing the francophone presence in St. Louis is first and foremost the role of French language teachers. By encouraging 100 to 130 high school students to participate in the Alliance Française annual writing contest, these students realize that they form a true community going beyond the classroom's walls. Today, educators also remind students that French is not only a language spoken in the French-speaking world, but that it also opens up professional opportunities. Dr. Pascal Perraudin, associate professor of French at Saint Louis University, organized, as an example, a successful "French career day" in 2008. On this occasion 435 participants, the majority of them high school students, came to meet the representatives of Sigma

Aldrich and Nestlé, who explained to them how the study of French had been useful in their careers.

Education is also the role of the association founded by Elizabeth Gentry Sayad who explained that "Les Amis conducts monthly programs with compelling speakers about our heritage, tours of the environs as well as other French pockets throughout the country, such as Mobile, Natchez, New Orleans, Northern Michigan." Les Amis has pursued the possiblity of the Creole Corridor being designated a UNESCO World Heritage Site. Whether that occurs or not, Mrs. Sayad considered that "this initiative has brought all the French communities of the Corridor together actively *for the first time since the colonial period.*"

Indeed, history has demonstrated that these Francophile associations have the most significant impact when they collaborate. Such is the case when the local chapter of the American Association of Teachers of French (AATF), the Alliance française de St. Louis, and area universities (Washington University in St. Louis, St. Louis University (SLU), University of Missouri St. Louis (UMSL), Webster University) collaborate each year in order to bring a French theater company. Led by André Nerman, La Compagnie Caravague performs classics such as *Huis Clos*, or singing performances in hommage to Jacques Brel or Guillaume Apollinaire. The annual success of such events can be attributed to the efforts of the AATF, which organizes a series of workshops that enable high school teachers *and* university professors to integrate the subject of the play into their course curriculum.

Francophone 2.0

It is the Internet revolution however, that has modified the proportions and the synergy of the francophone community in St. Louis the most. Today the activities of all associations are advertised on their websites and on bulletins circulated to Listservs. The same information is frequently relayed several times through various social networks, via Facebook in particular. Isabelle Heidbreder observes: "our new (AFSTL) web page and our presence on Facebook is certainly what allows us to reach members of the francophone/ Francophile community that would not otherwise know what events we are offering." In founding a francophone group on Facebook,

I wanted to create a platform that could synthesize the calendar of events of all these diverse organizations: this group now has 650 members, and counting. This web presence has created a new responsiveness and sense of community in the younger generation. When a young woman from Burkina Faso arrived in St. Louis in August 2014 with her two-year-old daughter who had to undergo heart surgery, I asked our members if they could visit her and donate food and clothing. The response was immediate, and many members went to see her at Haven House, where they could express support in French.[13] Such was also the case for the gathering at the Laclède Statue, in solidarity with the people of Paris during the Charlie Hebdo attack.[14] The Internet thus plays the role that word of mouth once did in uniting the former French quarter on the banks of the Mississippi.

Since 2010, French-speaking microgroups have indeed emerged on the Internet, thanks in particular to the Meetup platform, where people who are often not affiliated to traditional associations such as the Alliance Française gather informally in cafés or restaurants to converse in French. For Tsila Schvartz, who grew up learning French in Jerusalem and now lives in St. Louis, "Meetup is very inviting, and we discover more new people each week." What this type of platform gains in spontaneity (an Eiffel Tower in Legos in a café is the visual meeting point) is, however, lost in stability. And Meetup might also fragment other conversation groups. L'amicale française, a discussion group founded in 1985 by Hiro Mukai, provides a case in point: "In the nineties we counted 30 participants in every meeting. Now, although the roster exceeds 150, and perhaps because the Internet provides other groups and other means of practicing French, each meeting numbers 5 to 10." In short, as it has for social life in general, the impact of the internet on the francophone community of St. Louis has pros and cons, enhancing the possibility of networking while diminishing socializing in real time and space.

Soft Power . . . and Hidden French Communities

Thanks to the Internet, the francophone community has become more responsive, but can we also claim that its Web presence has enabled it to expand? As Isabelle Heidbreder concedes, many francophones do not feel attracted to the traditional associations: "They are not necessarily attracted to our organization (Alliance Française) as they feel—wrongly—that it is either a high-end social club (and they do not feel like they would belong there) or a place to learn French (which they already know)."

When I founded the Centre Francophone in 2012, my first goal was to strengthen the French presence in St. Louis by working closely with the Cultural Services of the French Consulate in Chicago, the Institut français, and Campus France. I brought to St. Louis renowned contributors to French culture, including writers such as Pascal Quignard, illustrators who could offer workshops at the Ecole française, or politicians such as the former minister of justice, Christiane Taubira, who accepted the invitation and requested to meet with members of the Ferguson commission. The Centre is also the main partner in Missouri of the Marianne Midwest Series, in collaboration with the University of Chicago: we host webinars in a dedicated conference room where our audience of Francophiles, academics, and students are able to engage dynamically in a virtual dialogue with economist Thomas Piketty, director Agnès Varda, and Haitian Canadian author Dany Laferrière. By working closely with the French cultural services, I was also able to offer continuous education—free of charge—to area French teachers through unique workshops (*Ateliers de formation*) on various topics including comics (Janine Kotwika), advertising (Bernard Gruas), and using the French press in schools (Elsa Santamaria, CLEMI), to name a few. The Centre is also the only partner of the French Art Discovery Midwest Network. With the SLAM (St. Louis Art Museum) and the Kemper Museum (Washington University), the Centre has created pedagogical worksheets on the French artists in the collections of these extraordinary museums. Ultimately, my goal is for all French teachers in the area to visit our museums with their students and discuss the artwork in French. It is therefore by reaching out to an outside partner based in Chicago that I was able to consolidate a small cultural fort in St. Louis, less well armed than Fort de Chartres, but just as determined to support cultural activities in a city founded by the French. Under the name of French ConneXions, the new French cultural center is further increasing its visibility by being housed, since September 2020, in the Department of Romance Languages and Literatures at Washington

University in St. Louis, one of the most prestigious universities in the Midwest, which has succeeded in ranking among the top fifteen universities in the country. By working closely with us, the French Embassy seems to have acknowledged the cultural strategic interest of St. Louis as a way to increase its "soft power."

In order to widen the traditional circle of Alliance Française members, I also used Graph Search, a semantic search engine introduced by Facebook (March 2013–December 2014) that has since devolved due to privacy issues.[15] I could type "people who live in St. Louis who speak French" and see all individuals on Facebook who had written this interest in their profile. This search uncovered a new francophone community or, rather, communities. I discovered that roughly three hundred Senegalese and one hundred Haitians live in St. Louis, whom one can befriend with a click. At that time I read the Facebook page of Coumba, a young Senegalese woman, who had posted (January 16, 2014) a commentary in French about a song by Diams, a French rap singer, confessing that she recognized her personal story in the lyrics. When a young Senegalese woman identifies with the words of a Franco-Cypriot singer, in turn provoking a series of commentaries in French by her Facebook friends living in St. Louis (Missouri) *and* in Senegal, we can see that the reach and definition of the French presence in St. Louis has indeed evolved.

I have since reached out to Coumba, who has become a French teacher at the St. Louis Immersion School (SLLIS). When contacted, she explained that the Senegalese Association in Saint Louis (SAS) was created in December 2007 with Ousmane Thiam as president, and a subgroup led by younger people called SAYS (Senegalese Association Youth Session) now totals eighty dues-paying members (2017). She confirmed that "Senegalese people in the United States in general and SAS members in particular are now more subject to mingling Wolof, French, and English together and everyone understands just fine!" To celebrate the Franco-American friendship, it was important for the Centre to commemorate the centennial of the First World War, in 2014, by hosting and presenting a cycle of French films in partnership with the French Consulate of Chicago and the Institut Français. I am proud that one of these films, *The Senegalese Riflemen*, provided an opportunity to connect with the Senegalese community in St. Louis who showed up massively, old and young.

To conclude on yet another high note, I would like to share three proposals for reinforcing and expanding the francophone community in St. Louis. Allison Prabhakar, a young French high school teacher, suggests that we organize cultural celebrations not in private clubs and organizations, but downtown: democratic celebrations that will attract media attention along the lines of the Wine Festival organized in Charlotte. Similarly inspired, Isabelle Heidbreder considers that the city could expand on the *Fête de la musique* (June 21) an international event originated in France, which could bring together local musicians, restaurants, and cafes. As for Jane Robert, one of the most active patrons of French culture in St. Louis, she proposes that we create an interdisciplinary workbook that could be used by high school teachers to make their students more aware of St. Louis's French heritage; a workbook that could include the reading of the comic book *Capitaine Perdu* by Jacques Terpand, which narrates the life of St. Ange de Bellerive, who might be the real "founder" of St. Louis, according to Dr. Carl Ekberg.[16] If I have learned a lesson from my investigation, it is that we must continue to reach out to the younger generation and to enlarge the scope of the more traditional Francophile groups in order to include the global francophone communities. Otherwise our local community may come to resemble a real-life version of Asterix's *"petit village gaulois,"* *"irréductible"* indeed—but isolated.

NOTES

1. For a pronunciation in French of these street names, see my contribution: "Pard' My French: St. Louis' Peculiar Way of Saying Local Street Names," St. Louis Public Radio, February 27, 2014, http://news.stlpublicradio.org/post/pard-my-french-st-louis-peculiar-way-saying-local-street-names#stream/0. Eight original French street signs were renamed in downtown St. Louis thanks to the association "Les Amis." For information about this group, see "History," Les Amis, accessed January 10, 2021, https://les-amis.org/history.

2. "Ce qui reste d'une chose disparue ou qui a été détruite," TLF (Trésor de la Langue Française), accessed January 10, 2021, http://www.cnrtl.fr/definition/vestige.

3. Gitlin, *Bourgeois Frontier*, 124. See also the essay in this book by Robert Moore.

4. Quoted in Bouchard, *Obsessed with Language*, 237. (Originally published as *La langue et le nombril: histoire d'une obsession québécoise* [Montréal: Fides, 1998]).

5. See the discussion in an important new book, Gosnell, *Franco-America*, 29–31.

6. U.S. Census Bureau, *American Community Survey*, 2015, *1-Year Estimates*, accessed January 10, 2021, https://www.census.gov. Thanks to Leah Hill and Dennis Pruitt, CECD, vice president of International Business Recruitment, Missouri Partnership.

7. U.S. Census Bureau, *American Community Survey, U.S. Census Bureau*, 2015, 5-year estimates.

8. In the first round of the legislative election, the participation of the French of North America is less than 19 per cent, "Résultats législatives 2017: les candidats pro-Macron en tête dans 10 circonscriptions sur 11 chez les Français de l'étranger," Huffigtonpost.fr, June 5, 2017.

9. Mark Evans, "National Park Could Be Established by October," *Ste. Genevieve Herald*, July 29, 2020.

10. "Missouri Connection: France," courtesy of Dennis Pruitt, https://www .google.com/url?sa=t&rct=j&q=&esrc=s&source=web&cd=&ved= 2ahUKEwipyOPxqd_sAhWEQc0KHe73CwMQFjAAegQIJhAC& url=https%3A%2F%2Fwww.missouripartnership.com%2Fwp-content %2Fuploads%2F2019%2F04%2FMO-Connections_France.pdf&usg= AOvVaw00g07PRat7jNT9-FkEqbDp.

11. The Impressionists are of course the main ambassadors of French culture in St. Louis, and exhibitions have to extend their run. Sarah Bryan Miller, "SLAM extends run of 'Impressionist France: Visions of Nation from Le Gray to Monet,'" *St. Louis Post Dispatch*, Jun 11, 2014.

12. "Paw Paw French: Two 20-Somethings Bet St. Louis Can Save a Vanishing Dialect," St. Louis Public Radio, July 13, 2015, https://news.stlpublicradio.org /show/st-louis-on-the-air/2015-07-13/paw-paw-french-two-20-somethings -bet-st-louis-can-save-a-vanishing-dialect.

13. HavenHouse St. Louis is a hospital hospitality house with the mission to provide the comfort of home and community of support to patients and their families traveling more than twenty-five miles to receive medical care. It operates within the DoubleTree by Hilton Hotel St. Louis-Westport in Maryland Heights, Missouri. HavenHouse website, accessed January 10, 2020, http:// www.havenhousestl.org/.

14. "St. Louisans Show Solidarity with France, Hold Vigil for Slain Cartoonists," St. Louis Public Radio, January 11, 2015, https://news.stlpublicradio.org

/government-politics-issues/2015-01-11/st-louisans-show-solidarity-with
-france-hold-vigil-for-slain-cartoonists.

15. Guillaume Decugis, "The Big Problem with Facebook's Graph Search: Privacy Constraints," January 22, 2013, https://www.fastcompany.com/3004952/big -problem-facebooks-graph-search-privacy-constraints.

16. "Capitaine Perdu," Glénat Quebec, accessed January 10, 2021, https://www .glenat.com/bd/series/capitaine-perdu. See also Ekberg and Person, *St. Louis Rising*.

BIBLIOGRAPHY

Bouchard, Chantal. *Obsessed with Language: A Sociolinguistic History of Quebec.* Toronto: Guernica, 2009.

Ekberg, Carl J., and Sharon Person. *St. Louis Rising: The French Regime of Louis St. Ange de Bellerive.* Urbana: University of Illinois Press, 2015.

Gitlin, Jay. *The Bourgeois Frontier: French Towns, French Traders, and American Expansion.* New Haven CT: Yale University Press, 2011.

Gosnell, Jonathan K. *Franco-America in the Making: The Creole Nation Within.* Lincoln: University of Nebraska Press, 2018.

CONCLUSION

The Founding and Lasting Significance of St. Louis

JAY GITLIN

What can historical scholarship best contribute to a moment of commemoration like the anniversary of the founding of a city? It is not a trivial question, for surely history and heritage, community building and memory, all have a place in such a moment. When the authors in this volume arrived in St. Louis for the conference that we described in this book's introduction—the original occasion for bringing us all together—it was hard to miss the enthusiasm that audience members brought to the event. (As the editors have frequently remarked to each other, it was one of the few occasions any of us can remember when academic history lectures were received not just by polite applause, but by shouts and whistles!) St. Louis—like many communities—cares deeply about its past. For historians like us whose vocation focuses essentially on bringing the past to life and making it speak to the present, the challenge in such a moment is finding creative ways to enrich historical memory and consciousness with new insights, to tell stories that resonate with a passionate community, to think again about what the past means for those both inside and outside of that community. For while we knew this St. Louis audience felt unusual enthusiasm, we also knew that there were multiple perspectives on these founding moments, and different communities with different connections to this past, and indeed different investments in how they are remembered. Perhaps the goal in such a moment is not so much to debunk, but rather to enliven our perspective, and elevate our vision to the historian's favorite question: *So what?*

St. Louisans should not be put off by this question. For by asking it critically, it turns out that historians over the past generation have only found ever more reasons to insist that St. Louis was indeed a centrally important place, in many stories, in many contexts, and to many processes. In the past generations—and I view my own efforts in *Bourgeois Frontier* as part of this phenomenon—historians have begun to situate St. Louis and its French colonial past in the largest trajectories, at once elevating the significance of the city, and at the same time challenging certain distortions that traditional frameworks have always contained. A north-south axis truly *was* the most important geographical reality in the early history of the mid-continent, not east-west. French colonial beginnings were not quaint "prehistory," full of traditional peasants and absolutist institutions waiting for enterprising Anglos to press the "start button" on National development; patterns of the French colonial past centrally shaped the development of the early nation and its economy from the start. In short, pursuing answers to the question of why St. Louis matters to larger contexts only makes the place and its people larger and more central, not more parochial and marginal.

And so this is what professional historians have been doing so successfully, indeed for a whole generation, elevating St. Louis's significance, sometimes without even caring much about St. Louis *as such*. Some notable examples are easy to cite. In 1999 Stephen Aron and Jeremy Adelman wrote an article in the field-leading *American Historical Review* entitled "From Borderlands to Bordered Lands," about early modern state building.[1] Easily one of the most discussed articles in scholarly circles for many years, the article laid out a new framework for thinking about an important historical process—the process by which contested political *borderlands* are transformed by state power into more rigidly controlled and divided *bordered lands*. In Aron and Adelman's powerful concept, this was a process that happened across the world in many contexts, representing a trajectory that links together disparate histories in a singular experience. To illustrate their concept, importantly, Aron and Adelman chose the central Mississippi Valley— the region of St. Louis. Similarly, the historian John Mack Faragher was only tangentially interested in St. Louis as such when he began investigating communities and identity creation in the early American West of the early national period. Articulating a framework for thinking about racial formation and processes of social differentiation and exclusion, Faragher was interested in one of the central themes of the history of the American West. But to illustrate his story he chose the lower Missouri Valley, the region of St. Louis.[2]

All of this is to say that early St. Louis matters in many contexts, and we often see our role as historians to amplify these, to bring them to life, and to add them to a historical consciousness that can too often exclude them. Early mythmakers and local boosters oriented early St. Louis history as part of a local story, or at best, part of a relatively constrained national story.[3] Such framings are what too often restrict our vision to founding fathers, to the creation of certain kinds of institutions, to the supposedly local roots of culture. To our eyes as outsiders, it is not that local history like this is irrelevant, but we see it as connected to so many other contexts and processes beyond the city's limits, processes that often explain what was really going on. St. Louis was of course part of colonial America, which eventually became the United States. And it played a very important role in the early development of the American West. But it was much else besides.

As we have shown in this book, there has been exciting new work on early St. Louis in recent years. Some of the new work on early St. Louis has involved discoveries of new sources and the application of new methods. Just as important has been recent work that does not so much discover new materials, but instead changes the way we think about old material. What historians can offer is old wine in new bottles.

Witnessing the engagement of historians and a local community over many years, I have learned much about St. Louis and its significance. I close this book with four key lessons about how to think about the city's founding, lessons that I hope help to summarize the key contributions in this book while amplifying the message of St. Louis's centrality in many dimensions.

Lesson 1: Context Is Key

At the beginning of 1762, a court order gave permission for streets to be laid for the new town of St. Louis. Plots within the new town were to be sixty yards long, half of that space to be used for a house with perhaps a courtyard, the other half to be used for a flower or vegetable garden. The territory had been secured for France by the military prowess of Roland-Michel Barrin, the Marquis de la Galissonnière.[4]

I hope you are scratching your head. Wasn't St. Louis founded in 1764 on February 14? Well, yes it was—*in the Mississippi Valley*. But I am describing the founding of St. Louis on the island of Minorca, not the one in Missouri—or rather, Upper Louisiana. And according to Charles Peterson's book on colonial St. Louis, the typical house lot in our colonial St. Louis was 120 feet by 150 feet, not so different from those in the Minorcan new town.[5] As for La Galissonière, he had been the governor of New France from 1747 to 1749, a successful administrator who had done his best to strengthen the French position at Detroit and in the Ohio Valley. His mother was the sister of Michel Bégon, the intendant of New France from 1712 to 1726. He accepted the king's commission as admiral of the Minorca squadron, against the advice of his doctors. Having forced the British squadron under Admiral Byng to withdraw, La Galissonière and the commander of the mission, the Duc de Richelieu, became heroes back in France. The conquest of Minorca—a desperately needed French victory in the European theater of the Seven Years' War—provoked fireworks displays, the ringing of church bells, and the erection of an arch in Paris. Odes were written for Richelieu. Louis XV was ready to grant La Galissonière the Grand Cross of the Order of Saint Louis, but the aging warrior died on his way to court.[6]

The Minorcan St. Louis never became a full-fledged city. It is but a small suburb of the island's capital city, Port Mahon. A beautiful white church, dedicated to Saint Louis and constructed from local freestone, remains. A local French magistrate named Chatillon—not our local Henri—supervised the church's construction. The French occupied the island in 1756 and left in 1763. The local population continues to speak Castilian and Catalan; however, French historian Georges Lacour-Gayet visited the town at the end of the nineteenth century and wrote that it still possessed the "rustic memory of France." We know little about Minorca or this long forgotten occupation; however, when the Duc de Richelieu ordered a sauce for his dinner and his chef could find neither cream nor butter, he blended eggs and olive oil and produced the sauce of Mahon or "Mahonesa"—known, of course, to us as mayonnaise.[7]

I employed this bit of historical sleight of hand for a reason. Our St. Louis is one of several colonial towns with that name. The French founded a settlement named St Louis in Maragnan in 1612. Today it is a city of close to a million inhabitants, the capital city of the Brazilian state of Maranhão.[8] A book published in France on French towns of the New World lists another St. Louis in St-Domingue and forts named St Louis in Quebec, Guadeloupe, Martinique, and Guiana. And, by the way, there is a parish municipality in eastern Quebec with the name Saint-Louis-du-Ha! *Ha!* Once we understand that there were and are multiple towns named St Louis, we begin to look beyond Missouri to ask why that is so, to seek a broader context in explaining the significance of our city. Obviously the name had military and religious connotations, and French towns in the New World often had fortifications shaped by the designs of royal engineers. In addition to *l'espace du pouvoir*, there must also be sacred space, the *sacré coeur* of French settlements. My point is that all the towns named St. Louis were stamped with the same French colonial prototype. As French historian Laurent Vidal has noted, French colonial towns might have lacked the "unifying model," the *plaza mayor* of Spanish colonial urbanism; however, French towns in the New World still "obeyed *quelques règles élementaires*," or basic principals. He identifies them as security, hygiene, and accessibility, or the use of natural defenses, escarpments, and rivers for travel and communication.[9] Commerce and mobility were critical to the success of a new town. Cultural historian Ryan Brasseaux has observed that to be colonial is to be worldly—colonial places must be legible and connected to the imperial homeland through networks of authority and trade.[10] I would add that to be colonial is also to be modern. Most French colonial new towns begin as a grid—property must be allocated and conveyed with some measure of precision. Conceived before they are actually settled, colonial new towns are like newborn children. Their founders or parents have expectations, reinforced by investment. Colonial new towns did not resemble medieval European places with their convoluted and often dense pedestrian-oriented centers.

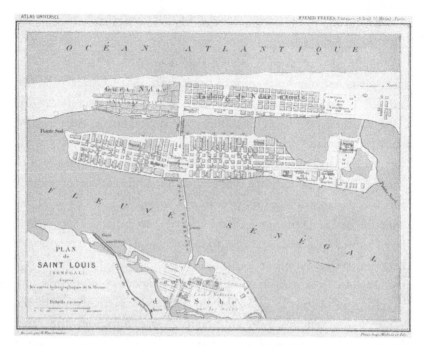

FIG. 29. A hydrographic map or chart showing the "Plan de Saint Louis (Sénégal)," drawn and engraved by R. Hausermann and published by Fayard Frères in *Atlas Universel* (Paris, 1877). Saint-Louis (Ndar) became a center of French colonial activity with the construction of a fort in 1659. It is known as one of the *Quatre Communes*. General Collection, Beinecke Rare Book and Manuscript Library, Yale University.

Engineered, designed, and planned: colonial towns are modern with street patterns meant to maximize circulation.

This was not simply a New World phenomenon. Towns and cities in the Old World were also changing in the eighteenth century. There was a new quest for orderly and wider streets, straight and often diagonal boulevards and avenues, and better lighting in public spaces. In their quest for a New France—both in Europe and North America—planners, engineers, and mercantile elites were refashioning their cities. To give one example: In 1754 Louis de Mondran—architect, economist, and engineer—submitted two plans for the remaking of Toulouse. Call it beautification or eighteenth-century urban renewal, Mondran's ambitious plans, partially realized, transformed Toulouse over the next fifty years. As historian Robert Schneider has observed, the city's new design facilitated the circulation of people and goods and reflected the emergence of a new elite, more commercial in orientation, that cared less for local matters and had fewer ties to the city's lower classes. Social tensions within the city increased. At the same time, the city and its new elites became more cosmopolitan and looked to Paris and beyond to reposition themselves in the world.[11]

Our St. Louis, the last city founded during the French regime, was a part of this eighteenth-century quest for a new urban order, a new France both in Europe and America. The history of St. Louis is a part of the colonial and imperial past and must be studied that way. It is high time that all academics and civilians interested in colonial history acknowledge that the eastern seaboard does not have a monopoly over this field. Colonial Ste. Genevieve is as important as colonial Williamsburg. Frankly, I think the Holy Family Church in Cahokia and the Bolduc House in Ste. Gen are more instructive and fascinating. They encourage a visceral response to the colonial past and push us to ask new questions about what I would call early modern American history. But perhaps I am biased.

Lesson 2: Take It Literally

Moving on, we turn now to a different part of our city. There was not only more than one St. Louis in the eighteenth century, there was more than one Vide Poche. Vide Poche was a nickname for Carondelet, a suburban village, now neighborhood, south of the city. Originally a Creole village, many German immigrants later moved there, and the village was annexed by St. Louis in 1870.

A little over a year ago, I received a delightful and rather long email from M. Jean-Pierre Gendreau-Hétu of Gatineau, Quebec—the fourth largest city in the province located across the river from Ottawa, of course, the capital of Canada. M. Gendreau-Hétu is trained in linguistics and does research in onomastics, the study of the history and etymology of proper names. His wife, Marie-Hélène Côté, is the chair of the Linguistics Department at the University of Ottawa. M. Gendreau-Hétu's first email began:

Cher professeur Gitlin,

I must first let you know how much I enjoyed reading your book *The Bourgeois Frontier*. . . . It starts filling an abysmal gap in US history that academics left unattended for too long. It might also inspire Quebec researchers to consider working seriously on this quite neglected heritage of ours.

Of course, I knew the other shoe would eventually drop—and so it did, but in the most lovely and educational way. Jean-Pierre had gone through the book to pick out certain problems in the French quotes—but always with the understanding that some of the linguistic problems might have come from the sources themselves. We went on to exchange over a dozen emails and become good friends. And one of my lessons on the significance of early St. Louis comes directly from our correspondence.

"Vide Poche" is often translated as "empty pocket." Jean-Pierre wrote:

I might be wrong here, but your translation is not the one I would favor. "Empty pocket" would rather be "Poche vide" to me. As a native speaker, I interpret the inversion of the noun and adjective sequence as meaning "Pocket emptier," i.e., "the one who empties pockets." So "Poche vide" and "Vide poche" actually mean two different things.

Jean-Pierre, who has a little detective in him, then pursued the matter. Here is what he found. "Bonjour Jay"—and I will mostly translate from here:

I have found a reference to another Vide-Poche on the road between Yamachiche and St.-Barnabé [this is just west of Trois-Rivières in Quebec]. As to the origins of the name, it is said that the road there is so bad that the farmers had the displeasure of losing the contents of their pockets as they rode in their wagons.

A week later, Jean-Pierre wrote again, having discovered another place named "Vide-Poche," one described as a "rang," a kind of rural neighborhood in Quebec with farmhouses stretched along either side of a road with perpendicular longlots. This one was near St-Raphaël de Bellechasse/ Kamouraska, south of the St. Lawrence near Quebec City.

Dear Jay—I believe all "Vide-Poche" etymologies ... should at least mention the fact that "vide-poche(s)" was a common noun referring to a once very common dish (Picture of un petit plat) dedicated to receive one's pockets' content. It should also correctly translate "vide" as a verb, not as an adjective ... with the alternative spelling "Vide-poches" (plural) proving it, with the verb not agreeing in number with the noun. French syntax (no matter what variety one speaks) simply prevents the "empty pocket" interpretation. Only the "pocket-empty-er" one makes sense. I seem to be the first to notice that in both places, the emergence of the toponym happens simultaneously with the settling down of Acadian refuges from 1755 on. Both place names are recorded only a few years after Acadian refugees arrived in the area. This might be a coincidence, but a suspicious one for sure. Common themes in the folk etymologies are money (or lack of it) and alcohol. Interestingly enough, Acadians were well-known throughout the Atlantic world for bootlegging. Both areas with the "Vide-Poche" toponyms were also called "Petite Cadie" at one time. Further work on the St. Louis "Vide Poche" might be the key to it all.

Jean-Pierre has now found five different places named Vide-Poche in Quebec and written up his findings in an article. The first recorded use of the name in all five cases—and in our local Vide Poche as well—occurs in the 1760s, which fits his thesis about Acadian refugees. What I have learned from all this is that we cannot fully understand our local French history and heritage without casting a broader net over the whole. The history of this Creole Corridor is part of the history of French North America: this whole informs the part and vice versa. Many Americans and Canadians assume that francophone culture occupies only a quaint space in Louisiana and an occasionally troublesome space in Quebec. When we begin to understand that the francophone world of mid-America was a meaningful place with centers in New Orleans, St. Louis, and Detroit, then the map looks very different. In short, St. Louis and the area's Creole Corridor, as Jean-Pierre noted, "might be the key to it all."[12]

Another example I came across recently: When the rebellion of 1837 that almost created a new Canadian nation was suppressed, French Canadian refugees and political exiles fled to such border towns as Burlington, Vermont, and Plattsburgh, New York. Quebecois historian Jean-Paul Bernard wrote that some settled in St. Louis, Missouri, and corresponded with exiled journalist Ludger Duvernay.[13]

Lesson 3: French North American History Is U.S. History

If lesson 2 suggests the French language is rich with insights into the past, our third lesson is to remember that its speakers were more pervasive and its echoes more audible than we often remember. Consider the 1860s, a decade Americans think of in terms of Blue and Gray, Black and White. That decade looks very different from a French North American perspective. The birth of Canada in 1867 becomes the birth of Quebec. The secession in Louisiana in 1861, at least in part, must be seen as a struggle to resist the eradication of a bilingual political structure and a francophone social and cultural existence. The convention that voted for secession immediately declared the birth—in French—of the *République de la Louisiane*. And, by the way, the French national anthem, "La Marseillaise," became one of the most popular songs in the Confederacy during the Civil War. These two francophone places, Quebec and Louisiana, were in conversation with each other throughout the decade. General Beauregard, not surprisingly, was a hero in Quebec. We might add that when Louis Riel led the Red River Rebellion of the Métis in 1869, it was, again in part, another francophone emergence. And let us not forget that the Supreme Court case that tested the legitimacy of segregation in 1896—Plessy v. Ferguson—was brought by the Comité des Citoyens, a group of Creoles of color led by Louis Martinet and Homère Patrice Plessy, the son of two French-speaking Creoles of color. Plessy's grandfather was born in Bordeaux.

Recovering the perspective of French North America requires a consideration of its many parts. St. Louis and its region are also, I would argue, critical to our understanding of American history—that is, the history of the United States. Let us briefly look again at the period of the Revolution. After the Seven Years' War, the French in both Upper and Lower Louisiana—as the Spanish would designate what today corresponds roughly to Missouri and Louisiana—had become colonial orphans. We might say that the French inhabitants of this vast region, separated by treaty from their mother country, became rogue colonials. In addition, in the Illinois Country, "the Mississippi River had once been the central, unifying artery" of the region. It had now become an international boundary dividing friends, neighbors, and families. Spanish officials on the west side and British officials on the east "complained constantly that trade was being siphoned off to the other side. Contraband was a fact of life. As one British official had noted, 'Smuggling with them [the French] . . . amounts to so considerable a sum as to become a National Object.' It could hardly have been otherwise. The road that connected the two main settlements of Spanish Illinois, St. Louis and Ste. Genevieve, ran along the coast of British Illinois."[14] Merchants on both sides kept track of business conditions. When one substantial French trader, Charles Gratiot, felt that a move across the river to St. Louis might be in order, he wrote "that if business continues any longer on this footing, I shall be obliged in spite of my inclinations to become a Spaniard."[15] In short, among the French in mid-America, identity had become situational and loyalty was increasingly based upon economic, commercial considerations.

These were the preconditions of revolt, and in Lower Louisiana that revolt came in 1768, seven years before the American Revolution. The central factors behind the revolt were economic. As summarized by historian Shannon Dawdy in her book on French colonial New Orleans, the demands of the Superior Council included the maintenance of the colony's traditional "privileges and exemptions"; the issuance of "passports . . . to residents allowing them to go and trade wherever they pleased"; the allowance of "ships from any nation . . . to enter the river 'according to the custom which has hitherto prevailed'"; and—in sum—the granting of "'liberty of commerce.'" The rebels demanded that New Orleans be a free and open port.[16] It was a businessman's bill of rights. Perhaps we might describe this as liberty, agency, and the pursuit of profit.

Were the French of Upper and Lower Louisiana revolutionaries? I would argue that the French had long since taken the measure of imperial regulations and royal officials and had assumed some sense of what independence might mean. When George Rogers Clark invaded the Illinois Country with his small band of Kentucky militiamen, he received critical support from many local French inhabitants ready to abandon the British. That support included a vital extension of credit from merchant Charles Gratiot. Gratiot, in turn, was paid in worthless Virginia scrip. Long before the Louisiana Purchase, the French had also learned a few things about the Americans—whom one referred to as *Américoquins*. When the Americans took possession of St. Louis, I think their French hosts might best be described as practical and somewhat skeptical westerners and businessmen used to regime change. As Charles Gratiot wrote to a friend in London in 1796, "The Americans can consider themselves the masters of the trade of this colony, under their Flag they can enter all parts of the world, and the neighboring territory on the west will become the empire, more and more flourishing, of the American union."[17] Far from being converted republicans, the French Creoles anticipated a new empire under which they might—and in fact, did—prosper. Abandoned by their own mother country and invested in illicit trade and smuggling that they considered both legitimate and necessary for their own well-being, the French in the Louisianas embraced the promise of America in their own unique ways.

In Louisiana, Creoles celebrated their traditions and achievements every year on January 8, Andrew Jackson Day—that is, the day Jackson defeated the British in the Battle of New Orleans. In short, for the Creoles, the best Americans were those who spoke French. The *Missouri Gazette* for July 14, 1819, reported that Col. Auguste Chouteau had presided over an Independence Day celebration at Pierre Didier's orchard. The festivities featured a full-length portrait of General Washington surmounted by a large, live eagle. After many toasts and a sumptuous dinner, the crowd sang a rousing chorus of "Yankee Doodle."[18] I have always presumed that Chouteau must have then sang "Yankee Doodle" in French, for he died without learning English. In any event, this perspective needs to be included in our understanding of this revolutionary era, which after all included uprisings all over the Americas. There was more going on here than a struggle over the rights of Englishmen.

Consider the invasion of Canada in November of 1775. To my students, I refer to this as the first American attempt to export democracy. The Continental Congress sent troops and propaganda messages to French Canada, hoping there might be interest there in throwing out the British and becoming the fourteenth colony. They received a mostly positive reception; indeed, the father of Pierre Menard of Kaskaskia, Jean Menard, raised a company of French Canadian volunteers, and was said to be "very zealous and active in the cause of the United States of America."[19] The elder Menard became a prisoner of war in Montreal in 1778, and several years later his son Pierre found his way to the Illinois Country by way of Detroit and Vincennes. French Canadian enthusiasm for the American cause quickly dissipated when Brigadier-General David Wooster was left in command in Montreal when General Richard Montgomery left to join in the siege of Quebec City. Wooster "forbade mass on Christmas Eve—a decision that was bound to offend even the most unenthusiastic of Catholics."[20] He also arrested twelve residents suspected of loyalist activities. One, Simon Sanguinet, upon his release, told his compatriots to kick the invaders out. Wooster was an all too obvious reminder to the French Canadians that they were caught once more in the middle, this time between the British and the *Bostonnais*—the standard French term for Anglo-Americans, even as far west as the Creole town of St. Louis.

Lesson 4: Legacies Appear in Surprising Places

When the United States acquired St. Louis and Upper Louisiana in 1803, it gained a rich region and an already cosmopolitan young city with a savvy population. The leading families of this place already viewed themselves as natives or Creoles and were not about to relinquish their culture, language, religion, or property. They had priority. Located on the periphery of their new nation and outside the English-speaking circles of power in New

England and Virginia and the like, French Creole merchants in St. Louis, along with their fur trade business associates, such as John Jacob Astor, pioneered the use of lobbying in Congress in order to shape the direction of Indian policy, pass advantageous Indian treaties, and confirm private land claims. Although little has been written on this subject, the history of lobbying must have a central chapter on St. Louis businesses.[21] It was General Charles Gratiot Jr. who served the family company's interest while stationed in Washington DC, ultimately as the chief of the Army Corps of Engineers.[22] Perhaps it is a dubious legacy, but Gratiot may have been one of the first great lobbyists in the nation's history. Seen in context, we may observe that lobbying was simply an ancien régime practice of cultivating a personal relationship in the negotiation of power and privilege, a somewhat fuzzy line between private and public interests. Given the cultural and physical distance between St. Louis in the West and Washington and the eastern centers of authority, it was an absolute necessity to find some means of communicating both the needs and expertise of various interest groups. In this way and in so many others, American history must be informed by the history of this place and its people. As Peter Kastor wrote about the situation in Lower Louisiana: "It was Louisiana that helped Americanize the United States."[23]

It was Pierre Chouteau III—a direct descendant of Pierre Sr. and the son-in-law of General Gratiot—who well understood that his St. Louis and its founding families must be included in a variety of historical narratives. Proud of being French, a St. Louisan, and an American, this Pierre, one of the civic leaders responsible for the St. Louis World's Fair of 1904, fiercely opposed such statements as the one uttered by historian C. W. Alvord in 1906: "From these French settlers did not spring the forces that have made Illinois one of the great States of our Union. Our true history begins with the coming of the Virginians."[24]

It would be this Chouteau who made sure his vast collection of documents went to the Missouri Historical Society and also supported the pioneering work of historians Louis Houck and Hiram Chittenden. Understanding that the past of his community was in danger of being lost or pushed aside, he wrote that the "furnishings [of Upper Louisiana] . . . compared favorably with those in use in the English colonies," and "as for Creole mothers, they 'made Creole cooking the best cooking in the world to those who understand what good cooking is.'"[25] He insisted on the legacy of the French and the centrality of their story in American history.

Conclusion

As the chapters of this book have collectively argued, the history of St. Louis belongs to many contexts, each of which allows us to view the city and the region in broader perspective and gain new insight. One last context I must mention briefly is that of Indigenous history. From its inception, St. Louis has been, as Fred Fausz has reminded us, a place in Indian country. The example of St. Louis reminds us that Native people were the co-founders of many such American places. The connection between the Osage community and St. Louis certainly did not end when their last lands in Missouri were sold in 1825.

One Chouteau—Edward, the son of Paul Liguest and grandson of Pierre Sr.—was said by a French traveler (Victor Tixier) to be the "only white man who spoke [the Osage language] like an Osage."[26] His daughter Sophie, a leader in her Osage community, was interviewed later in her life and remarked, "I have never been to St. Louis, but I may go during the 'World's Fair.' The Chouteau kindred live in St. Louis, but it has been a long, long time since I have seen any of them."[27] The memory clearly lingered on. To refer back to lesson 1, I must mention one last St. Louis, and that is the St. Louis Academy in Pawhuska, Oklahoma, the capital of the Osage Nation. That school for Osage girls was founded in 1887 by the Franciscan sisters and remained open until 1949. As another example of this connection, we acknowledge Professor Carter Revard, a widely respected expert on British medieval manuscripts and an Osage poet. Born in Pawhuska, Revard began his long teaching career at Washington University in St. Louis in 1961, where he is now emeritus professor of English. Revard has also served as the secretary and president of the American Indian Center of St. Louis. He earned a Rhodes Scholarship to Oxford and received his PhD at Yale in 1959. We were honored to have the Assistant Principal Chief of the Osage nation, Scott BigHorse, with us at the celebration and commemoration of the founding as a central participant and honoree.

And so St. Louis is a place of great historical significance because it has been and continues to be shaped by many frameworks—it is a place on many maps. At the same time, it is unique and provides a distinct perspective. Situated at the heart—*la sacré coeur*—of the Creole Corridor, St. Louis has been and remains a Creole city. Ragtime flourished in St. Louis. A line repeated in the traditional song sung on New Year's Eve in the older French communities of the region, "*La Guignolée*," is "dansons la guenille"—"do the rag dance." Let us end as we began: French and American, eastern and western, southern and northern, multiracial, multicultural, and multilingual, St. Louis may not be the geographic center of the nation, but its history—and its future—may hold the key to understanding our sense of self and our sense of purpose. Many strands of our past intersect at this place where rivers and people—as Judy Garland sang—meet. We can hope that history will help us to understand and honor the many paths that led us here.

NOTES

1. Adelman and Aron, "From Borderlands to Borders."
2. Faragher, "'More Motley than Mackinaw.'"
3. Hoover and Ames, *Auguste Chouteau's Journal*.
4. Sloss, *Small Affair*, 63–71.
5. Peterson, *Colonial Saint Louis*, 8.
6. Sloss, *Small Affair*, 29–30.
7. Sloss, *Small Affair*, 16, 66.
8. Vidal and d'Orgeix, *Les villes françaises*, 88–89.
9. Vidal and d'Orgeix, *Les villes françaises*, 57.
10. Ryan Brasseaux, personal correspondence with the author, January 2010.
11. Schneider, *Public Life in Toulouse*, 344–52. On the idea of creating a New France both in North America and in Europe, see the recent book by McShea, *Apostles of Empire*.
12. Email correspondence between the author and M. Jean-Pierre Gendreau-Hétu of Gatineau, Québec, from January 17, 2013, to March 14, 2013. My thanks to him.
13. Jean-Paul Bernard, "Vermonters," 257.
14. Gitlin, *Bourgeois Frontier*, 35.
15. Gitlin, *Bourgeois Frontier*, 39.
16. Dawdy, *Building the Devil's Empire*, 221.
17. Gitlin, *Bourgeois Frontier*, 45.

18. Foley and Rice, *First Chouteaus*, 198; Billon, *Annals of St. Louis*, 72.

19. Spence, Seineke, and Adler, *Guide to the Microfilm Edition*, 1.

20. Baumgartner, "General David Wooster," 7. See also, Lagrave, *Voltaire's Man in America*.

21. See Pasley, "Private Access," 100–138. Pasley and others see the rise of lobbying as having its origins in the practice of petitioning the government, a common rite of popular expression in England and the colonies. The French communities in Canada and the Illinois Country were also quite accustomed to using petitions to seek redress of grievances. Using a case study of stagecoach operators and the postal agents from the 1790s on, Pasley shows the transition of the petition from a form of expression to a tool of governance. Pasley notes that such petitions were often drafted by "members of the local gentry" and signed by "an impressive array of local notables, with merchants or lawyers heading the list" (104). Thus, the French Creole business leaders of St. Louis were in a perfect position to seek the recognition of their interests from members of Congress. Further studies of petitions from French communities are long overdue.

22. Gitlin, *Bourgeois Frontier*, 71.

23. Kastor, *Nation's Crucible*, 15.

24. Alvord, "Kaskaskia Records," 31.

25. Gitlin, "From Private Stories," 10.

26. Gitlin, *Bourgeois Frontier*.

27. Gitlin, *Bourgeois Frontier*, 100.

BIBLIOGRAPHY

Adelman, Jeremy, and Stephen Aron. "From Borderlands to Borders: Empires, Nation-States, and the Peoples in between in North American History." *American Historical Review* 104, no. 3 (1999): 814–41.

Alvord, Clarence Walworth. "The Finding of the Kaskaskia Records." In *Transactions of the Illinois State Historical Society for the Year 1906*. Springfield: Illinois State Historical Society, 1906.

Baumgartner, Alice. "General David Wooster in Montréal and the Failure of the American Occupation, 1775–76." Seminar Paper: Quebec and Canada from 1791 to the Present, Yale University, 2009.

Bernard, Jean-Paul. "Vermonters and the Lower Canadian Rebellions of 1837–1838." *Vermont History* 58, no. 4 (1990): 250–63.

Billon, Frederic Louis. *Annals of St. Louis in Its Territorial Days, from 1804 to 1821 Being a Continuation of the Author's Previous Work, the Annals of the French and Spanish Period*. St. Louis: Printed for the author, 1888.

Dawdy, Shannon. *Building the Devil's Empire: French Colonial New Orleans*. Chicago: University of Chicago Press, 2008.

Faragher, John Mack. "'More Motley than Mackinaw': From Ethnic Mixing to Ethnic Cleansing on the Frontier of the Lower Missouri, 1783–1833." In *Contact Points: American Frontiers from the Mohawk Valley to the Mississippi, 1750–1830*, edited by Andrew R. L. Cayton, and Fredrika J. Teute, 304–26. Chapel Hill: University of North Carolina Press, 1998.

Foley, William E., and C. David Rice. *The First Chouteaus: River Barons of Early St. Louis*. Urbana: University of Illinois Press, 1983.

Gendreau-Hétu, Pierre. "Vide-Poche, toponyme générique d'Amérique française?" *Onomastica Canadiana* 97, no. 1 (2018): 1–52.

Gitlin, Jay. *The Bourgeois Frontier: French Towns, French Traders, and American Expansion*. New Haven CT: Yale University Press, 2011.

———. "From Private Stories to Public Memory: The Chouteau Descendants of St. Louis and the Production of History." In *Auguste Chouteau's Journal: Memory, Mythmaking & History in the Heritage of New France: Essays Accompanying a New, Annotated Translation of the Narrative of the Settlement of St. Louis Together with a Reprint of John Francis McDermott's Glossary of Mississippi Valley French*. Edited by John Neal Hoover and Gregory Ames, 3–16. St. Louis Mercantile Library, University of Missouri-St. Louis, 2010.

Hoover, John Neal, and Gregory Ames, eds. *Auguste Chouteau's Journal: Memory, Mythmaking & History in the Heritage of New France: Essays Accompanying a New, Annotated Translation of the Narrative of the Settlement of St. Louis Together with a Reprint of John Francis McDermott's Glossary of Mississippi Valley French*. St. Louis Mercantile Library, University of Missouri-St. Louis, 2010.

Kastor, Peter J. *The Nation's Crucible: The Louisiana Purchase and the Creation of America*. New Haven CT: Yale University Press, 2004.

Lagrave, Jean-Paul De. *Voltaire's Man in America*. Montréal: Robert Davies, 1998.

McShea, Bronwen. *Apostles of Empire: The Jesuits and New France*. Lincoln: University of Nebraska Press, 2019.

Pasley, Jeffrey L. "Private Access and Public Power: Gentility and Lobbying in the Early Congress." In *The House and Senate in the 1790s: Petitioning, Lobbying, and Institutional Development*. Edited by Kenneth R. Bowling and Donald R. Kennon, 100–138. Perspectives on the History of Congress, 1789–1801. Athens: Published for the United States Capitol Historical Society by Ohio University Press, 2002.

Peterson, Charles E. *Colonial St. Louis: Building a Creole Capital*. Saint Louis: Missouri Historical Society, 1949.

Schneider, Robert Alan. *Public Life in Toulouse, 1463–1789: From Municipal Republic to Cosmopolitan City.* Ithaca NY: Cornell University Press, 1989.

Sloss, Janet. *A Small Affair: The French Occupation of Menorca During the Seven Years War.* Tetbury, UK: Bonaventura Press, 2000.

Spence, Paul D., Kathrine Wagner Seineke, and Emily W Adler. *Microfilm Edition of the Pierre Menard Collection in the Illinois State Historical Library.* Springfield: Illinois State Historical Society, 1972.

Vidal, Laurent, and Emilie d'Orgeix, eds. *Les villes françaises du nouveau monde: Des premiers fondateurs aux ingénieurs du roi, XVIe-XVIIIe siècles.* Paris: Somogy, 1999.

CONTRIBUTORS

PATRICIA CLEARY is professor of history at California State University, Long Beach. She is the author of *The World, the Flesh, and the Devil: A History of Colonial St. Louis* (University of Missouri Press, 2011) and *Elizabeth Murray: A Woman's Pursuit of Independence in Eighteenth-Century America* (University of Massachusetts Press, 2000) and the NEH-funded website: *The Elizabeth Murray Project: A Resource Site for Early American History*. Her current book project is *Mound City: The Place of the Indian Past and Present in St. Louis*, under contract with University of Missouri Press.

ANNE JUNEAU CRAVER, a St. Louis native, has held a variety of positions over the years as a U.S. Department of Defense translator, professor of French and comparative literature, and attorney. In 2001 the French government awarded her the *Chevalier dans l'Ordre des Palmes Académiques*. She is currently working on a book on *La Revue de l'Ouest*, the most successful French newspaper published in St. Louis in 1854, and its editor and publisher, Louis Cortambert.

LIONEL CUILLÉ is Teaching Professor of French at Washington University in St. Louis. His teaching and research focus on nineteenth- and twentieth-century French literature. In 2012 he founded the first francophone cultural center in St. Louis, at Webster University. In 2020 he became the director of the new French cultural center "French Connexions," hosted by Washington University in St Louis.

ROBERT ENGLEBERT is an associate professor of history at the University of Saskatchewan, Canada. He is coeditor of *French and Indians in the Heart of North America, 1630–1815*. His research focuses on French social and commercial networks, the fur trade, and the history of French North America. He recently published articles on French law and métissage in Illinois Country in French Colonial History (2017) and Ohio Valley History (2018). His forthcoming coedited book with Andrew Wegmann, *French Connections: Cultural Mobility in North America and the Atlantic World, 1600–1875*, will appear fall 2020.

J. FREDERICK FAUSZ is an emeritus history professor and honors college dean who has won prestigious awards for publications about seventeenth-century Virginia and Maryland and the 1825 U.S. treaty with the Osage Indians. He is the author of four books, including two on St. Louis history, and has loaned the new "Museum of Westward Expansion," under the Gateway Arch, many rare fur trade artifacts.

JAY GITLIN is senior lecturer in the History Department and chair of the Committee on Canadian Studies, the MacMillan Center at Yale. His first book, *The Bourgeois Frontier: French Towns, French Traders, and American Expansion*, received the 2010 Alf Andrew Heggoy Prize from the French Colonial Historical Society. His most recent book is *Country Acres and Cul-de-Sacs* (Wesleyan University Press, 2018) about the rebranding of Connecticut from 1938 to 1952.

PETER J. KASTOR is Samuel K. Eddy Professor and professor of History at Washington University in St. Louis. His teaching and research focuses on the early American republic. He is author of *The Nation's Crucible: The Louisiana Purchase and the Creation of America* and *William Clark's World: Describing America in an Age of Unknowns*. He is currently at work on *Creating a Federal Government*, which combines a book on early federal policymaking with a major digital archive that reconstructs the federal workforce.

JOHN H. LAWRENCE (now retired) was director of Museum Programs at the Historic New Orleans Collection, where he was responsible for planning and implementing museum exhibitions, lectures, seminars, and related activities. He was also the head of Curatorial Collections, with oversight of pictorial and object holdings numbering in excess of five hundred thousand items. He served as principal or guest curator for dozens of exhibitions on a variety of historical topics. Lawrence chaired the Williams Prize Committee of the Louisiana Historical Association.

ROBERT MICHAEL MORRISSEY is associate professor of history at University of Illinois in Urbana-Champaign, where he teaches courses on early America and North American environmental history. He has published extensively on the history of French colonial Illinois Country, the indigenous history of the Midwest, and ecological history in the Great Lakes and Mississippi Valley. He is at work on a history of the tallgrass prairie region of North America from the distant past through the nineteenth century.

ROBERT J. MOORE JR. is the historian for the National Park Service at Jefferson National Expansion Memorial in St. Louis, Missouri. He is a senior lecturer in the Sam Fox School of Design and Visual Arts at Washington University in St. Louis. He is the author of eight books, including *The Gateway Arch: An Architectural Dream*; *Lewis and Clark: Tailor Made, Trail Worn*; and *Native Americans: The Art and Travels of George Catlin, Karl Bodmer, and Charles Bird King*.

An emeritus professor of history at Tulane, **LAWRENCE N. POWELL** is the author of *The Accidental City: Improvising New Orleans*; *Troubled Memory: Anne Levy, the Holocaust, and David Duke's Louisiana*; and *New Masters: Northern Planters during the Civil War and Reconstruction*. He is currently writing a history of antebellum New Orleans.

ANDREW N. WEGMANN is associate professor of history at Delta State University, where he teaches courses on the Early American Republic and the Atlantic World. A scholar of race and identity in the urban Atlantic, he is the author of *An American Color: Race and Identity in New Orleans and the Atlantic World* and coeditor, with Robert Englebert, of *French Connections: Cultural Mobility in North America and the Atlantic World, 1600–1875*. A native of New Orleans, he lives in Cleveland, Mississippi.

INDEX

Page numbers in italics refer to illustrations.

Clamorgan, Cyprian, 157, 161, 162, 163, 166, 174n2, 178n29

Clamorgan, Eutrope, 164, 174n1

Clamorgan, Henry, 162–63, 164

Clamorgan, Jacques, 174n1

Clamorgan, Louis, 162–63, 164

Clamorgan family, 157, 158, 162, 169, 176n12, 176n14

Clark, Emily, 38

Clark, George Rogers, 40, 296

Clark, William, 78, 79, 80, 87n35, 237n47, 237n49

Classic French Film Festival, 276

Cleary, Patricia, 4–5

clothing and fashion, 93–123; artifacts and texts on, 95–96; elite colonial, 104–8, *105, 107, 109, 110*; European consumption of Indian, *120,* 121–22; and global variety of fabrics, 99–100; Indian consumption of European, 97, 100–102, 104, 116–21, *117, 118, 119*; legislation, 94–95, 111, 113; and lucrative mercantile careers, 98–99; political and cultural affiliations displayed through, 112–15; and poverty, 111–12

Code Noir (1724), 235n37

Colbert, Louis, 23

Collot, Georges Henri Victor, 195, *210–11*

colonialism, settler, 77–78

Comanche, 27

commerce. *See* clothing and fashion; fur trade; trade and commerce; transcolonial economy

La Compagnie Caravague, 278

Conde, Auguste, *190*

consumer culture. *See* clothing and fashion

Corbett, Katharine, 48

Le Corbusier, 192

Coronelli, Vincenzo, *26*

correspondence practices, 49–51

Cortambert, Eugène, 244

Cortambert, Isa, 268n61

Cortambert, Louis, Jr, 246, 258

Cortambert, Louis Richard, 245; biographical sketch, 244, 246, 258, 268n63, 268n64; and Catholicism, 263n31; on French spirit, 243, 249, 257; *Histoire de la Guerre Civile Américaine,* 246; philosophical and political views, 244–46, 247–49, 262n29, 263n33; resignation as vice-consul of France, 244, 262n26; and *Le Telegraphe,* 261n14; *Voyage au Pays des Osages,* 246, 261n20

Cortambert, Melanie Racine, 246, 258, 261n19, 268n61, 268n63

Cortambert, Richard Anne, 244, 268n64

Cortambert, Susanne Chouteau, 244, 260n8, 261n19

cosmetics, 100, *101*

Côté, Marie-Hélène, 291

Coton-Maïs, Adélaïde Jacquitte, *165,* 168

Coton-Maïs, Antoine, *165,* 166, 178n28

Coton-Maïs, Charles, 164–66, *165,* 168, 169, 170, 173

Coton-Maïs family, *165,* 167

cotton production, 145–47

Le Courrier de St. Louis (newspaper), 259

Creole Corridor, as term, 131, 177n14, 179n38

Creoles of color. *See* free people of color

Crevier family, 158, 169

Cruzat, Francisco, 111, 113

culture. *See* French culture

Custis-Freeman Expedition, 237n49

Daugerot, Joseph, 237n51

Dawdy, Shannon Lee, 4, 295–96

Decrès, Denis, 225

Delaistre, Louise Henriette, 244

Delassus, Charles Dehault, 76, 233n14, 236n46

Delassus, Pierre Dehault, 233n14

DeMenil, Alexander de, 244–46, 258, 263n33

of crimes, 76–77, 86n27; U.S. criticism
of, 78–79
French Regional and American Museum
Exchange Consortium (FRAME), 276
The French Society of St. Louis, 253
Frères, Fayard, 290
fur trade: appeal of career in, 98–99; and
exchange of European goods, 97, 102–3;
and expansion vs. compact French
imperial plan, 23, 25, 27; French-
American partnerships in, 80; fur and
hide types, 236n44; and multitribal
diplomacy, 70–71; Osage dominance of,
68–69, 72, 102–3; profits, 72; significance of, for St. Louis's economy, 73–76;
steamboat usage, 134–35; store buildings, 200; women's participation in, 37

Galloway, Patricia, 69
Galvez, Bernardo de, 220, 234n27
Garesché, Juliette McLane, 265n50
Garesché, Katherine "Kitty" Milligan,
265n50
Garesché, Peter Bauduy, 253, 265n50
Gateway Arch and Jefferson National
Expansion Memorial, 188, 192–93, 196,
201–2, 260n2, 264n40, 271
Gayoso de Lemos, Manuel, 112–13
gendered societal norms: and family businesses, 40, 46; historiography, 37–38;
and marriage alliances, 42; in Osage
culture, 68–69
Gendreau-Hétu, Jean-Pierre, 291–94
German immigrants, 223, 259, 269n67
Giard, Antoine, 39
Giard, Marie-Catherine: correspondence,
49–50; daughters' marriage alliances,
41–43; family exchange of goods, 44;
family wealth, 39–40, 45; relocation
to St. Louis, 40–41; slaves of, 45–47;
travels, 48

Gibeau, Marie-Louise, 37
gift giving, 71–72, 73, 76–77, 96, 103–4,
116, 218
Girardin, Emile de, 264n39
Gitlin, Jay, 3–4, 23, 39, 80, 122, 131, 132,
175n6, 179n38, 266n53
Godchaux, Leon, 148
grain trade, 46, 56n71, 139–40
Gratiot, Charles, 30, 40, 96, 295, 296
Gratiot, Charles, Jr., 298
Gravier, Jacques, 27
Great Fire of 1849, 253, 266n51
Grenier, Fernand, 38
Griveaud, Emanuel, 164
Gruas, Bernard, 280

hair styles, 95, 115
Haiti, 213, 232n9
Harrison, William Henry, 78
Hausermann, R., 290
Haven House, 279, 283n13
Heberer, Charles, 198, 199
Heidbreder, Isabelle, 274, 278, 279–80, 282
hemp cultivation, 220, 234n28
Hennepin, Louis, 25
Hill, Meghan, 274, 277
Hoblitzelle, Clarence, 190–91, 199
Houck, Louis, 298
How, John, 266n53, 267n54
Howe, George, 192
Hunter-Dunbar Expedition, 237n49

Illinois Country, 21–31; alliance with Illinois Indians, 23, 25–27, 29; collaborative
political culture, 22–23, 27–31; desire
for British imperial support, 21–22;
expansion vs. compact imperial plan,
23–25, 26
Illinois Indians, 23, 24–27, 28, 29
Immaculate Conception (Jesuit mission),
24–25

To order or obtain more information on these or other University
of Nebraska Press titles, visit nebraskapress.unl.edu.

CPSIA information can be obtained
at www.ICGtesting.com
Printed in the USA
LVHW091306260721
693693LV00001B/24